THE THEORY AND PRACTICE OF GROUP PSYCHOTHERAPY

THE THEORY AND PRACTICE OF GROUP PSYCHOTHERAPY

IRVIN D. YALOM

Basic Books, Inc., Publishers

NEW YORK   LONDON

© 1970 by Basic Books, Inc.
Library of Congress Catalog Card Number: 71–94305
SBN 465–08445–1
Manufactured in the United States of America
DESIGNED BY VINCENT TORRE
74 75 76   10

To the memory of my father
BENJAMIN YALOM

PREFACE

Half of this book was written in London, the other half in California. The practice of group therapy is so different in the two settings that in the former I felt like a radical and in the latter an arch conservative. Even a cursory examination of the field of group therapy reveals great diversity in practice. The term "group therapy" is an oversimplification; one should speak instead of the group therapies. Alcoholics Anonymous is group therapy, and so is a group for pregnant women in a prenatal clinic, a group of schizophrenics in a chronic hospital ward, a group of parolees at a probation officer's office, or a group of relatively well-functioning individuals with neurotic or characterologic disorders meeting in an outpatient clinic or a psychotherapist's private office.

The current picture is complicated still further by the emergence of a large variety of new groups; a recent survey[1] of representative groups run in the Northern California Bay area discloses a bewildering array of approaches: psychoanalytic groups, psychodrama groups, crisis groups, Synanon, Recovery, Inc., Alcoholics Anonymous, marital couples groups, marathon encounter groups, family therapy groups, traditional T-groups, personal growth T-groups, nude therapy groups, multi-media groups, nonverbal sensory awareness groups, transactional analysis groups, and Gestalt therapy groups. Many of these are designated as therapy groups; others straddle the blurred boundary between personal growth and therapy (see Chapter 14 for a discussion of this issue).

With so much apparent diversity and flux in the field, it was with considerable hesitation that I ventured to write a book which might have relevance to all the group therapies. My first strategy was simplification; I attempted to introduce order by separating "front"[2] from "core" in each of the group therapies. The "front" consists of the trappings, the form, the techniques, the specialized language, and the aura surrounding each of the schools of therapy; the core consists of those aspects of the experience which are intrinsic to the therapeutic process—that is, the bare-boned mechanisms of change. Disregard the "front," consider only the actual method of effecting change in the patient, and one will find that these methods are limited in number and remarkably similar across groups. Therapy groups which appear totally different in form may rely on identical mechanisms of change. I have, perhaps too expansively, referred to these mechanisms of change as "curative factors," ten of which are identified and discussed in this book.

By classifying groups according to their curative factors rather than to their "front," the array of group therapies seems less variegated and more ordered. It is my contention that groups with similar goals use similar curative factors. The goals of group therapy, which depend on the set of the leader and the composition of the group, may vary from support, suppression, and inspiration (Alcoholics Anonymous, Recovery, Inc.) to the maintenance of reality testing and prevention of ward friction (groups on chronic psychiatric wards), to the restoration of functioning and the reinstitution of old defenses (groups on acute, rapid-turnover psychiatric wards), to the building of new defenses and a change in coping style and characterologic structure (groups of patients with neurotic and characterologic problems).

Consider, for example, the ambitious goal of characterologic change. Therapy groups which effect this change rely heavily on the curative factors of cohesiveness and interpersonal learning (Chapters 2 and 3). Regardless of whether the group leader espouses Freudian, neo-Freudian, Rogerian, Adlerian, or eclectic viewpoints and techniques, the actual mechanism of change in the patient in groups with these goals is the same. (Member interaction plays such a crucial role in group therapy with the goal of character change that throughout this book I have referred to intensive group therapy as "interactional group therapy.")

Although the curative factors are the primary agents of change, the "front" of the group is by no means expendable. Each therapist, depending upon his professional training and his personal style, will master a system of therapy which enhances the operation of the curative factors. Often the enthusiasm and dedication of the therapist to a particular style of therapy is itself a critical aid in the initial stages of therapy; the patient's faith and positive expectations are heightened, he is more prone to value the group, to attend more regularly, and to participate more actively. Without question the "front" has its value; the danger comes in not distinguishing "front" from core. If the "front" is considered to be the agent of change, then the curative factors may be neglected, as the "front" becomes more elaborate and revered. Occasionally this has resulted in an elaborate façade which, like Gaudi's Sagrada Familia in Barcelona, has no interior.

This book approaches the field of group therapy through these curative factors. The first four chapters describe the derivation and operation of the curative factors: Chapter 1 discusses the minor curative factors (minor from the perspective of intensive interactional group therapy with ambitious goals); Chapters 2 and 3 discuss the major factors, group cohesiveness and interpersonal learning; while Chapter 4 discusses the comparative importance and the interdependence of the curative factors. The next nine chapters are an inductive sequence describing a system of therapy based on these curative factors: Chapters 5 and 6 consider basic principles regarding the therapist's role and technique; while Chapters 7 through 13 present a chronological view of the therapy group, emphasizing group phenomena and therapist techniques relevant to each stage. Chapter 14 describes the rapidly expanding world of the T-group or encounter group, with special attention to the relationship between these groups and therapy groups. (Some readers whose primary background is in human relations training may prefer to read Chapter 14 first.) The final chapter presents an overview of the dual goals of this book: (1) to provide a guide for the training of group therapists and (2) to describe the scientific basis of group therapy.

The dual research-clinical orientation of this book reflects, of course, my own interests and values. I have over the past few years become increasingly conscious that the field urgently needs a dual humanistic-scientific foundation if it is to deal effectively with the mounting human stresses created by a machine-oriented scientific technology. In preparation of this book I have often, while searching through library stacks, browsed through ancient psychiatric texts. It is unsettling to realize that the devotees of therapy through venesection, cold-water immersion, starvation, purgation, and trephining were obviously men of high intelligence, dedication, and integrity. The same may be said of the last generation of therapists who advocated hydrotherapy, leucotomy, insulin coma, and carbogen inhalation. Their texts are as well written, their optimism as unbridled, and their reported results as impressive as those of practitioners of the most modern current techniques.

Many other fields have left us far behind because they have applied the principles of the scientific method in research. Without methodological refinement it is quite obvious that the workers of today who are enthusiastic about current treatment modes—analytic therapy, Gestalt therapy, marathon groups, conjoint family therapy, etc.—are tragically similar to the hydrotherapists of yesterday. Without utilization of scientific method to test basic principles and relative treatment efficacies, the field remains unstable and at the mercy of passing current fashions. Throughout this book I have therefore attempted to cite the hard relevant research data where it exists and to call attention to areas in which research seems especially necessary and feasible. Some areas (for example, group composition) have been heavily (though not definitively) studied, while others (for example, "working through" or countertransference) have been virtually untouched by research. Naturally the relevant chapters reflect this distribution of research emphasis: some chapters may appear, to clinicians, rarefied and irrelevant, while other chapters may appear, to research-minded colleagues, to lack rigor.

It would be unrealistic to expect research to effect a rapid major change in the practice of psychotherapy. Therapists faced with suffering patients have obviously been unable to wait for science. Complex systems of therapy have been constructed which will change slowly and only in the face of very substantial evidence. Beyond this there is yet another consideration: unlike the physical sciences, many aspects of psychotherapy defy quantification. Psychotherapy is both art and science. Research findings will ultimately guide the broad brush strokes of therapy, but the human encounter will always be a deeply personal, nonmeasurable experience.

The field of group therapy has become ideologically cosmopolitan. Readers of this text will probably stem from many disciplines: psychiatry, psychology, social work, nursing, the ministry, corrections, education, and organizational behavior. Furthermore, the ideological differences within any of these disciplines may be greater than between disciplines. This book reflects my own eclectic ideological background beginning with a grounding in Freudian psychoanalytic theory and technique which was, over the years, complemented by a series of other influences: neo-Freudian theorists (especially Sullivan and Horney), brief-therapy approaches including behavior and somatic therapy, in-patient therapeutic community groups, conjoint family therapy with a period of valuable collaboration with the late Don Jackson, social psychology and small-group dynamics, and sensitivity group work and affiliation with the National Training Laboratories. Throughout I have been influenced by such rigorous behavioral scientists as Jerome Frank, David Hamburg, and Morris Parloff. My group work has spanned all these ideological phases and has, I think, drawn on all of them to produce the system presented in this book. The method of therapy I describe is not original and is to a large extent already used by the majority of American group therapists. This book attempts to suggest a scientific basis for the method and to offer a systematization so as to facilitate the training of students. Although my group work has been in many settings, this book chiefly emphasizes outpatient group therapy, which has the ambitious goal of characterologic change for its members. It is my hope, however, that the broad principles of theory and technique presented herein will have general value for all group therapists.

December, 1969   IRVIN D. YALOM

REFERENCES

1. M. Lieberman, P. Golde, and I. Yalom, unpublished data, 1969.
2. E. Goffman, *The Presentation of Self in Everyday Life* (Garden City, New York: Doubleday Anchor Books, 1959).

ACKNOWLEDGMENTS

Many have helped me in the preparation of this book. Drs. C. Peter Rosenbaum, Jerome Frank, and Morris Parloff have reviewed the entire manuscript and provided invaluable encouragement and substantive assistance. Several colleagues have read critically sections of the manuscript. These include Drs. Morton Lieberman, Herbert Leiderman, David Hamburg, Peggy Golde, Rudolf Moos, Daniel Miller, Leonard Solomon, and a large number of Stanford psychiatric residents.

My wife, Marilyn, offered moral support, as well as considerable advice on stylistic matters.

My secretary at Stanford, Mrs. Nancy Phillips, did a superlative job. She has struggled with the manuscript from the earliest fragmented scribblings to the final draft.

Stanford University and the Tavistock Clinic were extraordinarily cooperative and generous to me during the two years of preparation of this book.

To all, my thanks. Most of all, however, I am indebted to my teachers: Drs. John Whitehorn, Jerome Frank, and David Hamburg. All three have offered me invaluable guidance, stimulation, and support; they have contributed significantly to my substantive education, and they have become models for me of professional excellence and personal integrity.

CONTENTS

THE THEORY
AND
PRACTICE OF
GROUP
PSYCHOTHERAPY

1

THE CURATIVE
FACTORS IN
GROUP THERAPY

❦

Introduction

How does group therapy help patients? This seemingly naïve question is
the keystone of a general treatise on group therapy. If we can answer it
with precision and certainty, we shall have at our disposal a central organizing principle by which to approach some vexing and controversial problems. For example, the selection of patients, the composition of the group,
the tactics and strategy of the leader should all be directed toward enhancing the development and potency of the major curative factors. But
how can we answer so crucial a question when our sources of information
(therapists and patients) are not objective and our methods of research
limited and unsophisticated?

From the group therapists we obtain a variegated and internally inconsistent inventory of curative factors (see Chapter 4). Therapists are by no
means disinterested or unbiased observers. They have invested considerable time and energy in mastering a certain therapeutic approach, and
their answers will be largely determined by their particular school of conviction. Even among therapists who share the same ideology and speak
the same language, there may be no consensus as to *why* patients improve.
All therapists have treated patients who made vast improvements for reasons entirely obscure to the therapists. The history of medicine abounds
with healers who were effective but not for the reasons they supposed.[1]

3

From the group therapy patients at the end of a course of treatment we can obtain data concerning those therapeutic factors which they consider as most and least helpful; or, during the course of therapy, they can after each group meeting supply evaluations of the significant aspects of that meeting. For these purposes an interview or a variety of data-collecting approaches may be employed, and yet we recognize the patients' evaluations will be subjective. Will they not, perhaps, focus primarily on superficial factors and neglect some profound healing forces which may be beyond their awareness? Will their responses not be influenced by a variety of factors difficult to control? For example, their views may be distorted by the nature of their relationship to the therapist or to the group.* In addition, the patient's experience in the group is very personalized; research has demonstrated the extent to which different group patients perceive and experience the same event in different ways. [3,4] The same event may be important or helpful to some members and inconsequential or even harmful to others. The search for collective curative factors is thus further compounded. Nevertheless, patient reports are a fertile and relatively untapped source of valuable data about the therapeutic process and should not be treated with disdain, like that of one British colleague who asserted that they represent nothing more than the testimonials of "satisfied customers." Although their appraisals are obviously partial and subjective, there is no reason not to take seriously what patients *do* say.

A third way of determining the curative factors is through a systematic research approach. One method is to correlate a series of in-therapy variables with ultimate patient outcome in therapy. By discovering which variables are significantly related to successful outcome, one can establish a reasonable base from which to begin to delineate the curative factors. However, there are many problems inherent in this research approach: the measurement of outcome is itself a methodological morass. The selection and measurement of the in-therapy variables is equally problematic; generally the accuracy of the measurement is directly proportional to the triviality of the variable.

These three methods have been used in the derivation of the curative factors which are presented in the first four chapters of this book. The definition and description of the curative factors based on therapist and patient sources and on research, as well as on my own clinical experience, are not presented as conclusive; rather, they are offered as provisional

---

* Feifel and Eells [2] examined patients at the end of therapy and once again four years later and found that patients, at the immediate conclusion of therapy, rarely commented on nonhelpful or harmful aspects of their group experience; four years later, however, three times as many patients were willing to "speak up" about these aspects.

guidelines which may be tested and perhaps expanded by other clinical researchers. For my part, I am satisfied that they derive from the best available evidence and constitute the basis of an effective approach to therapy.

The curative factors to be discussed operate in every type of therapy group. However, they assume a differential importance depending on the goals and compositions of the specific group; factors which are minor or implicit in one group approach may be major or explicit in another. Furthermore, patients in the same group may be benefited by widely differing clusters of curative factors. Although stylistic clarity demands that these factors be discussed singly, the discriminations are, in actuality, quite arbitrary and many of the factors are interdependent: they neither occur nor function separately. Moreover, these factors may represent different parts of the change process; some refer to actual mechanisms of change, while others may be more accurately described as conditions for change. (All of these issues are discussed more fully in Chapter 4.) From my viewpoint, natural lines of cleavage divide the curative factors into ten primary categories:

1. Imparting of information
2. Instillation of hope
3. Universality
4. Altruism
5. The corrective recapitulation of the primary family group
6. Development of socializing techniques
7. Imitative behavior
8. Interpersonal learning
9. Group cohesiveness
10. Catharsis

The rest of this chapter will discuss the first seven factors. I consider "interpersonal learning" and "group cohesiveness" so important and complex that they are treated separately in the next two chapters. "Catharsis" is intricately interwoven with other factors and will be discussed in Chapter 4, "Curative Factors—Overview."

Imparting of Information

Under this general rubric I include the didactic instruction about mental health, mental illness, and psychodynamics given by the therapists, as well as advice, suggestions, or direct guidance about life problems offered either by the therapist or other patients. Generally, when therapists or patients retrospectively examine their experience in interactional group therapy, they do not highly value this curative mode.

Most patients, at the conclusion of successful interactional group therapy, have learned a great deal about psychic functioning, the meaning of symptoms, and the process of psychotherapy. However, the educational process is a very implicit one; most group therapists do not offer explicit didactic instruction in interactional group therapy. There are other group therapy approaches in which formal instruction is an important part of the program. For example, Maxwell Jones [5] in his early work with large groups devoted three hours a week to lectures which instructed patients about the structure and function of the central nervous system and the relevance of this material to psychiatric symptoms and disability. Klapman [6] developed a form of didactic group therapy for outpatients in which he used formal lectures and textbook assignments. Marsh [7] also organized groups of patients into classes and instilled a classroom atmosphere by means of lectures, homework, and grading procedures.

Recovery, Inc., is basically organized along didactic lines.[8] This self-help organization was founded in 1937 by the late Abraham Low, M.D., and by 1960 had 250 operating groups with a regular attendance of over four thousand individuals. The membership is completely voluntary and consists of individuals complaining of any type of psychological problem. The leaders spring from the membership, and there is no formal professional guidance. But the process of the meetings has been highly structured by Dr. Low, and parts of his textbook *Mental Health Through Will Training* [9] are read aloud and discussed at every meeting. Psychological illness is explained on the basis of a few simple principles which are memorized by the members: the neurotic symptom is distressing but not dangerous; tension intensifies and sustains the symptom and should be avoided; the use of free will is the solution to the nervous patient's dilemmas, etc.

Malamud and Machover [10] report an exciting, innovative approach organized on a didactic base. They organized "workshops in self-understanding" consisting of approximately twenty patients drawn from a psy-

6

chiatric clinic waiting list. The workshop's goal was to prepare patients for group psychotherapy and consisted of fifteen two-hour sessions which were carefully planned to clarify important reasons for psychological dysfunction as well as methods of self-exploration. The technique was not only successful in preparing patients for further treatment but proved to be an effective therapy modality; at the conclusion of the workshop many patients felt sufficiently improved so that no further treatment was required.

Groups in prenatal clinics for primiparous mothers [11] and groups in Peace Corps training centers [12] also use considerable didactic instruction. The new mothers are informed of the physiological basis of the physical and psychological changes they are undergoing, the actual mechanics of labor and delivery are clarified, and an attempt is made to dissipate irrational fears and beliefs by an appeal to reason. Peace Corps training groups often use an "anticipatory guidance" approach in which the stresses and conflicts likely to be encountered in the new culture are predicted and discussed. In my work with the Peace Corps, I have found it useful to include a staff member from the country to which the trainees are going. He is able, through didactic means, to describe the culture realistically and undermine many of the groundless fears of the trainees.

My colleagues and I have used an analogous type of anticipatory guidance for psychiatric patients about to enter a new culture—the psychotherapy group.[13] By predicting patients' fears, by providing them with a cognitive structure, we helped them to cope more effectively with the initial "culture shock." (This research is described in detail in Chapter 9.)

Didactic instruction has thus been employed in a variety of fashions in group therapy: to transfer information, to structure the group, to explain the process of illness. Often it functions as the initial binding force in the group until other curative factors become operative. In part, however, explanation and clarification function as effective curative agents in their own right. Man has always abhorred uncertainty and through the ages has sought to order his universe by providing explanations, primarily religious or scientific. The explanation of a phenomenon is the first step toward control of the phenomenon. If a volcanic eruption is caused by a displeased volcanic god, then there are methods of pleasing and eventually controlling the god. Frieda Fromm-Reichman[14] underscores the role of uncertainty in the production of anxiety. She points out that the individual's awareness that he is not his own helmsman, that his perceptions and behavior are controlled by irrational forces, is in itself an important source of anxiety. Jerome Frank[15] in a study of Americans' reactions to an unfamiliar South Pacific disease (Schistosomiasis) demonstrates that secondary anxiety stemming from uncertainty often creates more havoc than the pri-

7

mary disease. Similarly with psychiatric patients: fear and anxiety which stem from uncertainty of the source, meaning, and seriousness of psychiatric symptoms may so compound the total dysphoria that effective exploration becomes vastly more difficult. Didactic instruction, though not a "deep" therapeutic agent, has intrinsic value and deserves a place in our repertoire of therapeutic instruments. (See Chapter 6 for a more complete discussion of this issue.)

Unlike explicit didactic instruction from the therapist, direct advice from the members occurs without exception in every therapy group. In dynamic interactional therapy groups it is invariably part of the early life of the group and occurs with such regularity that it can be used to estimate the age of the group. If I observe or hear a tape of a group in which the patients with some regularity say, "I think you ought to . . ." or "What you should do is . . ." or "Why don't you . . ." then I can be reasonably certain that the group is either a young group or that it is an older group in some difficulty which has either impeded its development or effected a temporary regression or flight. Despite the fact that advice-giving is common in early interactional group therapy, I can recall few instances in which a specific suggestion or guidance about some problem or life situation was of any direct benefit to any patient. Indirectly, however, it serves a purpose; the process of advice-giving rather than the substantive advice may be of benefit, as it implies and conveys a mutual caring and interest.

Advice-giving or advice-seeking behavior is often an important clue to the elucidation of interpersonal pathology. The patient who, for example, continuously pulls advice and suggestions from others only to reject it ultimately and frustrate others is well known to group therapists as "the help-rejecting complainer" [16] or the "yes . . . but" [17] patient. (See Chapter 12.) Other patients may bid for attention and nurturance by asking for suggestions about a problem which is either insoluble or which is already a "fait accompli." A turning point once occurred for a patient when the group, after long months, confronted him with the fact that he "soaked up advice and reassurance like a sponge" and yet had never reciprocated to any of the other equally needy members.

Other types of groups, noninteractionally focused, make explicit and effective use of direct suggestions and guidance. For example, discharge groups (preparing patients for discharge from a hospital), Recovery, Inc., Alcoholics Anonymous, all proffer considerable direct advice. Discharge groups may discuss the events of a patient's trial home visit and offer suggestions for alternative behavior. Alcoholics Anonymous makes use of guidance and slogans; for example, patients are asked to remain abstinent for only the next twenty-four hours, one day at a time. Recovery, Inc., teaches members how to "spot symptoms," how to "erase and retrace," "rehearse and reverse," how to apply will power effectively.

Instillation of Hope

The instillation and maintenance of hope is crucial in all of the psychotherapies; not only is hope required to keep the patient in therapy so that other curative factors may take effect, but faith in a treatment mode can in itself be therapeutically effective. Several research inquiries have demonstrated that a high pretherapy expectation of help is significantly correlated with positive therapy outcome.[18] Consider also the massive data documenting the efficacy of faith healing and placebo treatment, therapies entirely mediated through hope and conviction.

Therapy groups invariably contain individuals who are at different points along a coping-collapse continuum. Patients see or hear about other group members who have improved in the group. They also often encounter patients who have had problems very similar to their own and have coped with them more effectively. Hadden,[19] in his description of group therapy with homosexuals, argues that there should be, for this very reason, patients in the group at varying stages of recovery. I have often heard patients remark at the end of their therapy how important it was for them to have observed the improvement of others. Group therapists should by no means be above exploiting this factor by periodically calling attention to the improvement that members have made. Therapy group members themselves often proffer spontaneous testimonials when new, unconvinced members enter the group.

Some of the other group therapies place heavy emphasis on the instillation of hope. A major part of the Recovery, Inc., and Alcoholics Anonymous meetings is dedicated to testimonials. Recovery, Inc., members give accounts of potentially stressful incidents in which they avoided tension by the application of Recovery, Inc., methods. Successful Alcoholics Anonymous members tell their story of downfall and salvation at each meeting. One of the great strengths of Acoholics Anonymous is the fact that the leaders are all ex-alcoholics—living inspirations to the others. Synanon, also, mobilizes hope in the patient by using recovered drug addicts as group leaders. The members develop a strong conviction that they can be understood only by someone who has trod the same path as they and who has found the way back.

Universality

Many patients enter therapy with the foreboding thought that they are unique in their wretchedness, that they alone have certain frightening or unacceptable problems, thoughts, impulses, and fantasies. There is a core of truth in this since many patients have had an unusual constellation of life stresses and are commonly flooded by generally unconscious psychic elements. Their sense of uniqueness is often heightened by their social isolation; because of interpersonal difficulties, opportunities for frank and candid consensual validation in an intimate relationship are often not available to patients. In the therapy group, especially in the early stages, the disconfirmation of their feelings of uniqueness is a powerful source of relief. After hearing other members disclose concerns similar to their own, patients report feeling more in touch with the world and describe the process as a "welcome to the human race" experience. Simply put, the phenomenon finds expression in the cliché, "We're all in the same boat," or perhaps more cynically, "Misery loves company." Nor is this form of aid limited to group therapy. Universality plays a role in individual therapy also, although in that format less of an opportunity for consensual validation exists. Recently I reviewed with a patient his 600-hour experience in individual analysis with another therapist. When I inquired about his recollection of the most significant event in his therapy, he recalled an incident in which he was profoundly distressed about his feelings toward his mother. Despite strong concurrent positive sentiments, he was beset with death wishes for her so that he might inherit a very sizable estate. His analyst, at one point, commented, "That seems to be the way we're built." The statement offered considerable relief and furthermore enabled him to explore his ambivalence in great depth.

Despite the complexity of human problems, certain common denominators are clearly evident, and the members of a therapy group are not long in perceiving their similarities. An example is illustrative: for many years I have asked members* of T-groups to engage in a "top secret" task. The group members are asked to write, anonymously, on a slip of paper their top secret—the one thing they would be most disinclined to share with the group. The use of this task to facilitate learning is not central to the present discussion. Briefly, however, the leader may proceed in several ways. He

* Nonpatients, primarily medical students, psychiatric residents, nurses, psychiatric technicians, and Peace Corps volunteers. This exercise was first suggested to me by Gerald Goodman, Ph.D., of the University of California, Los Angeles.

may, for example, collect the anonymous secrets and redistribute them to the members, each one receiving another's secret. Each member is then asked to read the secret aloud and to reveal how he would feel if he had such a secret. This usually proves to be a valuable demonstration of universality, empathy, and the ability of others to understand.

The main point I wish to make relates to the content of the top secrets. They prove to be startlingly similar with a couple of major themes predominating. Perhaps the most common secret is a deep conviction of basic inadequacy—a feeling that if others could really see him, they would know of his incompetence, his intellectual bluff.* Next in frequency is a deep sense of interpersonal alienation. Individuals report that they do not or cannot really care for or love another person. The third most frequent category is some variety of sexual secret, often concerns about homosexual inclinations. These chief concerns, in nonpatients, are qualitatively the same in individuals seeking professional help, who become labeled as patients. Almost invariably patients experience deep concern about their sense of worth and their sense of interpersonal relatedness.

Universality, like the other curative factors, cannot be appreciated separately. As patients perceive their similarity to others and share their deepest concerns, they benefit further from the accompanying catharsis and from the ultimate acceptance ("cohesiveness") by the other members.

Altruism

Altruistic acts often set healing forces in motion in group therapy. Throughout the course of therapy patients help one another. They may offer support, suggestions, reassurance, insights, or share similar problems with other members. Quite frequently it is the patients rather than the therapists who will point out each other's strengths and assets. Psychiatric patients entering therapy, demoralized, with a low level of self-esteem, are of the conviction that they have nothing of true value to offer others. Frequently this conviction is manifested in disguised form in the initial interview. When group therapy is offered to a new patient, one often hears him say that he doesn't see how group therapy can help. "What can I get from other patients as mixed up as I am?" "How can the blind lead

---

* One cannot but reflect on the tragic aspects of this phenomenon. How disquieting it is that representatives of our intellectual elite, students in one of our nation's leading universities, should be so imbued with a sense of incompetence. Surely there is a malignant process at work in a culture which generates these feelings in its youth.

the blind?" Exploration of this sentiment usually reveals that the patient is really saying, "What do I have to offer anyone?" This resistance to entering the group is best worked through from the direction of the patient's critical self-evaluation.

Psychiatric patients often have long considered themselves as burdens to others, and it is a refreshing, self-esteem-boosting experience to find that they have been important to others; a morbid self-absorbtion is temporarily relieved. Jerome Frank, in his study of comparative psychotherapeutic systems,[20] has underscored the importance of altruism in many different modes of healing. In primitive cultures, for example, the patient is often given the task of preparing a feast or performing some type of service to the community. Altruism plays an important part in the healing process at Catholic shrines such as at Lourdes, where the sick pray, not for themselves, but for each other. Warden Duffy is reputed to have claimed that the best way to help a man is to let him help you. People need to feel they are needed. I have known ex-alcoholics who have continued their AA contacts for years after they achieved complete sobriety; one worker said he had told the story of his downfall and subsequent reclamation at least a thousand times.

The Corrective Recapitulation of the Primary Family Group

Without exception patients enter group therapy with the history of a highly unsatisfactory experience in their first and most important group— their primary family. The group resembles a family in many aspects: the members are considerably dependent on the leader,* whom they imbue with unrealistic knowledge and power; there may be considerable inter-member competition for his favors; members grow up, as it were, in the group and, often with great difficulty, strike out into the world on their own. There is considerable emotional interplay between the therapy group and the primary family group experience. Experiences in the family will influence the patient's behavior in the group and his attitudes toward the leaders (the parents) and the other members (the siblings). The therapy group experience may evoke many early memories of the family; working out problems with other members or with the therapist may, in a

* Some therapists advocate the use of male-female co-therapists to simulate more closely the parental configuration.

sense, be working through unfinished business from the past.* The recapitulation of the primary family can be a corrective one, in that maladaptive, growth-inhibiting relationships are not permitted to freeze into the rigid, impenetrable system that characterizes many family structures. Instead, behavior stereotypes are constantly challenged, and ground rules of reality testing, exploration of relationships, and testing out of new behaviors are constantly encouraged.

Development of Socializing Techniques

Social learning—the development of basic social skills—is a curative factor which operates in all therapy groups, although the nature of the skills taught and the explicitness of the process varies greatly depending upon the type of group therapy. In some groups—for example, groups preparing long-term hospitalized patients for discharge, or adolescent groups—there may be an explicit emphasis on the development of social skills. Role playing may be employed in which patients learn to approach prospective employers for a job or in which adolescent boys learn to ask a girl to a dance. In dynamic group therapy with ground rules encouraging open feedback, patients may obtain considerable information about maladaptive social behavior. They may, for example, learn about their disconcerting tendency to avoid looking at the person with whom they are conversing; or they learn about other's impressions of their haughty, regal attitude or a variety of other social habits which, unbeknownst to them, have been undermining their social relationships. Often, for individuals lacking intimate relationships, the group represents the first opportunity for accurate interpersonal feedback. One patient, for example, who obsessively included endless, minute, irrelevant detail in his social conversation realized this for the first time in a therapy group. For years he had been aware only that others either avoided or curtailed their social contacts with him. Obviously therapy involves far more than the simple recognition and deliberate alteration of social behavior, but as we shall show in Chapter 3, these gains are more than fringe benefits and are often exceedingly instrumental in the initial phases of therapeutic change.

* We shall return later, in Chapter 6, to the highly controversial question of how explicit this working-through process need be made in therapy.

Imitative Behavior

Pipe-smoking therapists often beget pipe-smoking patients. Patients during psychotherapy may sit, walk, talk, and even think like their therapists. In groups the imitative process is more diffuse, as patients may model themselves upon aspects of the other group members as well as of the therapist. The importance of imitative behavior in the therapeutic process is difficult to gauge, but recent social psychological research suggests that we may have underestimated its importance. Bandura, [21, 22] who has long claimed that social learning cannot be adequately explained on the basis of direct reinforcement, has experimentally demonstrated that imitation is an effective therapeutic force. For example, he has successfully treated a large number of individuals with snake phobias by asking them to observe their therapist handle a snake. In group therapy it is not uncommon for a patient to benefit by observing the therapy of another patient with a similar problem constellation—a phenomenon generally referred to as "vicarious" or "spectator" therapy.[23] Even if specific imitative behavior is short-lived, it may function to help the individual "unfreeze" by experimenting with new behavior. In fact it is not uncommon for patients throughout therapy to try on, as it were, bits and pieces of other people and then relinquish them as ill-fitting. This process may have solid therapeutic impact; finding out what we are not is progress toward finding out what we are.

REFERENCES

1. R. Hunter and I. Macalpine, *Three Hundred Years of Psychiatry: 1535–1860* (London: Oxford University Press, 1963).
2. H. Feifel and J. Eells, "Patients and Therapists Assess the Same Psychotherapy," *J. Consult. Psychol.*, 27: 310–318, 1963.
3. F. Taylor, *The Analysis of Therapeutic Groups* (London: Oxford University Press, 1961).
4. B. Berzon and R. Farson, "The Therapeutic Event in Group Psychotherapy: A Study of Subjective Reports by Group Members," *J. Indiv. Psychol.*, 19: 204–212, 1963.
5. M. Jones, "Group Treatment with Particular Reference to Group Projection Methods," *Am. J. Psychiat.*, 101: 292–299, 1944.
6. J. W. Klapman, "The Case for Didactic Group Psychotherapy," *Dis. Nerv. Sys.*, 11: 35–41, 1950.

7. L. C. Marsh, "Group Therapy and the Psychiatric Clinic," *J. Nerv. Ment. Dis., 82:* 381–390, 1935.
8. H. Wechsler, "The Self-Help Organization in the Mental Health Field: Recovery, Inc.—A Case Study," *J. Nerv. Ment. Dis., 130:* 297–314, 1960.
9. A. A. Low, *Mental Health Through Will Training* (Boston: Christopher Publishing House, 1950).
10. D. I. Malamud and S. Machover, *Toward Self-Understanding: Group Techniques in Self-Confrontation* (Springfield, Ill.: Charles C. Thomas, 1965).
11. C. W. F. Burnett, *A Textbook of Obstetrical Nursing* (Oxford: Blackwell Scientific Publications, 1964), pp. 88–92.
12. G. Caplan, *Principles of Preventive Psychiatry* (New York: Basic Books, 1964).
13. I. D. Yalom, P. S. Houts, G. Newell, and K. H. Rand, "Preparation of Patients for Group Therapy: A Controlled Study," *Arch. Gen. Psychiat., 17:* 416–427, 1967.
14. F. Fromm-Reichman, *Principles of Intensive Psychotherapy* (Chicago: University of Chicago Press, 1950).
15. J. Frank, "Emotional Reactions of American Soldiers to an Unfamiliar Disease," *Am. J. Psychiat., 102:* 631–640, 1946.
16. J. Frank *et al.,* "Behavioral Patterns in Early Meetings of Therapy Groups," *Am. J. Psychiat., 108:* 771–778, 1952.
17. E. Berne, *Games People Play* (New York: Grove Press, 1964).
18. A. P. Goldstein, *Therapist Patient Expectancies in Psychotherapy* (New York: Pergamon Press, 1962).
19. S. Hadden, "Treatment of Male Homosexuals in Groups," *Int. J. Group Psychother., 16:* 13–22, 1966.
20. J. Frank, *Persuasion and Healing, A Comparative Study of Psychotherapy* (New York: Schocken Books, 1963).
21. A. Bandura, E. B. Blanchard, and B. Ritter, "The Relative Efficacy of Desensitization and Modeling Approaches for Inducing Behavioral, Affective, and Attitudinal Changes," *J. Personal. Soc. Psychol.,* in press.
22. A. Bandura, D. Ross, and S. Ross, "Vicarious Reinforcements and Imitative Learning," *J. Abnorm. Soc. Psychol., 67:* 601–607, 1963.
23. J. L. Moreno, "Psychodramatic Shock Therapy," *Sociometry, 2:* 1–30, 1939.

2

INTERPERSONAL

LEARNING

❧

Interpersonal learning, as I define it, is a broad and complex curative factor representing the group therapy analogue of such individual therapy curative factors as insight, working through the transference, the corrective emotional experience, as well as processes unique to the group setting. To define the concept of interpersonal learning and to describe the mechanism whereby it mediates therapeutic change in the individual, I shall first need to discuss three other concepts:

1. The importance of interpersonal relationships
2. The corrective emotional experience
3. The group as a social microcosm

The Importance of Interpersonal Relationships

As we study human society we find that, regardless of the magnification we employ, interpersonal relations play a crucial role. Whether we scan man's broad evolutionary history or scrutinize the development of the single individual, we are at all times obliged to consider man in the matrix of his interpersonal relationships. As Hamburg[1] has pointed out, there is convincing data from the study of primitive human cultures and nonhuman primates that man has always lived in groups which have been characterized by intense and persistent intermember relationships. Man's interpersonal behavior has been clearly adaptive in an evolutionary sense;

16

without intense, positive, reciprocal interpersonal bonds, both individual and species survival would not have been possible. Bowlby,[2] from his studies of the early mother-child relationship, concludes also that attachment behavior is built into us. If the mother and infant are separated, both experience marked anxiety concomitant with their search for the lost object. If the separation is prolonged, the consequences will be proportionately profound. Goldschmidt,[3] on the basis of an exhaustive review of the ethnographic evidence, states:

Man is by nature committed to social existence, and is therefore inevitably involved in the dilemma between serving his own interests and recognizing those of the group to which he belongs. Insofar as this dilemma can be resolved it is resolved by the fact that man's self-interest can best be served through his commitment to his fellows. . . . Need for positive affect means that each person craves response from his human environment. It may be viewed as a hunger, not unlike that for food, but more generalized. Under varying conditions it may be expressed as a desire for contact, for recognition and acceptance, for approval, for esteem, or for mastery. . . . As we examine human behavior, we find that persons not only universally live in social systems, which is to say they are drawn together, but also universally act in such ways as to attain the approval of their fellow men.

Similarly, eighty years ago, William James said, "We are not only gregarious animals liking to be in sight of our fellows, but we have an innate propensity to get ourselves noticed, and noticed favorably, by our kind. No more fiendish punishment could be devised, were such a thing physically possible, then that one should be turned loose in society and remain absolutely unnoticed by all the members thereof." [4]

Although all modern schools of psychiatric thought are interpersonally based, none is as explicit and systematic as Harry Stack Sullivan's interpersonal theory of psychiatry. Sullivan's formulations are exceedingly helpful for understanding the group therapeutic process.

A comprehensive discussion of his interpersonal theory of psychiatry is obviously beyond the scope of this book and the reader is referred to Sullivan's works [5, 6] or, because of Sullivan's often obscure language, to a complete review of his concepts.[7] However, mention of a few key concepts is in order. Sullivan contends that the personality is almost entirely the product of interaction with other significant human beings. Man's need to be closely related to others is as basic as any biological need and, considering the prolonged period of helpless infancy, equally necessary to survival. During development the child, in his quest for security, tends to develop those traits and aspects of himself which meet with approval and will squelch or deny those aspects which meet with disapproval. Eventually the individual develops a concept of himself (self-dynamism) which is based on these perceived appraisals of significant others.

The self may be said to be made up of reflected appraisals. If these were chiefly derogatory, as in the case of an unwanted child who was never loved, of a child who has fallen into the hands of foster parents who have no real interest in him as a child; as I say, if the self-dynamism is made up of experience which is chiefly derogatory, it will facilitate hostile, disparaging appraisals of other people and it will entertain disparaging and hostile appraisals of itself.[8]

Sullivan used the term "parataxic distortions" to describe the individual's proclivity to distort his perceptions of others. A parataxic distortion occurs in an interpersonal situation when one person relates to another, not on the basis of the realistic attributes of the other, but wholly or chiefly on the basis of a personification existing chiefly in his fantasy. Parataxic distortion is similar to the concept of transference but broader in scope. It refers, not only to the therapeutic, but to all interpersonal relationships. It includes not only the simple transferring of attitudes from real life figures but also the distortion of interpersonal reality in response to intrapersonal needs.*

Interpersonal distortions tend to be self-perpetuating. An individual may, through selective inattention, distort his perceptions of another so that an individual with a derogatory, debased self-image may incorrectly perceive another to be a harsh, rejecting figure. Moreover, the process compounds itself because he may gradually develop mannerisms and behavioral traits, for example servility, defensive antagonism, or scorn, which eventually will cause others to relate to him as he expected. The term, "self-fulfilling prophecy," has been applied to this phenomenon.

Parataxic distortions, in Sullivan's view, are modifiable primarily through "consensual validation," through comparing one's interpersonal evaluations with those of others. This brings us to Sullivan's view of the therapeutic process. "Psychiatry is the study of processes that involve or go on between people." [9] Mental disorder, psychiatric symptomatology in all of its varied manifestations are translated into interpersonal terms and treated accordingly. "Mental disorder as a term refers to interpersonal processes either inadequate to the situation in which the persons are inte-

---

* Although their origins differ, operationally transference and parataxic distortions may be considered identical. Most therapists today use the term transference to refer to all interpersonal distortions rather than confining its use to the patient-therapist relationship.

grated, or excessively complex because of illusionary persons also integrated into the situations. It implies sometimes a greater ineffectiveness of the behavior by which the person is conceived to be pursuing the satisfactions that he requires." [10] Accordingly psychiatric treatment should be directed toward the correction of interpersonal distortions, thus enabling the individuals to lead a more abundant life, to participate collaboratively with others, to obtain interpersonal satisfactions in the context of realistic, mutually satisfying interpersonal relationships. "One achieves mental health to the extent that one becomes aware of one's interpersonal relationships." [11] Psychiatric cure is the "expanding of the self to such final effect that the patient as known to himself is much the same person as the patient behaving to others." [12]

Thus therapy is broadly interpersonal, both in its goals and in its means. An early task of the therapist is to help the patient understand his symptoms in interpersonal language. Often the patient is consciously aware of this translation from the symptomatic to the interpersonal. In an outcome study,[13] my colleagues and I demonstrated that group therapy patients, somewhere between the third and sixth month of therapy, often undergo a shift in their therapeutic goals. Their initial goal, relief of suffering, is modified and eventually replaced by new goals, usually interpersonal in nature. Thus goals changed from wanting relief from anxiety or depression to wanting to learn to communicate with others, to be more trusting and honest with others, to learn to love.

Sullivan's statement of the overall process and goals of therapy is clearly consistent with those of interactional group therapy. However, the emphasis on the patient's understanding of the past, of the genetic development of these maladaptive interpersonal stances, may be less crucial in the group than in the individual setting in which Sullivan worked (see Chapter 6).

Sullivan's professional fate has been similar to that of many another innovator. The conservative community responded to his ideas at first by ignoring them, then by attacking them, and finally by so assimilating them that their innovative nature is forgotten. The importance of interpersonal relationships is presently so much an integral part of the fabric of psychiatric thought that one feels trite in underscoring it. Empirical documentation of the critical nature of man's social needs is voluminous. Consider, for example, the studies of bereavement in which the surviving spouse has been shown to suffer increased incidence of physical illness,[14] mental illness,[15] and even an increased mortality rate.[16]

People need people—for initial and continued survival, for socialization, for the pursuit of satisfaction; at no time do we become immune to this axiom. A recent experience at a prison provided me with a forceful reminder of the potency of interpersonal needs:

An untrained psychiatric technician requested consultation with his therapy group composed of twelve inmates. The members of the group were all hardened recidivists, whose offenses ranged from aggressive sexual violation of a minor to murder. The group, he complained, was sluggish and persisted in focusing on extraneous extragroup material and was being controlled by one prisoner, John, who he felt was the least popular member of the group. I agreed to observe his group and suggested that first he obtain some sociometric information by asking each member privately to rank order everyone in the group for "general popularity."* Although we had planned to discuss these results before the next group session, unexpected circumstances precluded our pre-session discussion. During the next group meeting the therapist, enthusiastic but still unsophisticated and insensitive to interpersonal needs, decided that he would simply read out the results of the popularity poll. The group began the meeting in a somewhat agitated manner and, clearly frightened and threatened, soon made it very explicit that they did not wish to know the results of the poll. Several members spoke so vehemently of the possible devastation at learning that they might appear at the bottom of the list that the therapist quickly and permanently abandoned his plan of reading aloud the list. I suggested an alternative plan: Each member was asked to indicate whose vote he cared about most in the group and explain his choice. This, also, was too threatening and only one-third of the members ventured a choice. Nevertheless, the group shifted to an interactional level and developed a degree of tension, involvement, and exhilaration, previously unknown in the group. These human beings had received the ultimate message of rejection from society at large; they were imprisoned, segregated, and explicitly labeled as outcasts. To the casual observer these people, of all people, seemed calloused, hardened, and indifferent to the subtleties of interpersonal approval and disapproval; and yet they cared, and cared very much.

Peer appraisal from a primary reference group is always important, and if properly channeled, can be a potent therapeutic force; much of the therapeutic power of the therapeutic community stems from a harnessing of this factor. Rogers,[17] in speaking of the basic encounter group, makes a similar point:

* My reasons for this suggestion were twofold: first, that the leader might have the opportunity to check out his observations about John's being the least popular member of the group; and secondly, that a discussion of the task would induce the group to turn its attention onto itself. (John, incidentally, was selected as the *most* popular member of the group and the leader learned something about projection and the degree to which he had felt his leadership role threatened by John.)

As a phenomenon it has been both praised and criticized, but few people who have participated would doubt that something significant happens in these groups. People do not react in a neutral fashion towards the intensive group experience. They either regard it as strikingly worthwhile or deeply questionable. All would agree, however, that it is potent.

In summary, then, we have reviewed some aspects of personality development, mature functioning psychopathology, and psychiatric treatment from the point of view of interpersonal theory. Many of the issues that we have raised have a vital bearing on the curative process in group therapy: the enduring nature and potency of man's social needs, the concept that mental illness emanates from disturbed interpersonal relationships, the role of consensual validation in the modification of interpersonal distortions, and the definition of the therapeutic process as a clarification of interpersonal relationships.

The Corrective Emotional Experience

In 1946, Franz Alexander, when describing the mechanism of psychoanalytic cure, introduced the concept of the "corrective emotional experience." The basic principle of treatment, he stated, is "to expose the patient, under more favorable circumstances, to emotional situations which he could not handle in the past. The patient, in order to be helped, must undergo a corrective emotional experience suitable to repair the traumatic influence of previous experience." [18] Alexander underscores the importance of an emotional experience; intellectual insight alone is insufficient. Furthermore, the essence of the curative mechanism is the accompanying reality testing. The patient, while affectively interacting with the analyst in a distorted fashion because of transference (or parataxic distortion), gradually becomes aware of the fact that "these reactions are not suited to the analyst's reactions, not only because he (the analyst) is objective, but also because he is what he is, a person in his own right. They are not suited to the situation between patient and therapist, and they are equally unsuited to the patient's current interpersonal relationships in his daily life."[19]

These basic principles of therapy—the importance of the emotional experience in therapy, and the patient's discovery of the inappropriateness of his interpersonal reactions through reality testing—are equally crucial to the group therapeutic experience. In fact, the group setting offers far more opportunities for the generation of corrective emotional experiences; in the individual setting the corrective emotional experience, valuable as it is, may be hard to come by because of the insularity and unreality of the patient-therapist relationship. In fact, Alexander suggested that the analyst may have to be an actor and to play a role in order to create the desired emotional atmosphere.[20] Frank and Ascher [21] described two corrective emotional experiences in group therapy which significantly altered the course of therapy for the involved patients. In each of these incidents the appearance of the critical incident was facilitated by three therapeutic processes: support, affect stimulation, and reality testing. Patients must obtain enough support from the group so that they are willing to express themselves honestly and to work through the incident afterwards. The group offers considerable stimulation for the activation of noxious attitudes: "competition for the doctor, struggles for status, differences in background and outlook among patients, transference reactions to other group members, etc." [21] Furthermore the group, because of ground rules of honesty of expression, offers ample opportunity for consensual validation.

In a recent study [13] of twenty successful group therapy patients, I asked each whether he could recall some single critical incident in therapy which seemed to be a turning point for him, or which was the most helpful single event in therapy for him. Although the single critical incident is not synonymous with "curative factor," clearly the two are not unrelated and much may be learned from an examination of single important events. Of the twenty patients only two were unable to recall a critical incident; the other eighteen recalled a total of twenty-nine such incidents. Almost invariably, the incident involved some other group member, rarely the therapist, and was highly emotionally laden.

The most common type of incident reported, as well as the two described by Frank and Ascher, involved the patient's suddenly expressing strong feelings of anger or hatred toward another member. In each instance communication was maintained, the storm was weathered, and the patient experienced a sense of liberation from inner restraints as well as an enhanced ability to explore his interpersonal relationships more deeply.

The common characteristics of these critical incidents were:

1. The patient expressed strong negative affect.
2. This expression was a unique or novel experience for him.
3. The feared and fantasied catastrophe did not occur; no one left or died, the roof did not collapse.

4. Reality testing ensued in which the patient realized either that the affect he expressed was inappropriate in intensity or direction or that his prior avoidance of affect expression was irrational; he may or may not have gained some knowledge of the source of the distortion or the prior avoidance.
5. The patient was enabled to interact more freely and to explore his interpersonal relationships more deeply.

The second most common type of critical incident also involved strong affect, but in these instances positive affect. For example, a schizoid patient ran after and comforted a distressed patient who had bolted out of the group room; later he spoke of how profoundly he was affected by learning that he could care for and help someone else. Others similarly spoke of discovering their "aliveness" or feeling "in touch with" themselves. These incidents had in common the following characteristics:

1. The patient expressed strong positive affect, which was unusual for him.
2. The feared fantasied catastrophe did not occur; he was not rejected, derided, engulfed, nor were others damaged by his display of caring.
3. The patient discovered a previously unknown part of himself, which enabled him to relate to others in a new dimension.

The third most common category of critical incident was quite similar to the second. Patients recalled an incident, usually involving self-disclosure, which plunged them into greater involvement with the group. For example, a previously withdrawn reticent patient who had missed a couple of meetings disclosed to the group how desperately he wanted to hear the group say that they had missed him during his absence. Others, too, in one fashion or another openly asked the group for help.

To summarize, the corrective emotional experience in group therapy may have several components:

1. A strong expression of emotion which is interpersonally directed and which represents a risk taking on the part of the patient
2. A group supportive enough to permit this risk taking
3. Reality testing which allows the patient to examine the incident with the aid of consensual validation from others
4. A recognition of the inappropriateness of certain interpersonal feelings and behavior or of the inappropriateness of certain avoided interpersonal behaviors
5. The ultimate facilitation of the individual's ability to interact with others more deeply and honestly

The Group as a Social Microcosm

A freely interactive group, with few structural restrictions, will, in time, develop into a social microcosm of the participant members. I mean by this that, given enough time, every patient will begin to be himself, to interact with the group members as he interacts with others in his social sphere, to create in the group the same interpersonal universe which he has always inhabited. In other words, patients will begin to display their maladaptive interpersonal behavior in the group; no need for them to describe their pathology—they will sooner or later act it out before the group's eyes. This concept, of paramount importance in group therapy, is widely accepted by clinicians, although the therapist's perception and interpretation of group events and his descriptive language are determined by his school of conviction. Freudians may see patients manifesting their oral, sadistic, or masochistic needs in their relationship to other members; correctional workers may see "conning," exploitative behavior; certain social psychologists may see manifold bids for dominance, affection, or inclusion; students [22] of Karen Horney may see the detached resigned person, with his need to resist invitations for involvement, putting his energies into acting noncommittal and indifferent; or the perfectionist who, driven to follow the set of standards which are his master, must control the group by teaching what is proper and how it should be done; or the arrogant-vindictive person who must defeat others and prove himself right by proving others wrong.

The important point is that, regardless of the type of conceptual spectacles worn by the therapist-observer, each member's interpersonal style will eventually appear in his transactions in the group. Some life styles have greater inherent possibilities for interpersonal friction and will manifest themselves in the group more rapidly than others. Individuals who are, for example, angry, vindictive, harshly judgmental, self-effacing, or grandly coquettish will generate considerable interpersonal static early in the group. Their maladaptive social patterns will seem clear far earlier than those of individuals equally or more severely troubled who may subtly exploit others or achieve intimacy to a point but then, in panic, disengage themselves. The initial business of a group usually consists of dealing with the member whose pathology is most interpersonally blatant. Some interpersonal styles become crystal clear from a single transaction, others from a single group meeting, while others require months of observation to understand. The development of the ability to identify and put to therapeutic advantage maladaptive interpersonal behavior as seen in the social microcosm of the small group is one of the chief tasks of a training program for group psychotherapists. Some clinical examples may make these principles more graphic.

The Grand Dame

Mrs. Cape, a twenty-seven-year-old musician, sought therapy primarily because of severe marital discord of several years' standing. She had had considerable, unrewarding, individual and hypnotic uncovering therapy. Her husband she noted, was an alcoholic who was reluctant to engage her socially, intellectually, or sexually. Now the group could have, as some groups do, investigated her marriage interminably. They might have taken a complete history of the courtship, of the evolution of the discord, of her husband's pathology, of her reasons for marrying him, of her role in the conflict; they may have given advice for new behaviors, trial or permanent separations—but all would have been in vain. This approach not only disregards the unique potential of therapy groups but is also based on the highly questionable premise that the patient's account of the marriage is even reasonably accurate. Groups which function in this manner not only fail to help the particular protagonist but also suffer demoralization as the group becomes aware of its impotence. However, as one attended to Mrs. Cape's group behavior, several interesting patterns unfolded. First, her grand entrance, always five or ten minutes late. Bedecked in flamboyant, ever different garb, she swept in, sometimes throwing kisses, and immediately began talking, oblivious of the possibility that some other member may have been in the midst of a sentence, or indeed in the midst of a word. Here was narcissism in the raw! Her world view was so solipsistic that she did not consider that life might have been going on in the group before her arrival.

After a very few group meetings, Mrs. Cape began to give gifts in the group: to an obese female member, a copy of a Mayo diet; to a female with strabismus, the name of a good ophthalmologist; to a male homosexual patient, a subscription to *Field and Stream* magazine (to masculinize him); to a twenty-four-year-old virginal male, an introduction to a divorcee friend of hers. Gradually it became apparent that the gifts were not duty free. For example, she intruded in the relationship between the male member and her divorcee friend by serving gratuitously as a third-party go-between. In so doing she exerted considerable control over both individuals.

The therapist, too, became a challenge to her and various efforts to control him unfolded. The therapist by chance saw her sister in consultation and referred her to a competent therapist, a clinical psychologist. Mrs. Cape in the group congratulated him for his "brilliant tactic" of sending her sister to a psychologist; he "must have divined her deep-seated aversion for physicians." Similarly, on another occasion, the therapist made a comment to her and she responded, "How perceptive you were to have noticed my hands trembling." Now in fact, the therapist had not divined her sister's alleged aversion for physicians, he had simply referred her to the best therapist he knew to be available; nor had he noted her hands trembling. Entrapment was imminent: if he silently accepted her tribute, then he and Mrs. Cape became unwitting accomplices; on the other hand, if he admitted that he had not been sensitive to either the trembling of the hands or to the sister's aversion, then in a sense he has also been bested. In such situations, the therapist does well to concentrate instead on the process and to comment about the nature and the meaning of the trap. (We shall have a great deal more to say about relevant therapist technique in Chapter 6.)

She vied with the therapist in many ways. Intuitive and intellectually gifted, she became the group expert on dream and fantasy interpretation. On one occasion she saw the therapist between group sessions to ask whether she could take a book out of the medical library under his name. On one level the request was a reasonable one: the book (on music therapy) was related to her profession; furthermore she, as a layman, was not permitted the use of the library. However, in the context of the group process the request was a complex one in which she was testing limits, and which, if granted, would have meant to her and the rest of the group that she did occupy a "special place" vis-à-vis the therapist and the other members. The therapist clarified these contingencies to her and suggested further discussion in the next session. Following this perceived rebuttal, however, she called the three male members at home, after swearing them to secrecy, arranged to see them, and engaged in sexual relations with two: she failed with the third, a homosexual, only after a strenuous attempt.

The following meeting was a horrific one. It was extraordinarily tense, unproductive, and demonstrated the axiom (to be discussed later) that if something important in the group is being actively avoided, then nothing else of import is talked about either. Two days later Mrs. Cape, overcome with anxiety and guilt, asked to see the therapist and made a full "confession." It was agreed that the whole matter should be discussed in the next group meeting. This meeting was opened by Mrs. Cape, who said, "This is confession day, go ahead Charles!" and then later, "Your turn, Louis." The men performed as she bade them and later in the meeting received from her a critical evaluation of their sexual performance! Later in the course of the group Mrs. Cape accidentally let her estranged husband know of this event and soon he sent threatening messages to the men in the group, who then decided they could no longer trust Mrs. Cape and she was thereupon voted out of the group—the only occasion I have known of this. (She was continued in therapy with another group.) The saga does not end here, but perhaps we have gone far enough to illustrate the concept of the group as social microcosm.

To summarize, Mrs. Cape clearly displayed her interpersonal pathology in the group context. Her narcissism, her need for adulation, her need to control, her sadistic relationship with men, all unfolded in a dramatic sequence. Finally she began to receive crucial feedback as the men, for example, talked of their deep humiliation and anger at having to "jump through a hoop" for her and at having received "grades" for their sexual performance. They began to reflect that "No wonder your husband avoids you!" "Who wants to sleep with his mother?" etc. The female patients and the therapist also reflected their feelings about her insatiability, about the tremendously destructive course of her behavior—destructive for the group as well as herself. Most important of all she had to deal with this fact: she had started in the group with a number of troubled individuals who were anxious to help each other and whom she grew to like and respect; yet, in the course of one year, she had so poisoned her environment that, against her conscious wishes, she became a pariah, an outcast from a group of potentially intimate friends. It was the facing and working through of these issues in subsequent therapy that, in part, enabled her to change and to employ much of her considerable potential constructively in her future relationships and endeavors.

The Timid Homosexual

Mr. Flagge, a twenty-eight-year-old clerk, sought therapy because he felt that his life had "come to a grinding halt," had become constricted and stagnant; he repetitively became embroiled in "sick" unsatisfactory homosexual relationships; he was being exploited at work but was too timid to assert himself there and too anxious and unsure of himself to seek work elsewhere. His sexual expression was exclusively homosexual and he expressed no desire to change his orientation.

In the group his participation soon took on a characteristic pattern. He engaged animatedly in the sexual discussions and disclosed his intimate sexual life quite freely; however, he often became a nonparticipant for long intervals. Mr. Flagge never addressed a question to another patient nor, indeed, did he appear to share in any of the joys or travails or interests of the other members; only when sex was mentioned did Mr. Flagge stir, illuminated as though his master switch had just been thrown, rousing him from his arid world. The group became aware of this after living with Mr. Flagge in the sessions for many weeks, and one day a member told him, "You're a homosexual first and a human being second." Other members agreed and in various fashions confronted Mr. Flagge with the banal, restricted life space he had created for himself. In his friends, his conversations, his feeling life, his range of interests, he had isolated himself from all but a narrow slice of human experience.

One day in the group a member made a disparaging remark about a friend of Mr. Flagge's with whom he had seen him walking during the week; he continued to make some very insulting remarks about "queers" in general. Mr. Flagge flushed but did not comment and the incident was forgotten as the group became involved in another pressing issue. However, Mr. Flagge missed the next meeting and in the following session reported that for the first time in months he found himself extraordinarily sexually driven and had been relentlessly cruising gay bars, parks, Turkish baths, and public lavatories since his last group meeting. Furthermore, he described to the group, in great detail, the type of "sick" sex in which he had been engaging, including such perversions as copraphagia and bizarre sado-masochistic practices. Although the group was a mature, sophisticated one, this was more than

27

they could take and they responded with aversion and withdrawal from him. When we analyzed the process of these events, the pattern seemed clear. Mr. Flagge, instead of expressing his great anger to the other patient—the appropriate target—had reacted in a characteristic fashion. He had plunged himself into a cycle of activity that he personally experienced as degrading; furthermore, he castigated himself still more by behaving in the group in such a way as to invite rejection and scorn. This insight was a profound one for Mr. Flagge and it was of paramount relevance to his presenting problem: his inability to assert himself, to demand, to avoid being exploited. He appeared so fearful of expressing anger that he sought safety symbolically by self-degradation. Who will fear or harm the man at the bottom of the heap? Mr. Flagge eventually faced his anger in the group, directed it toward the proper target and survived. The incident was a crucial one for him and the eventual carryover to the outside world was considerable. Mr. Flagge's major interpersonal difficulties, therefore, were manifested in his relationships with the group members. His limited involvement, his overevaluation of the sexual basis of relatedness, his fear of assertiveness, and his maladaptive manner of dealing with his anger by turning it upon himself, all unfolded in the group and were available for analysis and change.

The Men Who Could Not Feel

One day the group was discussing the fact that the therapists, because of a last-minute exigency, had canceled the previous meeting. Miss Sands was greatly distressed and disclosed her profound loneliness. The group, in fact, seemed her only home, her only human contact, and she wept in despair. Mr. Farr, restless, started a long monologue in which he prescribed socializing techniques to her. Others tried in vain to stop him; finally, when he was in the midst of an endless comparison of parties and swimming pools and how one gets used to the water one toe at a time, Miss Sands tearfully exploded by shouting that he was a pompous ass. He responded only by pointing out that he hadn't been allowed to finish and doggedly pursued his metaphor.

Shortly after this, a male member who had been in the group for only a few meetings suddenly changed his seat from a chair next to the therapist to one across the room. When asked about the switch he seemed tremulous and on the verge of panic; he finally explained that he "felt sexually oppressed by the therapist." (This patient entered therapy because of strong unexpressed homosexual impulses which engendered considerable guilt and anxiety. He had not yet discussed this in the group.) Mr. Farr exclaimed jokingly, "Ye gods, how did sex get into this?"

As we examined these and other transactions of Mr. Farr's, the common denominator seemed evident: emotions must be avoided. He avoided his own emotions and endeavored to avoid interacting emotionally with others. Mr. Farr had entered therapy because of his inability to love and to marry. He had during his adolescence barely survived the horrors of a concentration camp and had long since avoided the danger and pain of deep interpersonal involvement.

In another group Mr. Steele, a sometime homosexual, sought therapy for a single, sharply delineated problem: "I want to be able to feel sexually stimulated by a woman." Intrigued by this conundrum, the group searched for the answer. They investigated his early life, sexual habits, fantasies, and finally, baffled, turned away. As life in the group continued, Mr. Steele, a regular attender, seemed peculiarly impassive. He spoke in a monotone and seemed entirely insensitive of others' pain. On one occasion, for example, a member in great distress announced in sobs that she was illegitimately pregnant and was planning to have a criminal abortion. During her account she also mentioned incidentally that she had had a bad marijuana "trip." Mr. Steele, seemingly unmoved by her tears, persisted in questioning her intellectually about marijuana effects and was puzzled when the group turned on him because of his insensitivity. So many similar incidents occurred that the group came to expect no emotions from him. When he was directly queried about his feelings, he responded as if he had been addressed in a foreign language. After some months the group formulated a new answer to his oft-repeated question, "Why can't I have sexual feelings toward a woman?" They asked him to consider instead why he couldn't have *any* kinds of feeling toward man *or* woman.

Changes in his behavior occurred very gradually, via an investigation of his autonomic expressions of affect. The group wondered about his frequent facial flushing; he described his gastric tightness during emotionally laden episodes in the group. On one occasion a very volatile girl in the group called him a "goddamned faggot" and said that she couldn't relate to a "psychologically deaf and dead" individual and threatened to leave the group. Mr. Steele again remained impassive, stating that he wasn't going to "get down to her level." However, the next week he told the group that after the meeting he had gone home and cried like a baby. When looking back at the course of his therapy this seemed to be a turning point, and gradually he was able to feel and express sorrow, fear, and anger with others. His relationship with people in the group changed from his being a tolerated mascot to his being accepted as a compeer.

These few clinical illustrations are sufficient to clarify this simple but basic concept in group therapy: patients, during their life in a group, will sooner or later be themselves and will, in their intragroup member relationships, manifest their interpersonal maladaptive behavior. They will also, of course, demonstrate their areas of strength, of resourcefulness, of sensitivity and empathy. Many of these aspects may become evident in a single meeting, or months may be required for patterns to be clear; the duration of time required for recognition is a function of the form of the

29

interpersonal pathology as well as of the sensitivity of the therapist and the group.

The concept of the group as a social microcosm implies, in part, an ahistoric, or as it is popularly called, a "here-and-now" approach to therapy. This approach, which has far-reaching implications for the tactics and strategy of the therapist, is by no means a recent trend in psychotherapy; in the history of Western psychotherapeutic practice it dates back at least forty years. These issues will all be fully discussed in Chapter 6.[*]

Overview

Let us now return to the primary task of this chapter: to define and describe the curative factor "interpersonal learning." All the necessary premises have been posited and described in our discussion of:

1. The importance of interpersonal relationships
2. The corrective emotional experience
3. The group as a social microcosm

If these principles are organized into a logical sequence, the mechanism of interpersonal learning as a curative factor becomes more evident.

1. Psychiatry, the study of human behavior, is the study of interpersonal relationships. Psychiatric symptomatology has both its origins and its contemporary expression in disturbed interpersonal relationships.
2. The psychotherapy group, provided its development is unhampered by severe structural restrictions, evolves into a social microcosm, a miniaturized representation of each patient's social universe.
3. The group members, through consensual validation and self-observation, become aware of significant aspects of their interpersonal behavior: their strengths, their limitations, their parataxic distortions, and their maladaptive behavior which elicits unwanted responses from others. Often the patient in the past has had a series of disastrous group experiences in which he has been rejected and consequently has gradually internalized a derogatory self-image. He has failed to learn from these experiences because the

---

[*] Slater,[23] in an interesting speculative work, expands the concept of microcosm yet further and argues that man's entire social and religious evolution is recapitulated in the development of the small group.

members, sensing his general insecurity, have not communicated to him the reasons for his rejection. He has never learned to discriminate between objectionable aspects of his behavior and a picture of himself as totally objectionable. The therapy group with its encouragement of accurate feedback makes such a discrimination possible.

4. The depth and meaningfulness of this awareness is directly proportional to the amount of affect associated with the transaction. The more real and the more emotionally laden the experience, the more potent is the impact; the more objectified and intellectualized the experience, the less effective the learning.

5. As a result of this awareness, the patient may gradually change or may more abruptly risk new types of behavior and expression. The likelihood that change will occur is a function of:
   a. the patient's motivation for change; the amount of personal discomfort and dissatisfaction with current modes of behavior;
   b. the patient's involvement in the group, his need for acceptance by the group, his respect and appreciation of the other members;
   c. the rigidity of the patient's character structure and interpersonal style.

6. The change in behavior may generate a new cycle of interpersonal learning via self-observation and feedback from other members. Furthermore, the patient appreciates that some feared calamity which had hitherto prevented such behavior was irrational; his new behavior did not result in such calamities as death, destruction, abandonment, derision, or engulfment.

7. The social microcosm concept is a bi-directional one; not only does outside behavior become manifest in the group, but behavior learned in the group is eventually carried over into the patient's social environment and alterations appear in his interpersonal behavior outside the group.

8. Gradually an *adaptive spiral* is set into motion, at first inside and then outside the group. As the patient's interpersonal distortions diminish, his ability to form rewarding relationships is enhanced. Social anxiety decreases, self-esteem rises, there is less need to conceal himself; others find this behavior likable and show more approval and acceptance to the patient, which further increases self-esteem and enhances further change. Eventually the adaptive spiral achieves such autonomy and efficacy that professional therapy is no longer necessary.

Before concluding the examination of interpersonal learning as a mediator of change, I wish to call attention to two terms conspicuous by their absence earlier in this chapter. The terms are "transference" and "insight," and they have played too important a role in previous formulations of the therapeutic process to be omitted without consideration. Transference, an indispensable principle and tool in individual dynamic psychotherapy, has been incorporated into our discussion under the general rubric of interpersonal or parataxic distortions. Working through transference distortions in individual therapy is, in the group therapy model, one phase of interpersonal learning. The patient's distortions, however, are not, of course, limited to the therapist, and consequently the therapist's orientation must shift from the investigation of the patient's relationship to him to the entire network of relationships in the group. Naturally, the leader, in whom the authority, the establishment, the parental imagos are embodied, may come to have a special significance and a special form of distortion for some patients. However, group therapy research dealing with group members' reconstruction of the curative process [24, 25, 26] indicates that the working through of the specific relationship to the group therapist is not considered by them as of paramount importance. We shall have a great deal more to say on this issue in Chapter 5.

I have avoided the term "insight" because it is not a unitary concept and defies definition. In the group therapeutic process, patients may obtain "insight" on at least four different levels:

1. Patients may gain a more objective perspective on their interpersonal behavior. They may for the first time learn how they are seen by other people—how they manifest themselves interpersonally. Are they tense, warm, aloof, seductive, bitter, etc.?

2. Patients may gain some understanding into *what* they are doing to and with other people. Unlike what occurs on the first level, they learn more than how their disparate bits of behavior are seen by others; they learn instead about their dealings with others over a longer time span. Are they exploiting others, rejecting others, courting constant admiration from others, seducing and then withdrawing from others, relentlessly competing with others? Are they so needy of acceptance and love that their effacing behavior elicits the opposite response from others? What do they want from the therapist? From the other men or women in the group?

3. A third level of insight might be termed "motivational insight." Patients may learn *why* they do what they do to and with other people. Aloof, detached patients may begin to learn what they fear so much about intimacy. Competitive, vindictive, controlling patients may learn about their needs to be taken care of, to be nurtured. Seductive-rejecting individuals may learn more about their hostility and their dread of its consequences. An apt generalization is that patients may begin to learn that they behave in various ways and have not been able to behave differently because of their fears of some interpersonal calamity. They assume that if they were to behave differently, some catastrophe would occur: they would be humiliated, scorned, destroyed, abandoned, engulfed, rejected, or perhaps would themselves become murderous or uncontrollable.

4. A fourth level of insight, "genetic insight," attempts to help patients under-

stand how they got to be the way they are. Through an exploration of his developmental history, the patient understands the genesis of present patterns of behavior. The theoretical framework and the language in which the genetic explanation is couched are, of course, largely dependent on the therapist's school of conviction.*

These four levels have been listed in the order of their implied degree of inference. An unfortunate and longstanding conceptual error has resulted, in part, from the tendency to equate a "superficial-deep" sequence with this "degree of inference" sequence. Furthermore, "deep" has become equated with "profound" or "good" and "superficial" equated with "bad," "obvious," and "inconsequential." Many have come to believe that the more profound the therapist, the deeper the interpretation (from a genetic perspective) and the more complete the treatment: there is, however, not a shred of evidence to support this contention.

First we should note that there is considerable question about the validity of many of our most cherished assumptions about the specific relationship between types of early experience and adult behavioral outcomes.[28, 29, 30] Modern developmental psychology is, so to speak, still in its infancy, and insufficient time has elapsed for the execution of definitive longitudinal studies.

In group therapy this "superficial-deep" (behavioral-genetic; low inference-high inference) continuum does not coincide with a "least curative-most curative" continuum. In terms of degree of occurrence and usefulness to the patient, there is a sharp downward gradient between level three and level four interpretations. Furthermore, all therapists have encountered the patient who has obtained a high degree of genetic insight based on some accepted child developmental theory, be it Freudian, Kleinian, Sullivanian, etc., and yet has made no therapeutic progress. On the other hand, it is commonplace for significant clinical change to occur with little insight involved and virtually none of the "genetic" category; nor is there a demonstrated relationship between the acquisition of genetic insight and the persistence of the change. It seems that in group therapy we need to disengage the term "deep" or "profound" from the concept of genetic insight: something that is deeply felt or has deep meaning and deep significance for the patient may, or as is usually the case, may not be related to the understanding of the genesis of behavior.

---

* Causality may be understood from a cross-sectional as well as from a longitudinal perspective. In his illuminating essay on Galilean and Aristotelian thought, [27] Kurt Lewin differentiates two types of causality: the historical (Aristotelian) and the ahistorical (Galilean). Aristotelian causality, an analogue of genetic causality, considers such factors as longitudinal individual development; while Galilean causality considers instead all the field forces currently acting on the object which will influence its behavior.

REFERENCES

1. D. A. Hamburg, "Emotions in Perspective of Human Evolution," in P. Knapp, (ed.), *Expressions of the Emotions of Man* (New York: International Universities Press, 1963).
2. J. Bowlby, "The Nature of the Child's Tie to His Mother," *Int. J. Psychoanal., 39:* 1–23, 1958.
3. W. Goldschmidt, as quoted by D. A. Hamburg, *op. cit.*, p. 308.
4. W. James, *The Principles of Psychology, Vol. 1* (New York: Henry Holt, 1890), p. 293.
5. H. S. Sullivan, *The Interpersonal Theory of Psychiatry* (New York: W. W. Norton, 1953).
6. H. S. Sullivan, *Conceptions of Modern Psychiatry* (New York: W. W. Norton, 1940).
7. P. Mullahy, *The Contributions of Harry Stack Sullivan* (New York: Hermitage House, 1952).
8. *Ibid.*, p. 22.
9. *Ibid.*, p. 10.
10. H. S. Sullivan, "Psychiatry: Introduction to the Study of Interpersonal Relations," *Psychiatry, 1:* 121–134, 1938.
11. Sullivan, *Conceptions of Modern Psychiatry*, p. 207.
12. *Ibid.*, p. 237.
13. I. D. Yalom, J. Tinklenberg, and M. Gilula, "Curative Factors in Group Therapy." Unpublished study.
14. C. M. Parkes, "Effects of Bereavement on Physical and Mental Health—a Study of the Medical Records of Widows," *Brit. Med. J., 2:* 274–279, 1964.
15. C. M. Parkes, "Recent Bereavement as a Cause of Mental Illness," *Brit. J. Psychiat., 110:* 198–204, 1964.
16. A. S. Kraus and A. M. Lilienfeld, "Some Epidemiological Aspects of the High Mortality Rate in the Young Widowed Group," *J. Chron. Dis., 10:* 207, 1959.
17. C. Rogers, "The Process of the Basic Encounter Group," mimeographed paper from Western Behavioral Sciences Institute, La Jolla, California, 1966.
18. F. Alexander and T. French, *Psychoanalytic Therapy: Principles and Applications* (New York: Ronald Press, 1946).
19. F. Alexander, "Unexplored Areas in Psychoanalytic Theory and Treatment," in G. Daniels (ed.), *New Perspectives in Psychoanalysis: Sandor Rado Lectures 1957–1963* (New York: Grune and Stratton, 1965), p. 75.
20. *Ibid.*, pp. 79–80.
21. J. Frank and E. Ascher, "The Corrective Emotional Experience in Group Therapy," *Am. J. Psychiat., 108:* 126–131, 1951.
22. B. B. Wassel, *Group Analysis* (New York: Citadel Press, 1966).
23. P. Slater, *Microcosm* (New York: John Wiley and Sons, 1966).
24. B. Berzon, C. Pious, and R. Farson, "The Therapeutic Event in Group Psychotherapy: A Study of Subjective Reports by Group Members," *J. Indiv. Psychol., 19:* 204–212, 1963.
25. G. Talland and D. Clark, "Evaluation of Topics in Therapy Group Discussions," *J. Clin. Psychol., 10:* 131–137, 1954.
26. J. Frank, "Some Values of Conflict in Therapeutic Groups," *Group Psychother., 8:* 142–151, 1955.
27. K. Lewin, "The Conflict Between Aristotelian and Galilean Modes of Thought in Contemporary Psychology," in *A Dynamic Theory of Personality: Selected Papers* (New York: McGraw-Hill, 1935), pp. 1–42.

28. L. W. Hoffman and M. Hoffman (eds.), *Review of Child Development Research,* *Vol. 1* (New York: Russell Sage Foundation, 1964).
29. L. W. Hoffman and M. Hoffman (eds.), *Review of Child Development Research,* *Vol. 2* (New York: Russell Sage Foundation, 1966).
30. P. Chodoff, "A Critique of the Freudian Theory of Infantile Sexuality," *Am. J. Psychiat., 123:* 507–518, 1966.

3

GROUP
COHESIVENESS

Beginning with the hypothesis that cohesiveness in group therapy is the analogue of "relationship" in individual therapy, this chapter deals with the available evidence for group cohesiveness as a curative factor and the various pathways through which group cohesiveness exerts a therapeutic influence.

For decades there has been strong clinical sentiment that successful individual therapy depends on the nature of the therapist-patient relationship; until recently, however, research confirmation has been lacking. In fact, Eysenck and others [1,2] have long maintained that the overall efficacy of psychotherapy has not been proven since their data indicate no measurable difference in outcome between treated and untreated patients. Hence they saw little point in determining critical variables in so-called successful therapy.

In the past few years Bergin[3] and Truax and Carkhuff[2] have marshaled evidence that "patients receiving psychotherapy show significantly greater *variability* in personality change indices at the conclusion of psychotherapy than do the no-treatment controls. . . . In other words, treatment may be for better or for worse."[4] Some psychotherapists help their patients while others may, in fact, do harm. If one, however, averages the effective and ineffective therapist recovery rates, only two-thirds of the patients will have been helped—the same figure cited by Eysenck for neurotics receiving no treatment.

Truax and Carkhuff pursued this finding by searching for the critical differences between effective and noneffective therapists. [5] In a series of rigorously controlled studies they found that the successful therapist establishes a relationship with his patients which offers them "high levels of accurate empathy, non-possessive warmth and genuineness." [6] Others have demonstrated that patients who are liked or consider themselves liked by their therapist are more likely to improve in therapy.[7, 8]

Furthermore, it has been long established that the quality of the relationship is independent of the individual therapist's school of conviction. Fiedler,[9, 10] in a series of studies, states that expert clinicians from different schools (Adlerian, Freudian, nondirective) resemble one another (and differ from nonexperts in their own school) in their conception of the ideal therapeutic relation and in the nature of the relationship they themselves establish with their patients.

Thus, effective therapists generate a specific type of therapeutic relationship with their patients. Furthermore, patients attribute their improvement to the nature of this relationship.[11, 12] The evidence supportive of the critical role of the relationship in individual therapy outcome is now so considerable that it compels us to ask whether "relationship" plays an equally critical role in group therapy. *It is obvious that the group therapy analogue of the patient-therapist relationship is a broader concept, encompassing the patient's relationship to his group therapist, to the other group members, and to the group as a whole.* At the risk of courting semantic confusion I shall refer to all these factors within the term "group cohesiveness."

Definition of Cohesiveness

Cohesiveness is a widely researched, poorly understood, basic property of groups. Several hundred research articles exploring cohesiveness have been written, many with widely varying definitions. In general, however, there is agreement that groups differ from one another in the amount of "groupness" present. Those with a greater sense of solidarity or "we-ness" value the group more highly and will defend it against internal and external threats; voluntary attendance, participation, mutual help, defense of the group standards are all greater than in groups with less esprit de corps. There are many methods of measuring cohesiveness, and a precise definition depends upon the method employed. In this book cohesiveness is broadly defined as "the resultant of all the forces acting on all the members to remain in the group," [13] or more simply "the attractiveness of a group for its members." [14] There is also a difference between total group

37

cohesiveness and individual member cohesiveness (or, more strictly, the individual's attraction to the group). The two, of course, are interdependent, and group cohesiveness is often computed by summing the individual members' level of attraction to the group; nevertheless, we must keep in mind that group members are differentially attracted to their group. At times we shall be referring to the therapy-facilitating effects of cohesiveness on the total group, while at other times we shall refer to the effects of an individual member's attraction to the group on his own process of therapy.

Before leaving the matter of definitions, it is well to remember that "group cohesiveness" is not per se a curative factor but instead a necessary precondition for effective therapy. When, in individual therapy, we say that "it is the relationship that heals," we mean that an ideal therapist-patient relationship creates conditions in which the necessary self-disclosure, intra- and interpersonal testing and exploration may unfold. In group therapy, similarly, group cohesiveness enhances the development of other important phenomena. Cohesiveness is not, for example, synonymous with intermember acceptance and understanding, but is interdependent with these factors. Cohesiveness is both a determinant and effect of intermember acceptance: the members of a highly cohesive therapy group will respond to each other in this manner more frequently than will the members of a noncohesive group; groups with members who show high mutual understanding and acceptance are, by definition, cohesive.

Cohesiveness as a Therapeutic Factor in Group Psychotherapy

Although we have discussed the curative factors separately, they are, to a great degree, interdependent. Universality and catharsis, for example, are part processes. It is not the sheer process of ventilation that is important, it is not only the discovery of others' problems similar to our own and the ensuing disconfirmation of our wretched uniqueness that is important; it is the affective sharing of one's inner world and *then* the acceptance by others that seems of paramount importance. Being accepted by others despite one's fantasies of being basically repugnant, unacceptable, or unlovable is a potent healing force. Provided he adheres to the group's procedural norms, the group will accept an individual regardless of his past life, transgressions, or perceived failings in his social universe. Deviant life styles, history of prostitution, sexual perversion, heinous criminal offenses—all can be accepted by the therapy group, provided norms of acceptance are established early in the group.

Very frequently psychiatric patients have had few opportunities for affective sharing and acceptance. Often we hear, "This is the first time I've ever told this to anyone." The decreased opportunities stem from the fact that patients have had fewer intimate relationships because of disturbed interpersonal skills. Furthermore, their conviction of the abhorrence of their impulses and fantasies have made interpersonal sharing even more difficult. I have known many isolated patients for whom the group represented their only deeply human contact. They may remember the sense of belonging and the basic acceptance years afterward, when most other recollections of the group have faded from memory. As one successful patient looking back over two and a half years of therapy put it, "The most important thing in it was just having a group there, people that I could always talk to, that wouldn't walk out on me. There was so much caring and hating and loving in the group and I was a part of it. I'm better now and have my own life, but it's sad to think that the group's not there any more."

Some patients describe the group as a haven from the stress of life, a source of strength for them. One reason that American prisoners did poorly during the Korean conflict was that they were not permitted this source of stability. Chinese captors disrupted cohesive group formation by methodically removing emergent group leaders. The Turks, on the other hand, maintained their morale and group structure. Leadership among them was determined completely on the basis of military rank and seniority; as soon as one leader was removed his role was filled automatically by the most senior remaining individual.

Patients may internalize the group. "It's as though the group is sitting on my shoulder, watching me. I'm forever asking, 'What would the group say about this or that?' " Often therapeutic changes persist and are consolidated because the members are disinclined to let the group down.[14]

Group membership, acceptance, and approval are of the utmost importance in the development of the individual. The importance of belonging to childhood peer groups, adolescent cliques, fraternities, the proper social "in" group can hardly be overestimated. There seems to be nothing of greater importance for the adolescent, for example, than to be included and accepted in some social group, and nothing more devastating than exclusion. Consider in the United States the "blackball" suicides following exclusion from fraternities, or in the West Indies the bone-pointing voodoo deaths, the latter mediated by total exclusion from the community, which regards the outcast as dead from the time the voodoo spell is cast.

39

Most psychiatric patients have an impoverished group history; never before have they been a valuable, integral, participating member of a group. For these patients the sheer successful negotiation of a group experience may in itself be curative.

Not only do we rely on others for approval and acceptance but also for continual validation of our important value systems. *When Prophecy Fails*[15] is a study of a religious cult which had predicted the end of the world. When the day passed without incident, the cult reacted by increasing its proselytizing efforts; doubt in the belief system of the group apparently required a greater degree of interpersonal validation.

Thus, in a number of ways, members of a therapy group come to mean a great deal to one another. The therapy group, at first perceived as an artificial group which doesn't count, may in fact come to count very much. Group members often experience a great deal of life together in their weekly meetings. I have known groups to experience together severe depressions, psychoses, marriage, divorce, abortions, suicide, career shifts, sharing of innermost thoughts, and incest (sexual activity among the group members). Relationships are often cemented by moving or hazardous adventures. How many relationships in life share such a panoply of vital experiences?

Evidence

Research evidence documenting the importance of group cohesiveness in the therapeutic process is rudimentary compared to the individual psychotherapy research. Nevertheless, there are a few relevant studies.

Dickoff and Lakin [16] in a study of former group psychotherapy patients find that, from the patients' point of view, group cohesiveness is of major therapeutic value.* They transcribed and categorized patients' explanations of the curative factors in their group experience. The investigators found that "more than half of the former patients indicated that the primary mode of help in group therapy is through mutual support." Patients who rejected the group more frequently complained of not having experienced meaningful social contact with the other members. Those patients who perceived their group as cohesive attended more sessions, experienced

* Twenty-eight patients who had been in either clinic or private outpatient groups were studied. The chief limitation of this exploratory inquiry is that the group therapy experience was of exceptionally brief duration (mean number of meetings attended = 11).

more social contact with other members, and judged the group as having offered a therapeutic mode. Those patients who either reported themselves improved or expressed regret at having to leave the group prematurely were significantly more prone to have:

1. Felt accepted by the other members
2. Perceived similarity of some kind among group patients
3. Made specific references to particular individuals when queried about their group experience

The authors conclude that group cohesiveness is in itself of therapeutic value and is essential for perpetuation of the group.

Kapp et al.[17] arrive at similar conclusions after a study of forty-seven patients who had been in twelve different psychotherapy groups for a mean duration of thirteen months. They administered a questionnaire designed to measure self-perceived personality change and the individual's assessment of the degree of cohesiveness among the members of the group. The findings indicate that self-perceived personality change correlates significantly with both the members' feelings of involvement in the group and with their assessment of total group cohesiveness. The authors conclude that perceived group unity (cohesiveness) may be an important factor in promoting personality change.*

A more rigorously designed study by Clark and Culbert [18] demonstrates a significant relationship between the quality of intermember relationships and outcome in a T-group of eleven subjects who met twice a week for a total of sixty-four hours. They correlated outcome† for the group members with intermember relationships.‡ Their results demonstrated that the

---

* These findings are tentative. The instruments to measure change were not, as recognized by the authors, standardized for reliability or validity. Furthermore, when personality change and group cohesiveness are tested simultaneously by a self-administered questionnaire, we cannot control for the possibility that patients who are attracted to their groups will be inclined to support their stance by reporting or perceiving themselves as improved. Cognitive dissonance theory teaches us that when an individual has made a decision he will misperceive, deny, and distort data which would discredit that decision.

† Outcome was measured by a well-validated rating scale designed by Walker, Rablen, and Rogers [19] to measure change in the individual's ability to relate to others, to construe his experience, to approach his affective life, and to confront and cope with his chief problem areas. Samples of each member's speech were independently rated on this scale by trained naïve judges from taped excerpts early and late in the course of the group.

‡ Intermember relationships were measured by the Barrett-Lennard Relationship Inventory,[20] which provided a measure of how each member viewed each other member (and the therapist) in terms of "unconditional, positive regard, empathic understanding, and congruence."

members who entered into the most two-person mutually therapeutic relationships showed the most improvement during the course of the group. Furthermore, the perceived relationship with the group leader was unrelated to the extent of change. The authors conclude that the quality of the member-member relationship is a prime determinant of individual change in the group experience.

My colleagues and I conducted two studies which document the importance of cohesiveness in the group therapeutic process. In one project (Yalom, Tinklenberg, Gilula),[21] twenty successful group therapy patients were studied, and the relative importance of all the curative factors described in this book were assessed. This project will be reported in detail in the next chapter. For the present it is sufficient to state that patients retrospectively considered cohesiveness to be of considerable import.

Yalom, Houts, Zimerberg, and Rand[22] examined at the end of a year all the patients (N=40) who had started therapy in five outpatient groups. The degree of improvement in symptoms, functioning, and relationships was assessed both in a psychiatric interview by a team of raters and by a self-assessment scale. Outcome was then correlated with a host of variables which had been measured in the first three months of therapy. Positive outcome in therapy correlated with only two predictor variables— "group cohesiveness" * and "general popularity." † That is, patients who were most attracted to the group (high cohesiveness) and who were rated as more popular by the other group members at the sixth week and the twelfth week had a better therapy outcome at the fiftieth week. The popu-

---

* Cohesiveness was measured by a post-group questionnaire filled out by each patient at the seventh and at the twelfth meetings, consisting of eleven questions (each answered on a five-point defined scale):

1. How often do you think your group should meet?
2. How well do you like the group you are in?
3. If most of the members of your group decided to dissolve the group by leaving, would you like an opportunity to dissuade them?
4. Do you feel that working with the group you are in will enable you to attain most of your goals in therapy?
5. If you could replace members of your group with other "ideal group members," how many would you exchange (exclusive of group therapists)?
6. To what degree do you feel that you are included by the group in the group's activities?
7. How do you feel about your participation in, and contribution to, the group work?
8. What do you feel about the length of the group meeting?
9. How do you feel about the group therapist(s)?
10. Are you ashamed of being in group therapy?
11. Compared to other therapy groups, how well would you imagine your group works together?

† Popularity was measured sociometrically: each member, at the sixth and twelfth meetings, was asked to rank order all the group members for general popularity.

larity finding, which is a stronger correlation than the cohesiveness, is, as we shall discuss shortly, quite relevant to group cohesiveness and sheds light upon the mechanism through which group cohesiveness mediates change. Note that this research demonstrates the relationship between outcome and individual members' cohesiveness (attraction to the group); the correlation between total group cohesiveness and outcome has not yet been directly demonstrated. That is, research has not yet clearly demonstrated that all or the majority of the members of a highly cohesive group will have better outcomes than the members of an equivalent but less cohesive group.*

SUMMARY OF FOREGOING

We have cited evidence that patients in group therapy consider group cohesiveness to be a prime mode of help in their therapy experience. There is tentative evidence that self-perceived positive therapy outcome is related to individual attraction to the group and to total group cohesiveness. Individuals with positive outcome have had more mutually satisfying intermember relationships. Positive patient outcome is correlated with individual attraction to the group and also to group popularity, a variable related to group support and acceptance. Although it is clear that further controlled research is necessary, these findings taken together do support the contention that group cohesiveness is an important determinant of positive therapeutic outcome.

There is, in addition to this direct evidence, considerable indirect evidence stemming from nontherapy group research. A plethora of studies demonstrate that in laboratory task groups increased group cohesiveness produces many results which may be considered as intervening therapy outcome variables. For example, group cohesiveness results in better group attendance, greater participation of members, greater influenceability of the members, and many other effects. We shall consider these findings in great detail shortly as we attempt to determine the mechanism through which cohesiveness fosters therapeutic change.

---

* There is, however, a formidable methodological obstacle in that a study involving a very large number of groups would be needed for such verification. In the Yalom, Houts, et al. study,[22] since only five groups were studied, near perfect rank ordering would be required for statistical significance. However, it should be noted the group that was the most cohesive at the twelfth meeting had a very successful therapy course. This group—the Dr. X. and Dr. G. group discussed in Chapter 8—demonstrated great stability, and virtually all the members had successful outcomes. The group with the lowest cohesiveness fragmented and was disbanded at the twenty-fourth meeting with poor outcome results for all members. However, no significant differences in outcome existed between groups 2, 3, and 4.

Mechanism of Action

INTRODUCTION

For the remainder of this chapter we shall discuss the various ways in which cohesiveness produces change in group patients. How do group acceptance, group support, intermember trust and acceptance help troubled individuals? Surely there is more to it than simple support or acceptance; therapists learn very early in their careers that love is not enough, that therapy does not consist of merely furnishing affective supplies for the patient. Although the quality of the relationship is crucial, therapy consists of more than relating warmly and honestly to the patient. The relationship creates favorable conditions for other processes to be set into motion. What other processes? And how are they important? In this discussion we shall approach this question from many different perspectives, all or some of which may be valid for any given patient.

Perhaps no one has thought more deeply about the therapeutic relationship than Carl Rogers. Let us start our investigation by examining his views about the mode of action of the therapeutic relationship in individual therapy. In his most systematic description of the process of therapy [23] Rogers states that when the conditions of an ideal therapist-patient relationship exist, a characteristic process is set into motion:

The patient is increasingly free in expressing his feelings.

He begins to test reality and to become more discriminatory in his feelings and perceptions of his environment, his self, other persons, and his experiences.

He increasingly becomes aware of the incongruity between his experiences and his concept of self.

He also becomes aware of feelings which have been previously denied or distorted in awareness.

His concept of self which now includes previously distorted or denied aspects becomes more congruent with his experience.

He becomes increasingly able to experience, without threat, the therapist's unconditional positive regard and to feel an unconditional positive self-regard.

He increasingly experiences himself as the focus of evaluation of the nature and worth of an object or experience.

He reacts to experience less in terms of his perception of others' evaluation of him and more in terms of its effectiveness in enhancing his own development.

Central to Rogers' views is his formulation of an "actualizing tendency," an inherent tendency of the organism to expand and to develop itself. The therapist in individual and in group therapy functions as a facilitator and must help create conditions favorable for self-expansion. The first task of the individual is self-exploration; he must begin to consider feelings and experiences previously denied awareness. This task is a ubiquitous stage in dynamic psychotherapy. Horney,[24] for example, emphasizes the individual's need for self-knowledge and self-realization, stating that the task of the therapist is to remove obstacles in the path of these autonomous processes. There is some experimental evidence that good rapport in individual therapy and cohesiveness in group therapy enable the individual to gain greater self-awareness. For example, Truax,[25] studying forty-five hospitalized patients in three heterogenous groups, demonstrated that patients in cohesive groups will be significantly more inclined to engage in deep and extensive self-exploration (measured by the Rogers-Rablen scale).[19]

Over the last few years Rogers has become increasingly interested in the group experience as a therapeutic medium; and although his views of the important growth-potentiating factors in groups are similar to his views of those in the individual relationship, he has commented upon additional powerful factors inherent in the group setting. He underscores, for example, that member-member acceptance and understanding may carry with it a greater power and meaning than acceptance by a therapist. Other group members, after all, don't have to care, don't have to understand, they're not paid for it, it's not their "job." [26] This peer acceptance occurs regularly in childhood but not for many of our patients, who find validation by other group members a vital experience. In the affluence of modern American society we have moved up the hierarchy of needs [27] from survival needs to emotional ones. Modern man, steeped in abundance, turns to the question, "With whom can I be personal?" With the breakup of the extended nuclear family and the isolation of contemporary life, the problem becomes a considerable one. The intimacy developed in a group may be seen as a counterforce in a culture "which appears to be bent upon dehumanizing the individual and dehumanizing our human relationships."[28] The deeply felt human experience in the group may be of great value to the patient, Rodgers believes; even if there is no visible carryover, no external change in behavior, the patient may still experience a more human, richer part of himself and have this as an internal reference point.

Group members' acceptance of one another, though crucial in the group therapeutic process, may be quite slow to develop. Acceptance by others and self-acceptance are mutually dependent; not only is self-acceptance basically dependent on acceptance by others, but acceptance of others is

45

fully possible only after the individual can accept himself. The members of a therapy group may experience considerable self-contempt and a deep contempt for others. A manifestation of this may be seen in the patient's initial refusal to join "a group of nuts" or his reluctance to become closely involved in the group for fear of being sucked into a maelstrom of misery. The importance of self-acceptance for the acceptance of others has been demonstrated in research by Rubin,[29] who studied fifty individuals before and after an intensive live-in two-week T-group laboratory. Increase in self-acceptance, measured by a sentence completion test,[30] was significantly correlated with increased acceptance of others, measured by a questionnaire focusing on changes in racial prejudice. These results are consonant with Fromm's statement many years ago that only after one is able to love himself is he able to love others. I would add, however, that only after he has once been loved and accepted will he be able to love himself.

GROUP COHESIVENESS AND SELF-ESTEEM

Although we have not yet used the term, we have begun to discuss a variable usually labeled "self-esteem," a core concept in any approach to personality change. Hamburg[31] has stated that all individuals seeking assistance from a mental health professional have in common two paramount problems: (1) a difficulty in establishing and maintaining meaningful interpersonal relationships and (2) a difficulty in maintaining a sense of personal worth (self-esteem). Although it is difficult to discuss these two interdependent areas as separate entities, nevertheless, since we have in the preceding chapter dwelled more heavily on the establishment of interpersonal relationships, we shall now concentrate on self-esteem.

In a scholarly review and analysis of identity and esteem, from which this discussion draws heavily, Miller[32] underscores the interdependence between self-esteem (the individual's evaluation of his identity) and public esteem (the group's evaluation of the worth of that aspect of his identity germane to that particular group). Self-esteem refers to the individual's conception of what he is really like, what he is really worth, and is indissolubly linked to his experiences in social relationships. Recall Sullivan's statement, "The self may be said to be made up of reflected appraisals."[33] The individual regards and values himself as he, during his ontogeny, believed others to have regarded and valued him. Depending upon the congruence of the individual's life experiences, he internalizes certain relationships and learns to evaluate himself with a measure of independence, but to a greater or lesser degree he is always concerned and influenced by his public esteem—the evaluation given by the groups to which he belongs.

How influenced the individual is by his public esteem in the group and how inclined he is to use the group's frame of reference depends on several factors: the importance of the group for him, the frequency and specificity of the group's communications to him about his public esteem, and the salience to him of the traits in question. (Presumably, in therapy groups, the salience is very great indeed, since the traits in question are close to his core identity.) In other words, the more the group matters to him, the more he subscribes to the group values, the more he will be inclined to agree with the group judgment.[34]

The self-esteem-public esteem system is thus closely related to the concept of group cohesiveness. We have said that the degree of a group's influence on self-esteem is a function of its cohesiveness. The more attracted an individual is to the group, the more he respects the judgment of the group, the more he will attend to and take very seriously any discrepancy between his public esteem and his self-esteem. A discrepancy between the two will place the individual in a state of dissonance and he will initiate activity to remove the dissonance.

If this discrepancy veers to the *negative* side—if the group evaluates him less highly than he evaluates himself—how can he resolve the discrepancy? One recourse is to misperceive, deny, or distort the group's evaluation of his public esteem. In a therapy group this development generates a vicious circle. His public esteem is low because of his nonparticipation in the group task, and any increase in communicational problems and defensiveness will only beget further devaluation of public esteem. Eventually the group's communication to him will break through unless he uses near-psychotic mechanisms to distort reality.

Another method of dealing with the discrepancy is to devaluate the group. He may rationalize, for example, that the group is an artificial one or one composed of highly disturbed individuals, and compare it unfavorably with some anchor group (for example, the church or an occupational group) which might evaluate him differently. This sequence, characteristic of the group history of "group deviants" described in Chapter 1, usually results in termination of membership.

A final and therapeutic method of resolving the discrepancy is for the individual to attempt to raise his public esteem by changing those traits and attitudes which have been criticized by the group. This method of resolution is more likely if the individual is highly attracted to the group and if the discrepancy between the low public esteem and higher self-esteem is not too great. Is this final approach—the use of group pressure to change individual behavior or attitudes—a form of conditioning? Is it not mechanical, neglecting deeper levels of integration, and thus destined for transience? Indeed group therapy does employ conditioning principles; in fact psychotherapy is, in all its variants, basically a form of learning. Even the most nondirective approach invokes operant conditioning techniques which are not, however, consciously employed by the therapist.[35] Patients learn through explicit statements or through more subtle implications what their therapists desire of them. However, these comments in no way imply a more superficial approach to behavior change or less enduring results nor do they imply a dehumanization of the therapy process. Aversive or operant conditioning of behavior and attitudes is, in my opinion, neither feasible nor effective when approached as an isolated technique.* In fact, as I have repeatedly stressed, all the curative factors are intricately interdependent and must be appreciated as part of a complex spiraling process. Behavior and attitudinal change, regardless of origin, begets other changes. The group changes its evaluation of the patient, he feels more satisfied with himself in the group and with the group itself, and the adaptive spiral described in the previous chapter is initiated.

Far more common, in the properly guided therapy group, is a discrepancy in the opposite direction: the group evaluates the individual more highly than he evaluates himself. Once again the patient, in a state of dissonance, will attempt to resolve the discrepancy. In some groups he might seek to lower his public esteem by revealing inadequacies. However, in therapy groups, this behavior has the opposite effect of raising public esteem still more, since disclosure of inadequacies is a cherished group norm and further enhances acceptance by the group. Instead, the individual may begin to re-examine and re-evaluate his low level of self-esteem. An illustrative clinical vignette may flesh out this bare-boned formulation.

Mrs. Ende, a thirty-four-year-old housewife with an emotionally impoverished background, sought therapy because of anxiety and guilt stemming from a series of extramarital affairs. Clinically her self-esteem was exceedingly low; she was self-derogatory about her physical appearance and about her functioning as a

---

* Although lasting patient improvement is often reported following a removal, by behavioral therapy techniques, of some disabling complaint, closer inspection of the process inevitably reveals that important interpersonal relationships have been affected. Either the therapist-patient relationship has been more meaningful than the therapist realized or some important changes, initiated by the symptomatic relief, have occurred in the patient's social relationships which have served to reinforce and maintain the patient's improvement.

mother and a wife. She had received some solace from her religious affiliation, though she had never considered herself good enough to socialize with the "church people" in her community. She had married a man whom she considered repugnant but nonetheless a good man and certainly good enough for her. Only in her sexual affairs, and particularly in an arrangement in which she had sexual relationships with several men at once, did she seem to come alive. Only here did she feel attractive, desirable, and able to give something of herself which seemed of value to others. However, this behavior clashed with her religious convictions and resulted in considerable anxiety and self-derogation.

Viewing the group as a social microcosm, the therapist soon noted characteristic trends in her group behavior. She related to the other members around sexual issues, and for many hours the group struggled with all the exciting ramifications of her sexual dilemma. At all other times in the group, however, she disengaged and offered nothing. She related to the group as to her social environment. She could not associate with the good church people and, in fact, felt she had nothing to offer save her genitals.

Her course of therapy consisted, in large part, of the gradual re-examination and eventual disconfirmation of her belief that she had nothing of value to offer others. As she began to respond to others, to exchange problems and feelings, she found herself increasingly valued by other members. The public esteem-self-esteem discrepancy eventually widened to the point that upward shifts in her self-esteem levels resulted. Her behavior changed to such a point that meaningful nonsexual relationships in and out of the group were possible and these in turn further enhanced self-esteem, thereby generating an adaptive spiral.

SELF-ESTEEM, PUBLIC ESTEEM, AND GROUP COHESIVENESS—EVIDENCE

Group therapy research has not specifically investigated the relationship between public esteem and shifts in self-esteem.* However, there are some interesting data on group popularity—a variable closely synonymous with public esteem. In the study [22] of forty group therapy patients previously described, we demonstrated that patients "elected" by the other members as most popular at the sixth and twelfth weeks of therapy had significantly better therapy outcomes than the other group members at the end of one year. Thus it seems that patients who have high public

* Lundgren and Miller [36] reported a relevant study on nonpatients in a Bethel T-group (see Chapter 14). They found that self-esteem decreased when public esteem (measured by sociometrics) decreased. Furthermore, the more a member underestimated his public esteem, the more acceptable he was to the other members; in other words, the ability to face one's deficiencies or even to judge oneself a little harshly increased one's public esteem.

49

esteem early in the course of the group are destined to have a better therapy outcome.

To understand this phenomenon the investigators studied the determinants of popularity. What factors seemed reponsible for the attainment of popularity in therapy groups? Three variables, which did not themselves correlate with outcome, correlated significantly with popularity, namely:

1. Previous self-disclosure.*
2. FIRO-B compatibility.† Individuals who had (perhaps fortuitously) those interpersonal needs which happen to blend well with those of the other group members become popular in the group.
3. Other sociometric measures; group members who were highly chosen as leisure companions or work committee colleagues became popular in the group.

A clinical study of the most popular and least popular members revealed that members, in their selection of popular patients, placed a premium on youth, education, intelligence, and the ability to introspect. The popular patients all assumed leadership in their groups, helping to fill the leadership vacuum which occurred early in the group when the therapist declined to assume the traditional leader role.

The most unpopular patients in our sample were markedly rigid, moralistic, nonintrospective, and least involved in the group task. Four were blatantly deviant in their groups and quickly became group isolates. They responded to this defensively, attacking the group and thereby insuring their exclusion. Others who were more schizoid appeared frightened of the group process and remained on the periphery, never joining the interactional wave length of the group.

To summarize these findings, patients attain popularity in therapy groups by dint of active participation, self-disclosure, self-exploration, and leadership behavior. In short we may say that patients gain approval (and ultimately improve) in the therapy group by participating maximally in the group task.

What is the task of a therapy group? Most therapy groups come to value:

---

* Before beginning therapy the patients completed a questionnaire (a modified Jourard self-disclosure questionnaire)[37] which indicated that individuals who had previously disclosed much of themselves (relevant to the other group members) to close friends or to groups of individuals were destined to become popular in their groups. In a recent study, Hurley [38] demonstrated, in a ten-week counseling group, that popularity was correlated with self-disclosure *in* the group as well as prior to group therapy.

† See Chapter 8 for a discussion of the FIRO-B questionnaire.

1. Acceptance of the patient role
2. Self-disclosure
3. Honesty about feelings toward oneself and other members
4. Nondefensiveness
5. Interest in and acceptance of others
6. Support of the group
7. Personal improvement

Adherence to these behaviors is rewarded by the group. As Homans [39] has indicated, the member who abides most closely to the group norms is the member who is considered by the rest of the group as the most popular and the most influential.*

It is important to note that, not only is the individual who adheres to the group norms rewarded by increased public esteem, but he also reaps other dividends. The behaviors required by the group norms will serve him in good stead in his relationships outside of the group. In other words, the social skills the individual uses in the group to attain popularity are reinforced by the popularity he achieves, and these skills are likely to help him deal more effectively with his interpersonal problems outside the group. Thus increased popularity in the group acts therapeutically in two ways: by influencing self-esteem and by reinforcing adaptive social skills.

GROUP COHESIVENESS AND GROUP ATTENDANCE

Continuation in the group is obviously a necessary, though not sufficient, prerequiste for successful treatment. Several studies indicate that interactional group therapy is long-term therapy and that patients who terminate early in the course of therapy receive little benefit.[22, 42, 43] Over fifty patients who dropped out of therapy groups within the first twelve meetings reported that they did so because of some stress encountered in the group. They were neither satisfied with their therapy experience nor improved; indeed many of Nash's [44] patients felt worse. Patients remaining in the group for at least several months, however, had a very high likelihood (85 per cent in one study)[22] of profiting from therapy.

The greater the patient's attraction to the group, the more inclined he will be to continue membership in therapy groups [45] as well as in labora-

---

* Bales [40] in his research with leaderless discussion and task groups has found that two leaders arise in the group: a "task executive" leader and a "social-emotional" leader. Only rarely are these two roles filled by the same person, "the great man." In therapy groups, however, when the therapist is omitted from the sociometric selection, the patients usually select the same person to fill these roles.[41]

tory and task groups.[46, 47] For example, Sagi et al.[46] found a significant correlation between attendance and group cohesiveness in twenty-three college student organizations.* Yalom and Rand [45] studied cohesiveness among forty members of five therapy groups and found that the least cohesive members terminated within the first twelve meetings. In another study Yalom et al.[22] found that the members with the highest cohesiveness scores at the sixth and at the twelfth meetings attended significantly more meetings during the year.†

The relationship between cohesiveness and maintenance of membership has implications for the total group as well. Not only do the least cohesive members terminate membership and fail to benefit from therapy, but non-cohesive groups with a high patient turnover prove to be less therapeutic for the remaining members as well.

Stability of membership is a necessary condition for effective group therapy. Most therapy groups go through an early phase of instability, as some members drop out and replacements are added. Following this, the groups often enter into a long stable phase in which much of the solid work of therapy occurs. In a study of four therapy groups [22] we found that despite a heavy turnover of patients during the first twenty meetings, there were no further dropouts between the twentieth and the forty-fifth meetings (the end point of the study). Some groups seem to enter this phase of stability early, while others never achieve it.‡ Dropouts at times beget other dropouts, some patients terminating soon after the departure of a key member. In a group therapy follow-up study [21] patients often spontaneously underscored the importance of membership stability. A study carried out in an inpatient facility for sexual offenders treated by group therapy indicated also that the overriding critical factor in success-ful outcome is a stable therapist-group relationship.[48] Board[11] reports analogous findings in an outcome study of individual therapy. The patients who have not had a stable relationship with a single therapist but have seen several successive therapists over a relatively brief period have poorer therapy outcomes and report confusion about their problems and their therapy experience.

---

* Cohesiveness was appraised by a self-administered cohesiveness questionnaire; attendance was tabulated for six months. Of interest also was the fact that the most popular members had significantly better attendance records than unpopular members.

† One methodological obstacle encountered is that the most dissatisfied patients drop out so quickly that the investigator does not have the opportunity to obtain cohesiveness measurements on them.

‡ A fifth group in the same study lost several members and finally disbanded completely at the twenty-fourth meeting.

GROUP COHESIVENESS AND THE EXPRESSION OF HOSTILITY

We must not mistakenly equate cohesiveness with comfort. Although cohesive groups may show greater acceptance, intimacy, and understanding, there is evidence that they also permit greater development and expression of hostility and conflict.

Unless hostility is openly expressed, persistent and impenetrable hostile attitudes may develop which increasingly hamper effective interpersonal learning. As Newcomb states, unexpressed or autistic hostility "arising when another is viewed as a threat . . . is likely to persist until modified by further interaction. If as a result of a hostile attitude . . . communication with the other person is avoided, the conditions necessary for eliminating the hostile attitude are not likely to occur." [49] The temptation, however, for an individual to break off communication with an enemy is very great. At the most fundamental level one simply does not enjoy contact with someone he dislikes; the resulting lack of communication bars the opportunity for attitude change.[50]

The same phenomenon occurs with small groups and such megagroups as nations. Sherif's [51] famed Robbers' Cave experiment offers experimental confirmation. A camp of eleven-year-old well-adjusted boys was divided at the outset into two groups which were placed in competition with one another in a series of hotly contested events. Soon each group developed a high degree of cohesiveness and internal organization as well as a deep sense of hostility toward the other group. Any meaningful communication between the two groups became impossible. If they were placed in physical proximity in the dining hall, the group boundaries remained impermeable and the members merely exchanged taunts, insults, and spitballs.*

In the therapy process communication must not be ruptured; the adversaries must continue to work together in a meaningful way, to take responsibility for their statements, and be willing to go beyond name calling. This is, of course, a major difference between therapy groups and social groups, in which conflicts often result in the permanent rupture of relationships. Patients' descriptions of the critical incident in therapy (see Chapter 2) usually involve an episode in which they expressed strong neg-

* The communications block between the members of the two groups was finally relieved only by instilling a degree of cohesion and allegiance in a single large group. Some superordinate goals were created which disrupted the small group boundaries and forced the boys to work together in a single large group. For example, a truck carrying food for an overnight hike was stalled in a ditch and could be rescued only by cooperative efforts of all the boys; a highly desirable movie could be rented only by the pooled contributions of the entire camp; the water supply was cut off and similarly could be restored only by the cooperative efforts of all campers.

ative affect. However, in each instance they were able to weather the storm, to continue relating (often in a more gratifying manner) to the other member.

Underlying these events is the condition of cohesiveness. The group and the members must mean enough to each other so that they will be willing to bear the discomfort of working through the conflict. Cohesive groups are, in a sense, like families with much internecine warfare but nonetheless a powerful sense of loyalty. Frank [52] has commented that members of a cohesive group are more prone to take each other quite seriously and continue communication regardless of how angry they become.

Once the conditions are such that conflict can be constructively dealt with in the group, therapy is enhanced in many ways. We have already mentioned the importance of catharsis, of risk taking, of gradually exploring previously avoided or unknown parts of oneself and recognizing that the anticipated dreaded catastrophe is chimerical. It is also important for many patients to have the experience of being aggressed against. In the struggle, as Frank [52] suggests, each may become better acquainted with the reasons for his position and learn to withstand pressure from another. The conflict may enhance self-disclosure, as each tends to reveal more and more of himself to clarify his position. As members are able to go beyond the mere statement of position, as they begin to understand the other's experiential world, past and present, and view the other's position from his frame of reference, they may begin to understand that the other's point of view may be as appropriate for him as their own is for themselves. The coming to grips with, working through, and eventual resolution of extreme dislike or hatred of another person is an experience of great therapeutic power.

Not only are cohesive groups more able to express intermember hostility, but there is evidence that they are also more able to express hostility toward the leader.* Regardless of the personal style or skill of the group

---

* A study by Pepitone and Reichling [53] is an example of such confirmation in laboratory task groups. Paid college student volunteers were divided into thirteen high and thirteen low cohesion groups. Cohesion was created in the usual experimental manner: members of high cohesive groups were told before their first meeting that their group had been composed of individuals who had been carefully matched from psychological questionnaires to ensure maximum compatibility. The members of low cohesive groups were given the opposite treatment and were told the matching was unsuccessful and that they would probably not get along well together. The groups, while waiting for the experiment to begin, were systematically insulted by a member of the research staff. After he had left, the members' discussions in the various groups revealed that the high cohesive groups were significantly more able to express their hostility about the authority figure with greater intensity and directness. Wright [54] obtained similar findings in research on nursery school groups.

leader, the therapy group will nonetheless come, often within the first dozen meetings, to experience some degree of hostility and resentment toward him. He does not fulfill their fantasied expectations, he does not care enough, he does not direct enough, he does not offer immediate relief. If the group does not express these feelings openly, then several harmful consequences may ensue. They may attack a convenient scapegoat, either another group member or some institution like "Psychiatry" or "Doctors"; they may suppress the anger only to experience a creeping irritation within themselves or the group; they may, in short, begin to establish norms discouraging open expression of resentment. On the other hand, it is clearly helpful to the group if they are able to express their hostility and then observe that no irreparable calamity has occurred. It is obviously better for the therapist to face this attack than some scapegoated member who will be far less able to withstand and to understand it. Furthermore, the process is a self-reinforcing one; a concerted effective attack on the leader serves to increase cohesiveness still further. For example:

One group in its eighth meeting spent much of the session on nonpersonal topics such as politics, hypnosis, vacations, etc. Since some members were obviously uninvolved, the therapist brought up the subject by quoting one patient who had said she was bored. He wondered why the group was dealing with boring issues. An onslaught on the therapist ensued, the first time the group had attacked him. Everyone asserted that he had been intensely interested in the discussion; they wondered what the therapist's function was anyway; he was accused of giving them all the same "line" before they entered therapy; and finally he was informed that the group was having a good controversial discussion before he "butted in and changed the subject."

The group, as part of ongoing research, filled out questionnaires after each meeting. Of great import was the fact that the members rated the meeting, along several parameters, as the best they had ever had.

GROUP COHESIVENESS AND OTHER THERAPY—RELEVANT VARIABLES

Research has demonstrated in laboratory groups and dyads that group cohesiveness has many other important consequences.[55, 56] Many of these appear to be of great relevance to the group therapeutic process; for example, it has been shown that the members of a cohesive group in contrast to the members of a noncohesive group will:*

* These findings stem from experimentally composed groups and situations. To illustrate the methodology used in these studies, consider an experiment by Schachter [57] who

1. Try harder to influence other group members [57]
2. Be more influenceable by the other members [58]
3. Be more willing to listen to others [59] and are more accepting of others [60]
4. Experience greater security and relief from tension in the group [61]
5. Participate more readily in meetings [60, 62]
6. Protect the group norms and, for example, exert more pressure on individuals deviating from the norms [57, 63]
7. Be less susceptible to disruption as a group when a member terminates membership [56]

My clinical observations suggest that similar consequents of cohesiveness prevail in therapy groups. There is to date, however, no group psychotherapy validating research. I agree with Goldstein [56] that there is a need for replication of these findings in the group therapy context. The relevance to therapy of each of these consequents is self-evident and, if demonstrated to occur in therapeutic groups, would clarify further how cohesiveness facilitates successful outcome.

Summary

By definition, cohesiveness refers to the attraction that members have for their group and for the other members. Members of cohesive groups are more accepting of each other, more supportive, more inclined to form meaningful relationships in the group. Cohesiveness seems to be a significant factor in successful group therapy outcome. In conditions of acceptance and understanding, patients will be more inclined to express and explore themselves, to become aware of and integrate hitherto unacceptable aspects of self, and to relate more deeply to others. Self-esteem is greatly influenced by the patient's role in a cohesive group. Social behavior demanded of highly cohesive members is heavily reinforced by the group and is eventually socially adaptive to the individual both in and out

---

organized groups of paid volunteers to discuss a social problem—the correctional treatment of a juvenile delinquent with a long history of recidivism, who is currently awaiting sentence. In the manner described previously, several groups of low and high cohesiveness were formed, and paid confederates were introduced into each group who deliberately assumed an extreme position on the topic under discussion. The content of the discussion, sociometric data, and other post-group questionnaires were then analyzed to determine, for example, the intensity of the efforts of the group to influence the deviant and the degree of rejection of the deviant.

of the group. In addition, highly cohesive groups are more stable groups with better attendance and less turnover. Evidence was presented to indicate that this stability is vital to successful therapy: early termination precludes benefit for the involved patient and impedes the progress of the rest of the group as well. Cohesiveness favors the constructive expression of hostility in the group—an expression which may facilitate successful therapy in several ways.

What we have yet to consider are the determinants of cohesiveness. What are the sources of high and low cohesiveness? What does the therapist do to facilitate the development of a highly cohesive group? These important issues will be discussed in the sections on the therapist's role in group composition and in the ongoing therapy process.

REFERENCES

1. H. J. Eysenck, "The Effects of Psychotherapy," in H. J. Eysenck (ed.), *Handbook of Abnormal Psychology* (New York: Basic Books, 1961).
2. C. B. Truax and R. R. Carkhuff, *Toward Effective Counseling and Psychotherapy: Training and Practice* (Chicago: Aldine Publishing Co., 1967), pp. 6–14.
3. A. E. Bergin, "The Effects of Psychotherapy: Negative Results Revisited," *J. Counsel. Psychol.*, 10: 244–250, 1963.
4. Truax and Carkhuff, *op. cit.*, p. 19.
5. *Ibid.*, p. 25.
6. *Ibid.*, pp. 82–143.
7. J. Seeman, "Counselor Judgments of Therapeutic Process and Outcome," in C. Rogers and R. Dymond (eds.), *Psychotherapy and Personality Change* (Chicago: University of Chicago Press, 1954).
8. M. B. Parloff, "Therapist-Patient Relationships and Outcome of Psychotherapy," *J. Consult. Psychol.*, 25: 29–38, 1961.
9. F. Fiedler, "Factor Analyses of Psychoanalytic, Non-Directive and Adlerian Therapeutic Relationships," *J. Consult. Psychol.*, 15: 32–38, 1951.
10. F. Fiedler, "A Comparison of Therapeutic Relationships in Psychoanalytic, Non-Directive and Adlerian Therapy," *J. Consult. Psychol.*, 14: 436–445, 1950.
11. F. A. Board, "Patients' and Physicians' Judgments of Outcome of Psychotherapy in an Outpatient Clinic," *Arch. Gen. Psychiat.*, 1: 185–196, 1959.
12. H. Feifel and J. Eells, "Patients and Therapists Assess the Same Psychotherapy," *J. Consult. Psychol.*, 27: 310–318, 1963.
13. D. Cartwright and A. Zander (eds.), *Group Dynamics: Research and Theory* (Evanston, Ill.: Row, Peterson, 1962), p. 74.
14. J. D. Frank, "Some Determinants, Manifestations and Effects of Cohesion in Therapy Groups," *Int. J. Group Psychother.*, 7: 53–62, 1957.
15. L. Festinger, H. W. Riecker, and S. Schachter, *When Prophecy Fails* (Minneapolis: University of Minnesota Press, 1956).
16. H. Dickoff and M. Lakin, "Patients' Views of Group Psychotherapy: Retrospections and Interpretations," *Int. J. Group Psychother.*, 13: 61–73, 1963.

17. F. T. Kapp *et al.*, "Group Participation and Self-Perceived Personality Change," *J. Nerv. Ment. Dis.*, *139*: 255–265, 1964.
18. J. B. Clark and S. A. Culbert, "Mutually Therapeutic Perception and Self-Awareness in a T-Group," *J. Appl. Behav. Sci.*, *1*: 180–194, 1965.
19. A. M. Walker, R. A. Rablen, and C. Rogers, "Development of a Scale to Measure Process Changes in Psychotherapy," *J. Clin. Psychol.*, *16*: 79–85, 1960.
20. G. T. Barrett-Lennard, "Dimensions of Therapist Response as Causal Factors in Therapeutic Change," *Psychol. Monogr.*, *76*: No. 43, 1962.
21. I. D. Yalom, J. Tinklenberg, and M. Gilula, "Curative Factors in Group Therapy." Unpublished study.
22. I. D. Yalom, P. S. Houts, S. M. Zimerberg, and K. H. Rand, "Prediction of Improvement in Group Therapy," *Arch. Gen. Psychiat.*, *17*: 159–168, 1967.
23. C. Rogers, "A Theory of Therapy, Personality and Interpersonal Relationships," in S. Koch (ed.), *Psychology: A Study of a Science, Vol. 3* (New York: McGraw-Hill, 1959), pp. 184–256.
24. K. Horney, *Neurosis and Human Growth* (New York: W. W. Norton, 1950), p. 15.
25. C. Truax, "The Process of Group Therapy: Relationships between Hypothesized Therapeutic Conditions and Intrapersonal Exploration," *Psychol. Monogr.*, *75*: No. 5111, 1961.
26. C. Rogers, personal communication, April 1967.
27. A. Maslow, "Notes on Unstructured Groups at Lake Arrowhead," unpublished mimeograph, 1962.
28. C. Rogers, "The Process of the Basic Encounter Group," unpublished mimeograph, Western Behavioral Science Institute, La Jolla, California, 1966.
29. I. Rubin, "The Reduction of Prejudice Through Laboratory Training," *J. Appl. Behav. Sci.*, *3*: 29–50, 1967.
30. R. J. Dorris, D. Levinson, and E. Haufmann, "Authoritarian Personality Studied by a New Variation of the Sentence Completion Technique," *J. Abnorm. Soc. Psychol.*, *49*: 99–108, 1954.
31. D. A. Hamburg, personal communication, 1965.
32. D. Miller, "The Study of Social Relationships: Situation, Identity, and Social Interaction," in Koch, *op. cit.*, pp. 639–737.
33. H. S. Sullivan, *Conceptions of Modern Psychiatry* (London: Tavistock, 1955), p. 22.
34. Miller, *op. cit.*, p. 696.
35. E. J. Murray, "A Content Analysis for Study in Psychotherapy," *Psychol. Monogr.*, *70*: No. 13, 1956.
36. D. Lundgren and D. Miller, "Identity and Behavioral Change in Training Groups," *Human Relations Training News*, *9*, Spring 1965.
37. S. Jourard, "Self-Disclosure Patterns in British and American College Females," *J. Soc. Psychol.*, *54*: 315–320, 1961.
38. S. Hurley, "Self-Disclosure in Small Counseling Groups," unpublished doctoral thesis, Michigan State University, 1967.
39. G. C. Homans, *The Human Group* (New York: Harcourt, Brace, 1950).
40. R. F. Bales, "The Equilibrium Problem in Small Groups," in A. Hare, E. Borgatta, and R. F. Bales (eds.), *Small Groups: Studies in Social Interaction* (New York: Knopf, 1962), pp. 424–456.
41. I. D. Yalom and P. S. Houts, unpublished data.
42. I. D. Yalom, "A Study of Group Therapy Dropouts," *Arch. Gen. Psychiat.*, *14*: 393–414, 1966.
43. G. Bach, *Intensive Group Therapy* (New York: Ronald Press, 1954).
44. E. Nash, J. Frank, L. Gliedman, S. Imber, and A. Stone, "Some Factors Related to Patients Remaining in Group Psychotherapy," *Int. J. Group Psychother.*, *7*: 264–275, 1957.

45. I. D. Yalom and K. Rand, "Compatibility and Cohesiveness in Therapy Groups," *Arch. Gen. Psychiat., 13:* 267–276, 1966.
46. P. C. Sagi, D. W. Olmstead, and F. Atalsek, "Predicting Maintenance of Membership in Small Groups," *J. Abnorm. Soc. Psychol., 51:* 308–311, 1955.
47. L. Libo, *Measuring Group Cohesiveness* (monograph; Ann Arbor, Mich.: Institute for Social Research, 1953).
48. S. W. Morgan, personal communication, 1967.
49. T. M. Newcomb, "Autistic Hostility and Social Reality," *Human Relations, 1:* 69–86, 1947.
50. J. Frank, *Sanity and Survival: Psychological Aspects of War and Peace* (New York: Vintage Books, 1968), p. 125.
51. M. Sherif, O. J. Harvey, E. J. White, W. R. Hood, and C. W. Sherif, *Intergroup Conflict and Cooperation: The Robbers' Cave Experiment* (Norman, Okla.: University of Oklahoma Book Exchange, 1961).
52. J. Frank, "Some Values of Conflict in Therapeutic Groups," *Group Psychother., 8:* 142–151, 1955.
53. A. Pepitone and G. Reichling, "Group Cohesiveness and the Expression of Hostility," *Human Relations, 8:* 327–337, 1955.
54. M. E. Wright, "The Influence of Frustration Upon the Social Relations of Young Children," *Character and Personality, 12:* 111–122, 1943.
55. D. Cartwright and A. Zander, "Group Cohesiveness: Introduction," in *Group Dynamics: Research and Theory*, pp. 69–74.
56. A. Goldstein, K. Heller, and L. Sechrest, *Psychotherapy and the Psychology of Behavior Change* (New York: John Wiley and Sons, 1966).
57. S. Schachter, "Deviation, Rejection and Communication," *J. Abnorm. Soc. Psychol., 46:* 190–207, 1951.
58. Cartwright and Zander, *Group Dynamics: Research and Theory*, p. 89.
59. K. Back, "Influence Through Social Communication," *J. Abnorm. Soc. Psychol., 46:* 398–405, 1951.
60. G. Rasmussen and A. Zander, "Group Membership and Self-Evaluation," *Human Relations, 7:* 239–251, 1954.
61. S. Seashore, *Group Cohesiveness in the Industrial Work Group* (monograph; Ann Arbor, Mich.: Institute for Social Research, 1954).
62. Goldstein *et al., op. cit.*, p. 329.
63. A. Zander and A. Havelin, "Social Comparison and Intergroup Attraction," cited in Cartwright and Zander, *Group Dynamics: Research and Theory*, p. 94.

4

CURATIVE FACTORS—
OVERVIEW

The inquiry into the curative factors in group therapy began with the rationale that the delineation of these factors would lead to the development of systematic guidelines for the tactics and strategy of the therapist. The compendium of curative factors presented in Chapter 1 is, I believe, a comprehensive one but yet not in a form which has great clinical applicability. For one thing, the factors have, for the sake of clarity, been considered as separate entities when in fact they are intricately interdependent. I have taken the therapy process apart to examine it and am now obliged to resynthesize its complex structure. One question this chapter will consider is: How do the curative factors operate when they are viewed not separately but as part of a dynamic process?

A second issue to be considered is the comparative potency of the curative factors. Obviously not all are of equal value. However, an absolute rank ordering of curative factors is not possible. Many contingencies must be considered. The importance of various curative factors depends upon the type of group therapy practiced. Some are important at one stage of the group, while others predominate at another. Even within the same group, different patients benefit from different curative factors. Some factors are not mechanisms for change as much as they are conditions for change; for example, Chapter 1 describes how *instillation of hope* may serve largely to prevent early discouragement and to keep patients in the group until other, more potent forces for change come into play.

Attempts to evaluate and integrate the curative factors will be tentative and conjectural until investigative validation is available. Clinical research demonstrating the effects of any one of the curative factors is quite limited; the research bearing on a comparative study of these factors is very meager indeed.

Comparative Value of the Curative Factors— The Therapist's View

Many group therapists have published their opinions about group therapeutic curative factors. A review of this vast literature will reveal the range of curative factors but little about their comparative value. Moreover, it is possible that the various schools of conviction are not equally represented in the literature; the Rogerian school, for example, because of its academic roots and large number of Ph.D. dissertations and ancillary studies, commands a disproportionately large share of the literature.

Corsini and Rosenberg,[1] in a widely cited report, abstracted the curative factors from three hundred pre-1955 group therapy articles; 175 factors were clustered into nine major categories, which show considerable overlap with the factors I have described. Their categories and my analogous categories are:

1. Acceptance (analogous to "group cohesiveness")
2. Universalization (identical with universality)
3. Reality testing (includes elements of "recapitulation of the primary family" and "interpersonal learning")
4. Altruism (identical with "altruism")
5. Transference (includes elements of "interpersonal learning," "group cohesiveness," and "imitative behavior")
6. Spectator therapy (analogous to "imitative behavior")
7. Interaction (includes elements of "interpersonal learning" and "cohesiveness")
8. Intellectualization (includes elements of "imparting of information")
9. Ventilation (identical with "catharsis")

The considerable overlap between the two sets of curative factors increases confidence in the exhaustiveness of this series.

One pertinent issue that must be raised here is the question of whether the curative factors described by the therapists actually operate in the group; it is possible that the therapist's ideology will show little correlation with his actual behavior. There are some interesting studies that highlight this issue.

61

Fiedler's studies,[2, 3] described in Chapter 3, indicate that experts, regardless of their schools of conviction, closely resemble one another in the nature of their relationship with patients. Heine,[4] who studied the patients of therapists from different schools (psychoanalytic, Adlerian, nondirective), found that the successfully treated patients attributed their improvement to similar factors, regardless of the particular discipline of the therapist. Truax and Carkhuff's work,[5] discussed in Chapter 3, brings further evidence to support the conclusion that effective therapists operate similarly in that they establish a warm, accepting, understanding relationship with their patients. These studies suggest, then, that successful therapists closely resemble one another in several areas highly relevant to successful outcome and that the proclaimed differences between schools may be more apparent than real.

Two other studies approach this topic from another perspective and compare the views of the successfully treated patient and his therapist about the factors responsible for his successful outcome. Feifel and Eells[6] studied seventy-three patients and their twenty-eight psychoanalytically oriented therapists. They found that, although the patients attributed their successful therapy to relationship factors, their therapists gave precedence to technical skills and techniques. Blaine and McArthur [7] did a detailed retrospective study of the psychoanalytically oriented treatment of two patients. The patients and their therapists were interviewed and queried about the factors regarded as therapeutic turning points: significant insights, derepression, etc. There were startling differences between the patients and the therapist. Major differences occurred in the weighting of unconscious factors which were made conscious and the correlation between childhood experiences and present symptoms; the therapist placed great importance on these factors, while the patients "denied that this sort of thing had occurred in therapy." The patients valued the personal elements of the relationship, the encounter with a new, accepting type of authority figure, and their changed self-image and perception of other people. A turning point in the treatment of one of the patients starkly illustrates the differences. In the midst of treatment the patient had an acute anxiety attack, demanded and was granted an emergency interview with the therapist. Both therapist and patient regarded the incident as a critical one: the therapist because he thought that during the emergency session there had been a derepression of memories of early incestuous sex play and a subsequent freeing up and working through of oedipal material; the patient, on the other hand, considered the content of the emergency session unimportant and instead valued the meeting because of the relationship implications—the fact that the therapist would see him conveyed a caring and concern that was of the utmost importance.

These studies, then, demonstrate that although therapists of different disciplines may disagree cognitively about the curative processes in therapy, they resemble one another operationally. Furthermore, therapists and their patients have different views about the responsible curative factors in their therapy. Although all of these findings stem from individual psychotherapy research, it is highly likely that they have equal pertinence to group therapy. It is important to note that in the studies so far considered there is a common conceptual thread running through the patients' views about therapy. They consistently emphasize the importance of the relationship and the personal, human qualities of their therapist. Let us now look at the few studies dealing with the assessment by group psychotherapy patients of the curative factors in the therapy process.

Comparative Value of the Curative Factors—the Patient's View

There are four studies which bear on this issue: two which deal with patients' evaluations of single incidents; one which deals with patients' evaluations of curative factors after a short course in group therapy; and one which examines patients' evaluations of curative factors after long-term successful therapy.

Berzon et al.[8] studied eighteen members of two outpatient time-limited therapy groups which met for fifteen sessions. After each meeting the patients filled out a questionnaire in which they described the incident which they considered the most personally important. Two hundred and seventy-nine incidents were obtained and then sorted by three judges into nine categories which were, in order of frequency:

1. Increased awareness of emotional dynamics—a broad category in which the subject "was helped to acquire new knowledge about himself, his strength and weakness, his pattern of interpersonal relating, his motivations, etc."
2. Recognizing similarity to others
3. Feeling positive regard, acceptance, sympathy for others
4. Seeing self as seen by others
5. Expressing self congruently, articulately, or assertively in the group
6. Witnessing honesty, courage, openness, or expressions of emotionality in others

7. Feeling responded to by others
8. Feeling warmth and closeness generally in the group
9. Ventilating emotions

The authors noted that the main curative mechanisms were reported to reside in the interaction between group members; few of the reports involved the therapists. Interpersonal feedback enabled the patients to restructure their self-image and to validate the universality of problems. They concluded that a patient perceived personal benefit when he consciously experienced: "(a) a more realistic image of himself, (b) enrichment of his feeling life, (c) increased relatedness to others."

Talland and Clark [9] approached the same issue from a different direction. Forty-three members of seven outpatient analytic groups at the Maudsley Hospital were asked to rank in order of "helpfulness to the group" and "helpfulness to themselves" the following fifteen discussion content items: childhood memories, dreams, others in group, group doctor, people outside the group, shame and guilt, physical illness, marriage problems, money troubles, problems at work, quarrels, children, symptoms and anxieties, social position, sex. Their patients ranked symptoms and anxieties, sex, childhood memories, and shame and guilt as the most helpful areas of discussion. The significance of this research is difficult to evaluate because of the unclear relationship between "content areas" and "curative factors." Nevertheless, it is of interest that, as the authors note, "Topics which cannot be discussed outside the intimate atmosphere of the therapeutic situation, are thought to be the most valuable items in clinical discussion." The content item "group doctor," incidentally, was, as in the Berzon study, underchosen.*

Dickoff and Lakin [10] studied twenty-eight former members of two outpatient groups run by one psychiatrist. In a semistructured interview the patients' retrospective views about the curative factors in group therapy were discussed. Responses were taped, transcribed, and sorted by two judges into categories constructed a priori as they emerged from the data:

1. Support (reduction of isolation, universality, sharing problems, learning to express oneself)
2. Suppression (including catharsis)

---

* This study and the Berzon study clearly illustrate the role of investigator bias in this type of research. Berzon and her co-workers approached groups from the T-group interpersonal model, while the Maudsley groups were conducted along orthodox analytic lines. The research design of the studies plus the ongoing implicit communication to patients of the therapists' therapeutic values favor results which, in large part, support the orientation of the investigators.

3. Tools for action (understanding problems, insight of interpersonal and intrapersonal nature)

The results demonstrated that social support was experienced by the patients as the chief therapeutic mode. From the patients' point of view, group cohesiveness was seen as not only necessary for perpetuation of the group but in itself of great therapeutic value. The "tools for action" category was considered by far the least important by the patients; however, there was a significant correlation between high verbal I.Q. and the selection of this category.*

A study by Yalom, Tinklenberg, and Gilula,[11] the final one to be discussed, will be covered in more detail since I have drawn on it heavily throughout the book. This is in keeping with the general plan of attempting to make the reader aware of the nature of the data from which far-reaching conclusions are derived.

The investigators asked a number of group therapists who were leading groups of well-educated, middle-socioeconomic-class outpatients with neurotic or characterologic problems for their most successful patients who had recently terminated or were about to terminate group therapy. The subjects were required to have been in therapy a minimum of eight months.† The range of duration of therapy was 8 months to 22 months; the mean duration was 16 months, the median 17 months. All nominated subjects ($N = 20$) completed a curative factor Q-sort and were interviewed by the three investigators.

CURATIVE FACTORS—Q-SORT

Twelve categories of curative factors were constructed from the sources outlined throughout this book, and five items describing each category were written, making a total of sixty items.‡ (See Table 4–1.)

* It is important to note that this study deals only with early stages of group therapy; the patients had attended an average of only eleven group sessions.

† There were four checks to ensure that our sample was a successfully treated one: (1) the therapists' evaluation, (2) length of treatment (previous research [12] in the same clinic demonstrated that group patients who remained in therapy for that length of time had an extremely high rate of improvement), (3) the investigators' independent interview ratings of improvement along a 13-point scale in four areas—symptoms, functioning, interpersonal relationships, and self-concept, and (4) the patients' self-ratings along the same scale.

‡ The list of sixty curative factor items passed through several versions and was circulated among many senior group therapists for suggestions, additions, or deletions.

TABLE 4–1
Curative Factors

			Rank Order
1. Altruism	1.	Helping others has given me more self-respect.	40 T (tie)
	2.	Putting others' needs ahead of mine.	52 T
	3.	Forgetting myself and thinking of helping others.	37 T
	4.	Giving part of myself to others.	17
	5.	Helping others and being important in their lives.	33 T
2. Group Cohesiveness	6.	Belonging to and being accepted by a group.	16
	7.	Continued close contact with other people.	20 T
	8.	Revealing embarrassing things about myself and still being accepted by the group.	11 T
	9.	Feeling alone no longer.	37 T
	10.	Belonging to a group of people who understood and accepted me.	20 T
3. Universality	11.	Learning I'm not the only one with my type of problem; "We're all in the same boat."	45 T
	12.	Seeing that I was just as well off as others.	25 T
	13.	Learning that others have some of the same "bad" thoughts and feelings I do.	40 T
	14.	Learning that others had parents and backgrounds as unhappy or mixed up as mine.	31 T
	15.	Learning that I'm not very different from other people gave me a "welcome to the human race" feeling.	33 T

Some of the items are nearly identical, but it was convenient methodologically to have the same number of items representing each category. The twelve categories are: altruism; group cohesiveness; universality; interpersonal learning, "input"; interpersonal learning, "output"; guidance; catharsis; identification; family re-enactment; insight; instillation of hope; existential factors. They are not quite identical to those described in this book; we attempted, unsuccessfully, to divide interpersonal learning into two parts —input and output. The category "insight," poorly labeled, was included to permit examination of the importance of derepression and genetic insight. "Existential factors" was included at the suggestion of several colleagues.

Rank Order

4.	Interpersonal Learning, "Input"	16.	The group's teaching me about the type of impression I make on others.	5 T
		17.	Learning how I come across to others.	8
		18.	Other members honestly telling me what they think of me.	3
		19.	Group members pointing out some of my habits or mannerisms that annoy other people.	18 T
		20.	Learning that I sometimes confuse people by not saying what I really think.	13 T

5.	Interpersonal Learning, "Output"	21.	Improving my skills in getting along with people.	25 T
		22.	Feeling more trustful of groups and of other people.	10
		23.	Learning about the way I related to the other group members.	13 T
		24.	The group's giving me an opportunity to learn to approach others.	27 T
		25.	Working out my difficulties with one particular member in the group.	33 T

6.	Guidance	26.	The doctor's suggesting or advising something for me to do.	27 T
		27.	Group members suggesting or advising something for me to do.	55
		28.	Group members telling me what to do.	56
		29.	Someone in the group giving definite suggestions about a life problem.	48 T
		30.	Group members advising me to behave differently with an important person in my life.	52 T

7.	Catharsis	31.	Getting things off my chest.	31 T
		32.	Expressing negative and/or positive feelings toward another member.	5 T
		33.	Expressing negative and/or positive feelings toward the group leader.	18 T
		34.	Learning how to express my feelings.	4
		35.	Being able to say what was bothering me instead of holding it in.	2

67

8. Identification	36.	Trying to be like someone in the group who was better adjusted than I.	58
	37.	Seeing that others could reveal embarrassing things and take other risks and benefit from it helped me to do the same.	8
	38.	Adopting mannerisms or the style of another group member.	59
	39.	Admiring and behaving like my therapist.	57
	40.	Finding someone in the group I could pattern myself after.	60

9. Family Re-enactment	41.	Being in the group was, in a sense, like reliving and understanding my life in the family in which I grew up.	51
	42.	Being in the group somehow helped me to understand old hang-ups that I had in the past with my parents, brothers, sisters, or other important people.	30
	43.	Being in the group was, in a sense, like being in a family, only this time a more accepting and understanding family.	44
	44.	Being in the group somehow helped me to understand how I grew up in my family.	45 T
	45.	The group was something like my family—some members or the therapists being like my parents and others being like my relatives. Through the group experience I understand my past relationships with my parents and relatives (brothers, sisters, etc.).	48 T

10. "Insight"	46.	Learning that I have likes or dislikes for a person for reasons which may have little to do with the person and more to do with my hang-ups or experiences with other people in my past.	15
	47.	Learning why I think and feel the way I do (i.e., learning some of the causes and sources of my problems).	11 T

10.	"Insight" (continued)	48.	Discovering and accepting previously unknown or unacceptable parts of myself.	1
		49.	Learning that I react to some people or situations unrealistically (with feelings that somehow belong to earlier periods in my life).	20 T
		50.	Learning that how I feel and behave today is related to my childhood and development (there are reasons in my early life why I am as I am).	50
11.	Instillation of Hope	51.	Seeing others getting better was inspiring to me.	42 T
		52.	Knowing others had solved problems similar to mine.	37 T
		53.	Seeing that others had solved problems similar to mine.	33 T
		54.	Seeing that other group members improved encouraged me.	27 T
		55.	Knowing that the group had helped others with problems like mine encouraged me.	45 T
12.	Existential Factors	56.	Recognizing that life is at times unfair and unjust.	54
		57.	Recognizing that ultimately there is no escape from some of life's pain and from death.	42 T
		58.	Recognizing that no matter how close I get to other people, I must still face life alone.	23 T
		59.	Facing the basic issues of my life and death, and thus living my life more honestly and being less caught up in trivialities.	23 T
		60.	Learning that I must take ultimate responsibility for the way I live my life no matter how much guidance and support I get from others.	5 T

Each item was typed on a 3 x 5 card and the patient was given the stack of randomized cards and asked to sort them into seven piles. Each pile was labeled and the patient was asked to place a specified number of cards into each:

1. Most helpful to me in the group (2 cards)
2. Extremely helpful (6 cards)
3. Very helpful (12 cards)
4. Helpful (20 cards)
5. Barely helpful (12 cards)
6. Less helpful (6 cards)
7. Least helpful to me in the group (2 cards) *

INTERVIEW

Following the Q-sort, which took approximately thirty to forty-five minutes, each patient was interviewed for an hour by the three investigators. Their reasons for their choice of the most and least helpful items were reviewed and a series of other areas relevant to curative factors was discussed (e.g., other, nonprofessional therapeutic influences in their lives, critical events in therapy, goal changes, timing of improvement, curative factors in their own words).

RESULTS

A sixty-item, seven-pile Q-sort for twenty subjects makes for complex data. Perhaps the clearest way to consider the results is a simple rank ordering of the sixty items.† Turn again to the list of sixty items (Table 4–1). The number after each item represents its rank order. Thus item 48 ("discovering and accepting previously unknown or unacceptable parts of myself") was considered the most important curative factor by the consensus of patients; item 38 ("adopting mannerisms or the style of another group member") the least important, and so on. ("T" represents a tie.)

The ten items deemed most helpful to the patients were (in the order of importance):

48. Discovering and accepting previously unknown or unacceptable parts of myself.

* The number in each pile thus approaches a normal distribution curve and facilitates statistical assessment. For further information about the Q-sort technique, see J. Block, *The Q-Sort Method in Personality Assessment and Psychiatric Research*.[13]

† Arrived at by ranking the sum of the 20 pile placements for each item.

35. Being able to say what was bothering me instead of holding it in.
18. Other members honestly telling me what they think of me.
34. Learning how to express my feelings.
16. The group's teaching me about the type of impression I make on others.
32. Expressing negative and/or positive feelings toward another member.
60. Learning that I must take ultimate responsibility for the way I live my life no matter how much guidance and support I get from others.
17. Learning how I come across to others.
37. Seeing that others could reveal embarrassing things and take other risks and benefit from it helped me to do the same.
22. Feeling more trustful of groups and of other people.

If we turn our attention away from the individual items and on to the twelve general categories,* we see that they rank in order of importance:†

1. Interpersonal input
2. Catharsis
3. Cohesiveness
4. Insight
5. Interpersonal output
6. Existential awareness
7. Universality
8. Instillation of hope
9. Altruism
10. Family re-enactment
11. Guidance
12. Identification

Rather than discuss this study further, I shall instead incorporate these findings in a broader discussion of questions posited at the beginning of this chapter; *viz.* the interrelationships of the curative factors and their comparative potency.

CATHARSIS

This low prestige but irrepressible curative factor appears to operate in virtually every form of psychological healing endeavor. I was frankly surprised that our patients—a highly educated, psychologically sophisticated

* The twelve categories are used only for our analysis and interpretation. The patients, of course, were unaware of these categories and dealt only with the sixty randomized items.
† In considering these results we must keep in mind that the subject's task was a forced sort, which means that the least chosen items are not necessarily unimportant but are, instead, less important relative to the others.

sample—rated it so highly; the investigators estimated that the five cathar-sis items would have low social desirability. It appears that the strong expression of affect is an indispensable part of the therapeutic process, but is a part process and, in itself, not productive of change. Patients at the conclusion of group therapy point out that catharsis was important but only as part of an ongoing interpersonal process. Ventilating one's feelings in an empty closet or in a group of strangers is hardly helpful. If we look at the five items in the Catharsis category (items 31–35), we notice that "getting things off my chest" is greatly underchosen as compared with the others which have broader interpersonal implications (e.g., "expressing negative and/or positive feelings toward another member"). Thus catharsis—the expression of strong emotion—is a valuable part of the curative process but not a goal in itself. Strong expression of emotion enhances the devel-opment of cohesiveness; members who have expressed and worked through the mutual expression of strong feelings will develop more co-hesive bonds. We have already considered the role of catharsis in the corrective emotional experience. Each of the critical incidents or turning points in therapy recalled by patients had a very great affective com-ponent. The interpersonal learning that ensued after these critical inci-dents seemed directly proportional to the relative strength for that individ-ual of the affect expressed. Tears of compassion for another, a verbal ag-gressive confrontation, or running out of the room to aid a distraught member must be appreciated against a background of great emotional restriction for the involved patients.

INSIGHT

The category "insight" was constructed to permit investigation of the importance of derepression and the intellectual understanding of the rela-tionship between past and present, or, as we labeled it earlier, "genetic insight." The entire category was deemed by the patients as being moder-ately helpful. However, an inspection of the separate items in this cate-gory is informative in that the entire category is greatly supported by one item, No. 48, which, in retrospect, seems a misfit in this category. This item, "discovering and accepting previously unknown or unacceptable parts of myself," is the single most helpful item as selected by patients. When we questioned patients about the meaning of this item, we learned that more often than not patients had discovered *positive* areas of themselves—the ability to care for another, to relate closely to others, to experience compassion. There is an important lesson to be learned here.

Too often psychotherapy, especially in naïve, popularized, or 1920 conceptualizations, is viewed as a detective search, as a digging or a stripping away. Rogers, Horney, Maslow, and our patients as well, remind us that therapy is also exploration horizontally and upward; digging or excavation may uncover our riches and treasures as well as shameful, fearful, or primitive aspects of ourselves. Maslow states that "uncovering psychotherapy *increases* love, courage, creativity and curiosity while it *reduces* fear and hostility. This kind of therapy does not create from nothing; the implication is that it uncovers what was there in the first place." [14]

Genetic insight appeared to the patients to have limited therapeutic value; item 50, "Learning that how I feel and behave today is related to my childhood and development (there are reasons in my early life why I am as I am)," was distinctly underchosen.* Items 46 and 49, deemed of some importance by patients, are interpersonally based and refer to the concept of parataxic distortions.

Item 47, "Learning why I think and feel the way I do (i.e., learning some of the causes and sources of my problems)," is considered of moderate importance and does refer to an open-ended type of intellectual understanding. The role of the intellectual component in the therapeutic process is highly problematic. Clarification, the search for origins, cognitive restructuring—all are highly valued by patients and especially by therapists. We have learned from Dickoff and Lakin's [10] study that patients with a high I.Q. and high verbal facility especially value the intellectual component and from Talland and Clark's [9] study that patients of therapists who value this mode also come to value it. Thus the intellectual task may have over the years become part of the required role behavior for both therapists and patients.

There is a good deal of evidence, however, that the intellectual component in psychotherapy may have even more basic roots. Maslow[15] in his treatise on motivation posited that man has cognitive needs which are as basic as his needs for safety, love, and self-esteem. Monkeys in a solid enclosure will do considerable work for the privilege of being able to look through a window at the laboratory outside; furthermore, they will work hard and presistently to solve puzzles without any reward except for the satisfactions inherent in the puzzle solving itself.[14, 15] Most children are dangerously curious, and a lack of curiosity about their environment arouses concern. Considerable observational and experimental evidence indicates that psychologically healthy individuals are positively attracted to the mysterious and unexplained.[14, 16]

---

* We must keep in mind, however, that the group therapists were interpersonally oriented and did not, themselves, greatly value genetic exploration in the group.

There are several possible motives behind man's curiosity and need to explore: the effectance motive (his desire for mastery and power), the safety motive (his desire to render the unexplained harmless through understanding), and the pure cognizance motive [14] (his desire for knowledge and exploration for its own sake); very often it is difficult to separate one motive from the other.

The worried householder who explores a mysterious and frightening noise in his home; the young student who, for the first time, looks through a microscope and experiences the exhilaration of understanding the structure of an insect wing; the medieval alchemist or the New World explorer probing uncharted and proscribed regions—all receive their respective rewards: safety, a sense of personal keenness and satisfaction, and mastery in the guise of knowledge and wealth.

Present-day analysts ("the ego psychologists") postulate that sheer inquisitiveness is an autonomous ego function while others (for example, Hendrick[17] and Adler)[18] view curiosity only as a means to the end of power. Freud considered that adult curiosity was entirely a derivative of the childhood sexual instinct but was not always consistent about this, as when he said, "The voice of the intellect is soft but it *will* be heard." [19]

Knowledge for its own sake has always propelled man; the lure of the forbidden is an extraordinarily popular and ubiquitous motif in folk literature from the story of Adam and Eve to the saga of Peeping Tom. The history of mankind is dignified by men like Galileo, Socrates, and Vesalius, who have pursued knowledge and explanations in the face of considerable danger.

Knowledge to achieve mastery, ably discussed by White,[20] is closely intertwined with the search for knowledge in order to reduce anxiety. The unexplained and especially the fearful unexplained cannot be tolerated for long; all cultures, either through a scientific or a religious explanation, attempt to make sense of chaotic stimuli.

In psychotherapy, Maslow states, the task of the therapist is to help the patient search out the truth about himself. Freud stated, "To be completely honest with himself is the very best effort a human being can make." [19] Resistance in therapy is a way of fighting unpleasant or dangerous truths. Psychiatric illness is viewed by Maslow as a knowledge-deficiency disease. "I am convinced that knowledge and action are frequently synonymous, identical in the Socratic fashion. Where we know fully and completely, suitable action follows automatically and reflexly. Choices are then made without conflict, with full spontaneity."[14] While most psychotherapists would agree that Maslow's conclusions are somewhat overstated and oversimplified, there is unquestionably a measure of truth in the conclusion that knowledge may alleviate anxiety. There is a plethora of experimental evidence to document the contention that anxiety is diminished by the lessening of ambiguity.[21] To cite one well-known experiment: Dibner [22] exposed forty psychiatric patients to a psychiatric interview after dividing them into two experimental conditions: half were prepared for the interview and given cues about how they should, in a general way, conduct themselves; while the other half were given no such cues (high ambiguity situation). The results demonstrated that the subjects in the high ambiguity situation experienced, during the interview situation, a far greater degree of anxiety (as measured by several subjective, objective, and physiological techniques). The converse is, incidentally, also true: anxiety increases ambiguity by distorting perceptual acuteness. Anxious subjects show disturbed organization of visual perception; they are less capable of perceiving and organizing visual cues shown tachistoscopically [23] and are distinctly slower in completing and recognizing incomplete pictures in a controlled experimental setting.[24] Thus, unless the individual is able to order his world cognitively, he may experience anxiety which, if severe, may further reproduce itself by interfering with the perceptual apparatus; the ensuing perplexity and overt or subliminal awareness of perceptual distortion is in itself a potent source of anxiety.[25]

In psychotherapy, patients are enormously reassured by the belief that their chaotic inner world, their suffering, their tortuous interpersonal relationships are all explicable and thereby governable. Therapists, too, are made less anxious if, when confronted with great suffering and voluminous, chaotic material, they can believe in a set of principles which will permit an ordered explanation. Frequently therapists will cling tenaciously to their system in the face of considerable contradictory material; sometimes, ironically, in the case of researcher-clinicians, it is evidence which has issued from their own investigations. A belief system is valuable also in that it enables the therapist to preserve his equanimity in the face of considerable affect. Analysts working with adults who express powerful and primitive emotions maintain their bearings by referring to their beliefs about regression to the experiential world and expressive patterns of the infant.

Thus there are many explanations for the occurrence of the intellectual task in psychotherapy. However, it appears to me that frequently the intellectual component is overvalued. Often, rather than being the basic mechanism of therapy, the intellectual task is an epiphenomenon. Patients expect it, therapists highly prize their intellectual capacities and techniques, and the mutual intellectual enterprise serves, like mortar, to keep the patient and therapist joined together in the therapeutic relationship which, in time, will effect change. In these instances, however, the intellectual component is unduly credited with the entire fruits of the therapeutic venture. This is *not* to say that the intellectual task is dispensable; a meaningful therapeutic relationship must have a longitudinal component, it must be built around a common shared experience. The common experience, to be effective, must make sense for both parties: it must be relevant to the patient's suffering, it must be comprehensible and plausible, it must offer the hope of mastery via comprehension, and it must, over time, demonstrate a transfer value; that is, the patient must obtain some information and a set of general principles that will prove valuable, and thus be reinforced in his life outside the therapy hour.[26] Perhaps, given our inborn inquisitiveness, the set of the patient, the training of the therapist, and the valence placed on the intellect in our culture, the therapeutic relationship must, in part, be shaped around the intellectual task. One cannot *deliberately* develop a spontaneous therapeutic relationship with a therapist or, in group therapy, with the other members. One cannot dispense with mortar; the danger comes in not distinguishing between mortar and brick. This issue cannot be resolved here; we do not know enough to make it a resolvable issue. We shall return to it like a worrisome, aching tooth again and again in this book.

IMITATIVE BEHAVIOR

A few remarks about imitative behavior: successfully treated patients rated it as the least helpful of the twelve curative factors. However, in retrospect, the five items on imitative behavior seem to have tapped only a limited sector of this curative mode. (See Table 4–1.) They failed to distinguish between mere mimicry, which apparently has only a restricted value for patients, and the acquisition of general modes of behavior, which may have considerable value. To patients, conscious mimicry is an especially unpopular concept as a curative mode since it suggests a relinquishing of individuality—a basic fear of many group patients. On the other hand, patients may acquire from others a general strategy which may be used in a number of different situations. They begin to approach problems by considering, not necessarily on a conscious level, what some other member or the therapist would think or do in the same situation. For example, Rosenthal [27] has demonstrated that successful patients adopt the complex value system of the therapist. Sullivan, many years ago, described the use of imitative behavior by hospitalized schizophrenic patients which resulted in a form of "noblesse oblige sanity." [28]

A study of "social recoveries" in one of our large mental hospitals some years ago taught me that patients were often released from care because they had learned not to manifest symptoms to the environing persons; in other words, had integrated enough of the personal environment to realize the prejudice opposed to their delusions. It seemed almost as if they grew wise enough to be tolerant of the imbecility surrounding them, having finally discovered that it was stupidity and not malice. They could then secure satisfaction from contact with others, while discharging a part of their cravings by psychotic means.

Such a therapeutic result occurs within the confines of the patient's psychotic solution to his life stress. The therapeutic mechanism of imitative behavior in outpatient groups is considerably different. The initial imitation is, in part, an attempt to gain approval; however, it does not end there. The more intact patients retain their reality testing and flexibility and perceive that a change in their behavior elicits favorable and wanted responses from others. Increased acceptance can then act to change one's self-concept and self-esteem in the manner described in Chapter 3, and an adaptive spiral is instigated.

It is also possible for individuals to identify with aspects of two or more individuals which results in an amalgam.[29] Although parts of others are imitated, the resultant amalgam may be a novel, innovative pattern of behavior.

Furthermore, imitative behavior is a transitional curative factor in that patients make use of it in order to engage more fully in other aspects of therapy. For example, one of the five imitative behavior items was rated by the patients as the eighth (of 60) most important curative factors: "Seeing that others could reveal embarrassing things and take other risks and benefit from it helped me to do the same."

FAMILY RE-ENACTMENT

Family re-enactment, or the corrective recapitulation of the primary family experience, a curative factor highly valued by many therapists, is not considered helpful by the group patients. Few therapists will deny that the primary family of each group member haunts the group therapy room like an omnipresent specter. The patient's experience in his primary family obviously will, to a great degree, determine the nature of his parataxic distortions, the role he assumes in the group, his attitudes toward the group leaders, etc. In other words, there is little question but that the early experience members have had in the primary family imbues the therapy group with its power. Whether this phenomenon is suitable and available for interpretive work is another question entirely. I think not. Although a successful group experience may, in a sense, recapitulate the early experience in the family in a more gratifying and growth-inducing manner, the recapitulation remains on an unconscious level. To focus unduly on the sibling rivalries and incestuous, incorporative, or patricidal desires is to deny the reality of the group and the other members as a living experience in the here-and-now.

Curative Factors in Different Group Therapies

Different types of group therapies favor the operation of different clusters of curative factors. For example, Alcoholics Anonymous and Recovery, Inc., primarily encourage the operation of instillation of hope, imparting of information, universality, altruism, and some aspects of group cohesiveness. Discharge planning groups in psychiatric hospitals may use much "imparting of information" and "development of socializing techniques." Intensive interactional group therapy exerts its chief therapeutic power through "interpersonal learning" and "group cohesiveness"; nevertheless, the other curative factors play an indispensable role in the intensive therapy process. To appreciate the interdependence of the curative factors, we must consider the therapeutic process in its longitudinal dimension.

Curative Factors and Stages of Therapy

Many patients expressed difficulty in rank ordering curative factors because they found various factors helpful at different stages of therapy. Factors of considerable importance early in therapy may be far less salient late in the course of treatment. In the early stages of development the group is chiefly concerned with survival, with establishing boundaries and maintaining membership; in this phase, factors such as the instillation of hope, guidance, and universality seem especially important. A universality phase early in the group is inevitable, as members search out similarities and compare symptoms and problem constellations. The first dozen meetings of the group present a high risk period for potential dropouts, and it is often necessary to awaken hope in the patients in order to keep them attending through this critical phase. Factors such as altruism and group cohesiveness operate throughout the course of therapy; group cohesiveness operates as a curative factor at first by means of group support, acceptance, and the facilitation of attendance, and later by means of the interrelation of group esteem and self-esteem and through its role in interpersonal learning. It is only after the development of group cohesiveness that patients may engage deeply and constructively in the self-disclosure and confrontation essential in the process of interpersonal learning.

Patients' needs and goals change during the course of therapy. In Chapter 2 I described a common sequence in which patients first seek symptomatic relief and then, during the first months in therapy, formulate new goals—often interpersonal ones: they wish to be able to relate more deeply to others, to be able to love, to be honest with others. As patients' needs and goals shift during therapy, so too must the necessary therapeutic processes. Modern enlightened psychotherapy is often termed dynamic psychotherapy because it appreciates the dynamics, the motivational aspects of behavior, many of which are not in awareness. Dynamic therapy may be thought of also as changing, nonstatic, evolving psychotherapy; patients change, the group goes through a predictable developmental sequence, and so, too, the curative factors shift in primacy and influence during the course of therapy.

Curative Factors Outside the Group

Although major behavioral and attitudinal shifts would seem to require a degree of interpersonal learning, this is by no means necessarily evident in the group. Occasionally patients make major changes without making what would appear to be the appropriate investment in the therapeutic process. This brings up an important principle in therapy: the therapist or the group does not have to do the entire job. Personality reconstruction as a therapeutic goal is as unrealistic as it is presumptuous. Our patients have many adaptive coping strengths which may have served them well in the past, and not infrequently a boost from some event in therapy may be sufficient to help the patient to begin coping in an adaptive manner. We have previously used the term adaptive spiral to refer to the process in which one change in the patient begets changes in his interpersonal environment which beget further personal change. The adaptive spiral is the reverse of the vicious circle in which so many patients find themselves ensnared—a sequence of events in which dysphoria has interpersonal manifestations which weaken or disrupt interpersonal bonds and consequently create further dysphoria.

Documentation of these points comes when we ask patients about other, nontherapeutic influences on events in their lives which occurred concurrently with their therapy course. In one sample [11] of twenty patients, eighteen described a variety of extragroup therapeutic factors. Most commonly cited was a new or an improved interpersonal relationship with one or more of a variety of figures (member of the opposite sex, parent, spouse, teacher, foster family, or a new set of friends). Two patients claimed to have benefited by going through with a divorce that had long been pending. Many others cited success at work or school, which raised their self-esteem as they established a reservoir of real accomplishments; others became involved in some new social venture (YMCA groups or political committee work). It is possible, of course, that these factors were fortuitous, independent factors which deserve, along with group therapy, credit for the successful outcome. On closer examination, however, it is apparent that usually the external factor was an auxiliary to group therapy. The group mobilized the members to take advantage of environmental resources which, in fact, had long been available. The spouses, relatives, potential friends, social organizations, academic or job opportunities had long existed in the patient's life space but had never been utilized. The group may have given the patient only a slight boost, enough to allow him to exploit the other factors. Frequently the group members and the therapist are unaware of the importance of these factors and view the patient's improvement with skepticism or puzzlement.

Individual Differences and Curative Factors

It is important to note that the rank ordering of the curative factors in Table 4–1 is a mean or average value. There was, among the twenty patients studied, considerable individual variation in the ranking of the factors. The investigators explored several possible reasons for these differences. Do patients in one group differ from the patients in another group? Are the differences dependent on age, sex, length of time in treatment, degree of improvement, or the original reasons for seeking therapy? Statistical analysis demonstrated that none of these factors accounted for the individual differences.

This complex matter is clearly an important area for research. Not everyone needs the same things, or responds in the same way to group therapy; there are many therapeutic pathways through the group therapy experience.* For example, earlier we described the importance of catharsis; many restricted individuals are benefited by experiencing and expressing strong affect. Others, with contrasting problems of impulse control and great emotional lability may, on the contrary, profit from acquiring an intellectual structuring and from reining in emotional expression. Some narcissistic characters need to learn to share and to give (altruism), while others, self-defeating in their retiring self-effacement, need to learn to ask for and demand their rights. Most likely the manner in which an individual is helped in group therapy is the resultant of the interplay of several factors: his interpersonal needs, his strengths and weaknesses, his extragroup resources, and the composition and culture of his particular therapy group.

Although these issues require considerable research, certain conclusions seem heavily supported by all available studies. Group therapy draws its unique potency from its interpersonal and group properties. The agent of change appears to be the group and the intermember influence network. The effective group therapist must direct his efforts toward maximal development of these therapeutic resources. The next chapters will consider the role and the techniques of the group therapist from the viewpoint of the curative factors which we have considered.

* Research [8, 30] studying group members' responses to a single group incident demonstrates wide variation. Not only do patients differ greatly in their evaluation of the importance or value of incidents, but they may also perceive the meaning of an event in exceedingly different ways.

REFERENCES

1. R. Corsini and B. Rosenberg, "Mechanisms of Group Psychotherapy: Processes and Dynamics," *J. Abnorm. Soc. Psychol.*, *51*: 406–411, 1955.
2. F. Fiedler, "Factor Analyses of Psychoanalytic, Non-Directive and Adlerian Therapeutic Relationships," *J. Consult. Psychol.*, *15*: 32–38, 1951.
3. F. Fiedler, "A Comparison of Therapeutic Relationships in Psychoanalytic, Non-Directive and Adlerian Therapy," *J. Consult. Psychol.*, *14*: 436–445, 1950.
4. R. W. Heine, "A Comparison of Patients' Reports on Psychotherapeutic Experience with Psychoanalytic, Non-Directive and Adlerian Therapists," *Am. J. Psychother.*, *7*: 16–23, 1953.

5. C. Truax and R. Carkhuff, *Toward Effective Counseling and Psychotherapy* (Chicago: Aldine Press, 1967).

6. H. Feifel and J. Eells, "Patients and Therapists Assess the Same Psychotherapy," *J. Consult. Psychol.*, *27*: 310–318, 1963.

7. G. B. Blaine and C. C. McArthur, "What Happened in Therapy as Seen by the Patient and His Psychiatrist," *J. Nerv. Ment. Dis.*, *127*: 344–350, 1958.

8. B. Berzon, C. Pious, and R. Parson, "The Therapeutic Event in Group Psychotherapy: A Study of Subjective Reports by Group Members," *J. Indiv. Psychol.*, *19*: 204–212, 1963.

9. G. Talland and D. Clark, "Evaluation of Topics in Therapy Group Discussions," *J. Clin. Psychol.*, *10*: 131–137, 1954.

10. H. Dickoff and M. Lakin, "Patients' Views of Group Psychotherapy: Retrospections and Interpretations," *Int. J. Group Psychother.*, *13*: 61–73, 1963.

11. I. D. Yalom, J. Tinklenberg, and M. Gilula, "Curative Factors in Group Therapy." Unpublished study.

12. I. D. Yalom, P. S. Houts, S. M. Zimerberg, and K. H. Rand, "Prediction of Improvement in Group Therapy," *Arch. Gen. Psychiat.*, *17*: 159–168, 1967.

13. J. Block, *The Q-Sort Method in Personality Assessment and Psychiatric Research* (Springfield, Ill.: Charles C. Thomas, 1961).

14. A. Maslow, "The Need to Know and the Fear of Knowing," *J. Gen. Psychol.*, *68*: 111–125, 1963.

15. A. Maslow, *Motivation and Personality* (New York: Harper, 1954).

16. D. Berlyne, *Conflict, Arousal and Curiosity* (New York: McGraw-Hill, 1960).

17. I. Hendrick, "Work and the Pleasure Principle," *Psychoanal. Quart.*, *12*: 311–329, 1943.

18. H. Ansbacher and R. Ansbacher, *The Individual Psychology of Alfred Adler* (New York: Basic Books, 1956).

19. S. Freud, cited by A. Maslow, "The Need to Know and the Fear of Knowing."

20. R. W. White, "Motivation Reconsidered: The Concept of Competence," *Psychol. Rev.*, *66*: 297–333, 1959.

21. R. Lazarus, *Psychological Stress and the Coping Process* (New York: McGraw-Hill, 1966), p. 117.

22. A. S. Dibner, "Ambiguity and Anxiety," *J. Abnorm. Soc. Psychol.*, *56*: 165–174, 1958.

23. L. Postman and J. S. Brunner, "Perception under Stress," *Psychol. Rev.*, *55*: 314–323, 1948.

24. E. Verville, "The Effect of Emotional and Motivational Sets on the Perception of Incomplete Pictures," *J. Gen. Psychol.*, *69*: 133–145, 1946.

25. S. J. Korchin *et al.*, "Experience of Perceptual Distortion as a Source of Anxiety," *Arch. Neurol. Psychiat.*, *80*: 98–113, 1958.

26. D. A. Hamburg, personal communication, October 1968.

27. D. Rosenthal, "Changes in Some Moral Values Following Psychotherapy," *J. Consult. Psychol.*, *19*: 431–436, 1955.

28. H. S. Sullivan, cited in E. Goffman, *The Presentation of Self in Everyday Life* (Garden City, N.Y.: Doubleday Anchor Books, 1959), p. 18.

29. A. Bandura, personal communication, February 1968.

30. D. Stock and R. W. Whitman, "Patients' and Therapists' Apperceptions of an Episode in Group Psychotherapy," *Human Relations*, *10*: 367–383, 1957.

5

THE ROLE
OF THE THERAPIST:
BASIC
CONSIDERATIONS

The Group as the Agent of Change

There is a fundamental difference in the basic role of the individual therapist and the group therapist. In the individual format the therapist functions as the sole and direct agent of change; in the group therapeutic format he functions far more indirectly. The curative factors in group therapy are primarily mediated not by the therapist but by the other members, who provide the acceptance and support, the hope, the experience of universality, the opportunities for altruistic behavior, and the interpersonal feedback, testing, and learning. It is the therapist's task to help the group develop into a cohesive unit with an atmosphere maximally conducive to the operation of these curative factors.

The game of chess provides a useful analogy. The expert player, in the beginning of the game, does not strive for checkmate or outright capture of a piece, but instead aims at obtaining strategic squares on the board and increasing the power of each of his pieces. In so doing, he is indirectly moving toward effectance since, as the game proceeds, his superior strategic position will inevitably result in an effective attack and ultimate gain of material. So, too, the therapist methodically builds a group which will ultimately exert great therapeutic strength.

Basic Tasks of the Therapist:
Group Maintenance and Culture Building

The leader is, of course, solely responsible for creating and convening the group. His offer of professional help serves as its initial *raison d'être,* and he naturally sets the time and place for meetings. A considerable part of the maintenance task is performed before the first meeting and, as we shall elaborate in later chapters, the leader's expertise in the selection and the preparation of members will greatly influence the group's fate.

Once the group begins, he must attend to gate-keeping functions, especially the prevention of member attrition. Occasionally an unsuccessful group experience resulting in premature termination of therapy may play some useful function in the overall therapy career of a patient; for example, a failure or rejection by a group may so unsettle a patient that he is ideally primed for his next therapist. Generally, however, a patient who drops out early in the course of the group should be considered a therapeutic failure. Not only does the patient fail to receive benefit, but the progress of the remainder of the group is adversely affected. Stability of membership seems to be a *sine qua non* of successful therapy. If dropouts do occur, the therapist must, unless he is leading a closed group, add new members.

Initially the patients are strangers to each other and know only the therapist, who serves as a transitional object. He is the group's primary unifying force; the members relate to each other at first through their common relationship with him.

The therapist must recognize and negotiate any factors which foster or portend group dissolution. Continued tardiness, absences, subgrouping, disruptive extragroup socialization, scapegoating—all threaten the integrity of the group and command the intervention of the therapist.

The leader must assist in the development of therapeutic group norms. The previous chapters describe certain types of behavior which are conducive to therapy: these include free interaction among the group members, self-disclosure, high levels of involvement, nonjudgmental acceptance, acceptance of patient role (willingness to engage in critical self-examination), and expression of conflict and affection. These patterns of behavior are examples of group norms. Norms are implicit prescriptions for and proscriptions against certain types of behavior. For example, a group may have norms proscribing profanity or crying but prescribing self-disclosure. These prescriptions and proscriptions are shared by a significant proportion of the members; they have an important evaluative element in that members feel the behavior *ought* or *ought not* to be performed. This is not to say that the norms of the group are consciously formulated by the group members. On the contrary, direct questioning of the members is not a productive method of discovering norms. If presented with a list of behaviors, however, members are aware of which behavior is positively or negatively sanctioned.

Therapeutic norms do not come into being automatically or inevitably; in fact, groups often elaborate self-destructive norms. For example, in the well-known bank-wiring groups discussed by Homans,[1] the group established a production norm which was clearly below their capacity and counter to the best interests of workers and management. Members who violated the norms by being too productive were invariably punished in some manner in the group.

It is vital to the group therapeutic process that norms be established which are consonant with the aims of therapy. An important task of the therapist is to guide this norm-building process. The group looks to him for direction, and he, knowingly or unknowingly, is a powerful culture builder.

Psathas and Hardert,[2] conducting a careful analysis of the leader's interventions in a training group, demonstrated that the leader's statements to the group play a powerful, though usually implicit, role in determining the norms established in the group. Shapiro and Birk[3] observed that "whenever the leader made a comment following closely after a particular member's actions this person became a center of attention in the group and often assumed a major role in future meetings." Furthermore, the relative infrequency of the leader's comments augmented the strength of his interventions. Even in leaderless groups, which we shall discuss later, the leader's norm-building functions persist. If there is an official body organizing the leaderless group, norm formation may be deliberately programmed by means of written or taped instructions. Without this, norm formation is directed by the informal leader (often an experienced member) who emerges naturally from group membership and who may or may not encourage the building of a culture conducive to therapy.

Therapists are frequently unaware of their role in the norm-building process. However, virtually all of their early group behavior is influential. Moreover, what they do not do is often as important as what they do; the late Don Jackson frequently said that "one cannot not communicate." Recently I observed a group led by a British group analyst in which a member who had been absent the six previous meetings entered the meeting a few minutes late. The therapist in no way acknowledged the arrival of the patient and after the session explained to the observers that he chose not to influence the group since he preferred that they make their own rules about welcoming tardy or prodigal members. However, it appeared clear to me that his nonwelcome was an influential act and very much of a norm-setting message. His group had evolved, no doubt, as a result of many similar directives, into a noncaring, insecure group which sought methods of currying the leader's favor.

Norms are created relatively early in the life of a group and once established are difficult to change. Consider, for example, the small group in an industrial setting which forms norms of individual member output, or a delinquent gang which establishes codes of behavior, or a psychiatric ward which forms norms of expected staff and patient role behavior. To change these standards is notoriously difficult and requires considerable time and often large turnover in group membership.

An interesting laboratory experiment by Jacobs and Campbell [4] illustrates the tenacity and durability of norms. Group members in a darkened room were asked to estimate how much a point of light (which was, in fact, stationary) moved.* A numerical group norm from which the individual members departed only minimally was rapidly established. The experimenters then replaced members, until there had been several complete turnovers of membership. However, the group norm, which had been established by individuals long since departed from the group, remained fixed.

Basic Roles of the Therapist

The therapist can most effectively influence the development of the group culture (the aggregate of norms) early in the life of the group. To accomplish his basic tasks of group maintenance and culture building, the therapist may use a variety of techniques; he has, however, only two basic modes of presentation or roles in the group: he can be a technical expert and he can be a model-setting participant.

* The tendency of a point of light to appear mobile is called the autokinetic response and was first effectively employed in social psychological research by Muzafer Sherif. [5]

THE TECHNICAL EXPERT

When assuming the traditional role of expert, the therapist deliberately employs the technical knowledge and skills at his disposal. The therapist as a technical expert has been referred to by Lieberman [6] as a "social engineer," a term of considerable merit despite its connotations of impersonality. As a social engineer, the therapist uses his expertise to select patients, compose the group, prepare his patients for therapy, and institute, through ground rules, such norms as good attendance or confidentiality.

To evolve into a true social microcosm with subsequent interpersonal learning, the group must develop a freely interactive communication pattern. In schematic form the pathways of interaction should appear like the first, rather than the second diagram, in which communications are primarily directed to or through the leader.

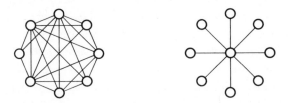

As social engineer the leader has a choice of techniques which can assist his group to achieve this interactive mode: he may explicitly instruct patients toward this end in his initial preparation; he may, repeatedly during the meetings, ask for all members' reactions to another member or toward a group issue; he may wonder why conversation is invariably directed toward himself; he may refuse to answer questions or may even close his eyes when he is addressed; he may ask the group to engage in exercises which teach patients to interact with one another—for example, a "go around" in which everyone is asked to describe his feelings toward the member sitting next to him.[7]

Similarly he must develop methods which help his patients to disclose themselves, to express themselves more honestly, and to integrate the knowledge they acquire about themselves. He must keep the group at work, helping to move it when it is becalmed and at other times preventing its flight from crucial issues. He must, to some degree, monitor the amount of affect in the group and deal with a myriad of potential group problems to be discussed in Chapter 12.

Although some of the social engineering is accomplished through overt intervention, the great bulk of the work is performed through the subtle technique of social reinforcement. Human behavior is continuously influenced by a series of environmental events (reinforcers) which may be positively or negatively valenced and which exert their influence on a conscious or subliminal level. Advertising science and political propaganda techniques are but two examples of a systematic harnessing of reinforcing agents. Psychotherapy, no less, relies on the use of subtle, often nondeliberate social reinforcers. Although no self-respecting therapist likes to consider himself a social reinforcing agent, nevertheless he continuously exerts influence in this manner, unconsciously or quite deliberately. He may positively reinforce some behavior by numerous verbal and nonverbal acts including nodding, smiling, leaning forward, an interested "Mmm," or a direct inquiry for more information. On the other hand, he may negatively reinforce some behavior which he does not deem salubrious by not commenting, not nodding, ignoring the behavior, turning his attention to another patient, looking skeptical, raising eyebrows, etc. Any obvious verbal directive from the therapist is an especially effective reinforcer because of the paucity of his interventions and his refusal to structure the group; intermittent reinforcement is more effective than continuous reinforcement. [3]

Every form of psychotherapy is a learning process, relying in part on a form of operant and aversive conditioning. I agree with Shapiro, who states that "therapy without manipulation is a mirage which disappears on close scrutiny." [3] Marmor,[8] speaking from the vantage point of psychoanalysis, says, "What goes on in the psychotherapeutic 'working through' process is a kind of conditioned learning in which the therapist's overt and covert responses act as 'reward-punishment' cues which reinforce more mature patterns of behavior and inhibit less mature patterns."

The manipulation in therapy is often covert, implicit, and unplanned; however, it may be overt, explicit, and planned without sacrificing therapeutic effectivess. Some recent research demonstrates that verbal conditioning in groups can influence behavior in an orderly predictable manner. Heckel *et al.*[9] eliminated silences in therapy groups by using a noxious noise which was triggered by a ten-second silence and turned off when a member spoke. Dinoff *et al.*[10] demonstrated that the percentage of personal or group comments in an inpatient schizophrenic group could be increased by verbal operant conditioning.

Liberman [11] reported a less contrived, more clinically pertinent study, involving two matched groups of neurotics, one led by a conventional therapist and the other by a therapist who was especially trained to use techniques of social reinforcement. Specifically, the latter therapist reinforced, by word and gesture, two types of behavior: (1) expressions of hostility and disappointment toward the therapist, and (2) intermember expressions of mutual interest, concern, and acceptance. Results of studies conducted throughout the groups' nine-month life span indicated that the experimental therapist powerfully influenced his group in the expected direction.*

Despite the evidence that they owe much of their effectiveness to these learning principles, psychotherapists often eschew the evidence because of the unfounded fear that such a mechanistic view will obviate the essential human component of the therapy experience. The facts are compelling, however, and an understanding of his own behavior does not strip the therapist of his spontaneity. The therapist who recognizes that he does exert great influence through social reinforcement and who has formulated for himself a central organizing principle of therapy will be more effective and consistent in his therapeutic interventions.

Still another manner in which the therapist, as technical expert, utilizes his specialized knowledge is to make interpretations which assist patients to gain insight into their maladaptive behavior. This is a broad statement and the types of interpretations which may prove helpful are varied. The therapist may help to identify and classify the patients' interpersonal behavior, their parataxic distortions, and their interpersonal impact on one another. When the patients have recognized the rigidity, the defensiveness, and the maladaptive, self-defeating quality of their behavior, the therapist may then turn his attention to the "why" of this behavior. As we have shown in Chapter 4, a search for a vertical or genetic explanation is often confounding and unprofitable for a therapy group. A "horizontal" explanation in which the therapist attempts to elucidate the conflicting conscious and unconscious forces presently operating behind interpersonal attitudes and behavior proves more feasible and appropriate for group work. For example, he can help clarify unconscious fears, prides, inappropriate demands, and the highly unrealistic catastrophies which patients sometimes expect will occur if they interact with others in an unaccustomed manner.

I do not consider interpretation to be the primary task of the therapist but part of his norm-setting function. Even more important† than the substantive content of the interpretation is the instillation into the group culture of an interpretive mode. Few group therapists will dispute the advisability

---

* Measuring techniques included the systematic coding of therapist and member behavior by an observer using the Interaction Process Analysis [12] and the sign process analysis [13] and sociometric, symptomatic, and personality questionnaires. The experimental group expressed more hostility to the therapist and developed greater independence and cohesiveness.

† Obviously I do not deny the importance of striving for accuracy and clarity of interpretive comments.

of a group culture which encourages, among other norms, introspection and self-understanding. However, interpretation is by no means the task of the therapist alone. With time and informal training in the group, patients are clearly capable, albeit in less sophisticated language, of arriving at interpretive conclusions as accurate and useful as those of the therapist. Moreover, as Foulkes[14] has stressed, interpretations emanating from other patients are often more effective than therapist interpretations of similar content;* patients frequently are more receptive to the interpretations made by their peers, provided that the interpreter has also accepted the patient role and does not offer interpretations primarily as a method of acquiring prestige, power, or a favored relationship with the leader. At times the therapist must learn, as Foulkes [15] suggests, to sit on his wisdom, to tolerate defective knowledge and to wait for the group to create its own solution.

These views on interpretation are not universally accepted. Indeed many therapists, especially followers of Bion and Ezriel, as well as those springing from an American psychoanalytic tradition, consider interpretation to be the primary and the sole task of the therapist. Their response to the view that patients may be equally capable of analyzing and interpreting behavior is that the therapist thereby "deskills himself" or that a "leveling down" process occurs when the leadership role is abdicated. Such an objection is, to my mind, invalidated by the group leader's other basic tasks, which we have already delineated. There is a danger in using interpretive profundity as a gauge for measuring the therapist's performance, and allowing this to take on a life of its own, which becomes isolated from any objective evaluation of patient outcome. For example, one leader [16] wrote that if the group accepted his interpretation, he knew it was correct but superficial and overobvious; if the group objected to and denied the interpretation, he knew he was close to the heart of the issue; if the group ignored the interpretation, then he knew he was entirely accurate. Conspicuous by its absence, however, is any type of response which would give the group leader cause to ponder on the correctness or usefulness of the interpretation. I have observed many groups led by senior clinicians in which the interpretations, though profound, were often puzzling or incomprehensible to the patients. To parody Shaw: the problem with elegant, complex, and profound interpretations is that they are so often wasted on the patient.

---

* Educators have long been aware that the most effective teacher is often a near peer, an individual who is close enough to the student to be accepted and who, by identifying with the students' mental processes is hence able to present material in a timely, accessible fashion.

THE MODEL-SETTING PARTICIPANT

In addition to being a technical expert, the therapist is both a model setter and a participant in the group. By demonstrating or modeling certain types of behavior, the leader helps to develop therapeutic group norms. By entering the group as a participant, the therapist helps patients work through their interpersonal relationships with him, which promotes a particularly valuable type of interpersonal learning. Let us consider each of these two functions in detail.

The Therapist as Model Setter. In the maximally effective therapy group patients must interact with one another in a confrontive, forthright, nondefensive, nonjudgmental manner. Obviously this requires that patients try out unaccustomed behavior, and one of the therapist's tasks is to assist the patients in such experimentation. How can the therapist demonstrate to the patient that new behavior will not have the anticipated aversive consequences? One method which has considerable research backing is via the observation of the therapist engaging freely and without adverse effects in the behavior under question. Bandura has demonstrated in many well-controlled research endeavors that individuals may be influenced to engage in more adaptive behavior (for example, the overcoming of specific phobias) [17, 18] or less adaptive behavior (for example, unrestrained aggressive behavior) [19] through observing and assuming the therapist's or therapist-surrogate's behavior.

The leader may, by offering a model of nonjudgmental acceptance and appreciation of others' strengths as well as their problem areas, help to shape a group which is health-oriented. If, on the other hand, he conceptualizes his role as that of a detective of psychopathology, the group members will follow suit. For example, one group patient had actively worked on the problems of other members for months but steadfastly had declined to disclose herself. Finally in one meeting she began to discuss her problems and "confessed" that one year previously she had been an inmate of a state psychiatric hospital. The therapist responded reflexly, "Why haven't you told us this before?" This comment, perceived as a punitive one by the patient, served only to reinforce her fear and distrust of others. Obviously there are questions and comments which will close people down and others which will help them to open up. The therapist, for example, might have commented upon the fact that she now seemed to trust the group sufficiently to talk about herself or might have commented about how difficult it must have been for her previously in the group, wanting and yet being afraid to share this disclosure.

The leader sets a model of interpersonal honesty and spontaneity; however, he keeps in mind the current needs of the members and demonstrates behavior which is understandable and congruent with the developmental stage of the group. Total disinhibition and unrestrained expression of all feelings is no more salubrious in therapy groups than in other forms of human encounter and if faithfully enacted may lead to the ugly, purposeless destruction portrayed in Albee's *Who's Afraid of Virginia Woolf.*[20] The therapist must set a model which includes honesty as well as judicious restraint. (The totally analyzed therapist who experiences no destructive feelings and fantasies toward his patients is, for the most part, illusory.)

The judicious use of the leader's own feelings resulted in one of the most effective interventions I have ever witnessed:

In the first session of a group of nonpatients (business executives) meeting for a five-day, intensive (fifty-hour) human relations laboratory, one member, a twenty-five-year-old, boastful, aggressive, swaggering individual who had obviously been drinking heavily that day, proceeded to dominate the meeting and make a fool of himself. He boasted of his accomplishments, belittled the group, monopolized the meeting, interrupted, outshouted, and insulted every other member. All attempts to deal with the situation failed. Feedback from members about how angry or hurt he made them feel, interpretations about the meaning and cause of his behavior—all were ineffective. Then my co-leader commented quite sincerely, "You know what I like about you? Your fear and lack of confidence. You're scared here, just like me; we're all scared about what will happen to us this week." At that point the patient instantaneously discarded his façade, eventually becoming a most valuable group member; furthermore, a softer, accepting style of relating became an important part of the group culture.

Interacting as a group member requires, among other things, that the therapist accept and admit his fallibility. The therapist who needs to appear infallible offers a perplexing and impeding example for his patients. He may be so disinclined to admit fallibility that he is withholding or devious in his relationship with the group.

Example: In one group, the therapist, who needed to appear omniscient, was to be out of town for the next meeting. He suggested to the group that they meet without him and tape record the meeting, promising to listen to the tape before the next session. He forgot to listen to the tape but, because of his need not to be wrong, was unable to admit this to the group. Consequently the subsequent meeting, in which the therapist bluffed by avoiding mention of the previous leaderless session, turned out to be diffuse, confusing, and discouraging.

Another example involved a neophyte therapist with similar needs. A patient attacked him by accusing him of making long-winded, confusing, flypaper-like statements. Since this was the first confrontation of the therapist in this young group, the members were tense and perched on the edge of their chairs. The therapist responded by wondering whether he didn't remind the patient of someone from the past. The attacking patient clutched at the suggestion and volunteered his father as a candidate; the crisis passed and the group members settled back in their chairs. However, it so happened that previously this therapist had himself been a member of a group (of psychiatric residents) and his colleagues had repeatedly focused on his tendency to make lengthy, unending, confused comments. In fact, then, what had transpired was that the patient had seen the therapist quite correctly but was persuaded to relinquish his perceptions. If one of the goals of therapy is to help the patient to test reality and to clarify his interpersonal relationships, then clearly this transaction was antitherapeutic. This is an example of a point made earlier in regard to "re-enactment of the primary family" as a curative factor. Undue emphasis on the past may serve to deny the immediate reality of the group.

Another consequence of the need to be perfect occurs when the therapist becomes overly cautious in his comments, lest he make an error. He weighs his words so carefully, interacting so deliberately and with such poor timing, that he sacrifices spontaneity and may mold a group which is stilted and lifeless. Often therapists who maintain an omnipotent, distant role are also saying, in effect, "Do what you will; you can't hurt or touch me." This pose may have the unwanted effect of aggravating a sense of impotence in the patients. As every group therapist knows, it is not easy to avoid falling back into a comfortable concealed position in the group. If the therapist really enters the group he will (as Foulkes noted in 1945):

. . . be taxed and exposed mercilessly and there will be no chance of escape. . . . No wonder it raises anxieties in the therapist. If, however, he has overcome in himself the claim to perfection, he is not afraid to be found wanting, imperfect, and ignorant, he can allow himself to be honest and sincere and stand firm on the grounds of reality. In doing so he exerts by his own example the most valuable and potent therapeutic influence.[14]

Occasionally less modeling is required of the therapist because of the presence of some "ideal" group patients who fulfill this function. In fact there have been two recent studies in which selected model-setting patients were deliberately introduced into the group. Schwartz and Hawkins [21] introduced a pair of experienced group patients to serve as models in each of two inpatient schizophrenic groups. It was known from their past group behavior that one pair of models habitually made affect-laden statements while the other pair made impersonal non-affect statements. The verbalizations of the other group members were recorded and analyzed.

The results confirmed a significant amount of imitative behavior: the group with the models who expressed affect showed an increment in the amount of affect expressed, while the other group increasingly made non-affect impersonal statements.

Goldstein *et al.*[22] report an exploratory study in which they introduced a confederate (a nonpatient psychology graduate student) into two out-patient groups. The "plants" pretended to be patients but met regularly in group discussions with the therapists and supervisors. Their role and be-havior were planned to facilitate, by their personal example, self-disclosure, free expression of affect, confrontation of the therapists, silencing of mo-nopolists, clique-busting, etc. The two groups were studied (through pa-tient-administered cohesiveness questionnaires and sociometrics) for twenty sessions. The results indicated that the plants, though not the most popular members, were regarded by the other patients as facilitating therapy; moreover, the authors concluded (though there were no control groups) that the plants served to increase group cohesiveness. Although a trained "plant" would contribute a form of deceit incompatible with the process of long-term group therapy, this use of such individuals has in-triguing implications. It is entirely feasible, for example, to "seed" new therapy groups with an "ideal" group therapy patient from another group who then continues therapy in two groups. Or a patient who has recently satisfactorily completed group therapy might serve as an auxiliary model-setting therapist during the formative period of a new group.

Despite these provocative possibilities, it is the therapist who, willingly or unwillingly, will continue to serve as the chief model-setting figure for the group patients. A provocative question is whether the therapist can assume the patient role and still continue to perform his other functions. Can the therapist, for example, facilitate the progress of the group by com-plete self-disclosure, by full and free expression of thoughts and feelings? Again the issue of timing must be considered: the therapist who at the beginning of his group assumes the role of a member has a completely different effect on the group from a therapist who assumes a member role only after the group has achieved considerable autonomy. The issue of therapist transparency is so highly controversial and complex that I shall pursue it in depth later in this chapter. First, however, let us pick up the threads of our discussion and turn from the therapist's function as a model setter to that of a participant who encourages interpersonal learning.

The Therapist as a Facilitator of Interpersonal Learning. No matter how much of a model setter or group participant the therapist becomes, he never becomes a full group member. He never relinquishes his concern with group maintenance and his special sense of responsibility for the group. He is often the only member who views the process from the perspective of the group's total development, mass movements, and obstacles. He, more than anyone else, has a sense of group history and illuminates the group patterns or sequences which have evolved over time. These distinctive characteristics of the therapist's behavior are easily noted by any systematic observational method.[2, 23]

A more elusive distinction between patient and therapist has its roots not in what the therapist does or what he is in reality but what he evokes in the fantasy of each patient. Each patient, to a greater or lesser degree, perceives the therapist incorrectly because of parataxic (or transference) distortions. Few are conflict-free in their attitudes toward such issues as parental authority, dependency, God, rebellion, and autonomy—all of which often come to be personified in the person of the therapist. Disabling conflicts in these areas can be ameliorated by a working through of the patient-therapist relationship; indeed many analytic group therapists consider the clarification of patient-therapist transference distortions as the paramount, and even the sole, mutative process in therapy.

It is my contention, however, that this process represents only one of several useful types of interpersonal learning. The clarification of patient-patient relationships is often equally important, since many patients are additionally or primarily conflicted in areas other than dependency and authoritarianism—for example, in their relationships with their peers, and in their feelings about intimacy, sex, aggression, or competition. The therapist has no monopoly on authoritarianism; it is not at all uncommon for patients to work through problems of authority or dependency with other domineering or controlling patients.

The difference between therapists who consider the resolution of therapist-patient transference as the paramount curative factor and therapists who attach equal importance to all parataxic distortions is more than a theoretical difference; in practice, marked differences of technique ensue. These two vignettes from a group led by a therapist-centered leader illustrate this point:

> The members of a group meeting for the twentieth time discussed at great length the fact that they did not know each other's first names. They then dealt with the general problem of intimacy, discussing, for example, how difficult it was to meet and really know people today. How does one make a really close friend? Now on two occasions during the course of this discussion members erred or forgot the surname of another member. From this data the group leader made a transference interpretation: namely, that by forgetting the others' names the members were each expressing a wish that all the other members would vanish so that he alone could have the therapist's sole attention.

95

In another group during a session in which two male members were absent, four women bitterly criticized the one male patient present, a homosexual, for his detachment and narcissism, which precluded any interest in the lives or problems of others. The therapist's interpretation was that the women attacked the male patient because he did not desire them sexually; moreover, he was an indirect target—the women really wanted to attack the therapist for his refusal to engage them sexually.

In each instance the therapist selectively attended to the data and, from the vantage point of his conception of the paramount curative factor, made an interpretation which was pragmatically correct since it focused the members' attention upon their relationship with the leader. However, in each instance the therapist-centered interpretation was an incomplete one and denied the important reality of intermember relationships; in fact, the members of the first group, in addition to their wish for the therapist's sole attention, *were* considerably conflicted about intimacy and about their desires and fears of engaging with one another. In the second group, the homosexual patient *had* in fact been narcissistic and detached in his relationship to the women in the group, and it was exceedingly important for him to recognize and understand his behavior.

The specialness of the therapist is evidenced in a number of diverse ways. Witness the difference caused by the therapist's entrance. The group is often engaged in animated conversation only to lapse into complete silence when the therapist enters the room. (Someone once said that the group therapy meeting officially begins when suddenly nothing happens!) The therapist's arrival is not only a reminder to the group of its task, but it also evokes early constellations of feelings about the adult, the teacher, the evaluator. Without him the group can frolic; his presence is experienced as a stern reminder of the responsibilities of adulthood.

Observations of seating patterns often demonstrate complex and powerful feelings toward the leader. Frequently the members attempt to sit as far away from him as possible; a paranoid member often takes the seat directly opposite him. If co-therapists sit close to each other with only one vacant chair between them, the members may be disinclined to occupy it. One member, after eighteen months of group therapy, still described a feeling of great oppression when seated between the therapists.

For years I have, for research purposes, asked group members to fill out a questionnaire following each meeting. One of their tasks is to rank order every member for activity (according to the total number of words spoken). There was excellent intermember reliability in their ratings of the other group members, but, notably, exceedingly poor reliability in their ratings of the group therapist. In the same meeting some patients rated the therapist as the most active member, while others considered him the least active. The powerful and unrealistic feelings of the members toward the therapist prevented an accurate appraisal, even on this relatively objective dimension.

Some members characteristically address all their remarks to the therapist, or they may speak to other members only to glance furtively at the therapist at the end of their statement. It is as though they speak to others in an attempt to reach the therapist, seeking his stamp of approval for all their thoughts and actions. They forget, as it were, their reasons for being in therapy, as they continuously seek to gain a conspiratoral eye contact with him, to be the last one to leave the session, to be in a multitude of ways his favorite child.

Others may imbue the leader with superhuman powers. They attribute to his skills improvements occurring to the group members, ignoring or distorting important contributions made by other members. Errors, *faux pas*, absences of the therapist are seen as deliberate techniques, which he employs to stimulate or provoke the group for its own good. Others, manifesting counter-dependency, challenge him continuously. They deny their feelings of helplessness in a counterphobic manner. Still others may validate their integrity or potency by attempting to triumph over the big adversary; a sense of exhilaration and power ensues from twisting the tail of the tiger and emerging unscathed.

Each of these postures toward the therapist has its distinctive ramifications in the patient's relationships with the other group members. The patients seeking the special favored position will view the others as competitors and hope for their departure; those viewing the therapist as omniscient will be inclined to devaluate the other members; those wishing to defeat him will search out allies or fellow conspirators in the group and may attempt to organize extragroup social activities from which the therapist is excluded.

We should note that the appearance of these attitudes does not always signify psychopathology in the group members.* It may instead be a response to the personality or technique of the therapist. Some therapists prefer being viewed as omniscient; others may operate in such a way as to discourage being challenged by the patients; others may be threatened by

---

* In any group there is a broad continuum of rational and irrational attitudes toward the therapist. One technique [24] which demonstrates these differential responses consists of the group members' writing down their estimate of the amount of money the leader (and co-leader, if present) has in his wallet. The wide range of guesses and subsequent discussion of the different amounts suggested by different members offers a graphic demonstration of varying attitudes to the leader.

the search for autonomy in their patients and unwittingly infantilize them; still others may be so caustic or provocative that somehow the group patients are forever banding together against them. Certain ways of running a group bring out common feelings about the leader but not necessarily conflicted ones. For example, the highly unstructured group approach of Bion, in which no cognitive guidelines are offered to the members, may in the early stages be so perplexing and threatening that dependency postures toward the leader, the one individual who knows what the group is about, are intensified.*

The general issues presented here are highly controversial ones among group therapists. Some therapists feel that every patient will experience marked transference distortions toward the therapist and that, if they are not readily apparent, the therapist should operate in such a way as to foster the development of unrealistic perceptions of him; they consider the chief mode of therapy to be the resolution of these transference distortions. More controversial yet is the subsequent question: how should the therapist operate to help the patients work through their distorted perceptions of him? Should he rely on an interpretive analytic mode, helping patients to understand the nature and sources of their distortions? Should he be transparent and self-disclosing, engaging the members in a personal encounter in order to facilitate their interpersonal learning? The degree of therapist self-disclosure is one crucial characteristic which differentiates the various schools of group therapy, and is so pressing a current issue that it deserves special consideration in a context larger than that of group psychotherapy per se.

The Psychotherapist and Transparency

Major "lasting" psychotherapeutic innovations appear and vanish with bewildering rapidity; only a truly intrepid observer would attempt to differentiate evanescent from potentially important and durable trends in the diffuse, heterodox American psychotherapeutic scene. Nevertheless, it

---

* This phenomenon has been interpreted by Bion and his followers as one of the natural forms of existence of the therapy group. As we shall discuss the matter later, however, this conclusion may be unwarranted and the basic assumption dependency group may often be an iatrogenic phenomenon—a response to a form of leadership which is deliberately enigmatic, a form of leadership which deliberately refuses to lead in the sense that the members have come to expect from previous group experiences and furthermore goes about this refusal in a deliberately mystifying manner.

seems that there are stirrings, in widely varying settings, of a shift in the therapist's basic presentation of himself. Consider the following vignettes:

The staff and the sixty acute and chronically ill patients of a state hospital meet together for a community meeting in which problems of a specific patient as well as those of the entire community are discussed. Following this, the entire ward, the professional staff (psychiatrists, psychologists, nurses, social workers), and the auxiliary staff (occupational and recreational therapists, etc.) meet for an hour to discuss staff relationships. In this meeting personal grievances are aired; for example, how the authoritarianism of a particular nurse or doctor is undermining others on the ward, or how a staff member is so anxious to be liked by the patients that he competes with other members of the staff for the patients' attention. They may additionally vent their collective feelings of frustration, puzzlement, or discouragement about a particular patient, a ward situation, or, for that matter, the field in general. This type of staff meeting is no longer unusual; the professional staff including the trained psychotherapists has, since the innovative writings of Maxwell Jones [25] and Stanton and Schwartz,[26] recognized the necessity of working out intrastaff tensions. What was unusual, however, was that most of the sixty patients were sitting around the periphery listening to and watching the staff group.

Therapists leading therapy groups which are observed through a one-way mirror reverse the roles at the end of the meeting. The patients are permitted to observe while the therapist and the students discuss or "rehash" the meeting.

At a university training center, a tutorial teaching technique has been employed in which four psychiatric residents meet regularly with an experienced clinician who conducts an interview in front of a one-way mirror. The patient is often invited to observe the post-interview discussion.

Similarly I have for many years used as a teaching vehicle a multiple therapy format [27] in which one patient is treated simultaneously by several therapists (usually four psychiatric residents and two experienced clinicians). One of the important ground rules is that there is no post-session rehash; everything that is said must be said in the presence of the patient, including disagreements about diagnosis, the appropriate plan of therapy, as well as criticism of one therapist by another.

Without discussing the merits or disadvantages of the approaches demonstrated in these vignettes, it can be said for now that there is no evidence that the therapeutic relationship or situation became corroded. On the psychiatric ward the patients, rather than lose faith in their all too human therapists, developed more faith in a process in which the therapists were willing to immerse themselves. The patients who observed their therapists in disagreement learned that, although "no one true way"

99

exists, the therapists are nonetheless dedicated and committed to finding ways of helping their patients.

In each of these vignettes the therapists abandon their traditional role and share some of their many uncertainties with their patients. Gradually the therapist is defrocked, the therapeutic process demystified. The past decade has witnessed the demise of the concept of psychotherapy as an exclusive domain of psychiatry. A short time ago therapy was indeed a private affair. Psychologists were under surveillance lest they be tempted to practice therapy; social workers could do "casework" but not psychotherapy. The eggshell era of therapy, in which the patient was considered so fragile and the mysteries of technique so deep that only the individual with the ultimate diploma dared treat him, is gone forever. Instead the past few years have witnessed the establishment of diverse programs, many sponsored by the National Institute of Mental Health, designed to train nonprofessionals to do psychotherapy. For example, Rioch [28] has, under the auspices of the Washington School of Psychiatry, established courses to train housewives in both individual and group therapy. Psychiatric technicians are being trained by intensive NIMH-sponsored courses to be group therapists in psychiatric hospitals.[29] Well-integrated college students have been successfully used as psychotherapists for disturbed adolescents at both Stanford University [30, 31] and Berkeley.[32]

The recent groundswell of interest in leaderless or patient-led groups is another case in point. Within the past few years many publications have described the rationale and course of these self-directed interactional groups [33, 34, 35, 36] (not to be confused with nonprofessional groups, such as Alcoholics Anonymous or Recovery, Inc., which are primarily suppressive and inspirational). The most thorough and systematic approach to patient-led groups has been made by Berzon,[35, 36] who for several years has attempted to program leadership functions into a group through a written or tape-recorded instructional manual to be used at each meeting. (This work is of such interest and significance that it will be discussed in detail in Chapter 13.)

Nor is this re-evaluation of the therapist's role solely a modern phenomenon. There are adumbrations of experimentation among the earliest dynamic therapists. Ferenczi, for example, because of his dissatisfaction with the therapeutic results of psychoanalysis, continually challenged the aloof, omniscient role definition of the classical psychoanalyst. During his last several years he openly acknowledged his fallibility to patients and, in response to a just criticism, felt free to say, "I think you may have touched upon an area in which I am not entirely free myself. Perhaps you can help me see what's wrong with me."[37] Foulkes[14] stated twenty years ago that the mature group therapist was a truly modest one—one who could sincerely say to his group, "Here we are together facing reality and the basic problems of human existence. I am one of you, not more and not less."

All of these approaches argue that therapy is a rational, explicable process. They espouse a humanistic attitude to therapy, in which the patient is considered a full collaborator in the therapeutic venture. No mystery need surround the therapist or the therapeutic procedure; aside from the ameliorative effects stemming from expectations of help from a magical being, there is little to be lost and perhaps much to be gained through the demystification of the therapy process. A therapy based on a true alliance between therapist and enlightened patient reflects a greater respect for the capacities of the patient and, with it, an increased reliance on self-awareness rather than on the easier but more precarious comfort of self-deception.

Greater therapist transparency is, in part, a reaction to the old authoritarian medical healer who, for many centuries, has resonated with distressed man's wish for succor from a superior being. Healers have harnessed and indeed cultivated this need as a powerful agent of treatment. In countless ways they have encouraged and fostered a belief in their omniscience: Latin prescriptions, specialized language, secret institutes with lengthy and severe apprenticeships, imposing offices, and avalanches of diplomas—all have contributed to the image of the healer as a powerful, mysterious, and prescient figure.

In unshackling himself from his ancestral role, the therapist of today has at times sacrificed his effectiveness at the altar of self-disclosure. However, the dangers ensuing from indiscriminate therapist transparency (which we shall consider shortly) should not deter us from exploring the judicious use of therapist self-disclosure.

THERAPIST TRANSPARENCY AND ITS EFFECT ON THE THERAPY GROUP

The primary sweeping objection to therapist transparency is based on the traditional analytic belief that the paramount curative factor is the resolution of patient-therapist transference. From this point of view it is necessary for the therapist to remain relatively anonymous or opaque in order to foster the development of unrealistic feelings toward him. It is our position, however, that other curative factors are of equal or greater importance and that the therapist who judiciously uses his own person increases the therapeutic power of the group by encouraging the development of these factors. He gains considerable role flexibility and maneuverability and may, without concerning himself about role spoilage, directly attend to group maintenance and to the shaping of the group norms. By decentralizing his position in the group, he hastens the development of group autonomy and cohesiveness.

One objection to self-disclosure, a groundless objection I believe, is the fear of escalation, the fear that once the therapist reveals himself the group will insatiably demand even more. My own clinical work is at times complicated by my occasionally leading human development laboratories (intensive T-groups), in which I am far more self-disclosing, and then returning to resume therapy groups. The "re-entry phenomenon" (discussed in Chapter 14) often results in abrupt but transient shifts in my role as a leader; yet I find that my therapy groups are neither confused nor, later, more personally demanding of me.

As a clinical illustration of this point as well as an example of therapist transparency, I shall describe a group therapy session which I held immediately after returning from a week-long residential human relations laboratory.

Four members, Don, Charles, Janice, and Martha, were present at the twenty-ninth meeting of the group; one member and the co-therapist were absent, one other member, Peter, had at the previous meeting dropped out of the group. The first group theme that emerged was the group's response to Peter's terminating. The group discussed this very gingerly from a great distance, and I commented that we had, it seemed to me, never honestly discussed our feelings about Peter when he was present and that we were avoiding them now even after his departure. Among the responses was Martha's comment that she was glad he left, that she had felt they couldn't reach him and that she didn't feel it was worth her while to try. She then commented on his lack of education and noted her surprise that he had even been included in the group—a thinly veiled swipe at the therapists. I felt that Martha's judgmentalism, her immediate rejection of others, had never been openly discussed in the group and I thought I might help Martha and the group to confront this issue by asking her to go around the group and describe those aspects of each person she found herself unable to accept. This proved to be very difficult for her and she generally avoided the task by phrasing her objections in the past tense—i.e., "I once disliked some trait in you but now it's different." When she had finished with each of the patients, I pointed out that she had left me out—indeed she had never expressed her feelings toward me except through indirect attacks. She proceeded to compare me unfavorably with the co-therapist, stating that she found me too retiring and ineffectual; with dispatch she then attempted to undo the remarks by commenting that "still waters run deep" and recalling a number of examples of my sensitivity to her.

The other members suddenly stated that they'd like to tackle the same task and did; in the process they revealed many long-term group secrets, such as Don's effeminacy, Janice's slovenliness and desexualized grooming and dress, Charles's lack of empathy with the women in the group. Martha was compared to "a golf ball, tightly wound up with an enamel cover." I was attacked by Don for my deviousness and lack of interest in him. The group then asked me also to go around the group in this manner; being fresh from a seven-day T-group, and no admirer of the Duke of Playa Toro who led his army from the rear, I agreed. I told Martha that her quickness to judge and condemn others made me reluctant to show myself to her, lest I, too, be judged and found wanting. I agreed with the golf ball metaphor and added that her judgmentalism made it difficult for me to approach her, save as an expert technician. I told Don that I felt his gaze on me constantly; I knew he desperately wanted something from me, and that the intensity of his need and my failure to reach him made me very uncomfortable at times. I told Janice that I missed a spirit of opposition in her, she tended to accept and exalt everything that I said to her so uncritically that it became difficult at times to relate to her as an autonomous adult. The meeting continued at an intense involved level, and after its end the observers expressed grave concerns about my behavior. They felt that I had irrevocably relinquished my leadership role and become a group member; that the group would never be the same; and that furthermore I was placing my co-therapist, who would return the following week, in an untenable position.

In fact, none of these predictions materialized. In subsequent meetings the group plunged more deeply into work; several weeks were required to assimilate the material generated in that single meeting. In addition the group members, following the model of the therapist, related to each other far more forthrightly than before and made no demands on the therapist for escalated self-disclosure.

Successfully treated patients, when interviewed at the conclusion of therapy, have usually expressed a wish that the therapist had been less aloof, more involved in the group. Yet none of the patients wanted the therapists to have contributed more of their personal lives or problems to the group. In actual practice it is relatively common for therapists to disclose their immediate feelings about a situation in the group or about a patient. It is much less common for therapists to go beyond this material, although some therapists agree with Berger who states that "it is at times very helpful for the therapist to share some past or current real-life problem and to afford a model for identification through his capacity to come through such a problem period constructively." [38]

PITFALLS INVOLVED IN THERAPIST TRANSPARENCY

Some time ago I observed a group led by two neophyte group therapists who were at that time much intrigued with existential thought. They formed an outpatient group and conducted themselves in an unflinchingly honest fashion, expressing openly in the first meetings their uncertainty about group therapy, their self-doubts and personal anxiety. In so doing, however, they jettisoned their group maintenance function; the majority of the members dropped out of the group within the first six sessions.

The new time-extended "marathon groups" (see Chapter 9) which meet from twenty-four to forty-eight consecutive hours place paramount emphasis on self-disclosure. I once attended such a group in which the leader's fiancée (a group member) burdened the group with the problem of her failure to achieve orgasm with her fiancé (the group leader).

For those still encumbered by scraps of physical or psychological concealment, three psychotherapists in a 1968 meeting reported enthusiastically on "group therapy in the nude," and *Time* magazine [39] recently reported on Southern California* nude marathons.

Many other illustrations could be cited to illustrate the paradox that freedom and spontaneity in extreme form can result in a leadership role which is as narrow and restrictive as the traditional blank screen leader. Under the present-day banner of "anything goes if it's genuine" (at any time, to any degree) the leader loses flexibility in his role. Consider the issue of timing. In the first example, the neophyte existential therapists overlooked the factor that leadership behavior which may be appropriate at one stage of therapy may be quite inappropriate at another. If patients need initial support and structure to remain in the group, then it is the therapist's task to provide it. There are situations when, as Maslow [41] puts it, "the good leader must keep his feelings to himself, let them burn out his own guts, and not seek the relief of catharting them to followers who cannot at that time be helped by an uncertain leader." The leader who strives only to create a mystique of egalitarianism between member and leader may in the long run provide no leadership at all. It is a naïve misconception to view effective role behavior of the leader as unchanging; as the group develops and matures, different forms of leadership are required. Furthermore, the "honest" comment of the dedicated leader may be the pragmatically correct response, rather than an indiscriminate ex-

---

* Many of the wilder innovations in therapy have sprung from Southern California. It brings to mind the fanciful notion in Saul Bellow's *Seize the Day*[40] of someone tilting the large flat map of the United States and observing that, "Everything that wasn't bolted or screwed down slid into Southern California."

pression of what may be the therapist's distortions or misperceptions. After all, as Parloff [42] states, "The honest therapist is one who attempts to provide that which the patient can assimilate, verify and utilize".*

Ferenczi years ago underscored the necessity for proper timing. The analyst, he said, must not admit his flaws and uncertainty too early. First the patient must feel sufficiently secure in his own abilities before he is called upon to face the defect in the one on whom he leans.[37]

In a sense, what may happen is that leader transparency becomes so cherished and romanticized that it achieves an independent autonomy; it is then considered as an end rather than as a means to an end. There has been an attempt to dignify this transformation by workers such as Mowrer [33] and Stoller,[44] who present self-disclosure as the keystone of an oversimplified approach to psychopathology and therapy. Jourard states, for example, that "people become clients because they do not disclose themselves in some optimal degree to the people in their life." [45] The corollary is that psychotherapy should reverse this process—with the therapist leading the way by his own personal example.

However, the therapist is not in the group primarily to be honest or to be authentic. In times of confusion about his behavior, the therapist may profit from a momentary stepping back and a reconsideration of his primary tasks in the group. Therapist self-disclosure is an aid to the group because it sets a model for the patients and because it assists some patients to reality-test their feelings toward the therapist. The therapist may ask himself, where is the group now? Is it a concealed, overly cautious group which may profit from a leader who models personal self-disclosure? Or is it a group which has already established vigorous self-disclosure norms and is in need of other assistance? The therapist must, as we have noted, consider whether his behavior will interfere with his group maintenance function. He must know when to recede into the background. Unlike the individual therapist, the group therapist does not have to do the entire job; in part he is midwife to the group, he must set a process in motion and may, if he insists on centrality, inhibit the progress of the group.

* A rich example of this principle is found in the novel *Magister Ludi*,[43] in which Hermann Hesse describes an event in the lives of two renowned healers. Joseph, one of the healers, severely afflicted with feelings of worthlessness and self-doubt, sets off on a long journey to seek help from his rival, Dion. At an oasis Joseph describes his plight to a stranger, who turns out to be Dion; whereupon Joseph accepts Dion's invitation to go home with him in the role of patient and servant. In time Joseph regains his former serenity, zest, and effectance and becomes the friend and colleague of his master. Only after many years have passed and Dion lies on his deathbed does he reveal to Joseph that when the latter encountered him at the oasis, Dion had reached a similar impasse in his life and was en route to request Joseph's assistance!

An overly restricted definition of the role of the group therapist, whether it be based on transparency or, for that matter, on any other criterion, may cause the leader to lose sight of the individuality of each patient's needs. The same caveat applies to leaderless groups or groups in which there is an attempt to create an automated leader. Despite his group orientation, the leader must retain some individual focus; not all patients need the same thing. The last chapter described, for example, how some, perhaps most, patients need to relax controls; they need to learn how to express their affect—anger, love, tenderness, hatred. Others, however, need the opposite; they need to gain impulse control because their life styles are already characterized by labile and immediately acted-upon affect.

One final consequence of more or less unlimited therapist transparency is that the cognitive aspects of therapy may be completely neglected. As we have noted previously, mere catharsis is not in itself a corrective experience. Some cognitive learning or restructuring seems necessary for the patient to be able to generalize his group experiences to his outside life; without this transfer or carryover, we have succeeded only in creating better therapy group members. Without the acquisition of some knowledge about general patterns in his interpersonal relationships, the patient may, in effect, have to discover the wheel anew in each of his subsequent interpersonal transactions.

REFERENCES

1. G. C. Homans, *The Human Group* (New York: Harcourt, Brace, 1950).
2. G. Psathas and R. Hardert, "Trainer Interventions and Normative Patterns in the T-group," *J. Appl. Behav. Sci.*, 2: 149–169, 1966.
3. D. Shapiro and L. Birk, "Group Therapy in Experimental Perspective," *Int. J. Group. Psychother.*, 17: 211–224, 1967.
4. R. C. Jacobs and D. T. Campbell, "The Perpetuation of an Arbitrary Tradition through Several Generations of a Laboratory Microculture," *J. Abnorm. Soc. Psychol.*, 62: 649–658, 1961.
5. M. Sherif, "Group Influences upon the Formation of Norms and Attitudes," in E. E. Maccoby, T. M. Newcomb, and E. L. Hartley (eds.), *Readings in Social Psychology* (New York: Holt, Rinehart, and Winston, 1958), pp. 219–232.
6. M. A. Lieberman, "The Implications of a Total Group Phenomenon: Analysis for Patients and Therapists," *Int. J. Group. Psychother.*, 17: 71–81, 1967.
7. G. Bach, *Intensive Group Therapy* (New York: Ronald Press, 1954).
8. J. Marmor, cited in R. Liberman, "Social Reinforcement of Group Dynamics: An Evaluative Study," presented at American Group Psychotherapy Association Convention, Chicago, January 1968.

9. R. V. Heckel, S. L. Wiggins, and H. C. Salzberg, "Conditioning Against Silences in Group Therapy," *J. Clin. Psychol., 18:* 216–217, 1962.
10. M. Dinoff, R. Horner, D. B. Kuppiewski, H. Rikard, and O. Timmons, "Conditioning the Verbal Behavior of a Psychiatric Population in a Group Therapy-Like Situation," *J. Clin. Psychol., 16:* 371–372, 1960.
11. Liberman, *op. cit.*
12. R. Bales, *Interaction Process Analysis* (Cambridge: Addison-Wesley, 1951).
13. L. Libo, *Measuring Group Cohesiveness* (monograph; Ann Arbor, Mich.: Institute for Social Research, 1953).
14. S. H. Foulkes, "A Memorandum on Group Therapy," British Military Memorandum ADM 11, BM (mimeographed), July 1945.
15. S. H. Foulkes and E. J. Anthony, *Group Psychotherapy: The Psychoanalytic Approach* (2nd ed.; Baltimore: Penguin Books, 1965), p. 153.
16. A. K. Rice, *Learning for Leadership* (London: Tavistock Publications, 1965).
17. A. Bandura, "Modelling Approaches to the Modification of Phobic Disorders," presented at the Ciba Foundation Symposium: The Role of Learning in Psychotherapy, London, 1968.
18. A. Bandura, J. Grusec, and F. Menlove, "Vicarious Extinction of Avoidance Behavior," *J. Personal. Soc. Psychol., 5:* 16–23, 1967.
19. A. Bandura, D. Ross, and J. Ross, "Imitation of Film Mediated Aggressive Models," *J. Abnorm. Soc. Psychol., 66:* 3–11, 1963.
20. E. Albee, *Who's Afraid of Virginia Woolf?* (New York: Atheneum, 1962).
21. A. M. Schwartz and H. L. Hawkins, "Patient Models and Affect Statements in Group Therapy," paper read at American Psychological Association Meetings, Chicago, September 1965.
22. A. Goldstein, S. Gassner, R. Greenberg, A. Gustin, J. Land, R. Liberman, and D. Streiner, "The Use of Planted Patients in Group Psychotherapy," *Am. J. Psychother., 21:* 767–774, 1967.
23. D. Stock and R. W. Whitman, "Patients' and Therapists' Apperceptions of an Episode in Group Psychotherapy," *Human Relations, 10:* 367–383, 1957.
24. D. Malamud and S. Machover, *Toward Self-Understanding: Group Techniques in Self-Confrontation* (Springfield, Ill.: Charles C. Thomas, 1965).
25. M. Jones, *The Therapeutic Community* (New York: Basic Books, 1953).
26. A. H. Stanton and M. S. Schwartz, *The Mental Hospital* (New York: Basic Books, 1954).
27. I. D. Yalom and J. H. Handlon, "The Use of Multiple Therapists in the Teaching of Psychiatric Residents," *J. Nerv. Ment. Dis., 141:* 684–692, 1966.
28. M. J. Rioch, E. Elkes, A. A. Flint, B. S. Usdansky, R. G. Newman, and E. Silber, "National Institute of Mental Health Pilot Study in Training Mental Health Counselors," *Am. J. Orthopsychiat., 33:* 678–689, 1963.
29. G. O. Ebersole, P. H. Leiderman, and I. D. Yalom, "Training the Non-Professional Group Therapist: A Controlled Study," *J. Nerv. Ment. Dis.,* in press.
30. *The San Mateo Times,* August 26, 1966, p. 22.
31. J. R. Hilgard and U. S. Moore, "Affiliative Therapy in the Treatment of Withdrawn Young Adolescents," *J. Acad. Child Psychiat.,* in press.
32. G. Goodman, "Companionship as Therapy: The Use of Non-Professional Talent," in J. T. Hart and T. M. Tomlinson (eds.), *New Directions in Client-Centered Psychotherapy* (Boston: Houghton-Mifflin, 1968).
33. O. H. Mowrer, *The New Group Therapy* (Princeton, D. Van Nostrand, 1964).
34. M. Harrow *et al.,* "Influence of the Psychotherapist on the Emotional Climate in Group Therapy," *Human Relations, 20:* 49–64, 1967.
35. B. Berzon and L. N. Solomon, "The Self-Directed Therapeutic Group: Three Studies," *J. Counsel. Psychol., 13:* No. 4, 1966.

36. B. Berzon, "Self-Directed Small Group Programs: A New Resource in Rehabilitation," Final Narrative Report, Vocational Rehabilitation Administration Project #RD1748, January 1968, Western Behavioral Science Institute, La Jolla, California, pp. 1–107.

37. M. Green (ed.), *Interpersonal Analysis: The Selected Papers of Clara M. Thompson* (New York: Basic Books, 1964).

38. M. M. Berger, "The Function of the Leader in Developing and Maintaining a Working Therapeutic Group," unpublished mimeograph, 1967.

39. *Time*, February 23, 1968, p. 42.

40. S. Bellow, *Seize the Day* (New York: Viking Press, 1956).

41. A. H. Maslow, "Notes on Unstructured Groups at Lake Arrowhead," unpublished mimeograph, 1962.

42. M. Parloff, "Discussion of Accelerated Interaction: A Time-Limited Approach Based on the Brief Intensive Group," *Int. J. Group Psychother., 28:* 239–244, 1968.

43. H. Hesse, *Magister Ludi* (New York: Frederick Unger, 1949), pp. 438–467.

44. F. Stoller, "Accelerated Interaction: A Time-Limited Approach Based on the Brief Intensive Group," *Int. J. Group Psychother., 28:* 220–235, 1968.

45. S. Jourard, *The Transparent Self* (Princeton: D. Van Nostrand, 1964), p. 21.

6

THE TECHNIQUE OF THE THERAPIST: BASIC CONSIDERATIONS

❦

The Here-and-Now Process

INTRODUCTION

A focus upon the here-and-now process is, to my mind, fundamental to effective group therapy technique. The words "here-and-now" make a deceptively simple phrase out of a complex therapeutic concept. They need to be understood in terms of their theoretical meaning and practical applicability.

The term "process," used liberally throughout this text, has a highly specialized meaning in a number of other fields—law, anatomy, sociology, anthropology, psychoanalysis, and descriptive psychiatry. In interactional psychotherapy, "process" refers to the ongoing nature of interpersonal relationships. A therapist who is process-oriented concerns himself not solely with the verbal content of the patient's utterance, but with the "how" and the "why" of the utterance, especially insofar as the "how" and "why" illuminate some aspects of the patient's relationship to others with whom he is interacting. The therapist considers the metacommunicational aspects of the message:* Why (from the relationship aspect) is the patient making the statement at this time, to this person, in this manner? Consider, for example, this transaction: During a lecture a student raised his hand and asked, "What was the date of Freud's death?" The lecturer replied, "1938," only to have the student inquire, "But sir, wasn't it 1939?" The student asked a question, the answer to which he knew, presumably for reasons other than a quest for information. We might infer that the process of the transaction was that the student wished to demonstrate his knowledge, or that he wished to humiliate or defeat the lecturer. Frequently, in the group therapy setting, the understanding of process becomes more complex; we search not only for the process behind a simple statement but for the process behind a sequence of statements made by a patient or by a number of patients. What does this sequence tell us about the relationship between one patient and the other group members, or between clusters or cliques of members, or between the members and the leader, or, finally, between the group as a whole and its primary task?

The phrase "here-and-now process" is, to be precise, tautological since "process," as we have defined it, encompasses the concept of the "here-and-now." Nonetheless, for added clarity and emphasis, I retain the phrase. A "here-and-now" or an ahistoric approach to therapy focuses on what is happening in the group in the present—at that very moment. There is a decreased emphasis on the patient's historical past or in the details of his current life problems; far more pertinent are the immediate patterns of interpersonal interaction in the group.

The rationale for such an approach is presented in detail in the discussion of the social microcosm concept in Chapter 2. Briefly, it is effective to focus on the here-and-now because the interpersonal behavior in the group of each patient is an accurate representation of his interpersonal behavior outside the group. By using this material, which is experienced by all the group members, rather than past material ("there-and-then") or material from the current life of one patient outside the group ("there-and-now"), which may concern only one patient, the leader may more meaningfully involve all the members in the group therapeutic work. By focusing on the here-and-now process, the therapist creates optimal conditions for the operation of the primary curative factors. The group's attention is turned upon itself, and the amount and intensity of interpersonal interac-

---

* Metacommunication refers to the communication about the communication. Compare, for example: "Close the window!" "Wouldn't you like to close the window? You must be cold." "I'm cold, would you please close the window?" "Why is this window open?" Each of these statements contains a great deal more than a simple request or command; each conveys a metacommunication—a message about the nature of the relationship between the two interacting individuals.

tion is increased, thereby enhancing the development of group cohesiveness and the opportunities for interpersonal learning.

CLINICAL ILLUSTRATIVE MATERIAL

Two clinical vignettes may further clarify the concept:

Early in the course of a group therapy meeting, Burt, a tenacious, bulldog-faced, intense graduate student, exclaimed to the group in general and to Rose (an unsophisticated astrologically inclined cosmetologist) in particular, "Parenthood is degrading!" This provocative statement elicited considerable response from the group, all of whom possessed parents and many of whom were parents, and the ensuing donnybrook consumed the remainder of the group session.

Let us consider the various perspectives available to the therapist and the group from which to view Burt's statement.

1. The statement can be viewed strictly in terms of substantive *content*. In fact, this is precisely what occurred in the group; the members engaged Burt in a debate of the virtues versus the dehumanizing aspects of parenthood—a discussion which was affect-laden but intellectualized and which brought none of the members closer to their goals in therapy. Subsequently the group felt discouraged about the meeting and angry with themselves and with Burt for having dissipated a meeting.

2. On the other hand, the therapist might have considered the *process* of Burt's statement, from any one of a number of perspectives.

a. Why did Burt attack Rose? What was the interpersonal process between them? In fact, the two had had a smoldering conflict for many weeks, and in the previous meeting Rose had wondered why, if Burt was so brilliant, was he still, at the age of thirty-two, a student. Burt had viewed Rose as an inferior being, who functioned primarily as a mammary gland; once, when she had been absent, he had referred to her as a brood mare.

b. Why is Burt so judgmental and so intolerant of nonintellectuals? Must he always maintain his self-esteem by standing on the carcass of a vanquished or humiliated adversary?

c. Assuming that Burt was chiefly intent upon attacking Rose, why did he proceed so indirectly? Is this characteristic of Burt's expression of aggression? Or is it characteristic of Rose that no one dares, for some unclear reason, to attack her directly?

d. Why did Burt, through an obviously provocative and indefensible statement, set himself up for a universal attack by the group? Although the words were different, this was a familiar melody for the group and for Burt, who had on many previous occasions placed himself in this position. Was it possible that Burt was most comfortable when relating to others in this fashion? He once stated that he had always loved a fight; indeed he almost licks his chops at the appearance of a row in the group. In fact, his early family environment was distinctively a fighting environment. Was fighting, then, a form (perhaps the only available form) of involvement for Burt?

e.   The process may be considered from the even broader perspective of the entire group. Other relevant events in the life of the group must be considered. For the past two months the session had been dominated by Kate, a deviant, disruptive, and partially deaf member who had, two weeks previously, dropped out of the group with the face-saving proviso that she would return when she obtained a hearing aid. Was it possible that the group needed a Kate and was Burt merely filling the required role of scapegoat? Through its continual climate of conflict, through its willingness to spend an entire session discussing in nonpersonal terms a single theme, was the group avoiding something—possibly an honest discussion of their feelings concerning Kate's rejection by the group or their guilt or fear of a similar fate? Or were they perhaps avoiding the anticipated perils of self-disclosure and intimacy?

Was the group saying something to the therapist through Burt (and through Kate)? For example, Burt may have been bearing the brunt of an attack that was displaced from the co-therapists. The therapists—bearded, aloof figures with a proclivity for rabbinical-like pronouncements—had, interestingly enough, never been attacked or confronted by the group (although the patients, in private, referred to the group as "the Smith Brothers' group!"). Surely there were strong, avoided feelings toward them, which may have been further fanned by their failure to support Kate and by their complicity through inactivity in her departure from the group.

Which one of these many process interpretations is correct? Which one could the therapist have employed in an effective intervention? The answer is, of course, that any and all may be correct; they are not mutually exclusive, each may be correct without invalidating the others. Each views the transaction from a slightly different vantage point. By clarifying each of these in turn, the therapist could focus the group on many different aspects of its life. Which one, then, should the therapist choose?

The therapist's choice should be based on one primary consideration—the needs of the group. Where is the group at that particular time? Has there been too much focus on Burt of late with the others feeling bored, uninvolved, and excluded? In that case the therapist might best wonder aloud about what the group is avoiding. He might remind the group of previous sessions spent in similar discussions which left them dissatisfied, or he might help one of the members varbalize this by inquiring about his inactivity or apparent uninvolvement in the discussion. If the group communications have been exceptionally indirect, he might comment on the indirectness of Burt's attacks or ask the group to help, via feedback, clarify what is happening between Burt and Rose. If, as was the case in this group, there was an important group event which was being strongly avoided (Kate's departure), then this should be pointed out. In short, the therapist must determine what he thinks the group needs most at that time and help it move in that direction.*

In another group, Kevin, an overbearing business executive, opened the meeting by asking the other members—housewives, lower income workers, and shopkeepers—for help with a problem confronting him. The problem was that he had received orders to cut his staff immediately by 50 per cent—he had to fire twenty out of forty men.

The content of the problem was intriguing and the group spent forty-five minutes discussing such aspects as justice versus mercy—i.e., whether one retains the most competent men or whether one should retain the men with the largest families or those who would have the greatest difficulty in finding another job. Despite the fact that most of the members engaged animatedly in the discussion, which involved important problems in human relations, the therapist strongly felt that the session was an unproductive one; the members remained in "safe" territory and the discussion could have appropriately occurred at a dinner party or any other social gathering; furthermore, as time passed, it became abundantly clear that Kevin had already spent considerable time thinking through all aspects of this problem and no one was able to provide him with novel approaches or suggestions.

How, then, might the therapist have proceeded to have made an intervention which would have been useful to the group? What data was available to elucidate the process of the transaction? As the meeting progressed, Kevin, on two occasions, revealed the amount of his salary (which was more than twice that of any other member); in fact the overall interpersonal effect of Kevin's presentation was to make others aware of his power and affluence. The process became ever more clear when the therapist recalled the previous meetings in which Kevin had attempted, in vain, to establish a special kind of relationship with the therapist (he had

---

* The here-and-now focus as I have described it is not, in the strictest sense, ahistoric since events occurring in the group weeks or months previously are considered in the therapist's formulations. The here-and-now therefore refers to experiences which the members have shared within the microcosm of the group.

sought some technical information about a projective psychological test to help him with a theological treatise on which he was working). Furthermore, in preceding meetings Kevin had been soundly attacked by the group for his strong religious convictions and labeled hypocritical because of his propensity for extramarital affairs and compulsive lying. He had also been termed "thick-skinned" because of his apparent insensitivity to the others. One other important aspect of Kevin's group behavior was his dominance; almost invariably he was the most active, central figure in the group meetings.

With this information, a number of alternatives were available to the therapist. He might have focused on Kevin's bid for prestige, especially following his loss of face in the previous meeting. Phrased in a nonaccusatory manner, a clarification of this sequence might have helped Kevin become aware of his desperate need for the group members to respect and admire him. At the same time the self-defeating aspects of his behavior could have been pointed out; despite his efforts to the contrary, the group had come to resent and, at times, even scorn him. Perhaps, too, Kevin was attempting to disclaim the appellation of "thick-skinned" by sharing with the group (or dramatizing) the agonies of his decision. The style of the intervention would have depended on Kevin's degree of defensiveness; if he had seemed particularly brittle or prickly, then one might have underscored how hurt he must have been at the previous meeting. If Kevin had been more open, then the therapist might have asked him directly what type of response he would have liked from the others. Other therapists might have preferred to interrupt the content discussion and ask the group what Kevin's question had to do with last week's session. Or the therapist might have chosen to call attention to an entirely different type of process by reflecting on the group's apparent willingness to permit Kevin to occupy the group center stage week after week. By encouraging the members to discuss their response to his monopolization, the therapist could have helped the group initiate an exploration of their relationship to Kevin.

FROM THE NONRELEVANT TO THE RELEVANT

In short, an intervention will be helpful as long as it focuses the group's attention upon either the interaction between group members or the group's avoidance of its primary task. The interpretation does not have to be diagnostically correct. As long as the therapist skillfully directs the group from the nonrelevant, from "then-and-there" to "here-and-now" material, he is technically correct. If a group spends time in an unproductive meeting discussing dull, boring parties and the therapist wonders aloud if they are indirectly referring to the present boring group session, there will be no method of ascertaining with any degree of certainty whether he is correct. How could such a hypothesis be tested? Nevertheless, by shifting the group's attention from "then-and-there" to "here-and-now" material, he performs a service to the group—a service which, consistently reinforced, will ultimately result in a cohesive, interactional group atmosphere maximally conducive to therapy. In this model, the effectiveness of an intervention can be gauged by its success in focusing the group upon here-and-now material.

Employing this principle, then, a group which dwells at length on poor health and a sense of guilt for remaining in bed during times of sickness might appropriately be asked whether "the group isn't really wondering about the therapist's recent absence from the group." Or a group suddenly preoccupied with death and the losses which each member has incurred might be asked whether they are also concerned with the impending four-week summer vacation for the group. One psychotherapy group in a prison, asked to meet in a different room to permit observation by some visiting psychiatrists, began its session with a lengthy discussion of new FBI computers which, at the press of a button, could deliver total information about any individual in a few seconds. The therapist made the interpretation that the group was dealing with the issue of being observed; he suggested that they were angry and disappointed with him and suspected that he, like the computer, had little regard for their feelings.

Obviously these interventions would be pointless if the group had already very thoroughly worked through all the implications of the therapist's recent absence, the impending four-week summer break, or the therapist's act of permitting observation. The technical procedure is not unlike the triage process in any traditional psychotherapy. Presented with voluminous data in considerable disarray, the therapist selects, reinforces, and interprets those aspects which he deems most helpful to the patient at that particular time. Not all dreams, not all parts of a dream are attended to by the therapist; however, a dream theme which elucidates a particular issue on which the patient is currently working is vigorously stalked.

Implicit here is the assumption that the therapist knows the most propitious direction for the group at a specific moment. As we have seen, this is not a precise matter; what is most important is that the therapist has formulated for himself the broad principles of what will ultimately be helpful to the group and to the members—this is precisely where a grasp of the curative factors is essential—and attempt to assist the group to develop in that direction. However, his interventions cannot disregard the concept of a developmental sequence—in other words, he must consider the matter of timing. A group or an individual may not be "ready" to understand or to make use of an intervention; ill-timed remarks may perplex or at times disrupt the group. It commonly occurs that patients find some interpretation or observation of great value, whereas the identical remark made previously in therapy was derided or ignored. The general issue of timing will be considered in more detail in Chapter 10 within a discussion of the developmental sequence of the therapy group.

PROCESS COMMENTARY AS THE THERAPIST'S TASK

It is quite common for the group members, especially in the early stages of therapy, to become so involved in the interaction that they are unable to objectify the transaction enough to be aware of or, for that matter, care about process. Process commentary is left to the therapist. This, of course, is one of the compelling objections to the leader's ever assuming full membership status; for if he became a full member, then he too would lose his perspective and be unable to step back, as it were, and see beyond the immediate content. The group, at that point, would provide its members with an emotional experience but not with a *corrective* emotional one. As the group proceeds and matures, members, modeling themselves after the leader, gradually assume some of the responsibility for commenting on process.* At the beginning, however, it is only the therapist who keeps perspective and who comments on process, only he who links up seemingly disconnected acts over time units.†

For example, two patients, Tim and Marjorie, had a sexual affair which eventually came to light in the group. The other members reacted in various ways but none so condemnatory or so vehemently as Diana, a forty-five-year-old nouveau-moralist who criticized them both for breaking group rules—Tim, for being "too intelligent to act like such a fool," Marjorie for "her irresponsible disregard for her husband and child," and the "Lucifer therapist" who had just

* A penetrating but humorous and accessible language for describing process like Eric Berne's glossary of games which people play [1] may hasten the assumption of process commentary by the patients.

† Stock and Whitman studied, microscopically, a single, crucial incident in a group session. They noted that the therapist's apperception of the group interaction differed from that of the patients in that the therapist "is likely to maintain a 'diagnostic' attitude and to see both the total group and individual dynamics in a fairly broad time perspective. Patients, on the other hand, are more likely to respond with direct affect to immediate group events." [2]

"sat there and let it happen." The therapist eventually pointed out that, in her formidable moralistic broadside, some individuals had been obliterated, that the Marjorie and Tim with all their struggles and doubts and fears whom Diana had known for so long had suddenly been replaced by faceless one-dimensional stereotypes. Furthermore, the therapist was the only one to recall the reasons for seeking therapy which Diana had expressed at the first group meeting: namely, that she needed help in dealing with her rage toward a nineteen-year-old rebellious, sexually awakening daughter, who was in the midst of a search for her identity and autonomy! From here it was but a short step for the group and then for Diana herself to enter the experiential world of her daughter and to understand with great clarity the nature of the struggle between mother and daughter.

Even when others are aware of an issue, it is often only the therapist who dares to comment on process. One neophyte therapist, when leading a training group of hospital nurses, learned through collusive intermember glances in the first meeting that there was considerable unspoken tension between the young progressive nurses and the older, conservative nursing supervisors in the group. The therapist felt that the issue, one reaching deep into tabooed regions of the authority-ridden nursing profession, was too sensitive and potentially explosive to touch. His supervisor assured him that it was too important an issue to leave unexplored and that he should broach it, since it was highly unlikely that anyone else in the group could do what he dared not. In the next meeting the therapist did so in a manner which is often effective in minimizing defensiveness: he stated his own dilemma about the issue—i.e., he told the group that he sensed a hierarchical struggle between the freshly trained nurses and the powerful senior nurses but that he was hesitant to bring it up for fear that the younger nurses would either deny it or so attack the supervisors that the latter would suffer injury and scuttle the group. His comment was enormously helpful and plunged the group into an open and constructive exploration of a vital issue.

Slowly the therapist, as he gains experience, begins to shift his set so that he automatically attends to process; he automatically attends not solely to *what* the patient is telling but what the patient is saying through the process of telling it.

Thus, in one group, at the end of the session, Mr. Glass, a young, rather fragile patient had, amidst considerable emotional upheaval, revealed for the first time his homosexual proclivities. At the next meeting the group urged him to continue. He attempted to do so but, nearly asphyxiated with emotion, he blocked and hesitated. Just then, with indecent alacrity, Mrs. Plough filled the gap with "*I* have a problem." Mrs. Plough, a husky, forty-year-old cabdriver, who sought therapy because of social loneliness and bitterness and who trichotomized the world into bold drivers, foolish drivers, and interfering but soon-to-be scurrying pedestrians, proceeded to discuss interminably a complex situation involving an unwelcome house-visiting aunt. For the process-oriented therapist the phrase "I have a problem" has a double entendre. Far more trenchantly than her words Mrs. Plough's behavior says, "I have a problem," and her problem is manifest in her insensitivity to Mr. Glass who, after months of silence, had finally mustered the courage to speak.

RECOGNITION OF PROCESS

Sometimes the process is clarified by attending not only to what is said but to what is omitted: the female patient who offers suggestions, advice, or feedback to the male patients but never to the other women in the group; the group that never confronts or questions the therapist; the topics (e.g., sex, money) that are never broached; the patient who is never attacked; or the one who is never supported—all these omissions are part of the transactional process of the group. (It is primarily through clinical experience that the therapist formulates expected norms and is able to understand process in terms of what is omitted.)

Physiologists commonly study the function of a hormone by removing the endocrine gland which manufactures it and observing the changes in the hormone-deficient organism. Similarly, in group therapy, we may learn a great deal about the role of a particular member by observing the here-and-now process of the group when he is absent. For example, if the absent member is an aggressive, competitive individual, the group may feel liberated and other patients who had felt threatened or restricted by the missing member may suddenly blossom into activity. If, on the other hand, the group has depended on the missing member to carry the burden of self-disclosure or to coax the other members into speaking, then it will feel helpless and threatened when he is absent. Quite often this occurrence elucidates interpersonal feelings which previously were entirely out of the group members' awareness, and the therapist should encourage the group to discuss these feelings toward the absent member both at the time and later in his presence. Similarly a rich supply of data about feelings toward the therapist often emerges in the leaderless or alternate meeting, which we shall discuss in Chapter 13.

Often the here-and-now process is obscure and eludes recognition unless the therapist relies heavily upon his own feelings—feelings which he comes to trust only after repeated episodes of consensual validation from previous similar incidents in his group therapy experience. For example, consider the following multiple therapy session (a psychotherapy teaching format in which one patient meets with several therapists with procedural rules similar to those of group therapy).[3]

In her fourth session Mrs. Straw, a severely ill narcotics addict with a marked inability to interact directly with others—a problem which the group had been exploring—began with an involved, detailed account of a family argument. With its endless procession of names of cousins, great-aunts, and neighbors, the story, whatever else it meant, had the effect of excluding the therapists from her world during the hour. Finally one commented that he felt impatient, frustrated, and very much shut out by the patient. She then took some paper out of her purse and read something that she said she had written to the group. It was a long, rather chilling allegory which involved her swimming aimlessly in circles, with children nearby trying to swim with weights on their feet which adults had placed on them to help them develop power. She shouted for help to passers-by on the shore and they encouraged her to swim harder and to rest in a boat, which, however, was full of holes and drew water. She knew that, although it was good to rest, she could never learn to swim in a boat.

The allegory was a poignant and intriguing one; but the therapists, when they recalled the group's primary task, verbalized once again their feelings of exclusion and frustration. The reading of the allegory had been an entirely autistic affair which effectively kept them at a great distance. Mrs. Straw then remarked that she had to tell the group that she was drowning. A therapist said that he sensed her feeling of drowning in the very first session and wondered why she had to tell them in this beautiful but devious fashion. In an unusual burst of directness, she replied that she wished to pique their interest in her by showing how sensitive and clever she was. Others pointed out that this was unnecessary and that they had, in fact, often thought and talked about her between sessions. They felt that though her strategy was in part successful (they *were* intrigued and impressed by the allegory), it also resulted in annoying and distancing them; it was after she had unveiled *both* the allegory *and* her need to impress them that their interest in her was greatest. Although literary devotees may shudder at this dismissal of her allegory as a much to be eschewed manifestation of interpersonal deviousness, it proved nonetheless good medicine for this patient, who had seen Kubla Khan too often in her beclouded, oblique course through an unpeopled world.

Often the therapist must rely on nonverbal communications in his quest for an understanding of process. The sluggishness, aliveness, tension, interest, or fragmentation of a group may become evident from a variety of nonverbal cues from the members. Are members looking at their watches or yawning? Are the chairs pulled away from the center of the table at the same time great interest is being verbally professed in the group? Are coats kept on? When in a single meeting or in the sequence of meetings are they removed? How quickly does the group enter the room? How do they leave it? What about cigarettes; who smokes and when; in what manner? (Berger[4] describes a beautiful self-possessed woman who smoked, not in moments of tension but only when the tension had subsided sufficiently to allow her to light and hold the cigarette with aplomb.) A near-infinite variety of postural shifts may betoken discomfort; foot flexion, for example, is a particularly common sign of anxiety. A change in dress or grooming is not uncommonly an indicator of change in a patient or in the atmosphere of the entire group. The first flicker of resentment to the leader from an unctuous, dependent male may be a change in group garb from a shirt and tie to an open-necked sport shirt. Indeed it is common knowledge that nonverbal behavior frequently expresses feelings of which the patient is yet unaware; the therapist, through observing and teaching the group to observe nonverbal behavior, may hasten the process of self-exploration.[4]

Neophyte group therapists are often taken aback at the concept of a basically ahistoric approach to group therapy. How, they ask, can a group of erstwhile strangers find sufficient here-and-now material to discuss? In fact, it is entirely possible to conduct a group using nothing but here-and-now material. I have often led training groups of medical students or psychiatric residents in which the basic ground rule, stated at the very beginning, was that *no* past or outside material was to be discussed. How can such a contract be maintained? What material is available to allow the group to begin? The leader may help the group work on a variety of initial common experiences. Once, several years ago, I was a participant in such a group when the leader began by asking us to write our names on cards in front of us. This data alone provided a rich source of material. I commented to a member who had filled his card with a large question mark that that seemed rather adolescent; he replied that I seemed as "four square as they come." We each had hit on a bit of truth for the other and the group was off with gusto.

Often the first here-and-now experience is the opening silence of the first meeting; the group members' feelings about the silence may provide significant data—for example, the varying degrees of tension, of shame, of a desire to speak, coupled with a fear of exposure. The group or the leader may raise the issue of group rules—for example, the rule about confidentiality. Should the group be permitted to discuss the meetings to outsiders? Or to spouses? I have seen many a valuable discussion stem from the concern about confidentiality which touches such areas as trust, shame, fear of disclosure, or degree of commitment to the group. Early in the group one may find a dichotomization of the members between those who want rules and structures and those who do not. In fact, almost any stimulus will elicit differential responses from the group members, which are reflective of important feelings about self and others. As the group builds up cohesiveness and trust, the process continues spiraling deeper, the members revealing more of themselves with each turn.

We are not suggesting, however, that in the effective therapy group discussion of the past or of current extragroup material is wholly dispensable. Part of the group cohesiveness building process depends on the sharing of symptoms and the finding of similarities between members. The curative factor of universality may be set into motion by non-here-and-now material. Furthermore, the therapist must not interpret the here-and-now process so quickly that the group affect is stifled; it must be allowed to live, to interact, to engage in a stage which Bach[5] aptly refers to as "cathartic free play." It is out of this non-here-and-now material, this grist for the interpersonal mill, that the process interpretations spring.

The Use of the Past

Past material from early life inevitably plays a part in the group therapeutic process; however, this material assumes a form and a function considerably different from that in traditional individual analytic therapy.* The past may be explored, not to explain the present, not to recapture repressed experiences, not to elucidate and (would that we could!) work through major past traumata, *but instead to aid in the development of group cohesiveness by increasing intermember understanding and acceptance.*

The method of studying the past material is not that of a general survey but generally a form of sector analysis [6] designed to explore the development of some particular interpersonal stance. If, for example, two members are locked in a seemingly irreconcilable struggle, each finding some

---

* It is not uncommon, for example, for group therapists to conclude a course of very successful therapy with a patient and yet be unfamiliar with such significant aspects of the patient's early life as number and age of siblings, occupation of parents, geographical moves, etc.

aspect of the other repugnant, often a full understanding of the developmental route whereby each arrived at his particular viewpoint can rehumanize the struggle. An individual with a regal air conveying hauteur and condescension, almost impossible to tolerate, may suddenly seem understandable and even winsome when one learns of his immigrant parents and his desperate struggle to transcend the degradation of his slum childhood. Individuals are benefited through being fully known by others in the group and being fully accepted; knowing another's process of becoming is a rich and often indispensable adjunct to knowing the person.

No doubt reworking the past serves other purposes, such as satisfying our needs for cognitive ordering, understanding, and mastery of hitherto diffuse, enigmatic data; too often, however, we make groping forays into the past because of our unswerving conviction that the past determines the present and the future. In a sense, perhaps it is more helpful (and not less accurate) to consider, too, that the present determines the past! As Frank[7] reminds us, patients, even in prolonged therapy, recall only a minute fraction of their past experiences and may selectively recall and synthesize the past so as to achieve consistency with their present view of themselves. (Goffman[8] suggests the term "apologia" for this reconstruction of the past.) As a patient, through therapy, changes his present image of himself, he may alter or reintegrate his past; for example, he may recall long forgotten positive experiences with a parent.* The past, in as real a form as we can know it, has been influenced by the present. It is possible that a circular process is set into motion and that the reinterpretation of the past may further alter or reinforce one's present self-image; however, great insights into the past do not in themselves alter the patient's present or future. The past is important only insofar as it influences the here-and-now therapist-patient relationship. As Rycroft[9] states, "It makes better sense to say that the analyst makes excursions into historical research in order to understand something which is interfering with his present communication with the patient (in the same way that a translator might turn to history to elucidate an obscure text) than to say that he makes contact with the patient in order to gain access to biographical data."

I am convinced that review and evocation of the past serve primarily to bind the group members together by providing them with a common, intriguing task, by increasing the likelihood of perceived similarities, and by stimulating self-disclosure and intermember empathy and acceptance.

---

* In group therapy patients often work on their past with no overt mention of this in the group. In follow-up outcome interviews patients frequently report attitudinal improvements in past, as well as current, interpersonal relationships despite the fact that no explicit work has been done in this area in the group.

Nor, for that matter, as I stated in Chapter 4, do I think the process is different in individual therapy where, too, the intellectual task, the exploration and integration of the past, serves primarily as cement to keep therapist and patient tied together until the relationship solidifies and its subsequent exploration becomes the paramount mutative force. Whether a therapist and his patients can know this and still explore the past with the zeal required to render the process worthwhile is another question. This is perhaps an ironic instance of self-deception in the service of self-understanding.

Interpretations*—Interpersonal and Total Group

To return, momentarily, to the first clinical vignette presented in this chapter in which a member exclaimed that "motherhood is degrading," we note that the several alternative here-and-now interventions available to the therapist fall into two broad categories: (1) interpersonal, in which the therapist clarifies some aspect of relationship between one member and one or more other members; (2) total or mass group, in which the therapist clarifies some trend of the group as a single unit.

INTERPERSONAL INTERPRETATIONS

The great majority of interventions made by American group therapists fall into this category. Generally the therapist comments on some aspect of the interpersonal relationships occurring between two or more group members or between himself and one or more members. Most often he attempts to clarify some important feature of the transaction, which is either not readily apparent to the participants or is totally out of their awareness. He may attempt in a descriptive manner to call attention to aspects of the relationship or he may hazard an interpretation designed to provide motivational insight. Some examples of types of interpersonal interventions are:

1. The therapist may point out that there is a displacement process occurring— i.e., one member may be attacking another instead of the rightful object of his anger, perhaps some other member or the therapist.

* I use the term "interpretation" in its broadest sense to refer to any type of clarifying, illuminating, or explanatory statement.

2. The therapist may point out that two or more members relate to each other very indirectly, i.e., they battle over issues or concepts instead of confronting deeply personal feelings about each other.

3. The therapist may identify "mirror reactions" [10]—the tendency of patients to respond strongly to a part of themselves which they sense in another. (See Chapter 11.)

4. He may identify parataxic distortions and may clarify these by, for example, eliciting consensual validation from the other members about some characteristic of a group member.

5. He may point out habitual maladaptive patterns of interpersonal behavior of some patients and wonder why they seem inclined to repeat behavior which results in undesired responses from others; he may wonder if the patient isn't forced into these patterns by some unconscious fear of a calamity should he attempt to relate in another way.

This list may be greatly extended, but these examples are sufficient to illustrate the options available to the therapist making an interpersonal intervention. The underlying principle is to increase the potency of the curative factors of cohesiveness and interpersonal learning. Interpersonal interventions focus the members' attention on what is alive and urgent in the group; the members' interest, affect, and degree of involvement is thereby deepened. In addition, through the clarification of interpersonal feelings and fantasies, the process of interpersonal learning is launched. Other curative factors, as we have shown, may play an important role at various stages of the group. For example, early in the group, universality is itself a potent source of relief as well as a mediator of group cohesiveness; therefore, the therapist may make an interpersonal intervention early in the group in which he points out that, despite clashes, two members have a great deal in common.

MASS GROUP INTERPRETATIONS

The other broad category of interventions available to the therapist is the mass or total group interpretation. In the therapist's statement there will be reference to "the group" or "we" or "all of us." For example, to return to the same "parenthood is degrading" vignette, the therapist might raise the issue of whether the "group" needs a scapegoat and whether, with Kate gone, Burt is filling the role; or whether the "group" is actively avoiding an important issue—i.e., their guilty pleasure and fears about Kate's departure. The mass group interpretation is a comment about some group phenomenon, generally about the group's attitude toward its primary task, toward the leader, or toward a unit of its membership (a single member or a subgroup).

Rationale of Mass Group Interpretations. The entire issue of mass group interpretations is an exceedingly complex and controversial one and, before embarking on an investigation of the matter, I would suggest a simplifying principle: *The purpose of a mass group interpretation is to remove some obstacle which has arisen to obstruct the progress of the entire group.* The two common types of obstacles are: anxiety-laden issues and antitherapeutic group norms.

ANXIETY-LADEN ISSUES. Often some issue arises which is so threatening that the group, on either a conscious or an unconscious level, refuses to confront the problem and takes some type of evasive action. This avoidance takes many forms, all of which are commonly referred to as "group flight." A clinical example of flight from an anxiety-laden issue may clarify this point:

Six members were present at the sixty-fifth group meeting; one member, John, was absent. For the first time and without previous mention, one of the members, Mary, brought her dog to the meeting. The group, usually an animated, active one, was unusually subdued and nonproductive. Their speech was barely audible and throughout the meeting they discussed safe topics on a level of impersonality appropriate to any large social gathering. Much of the content centered on study habits (three of the members were graduate students), on examinations, and on teachers (especially their failings and untrustworthiness). Moreover, the senior member of the group discussed former members who had long since departed from the group—the "good old days" phenomenon. The dog (a wretched, restless creature who spent most of the group session noisily licking his genitals) was never mentioned and finally the therapist, thinking he was speaking for the group, brought up the issue of Mary's bringing the dog to the meeting. Much to the therapist's surprise, Mary—a highly unpopular, narcissistic member—was unanimously defended; everyone denied that the dog was in any way distracting and left the therapist as a lonely protester.

The therapist considered the entire meeting as a flight meeting and accordingly made appropriate mass group interpretations which we will discuss. But first, what is the evidence that such a meeting is "flight"? And flight from what? We must consider the age of the group; in a young group, meeting, let us say, for the third time, such a session may be a manifestation not of resistance but of the group's uncertainty about their primary task and of their groping to establish procedural norms. However, this group had already met for fourteen months and, furthermore, the previous meetings had been strikingly different in character. Convincing evidence of flight occurs when the preceding group meeting is examined. At this meeting, John, the member absent from the meeting under consideration, had been twenty minutes late and happened to walk down the corridor at the precise moment when the door of the adjoining observation room was opened. John heard the voices of the other group members and saw a room full of observers viewing the group; moreover, the observers at that moment happened to be laughing at some private joke. Although John, like all the group members, had been told that the group was being observed by students, nevertheless this shocking irreverent confirmation stunned him. When John, in the last moments of the meeting, was finally able to discuss it with the other members, they were equally stunned. John, as we have seen, missed the next session.

This event was a catastrophe of major proportion for the group. It would be for any group, for that matter; it would raise serious questions in the minds of the members about the therapeutic situation. Was the therapist to be trusted? Was he, like his colleagues in the observation room, inwardly laughing at them? Was anything he said genuinely based? Was the group, once perceived as a human situation, in fact a sterile, contrived, laboratory specimen being studied dispassionately by a therapist who probably felt closer allegiance to "them" (the others, the observers) than to the group? Despite, or, we should say, because of, the magnitude of these painful group issues, the group declined to confront the matter. Instead they engaged in flight behavior which now begins to be understandable. Exposed to an outside threat, the group banded tightly together for protection; they spoke softly about safe topics so as to avoid sharing anything with the outside menace (the observers and, through association, the therapist). The therapist was unsupported when he asked about the obviously distracting behavior of the dog; the "good old days" was a reference to and a yearning for bygone times when the group was pure and the therapist could be trusted. The discussion of examinations and untrustworthy teachers was also a thinly veiled expression of attitudes toward the therapist.

The precise nature and timing of the intervention is largely a matter of individual style. Some therapists, myself included, tend to intervene when they sense the presence of some group flight even though they do not clearly understand its source. The therapist may, for example, comment that he feels puzzled or uneasy about the meeting and inquire as to whether "there is something the group is not talking about today" or whether "the group is avoiding something," or perhaps he might ask about the "hidden agenda." He increases the salience of his inquiry by citing the evidence—e.g., the whispering, the sudden shift toward neutral topics and a noninteractive mode of communication, his experience of being left out or of being deserted by the others in the dog issue.* Furthermore, he might add that the group is strangely avoiding all discussion both of the previous meeting and of John's absence today. In our clinical example it would not be a sufficient goal merely to get the group back on the track, back to a discussion of more meaningful material. The issues being avoided are too crucial to the group's existence to be left submerged. This is particularly relevant in a group whose members have insufficiently explored their relation to the therapist. Therefore, the therapist should repeatedly turn the group's attention back onto the main issue and not be misled by substitute behavior—e.g., the group's offering for discussion another theme, perhaps even a somewhat charged one. Some therapists prefer to wait longer until they have very full knowledge of the nature and the source of the flight and can make a complete interpretation to the group.

Another common way in which the group flight manifests itself is through intellectualization. For example, after a meeting in which two members disclosed their homosexuality, one group launched into a discussion of prejudice that lasted for two sessions. Prejudicial feelings *in abstracto* about Jews, Negroes, Orientals, and homosexuals were discussed. What was avoided, however, was a swarm of deeply personal feelings aroused by the two homosexual patients. The members avoided their scorn, their fears of the evocation of their own homosexual feelings, their anger toward the therapists for having chosen these two when, as one member stated later, "the group so badly needed men." The group may also avoid work by more literal flight, by absences or by tardiness. Whatever the form, however, the result is the same: in the language of the group dynamicist, locomotion toward the attainment of group goals is impeded, and the group is no longer engaged in its primary task.

ANTITHERAPEUTIC GROUP NORMS. Another type of group obstacle warranting a mass group interpretation occurs when antitherapeutic group norms are elaborated by the group. The therapist may note that some unusual procedural norms are being established by the group—norms that he deems antitherapeutic either on the basis of early events in the group or from his previous experience or training. For example, a group may, early in its life, establish a "take turns" format in which an entire meeting is devoted in turn to each member of the group. Such a format is an

* Mary, who had brought the dog, happened to have missed the previous session and was unaware of what had happened, so the important group issue was not why she brought it but their response to its presence.

undesirable one since members are often forced into premature self-disclosure with consequent humiliation at subsequent meetings. Furthermore, members, as their "turn" approaches, may experience extreme anxiety or even decide to terminate therapy. Or a group may have established a pattern of devoting the entire session to the first issue raised in that session; strong invisible sanctions have been erected against changing the subject. Another group (and I have especially noted this among college student groups) may establish a "can you top this" format in which the members engage in a spiraling orgy of self-disclosure. Or a group may become tightly knit, offering so hostile a welcome to new members that they soon terminate therapy.

In such instances the therapist's interpretations about the mass group phenomenon are more effective if the process is clearly described, the deleterious effects on the members or the group at large specifically cited, and the implication made that there may be alternatives to these normative patterns. For example, he might comment, "I notice that over the past few weeks we seem to have made a tradition of discussing, for the entire meeting, the first issue raised in the session and that no one seems to dare change the subject. And yet it seems as though most of the group is dissatisfied with this; several of you appeared bored and withdrawn today and it does not appear that Mr. X (the protagonist) has profited from the meeting. I wonder how and why this rule was established and how we can go about changing it."

Frequently one notes that the group, during its development, bypasses certain important phases or never incorporates certain norms into its culture. For example, a group may develop without ever going through a period of examining its views about the therapist, without ever confronting or attacking him; or a group may develop without a whisper of inter-member dissension, without status bids or struggles for control; or a group may meet for a year or more with no hint of real intimacy or closeness arising among the members. It is my impression that such a collaborative avoidance is a result of the group members' collectively constructing norms dictating this avoidance. If the therapist senses that the group is providing a one-sided or incomplete experience for the members, he may then comment on the missing aspect of group life in that particular group. (Such an intervention assumes, of course, that there are regularly recurring, predictable phases of small group development with which the therapist is thoroughly familiar—a topic which we will discuss in Chapter 10.)

Mass Group Interpretations—General Considerations. The general principle advanced earlier—that the purpose of a mass group interpretation is to remove some obstacle which has arisen to obstruct the progress of the entire group*—is a deceptively simple one; from both a theoretical and a practical standpoint, the matter is far more complex.

GROUP INTERVENTIONS AND GROUP-CENTERED THERAPY. Among various schools of group therapy, the issue of total group interpretations versus interpretations involving a smaller unit or a single group member is a highly controversial one; indeed some group therapists make only total group interpretations while others never or rarely do.† First we must disentangle the mass group interpretation from the concept of group-centered therapy. The approach described in this book clearly emphasizes total group forces—e.g., group cohesiveness as one of the paramount curative factors. Yet without being inconsistent, I would maintain that only a very small percentage of the therapist's interventions need be mass group ones. One assists a group to develop cohesiveness in a variety of ways, beginning with the selection and preparation of patients. The therapist may, for example, reinforce self-disclosure, reinforce members bringing in group dreams, clarify how the group goals are confluent with the individual member's goals, or encourage the expression of positive as well as negative intermember affect.

THE CONCEPT OF THE "GROUP." Gradually over the years the myth of the "group" has been elaborated and has generated considerable confusion in the field. As psychoanalysts entered the field of group therapy, they brought with them time-honored concepts and techniques of their disci-

---

* Both Spotnitz [11] and Foulkes [10] have drawn a parallel with the analysis of resistance in individual psychoanalysis. Although such a comparison adds little conceptually, it nevertheless is a useful aid for individuals, well grounded in psychoanalytic theory, entering the group field. The analysis of resistance has two functions: the work of analysis proper is permitted to proceed as the obstacles are removed and the patient, in the process of working through resistance, discovers a great deal about himself; in fact Freud regarded the overcoming of resistance as the paramount task of analysis. Much of the same is true in group therapy; clearly, by overcoming group resistances, the group is assisted in engaging in the primary task. At times, too, patients learn about themselves and group dynamics from an understanding of mass group phenomena; however, this type of learning is often not highly helpful and frequently the price (in terms of group time and possible dropouts) is exorbitant. It is only the therapist who has much interest in unraveling and understanding mass group dynamics. As I shall explain in Chapter 14, this is one of the significant differences between therapy groups and sensitivity-training groups.

† Parloff [12] in a recent comprehensive review classifies the current styles of analytic group therapy into three schools: the *classicists*, therapists who rely on intrapersonal interpretation and in essence do individual therapy in groups; the *interpersonalists*, who attempt to focus on the dyad or subgroup; and the *integralists*, who place major emphasis on group processes. The approach described in this book would in this system be described as "interpersonalist-integralist"; however, the guiding principle is not an allegiance to any theoretical position but instead a pragmatic attempt to implement what appear to be the curative factors in therapy.

pline. It was reasoned that traditional psychoanalytic techniques, with some modifications, could be employed in group therapy; however, the group and not the individual was now considered the patient, and vague concepts like "group ego" and "group superego" were formulated. Free association by an individual patient was then replaced by "group association."[13] The "group" became regarded as an autonomous organism: ". . . the group tends to speak and react to a common theme as if it were a living entity, expressing itself in different ways through various mouths. All contributions are variations on this single theme, even though the group are not consciously aware of that theme and do not know what they are really talking about." [14]

Now obviously the concept of the group as a system with characteristic properties is a valuable one; in many ways we have discussed the importance of attending to the group as a system. However, what has happened is that many workers have tended to anthropomorphize the group. Just as we have instilled life into a stock market which "attempts to fight off a selling wave" or "desperately guards the 900 Dow-Jones level," so too have we conceptually breathed life into the group. It is not, I feel, fatuous to point out that the group is not a living entity; it is but an abstraction created for our semantic and conceptual convenience. When it becomes so metapsychologized that it promotes not clarity but haziness of thought, then it no longer serves its original function.

As an example of the conceptual pitfalls involved, consider the process of diagnosing the state of the group. How do we know what is the dominant group culture, common group tension, or group mind? How many of the group members must be involved before we conclude it is the "group" speaking? This last question, particularly, is a source of considerable confusion; Bion and Ezriel, as we shall see, make the dubious assumption that silence by a group member signifies collusion or agreement with the individuals "speaking for the group." This results in a "group mind" or "group culture" interpretation made on the basis of a small percentage of the membership. As Parloff [12] suggests, this practice becomes antiscientific because "the greater the therapist's conviction regarding the nature of the conflicts which may be found in the group, the less evidence he requires for confirmation of his expectations."

We avoid becoming enmeshed in precious questions such as the group mind if we maintain an allegiance to pragmatic rather than metapsychological concerns. If the group therapist regularly reminds himself of curative factors in group therapy and addresses himself to the question of whether the group is moving toward or away from the implementation of the major curative factors, then he will have a valid guiding principle.

THE TIMING OF GROUP INTERVENTIONS. For pedagogical reasons interpersonal phenomena and mass group phenomena have been discussed as though they were quite distinct; in practice, of course, the two often overlap and the therapist is faced with the question of when to emphasize the interpersonal aspects of the transaction and when to emphasize the mass group aspects. This matter of clinical judgment cannot be neatly prescribed; as in any therapeutic endeavor, judgment develops from experience and supervision as well as intuition. As Melanie Klein stated, "It is a most precious quality in an analyst to be able at any moment to pick out the point of urgency" (cited by Strachey).[15]

The point of urgency is a far more elusive factor in group therapy than in individual treatment. As a general rule, however, *an issue critical to the existence or functioning of the entire group always takes precedence over a narrower interpersonal issue.* As an illustration let us return to the group which engaged in whispering, discussion of neutral topics, and other forms of group flight during the meeting after a member had inadvertently discovered the very indiscreet group observers. In the meeting under consideration, Mary (who had been absent at the previous meeting) brought her dog. Under normal circumstances this act would clearly have become an important group issue: Mary had not asked permission from the therapist or other members; she was, because of her great narcissism, an unpopular member, and the act of bringing the dog was representative of her lack of concern about others. However, in the meeting under consideration, there was a far more urgent issue—one threatening the entire group—and the dog was discussed, not from the aspect of facilitating Mary's interpersonal learning, but as he was used by the group in their flight. Only later, after the obstacle to the group's progress had been worked through and removed, did the group return to a meaningful consideration of their feelings about Mary's bringing the dog.

Should it occur, however, that the group is progressing well, considerable cohesiveness has developed, and the members are actively interacting and engaging in interpersonal exploration and learning, then there is no need for mass group interpretations in the group's therapy.

Total Group Interventions—Other Views. Other group therapists disagree and view the formulation of total group interventions, not as a method of removing obstacles, but as the chief or even the sole procedural task of the therapist. Systematic and influential approaches to mass group phenomena in therapy groups have been elaborated by Bion, Ezriel, and Whitaker and Lieberman.* These three approaches differ from my own

* It is not my intention to present a historical survey of the concept of the "group" in the group therapeutic process, but to describe systems which utilize mass group inter-

and from each other in (1) the nature of group phenomena described and (2) the use and the rationale of these phenomena in therapy.

BION. Wilfred Bion, a practicing Kleinian analyst, first became interested in group dynamics during the early 1940's when he, together with John Rickman,[16] first experimented with large and small group meetings in a military psychiatric hospital. Later, from 1947 to 1949, Bion conducted two therapy groups and a series of staff discussion groups at the Tavistock Clinic. After 1949 his interest turned to other areas,* and he permanently left the group therapy field.

Nature of the Group Phenomena. Bion studied his groups through holistic spectacles. Searching for total group currents, he noted that at times the group appeared to be pursuing its primary task† in a rational, effective fashion. Bion called this group culture the "work group" culture. At other times he noted that the group no longer seemed to be pursuing its primary task; instead it appeared to be dominated by certain massive emotional states which resulted in behavior incompatible with the primary task. Three types of basic, recurring emotional states (a "constellation of discrete feelings that permeate all the group's interactions") [19] were described: (1) aggressiveness, hostility, and fear; (2) optimism and hopeful anticipation; (3) helplessness or awe. From these primary observations [20] Bion postulated that in each of these emotional states the group was acting "as if" the members shared some common belief from which their affect stemmed. For example, while in an optimistic or hopefully anticipatory state the group acts "as if" its aim is to preserve itself by finding strength or a new leader from its peer membership; when it is in a helpless or awed state it acts "as if" its aim is to obtain support, nurturance, strength from something outside the group—generally the designated leader. When it is in an aggressive or fearful state it acts "as if" its aim is to avoid something by fighting or running away from it. Bion terms each of these three emotional states "basic assumption cultures" and thus speaks of three types of basic assumption groups: basic assumption pairing, basic assumption dependency, basic assumption flight-fight, respectively.

---

pretations in a manner significantly different from the approach I have described. For example, it seems likely that Foulkes [17] antedates most workers in his appreciation of total group forces. However, in his current practice, Foulkes rarely makes a total group intervention and, when he does, it is in an attempt to remove, in much the manner described here, some obstacle in the path of the group.[18]

* An exceedingly influential figure in the Kleinian branch of the British Psychoanalytic Society, he has been chiefly interested in the application of Kleinian analytic principles in the understanding and psychotherapy of the schizophrenias.

† Bion considered the primary task of the therapy group to be an exploration of its own intragroup tensions.

Thus at any given time a group may be described as either a work group, or as one of the three basic assumption groups, or in some transitional phase.

A basic assumption group may have a life span of a fraction of a meeting, or it may persist for several months. Note that the primary observation is the emotional state. "I consider the emotional state to be in existence and the basic assumption to be deductible from it." [21] This means that the basic assumption culture need not necessarily be conscious to the members or even observable to the leader but that if one makes the "as-if" assertion (i.e., the group is acting "as if" its purpose is to . . .) then the leader will be able to understand seemingly illogical and unconnected behavior on the part of the members.

Bion's focus on the individual group member centered on that member's relationship to the group culture. The concept of "valency" was developed to describe an individual's attraction to a particular group culture. This attraction, analogous to tropism in plants,[20] is a force which leads a member into being the chief spokesman or a participant or a major rebel in one of the basic assumption cultures.

One other important aspect of Bion's view of groups is that it is leader-centered. All three basic assumption states are oriented around the issue of leadership. Each type of group searches for a leader—one who will meet its needs: the basic assumption dependency group attempts in various ways to coax or coerce the professional leader to guide them; the flight-fight group searches for a member who will lead them in this direction; the pairing group optimistically pairs and waits, hopeful that the leader will "emerge from the offspring of the pair." [20]

Therapeutic Considerations. Bion's views on the technique of group therapy are not explicit in his writings and, with his departure from the field, have never been clarified. Basically it appears that Bion's ultimate goal was helping patients achieve the ability to become effective members of work groups. All of Bion's interpretations were mass group interpretations and were made immediately upon the therapist's recognition of the group situation. He repeatedly confronted the group with its basic assumption behavior, especially insofar as it related to the therapist. This behavior is depicted by Bion as characteristically illogical, impulsive, and non-reality-oriented. By confronting the group repeatedly in this manner, Bion attempted to reinstate the work group culture. He hoped that patients, as they became aware of the nature and unrealizability of their unrealistic demands, would gradually learn more realistic and adaptive methods of group functioning.

Three specific types of conflict which complicate group functions are described by Bion, who implies that it is the task of the therapist and the work group to expose, clarify, and work through these conflicts: (1) a desire on the part of the individual for "a sense of vitality by total submergence in the group" which exists alongside a desire for "a sense of individual independence by total repudiation of the group"; (2) the conflict between the group and the patient whose desires are often at cross-purposes to the needs of the group; and (3) the conflict between the problem-oriented work group and the basic assumption group.

At other times Bion suggests therapeutic approaches which imply that he places great emphasis on the working through of deeply unconscious material.

I must stress the point that I consider it essential to work out very thoroughly the primitive primal scene as it discloses itself in the group. This differs markedly from the primal scene in its classical description in that it is much more bizarre and seems to assume that a part of one parent, the breast or the mother's body, contains amongst other objects a part of the father . . . the group experience seems to me to give ample material to support the view that these fantasies are of permanent importance for the group. . . . Even in the "stable" group the deep psychotic levels should be demonstrated though it may involve temporarily an apparent increase in the "illness" of the group.[20]

Bion always interpreted the group to the entire group rather than to an individual member. He assumed that the effects would be wide and more effective since each individual would find all interpretations relevant to some degree.[22]

Overview of Bion's Approach. Bion himself seemed far more interested in understanding the dynamics of groups than in elaborating an effective system of group therapy. One of Bion's colleagues, who was associated with Bion while he conducted groups at the Tavistock Clinic (1947–1949) and who inherited his clinical groups, stated that "Bion's group technique seemed primarily suited to staff members whose goal was to understand group dynamics. Patients might be helped provided they had a level of sophistication high enough to grasp the relevance of the mass group interpretations for their own problems. Patients treated in this type of group therapy format without this degree of sophistication often responded with bewilderment and perplexity." [23] Accordingly Bion's influence has been greater in group dynamics research* and in the training group field than in group therapy per se. His direct influence on American group therapists

---

* A series of research inquiries based on Bion's formulations are reviewed in a monograph by Stock and Thelen.[24]

has been small indeed, perhaps in part, as Parloff [12] suggests, because of his use of Kleinian rather than Freudian concepts.

Bion's ingenious and highly original conceptualizations about group dynamics have intrigued many workers. An all-inclusive system satisfies one's need for closure and provides a group leader with a sense of mastery; all of the richly variegated, often confusing aspects of group life can be neatly classified. A citadel of such impregnability is erected that the therapist (as I recently observed) can, when the members are engaged in activity not easily classifiable, accuse the basic assumption fight group of deliberately attempting to confuse him!

Despite the ingenuity of the system, we must keep in mind that it is a highly speculative one arrived at intuitively by an individual who, though highly astute, did not continue to develop and refine his observations. Sherwood,[19] in a penetrating critical study of Bion's group theories, has described Bion's method as science by fiat and states that, examined from a logical, scientific vantage point, Bion's methodology and conclusions are wholly indefensible. Certainly many of the group phenomena Bion describes are readily observable in groups. However, there are, after all, only a limited number of ways in which individuals can respond to social or interpersonal stress. Horney pointed out that individuals can move *toward* others (a search for love), *against* others (a search for mastery), *away from* others (resignation, a search for freedom), or *with* others (a cooperative, mature collaboration). This social repertoire seems closely parallel to fight (against), flight (away), dependency (toward), work (with). Furthermore, as Parloff [12] notes, sex (pairing), aggression (fight-flight), dependency, and, I would add, self-actualization would appear to be an adequate classification of the motivational states of the members of any group. However, the appearance of these phenomena by no means validates the Bionic system. It is not necessary to postulate a highly elaborate system in order to explain the fact that the members of a group may be threatened by their designated task in the group and may engage in avoidance behavior. The degree of the threat and nature of the avoidance behavior is determined by the members' major conflicted areas and preferred styles of behavior and by the laws of group dynamics.*

Bion has proposed a system purported to represent the basic dynamics of all groups, and yet objective group workers will often be unable to classify events in their own groups according to Bionic theory. Bion, it must be remembered, studied group phenomena in a highly specialized type of group—a group which was confronted with a highly ambiguous

* For example, the effects of group pressure may, after a critical proportion of the membership is involved, result in unanimous group methods of avoiding the threat.

The Theory and Practice of Group Psychotherapy

task and an enigmatic leader. The preoccupation of his groups with leadership phenomena may be iatrogenic rather than a universal group truth.

Although Bion's direct influence on the practice of group therapy is limited, his indirect influence may have been considerable. His method of viewing the group as a whole, his focus on the here-and-now, his attempt to understand unconscious forces influencing group texture and activity were indeed innovative.

EZRIEL. Henry Ezriel, a contemporary of Bion, and a participating observer of some of Bion's early groups at the Tavistock Clinic, viewed group phenomena differently and developed a system of group therapy which, though less heroically group-based than Bion's, nevertheless relies on total group interpretations.[25, 26, 27, 28] Ezriel, in his individual analytic work, advocated a totally here-and-now view of the therapeutic situation. He directed his attention toward the therapist-patient relationship and noted that the patient is required to relate (the *required relationship*) to the therapist in one fashion in order to avoid the occurrence of a second type of relationship (the *avoided relationship*). The patient unconsciously attempts to avoid this second type of relationship because his unconscious fantasies make him believe that if it were to emerge into reality a third type of relationship, some dreaded *calamity*, would occur. Ezriel concludes that a recognition of these three relationships (required, avoided, and calamitous) is essential for the understanding of the dynamics of both individual and group sessions; in groups, however, two further concepts are necessary—the common group tension, and the common group structure.

In the group session each patient will give expression to his own three relationships. (He will overtly behave in the required manner and provide the perceptive analyst with clues about his unconsciously avoided relationship and the equally unconscious feared calamity.) The set of three relationships will differ from one patient to another and set up a tension in the group—the *common group* tension:

. . . which may be regarded as consisting of the various unconsciously determined pushes and pulls exerted by the members of the group on one another and on the therapist which make the patients react to one another, make them select, reject, and distort one another's remarks, model and remodel one another's interventions, until gradually a certain *common group structure* emerges. The common group structure is thus a vector, the resultant of the individual contributions of all members of the group. It contains the dynamically essential features of the three relationships of each patient, and so might be described as their common denominator.[29]

Ezriel thus attempts to understand the common group tension and common group structure in terms of the required, avoided, and calamitous relationships for the entire group as well as for each of the individual members. In one group, for example, the members may bid for his attention and favors, setting up a common group structure of considerable inter-member rivalry and obsequiousness to the leader. If the appropriate data is available from the material of the current session, the therapist will know, for example, that the group curries his favors (required relationship) in order to avoid attacking him because of their intense envy of him (avoided relationship) for fear that he might massively retaliate by injuring them or throwing them out of the group (calamity). After having clarified the common group structure and the three group relationships, the therapist can focus on the three relationships of individual members. For example, some of the male patients may be envious and angry because the therapist has a special relationship with the women in the group; secretly they would like to attack or banish the therapist but fear the calamitous consequences of such an act. A female patient may envy him his penis, which would result in the calamity of her losing the therapist on whom so much depends.[25]

Therapeutic Considerations. Ezriel's views about therapeutic mechanisms and techniques, though disputable, are nonetheless stated with remarkable clarity. The aim of both individual and group therapy is thought to be "the removal of unconscious conflicts and needs (and thus of the source of transference)."[30] The therapist should be "nothing but a passive projection screen except for his one active step of interpretation."[30] The therapeutic process thus consists of the therapist's helping the patient, through interpretation, to understand his transference distortions toward the therapist. The form of the interpretation is clearly stated: a three-part statement with a "because clause" joining the second and third parts—i.e., "You are behaving in one way to avoid behaving in another *because* you fear . . ." The essence of the therapeutic process is the *reality testing* which is induced by the interpretive process. Through the therapist's continued willingness to verbalize and to confront the calamity calmly, patients gradually realize the irrationality of the feared calamity. In the group therapy format the therapist first identifies the common group structure and interprets the three relationships for the group as a whole; then he makes a separate three-part interpretation for each of the group members, pointing out their overt contribution to the group structure (required relationship) and, insofar as the therapist perceives it, the patient's avoided relationship and the anticipated calamity. Thus every interpretation made by the therapist (and Ezriel suggests that the therapist participate in no other fashion in the group) is both a mass group interpretation and an individual interpretation.

Overview. Although beautiful in its simplicity and consistency, this approach to group therapy has several significant encumbrances. Chief among these is a rigidity in the conception of the therapist role that prevents the therapist from fulfilling the many other vital functions of the leader. Ezriel firmly advocates the blank projection screen therapist role and considers any therapist participation, other than interpretation or asking for repetition of a statement he has not heard, an error. In one group, in which the majority of members remained in therapy for nine years and three for eleven years, the members at the end of therapy discussed the changes that had occurred in each person; they all agreed that, aside from being a decade older, Dr. Ezriel had not changed whatsoever. "That," states Dr. Ezriel, "is good technique." [25] This rigidity of therapist role may be too high a price to pay for the dubious and unsubstantiated rewards of a purely interpretive approach. Besides, if, as Ezriel states, the essence of psychoanalytic treatment is reality testing, then the "projective screen" therapist role may be a logical inconsistency. For example, on one occasion Ezriel, in giving an interpretation to a patient, stated merely, "I know you want to bite me"; it was not necessary to say more since the remainder of the interpretation was nonverbal: the therapist by his accepting, understanding manner disconfirmed the patient's fantasied dreaded calamity.[25] If this is the central curative factor, why so severely limit the therapist? Why may not the therapist manifest himself more honestly so as to enhance the reality testing? The types of feared calamities are finite; the great majority of Ezriel's interpretations center about three calamities—the therapist will (1) be destroyed by the patient, (2) retaliate massively toward the patient, or (3) reject and abandon the patient. Surely an open, accepting, more transparent therapist will demonstrate the unrealistic nature of these fears by his actions more rapidly than will an impersonal opaque therapist by his words!

Not only is the therapist's role restricted, but the group too may become restricted. The therapist-centered interpretations of Ezriel (and Bion) may result in a leader-centered group with limited member-member interpersonal interaction, limited cohesiveness, and an unfavorable climate for interpersonal learning. Note that I have no quarrel with Ezriel's formulation of the analytic interpretation; the tripartite (required, avoided, and calamitous relationships) formulation is a clear and, in my opinion, a sound approach to one aspect of human relationships.* To therapists

* Ezriel has attempted to formulate the process of interpretation so systematically that a testable hypothesis can be constructed.[28] He postulates, for example, that if the

whose background is not in Freudian psychoanalysis, the content of Ezriel's interpretations may be unacceptable; he generally couches the avoided and calamitous relationships in the stark language of unconscious oedipal or pre-oedipal infantile sexuality. Nevertheless, the tripartite system is adaptable to other frames of reference. Our patients whose interpersonal relationships are maladaptive find themselves compelled by internal reasons to relate to others in relatively fixed ways; their styles are determined by a fear of some calamity (for example rejection, scorn, derision, engulfment, their own uncontrollable rage) should they attempt to relate differently. The choice of interpretive language is arbitrary and incidental.

The mass group interpretation is central to Ezriel's approach. Recall that each of his interpretations first describes the group structure and then each member's contribution to that structure. The requirement that the therapist wait until he understands (or thinks he understands) the group structure vastly complicates life for the therapist; not only is he restricted from usefully participating at other times but he is also burdened with the task of diagnosing, with exceedingly indistinct guidelines, the group structure. The recognition of the common group structure is, no less than with Bion's basic assumption cultures, a very arbitrary process. Ezriel, like Bion, suggests that the total material produced by all the members of the group is handled by the therapist as though it had been produced by one patient. Unanimity of the group membership is not necessary to enable the therapist to judge what the "group" is doing. Ezriel may, for example, diagnose the group structure on the basis of the verbal productions of only three out of nine members.[25] The silent members are adjudged, by dint of their silence, to be in agreement with the others ("communication by proxy").[25] Why it is that disagreement must actively be verbalized is unclear.

Given these objections, why bother with the mass group interpretation? What purpose does it serve? Ezriel states that one member's behavior is not understandable out of the context of the entire group. Furthermore, an interpretation about the entire group and each member's contribution to the group is one that compels interest in all the members. Most important of all, however, is that through a total group focus the therapist avoids the pitfall of engaging in individual therapy with any of the group members. This danger is more apparent than real, however, if the thera-

---

tripartite interpretation is correct, then the subsequent material produced by the patient will contain the avoided object relationship in a clearer—i.e., less repressed—form. Although he has to date not published his data, he has for many years studied tape recordings of patients' responses to interpretations.

pist has the mobility and flexibility of role which will enable him to deal with issues of favoritism and rivalry as they arise.

WHITAKER AND LIEBERMAN. Whitaker and Lieberman have applied Thomas French's focal conflict theory to therapy groups. Their position is clearly stated in a series of propositions.[31]

Proposition 1. Successive individual behaviors are linked associatively and refer to a common underlying concern about the here-and-now situation.

The comments and activities of a group therapy session are not diverse; they all hang together in relationship to some underlying issue. Seemingly unrelated acts gain coherence if one assumes that there is some concern which is shared by the members of the group.

Proposition 2: The sequence of diverse events which occur in a group can be conceptualized as a common, covert conflict (the group focal conflict) which consists of an impulse or wish (the disturbing motive) opposed by an associated fear (the reactive motive). Both aspects of the group focal conflict refer to the current setting.

For example, the members of a group may share a common wish to be singled out by the therapist for special attention (the disturbing motive) and yet they fear that such a wish will result in disapproval by the therapist and by other patients (reactive motive). The interaction between the wish and the fear is the group focal conflict.

Proposition 3: When confronted with a group focal conflict, the patients direct efforts toward establishing a solution which will reduce anxiety by alleviating the reactive fears and, at the same time, satisfy to the maximum possible degree the disturbing impulse.

In the group just described the members may arrive at the solution of searching for similarities among themselves; it is as if each were saying, "We are all alike, no one is asking for special favors." This solution, though it temporarily relieves tension, is by no means productive of growth; instead the disturbing wish (to be unique and be singled out by the therapist for special gratification) is merely suppressed in the service of comfort. Other solutions, however, may be more enabling of group and personal growth.

Proposition 4: Successful solutions have two properties. First, they are shared; the behavior of all members is consistent with or bound by the solution.

Second, successful solutions reduce reactive fears; individuals experience greater anxiety prior to the establishment of a successful solution, less anxiety after the solution is established.

Proposition 5: Solutions may be restrictive or enabling in character. A restrictive solution is directed primarily to alleviating fears and does so at the expense of satisfying or expressing the disturbing motive. An enabling solution is directed toward alleviating fears and, at the same time, allows for some satisfaction or expression of the disturbing motive.

For example, the disturbing motive in one group was the wish to express angry destructive feelings toward the therapist. The reactive motive (fear) was that the therapist would punish or abandon the group members. The group solution was to band together to express anger toward the therapist. Following one meeting they discussed the matter and found strength in an implicit agreement that each would express his anger toward the therapist.

However, the specific group focal conflict is not within the conscious awareness of the group members who are most involved, and the solution is not deliberately planned but is a vector, a course of action which "clicks" with the unconscious wishes and fears of each member. Should the solution be clearly unsatisfactory to one of the members, a new group conflict is created which culminates in a modified group solution. In this instance the reactive fear was alleviated by the mutual support of the group members, and the disturbing wish was therefore expressed. Such a solution will, over the long term, be enabling for the patients since only by gradual exposure and expression of their disturbing wishes can the necessary reality testing occur.

As Whitaker and Lieberman recognize, there is an overlapping between their tripartite schema and that of Ezriel's. Ezriel's required relationship is analogous to the group solution, the avoided relationship to the disturbing motive, and the calamitous relationship to the reactive motive. However, Ezriel considers the required relationship (group solution) to be a defensive, restrictive posture while Whitaker and Lieberman's focal conflict theory includes solutions which allow gratification of the disturbing motive while alleviating fears; thus the solution (required relationship) may be enabling rather than purely defensive and thereby subject to interpretation.

There is, however, a major difference between Ezriel's and Whitaker and Lieberman's therapeutic application of their group concepts. In their therapeutic approach Whitaker and Lieberman are most concerned with the nature of the group solution. Therapeutic intervention is required when a group solution appears which is restrictive to the group and to the members. Furthermore, an interpretation which elucidates the total group configuration is only one of a number of mechanisms which may be employed to influence the group. They suggest, for example, that the therapist may, with efficacy, deal with a restrictive solution by modeling for the patients a different form of behavior.[31] Thus the role of the therapist is a flexible one: he may ask questions, he may report on his personal reactions, he may focus on an individual's idiosyncratic mode of operating withiᵣ the group, or, as we have seen, he may focus on total group movement.

Whitaker and Lieberman do not lose sight of the fact that the tripartite (disturbing motive, reactive motive, and solution) system is but an abstraction rather than an entity in the animistic sense. Its purpose is to clarify the meaning and origin of behavior patterns which are restrictive for the group. Thus in their views about total group phenomena and in their application of this information to the therapy process Whitaker and Lieberman's approach, despite a semantic difference, overlaps significantly with the approach I have discussed earlier in this chapter.

The Ahistoric Approach—Historical Development

In this section we shall consider the developmental history of the "here-and-now" approach in psychotherapy. Perhaps an explanation is required; surely there is a certain inconsistency in studying the past history of a concept which decries the necessity of studying the past history! First, let me say that I am not concerned here or elsewhere in this book with paying tribute to the past, although there is clearly a place for homage in human culture. (We all, to some degree, abhor oblivion, and the ritual of bearing tribute carries with it the hope that the supplicant will in turn be remembered.) Instead I invoke the past in order to understand the present more fully. Just as understanding an individual's process of becoming enriches our understanding of him in the present, so, too, through understanding its evolution, we may more fully comprehend a concept. To see the various shapes the "here-and-now" approach has taken in the past will enhance our appreciation, our flexibility, and our originality in our current application of this therapy concept.

There is one other reason for a historical excursion at this juncture. The "here-and-now" approach is currently promulgated with such vigor by contemporary group therapists and sensitivity group trainers that it may be regarded as a hypermodern, untested, or highly experimental approach. I should like to disabuse the reader of this misconception; it is a venerable approach with roots in the very beginnings of modern dynamic psychiatry.

FREUD

The basic scaffolding of the here-and-now approach to therapy is found in Freud's writings, although he himself did not use the here-and-now as a primary modality and never relinquished the analogy of the therapist as archeologist. He always assigned the highest priority to the recall of the patient's early history. Thus, in "Constructions in Analysis," [32] written only two years before his death, he states that the work of analysis:

. . . involves two people to each of whom a different task is assigned. . . . We all know that the person who is being analyzed has to be induced to remember something that has been experienced by him and repressed; and the dynamic determinants of this process are so interesting that the other portion of the work, the task performed by the analyst, has been pushed into the background. The analyst has neither experienced nor repressed any of the material under consideration; his task cannot be to remember anything. What then is his task? His task is to make out what has been forgotten from the traces which it has left behind or, more correctly, to *construct* it. The time and manner in which he conveys his constructions to the person who is being analyzed, as well as the explanations with which he accompanies them, constitute the link between the two portions of the work of analysis, between his own part and that of the patient.

Later in the same article Freud makes the curious statement, which illustrates the weight he attaches to the reconstruction of the past, that even if the patient cannot remember, the therapist should endeavor to remember for him—to offer an acceptable reconstruction or construction of the past:

The path that starts from the analyst's construction ought to end in the patient's recollection; but it does not always lead so far. Often enough we do not succeed in bringing the patient to recollect what has been repressed. Instead of that, if the analysis is carried out correctly, we produce in him an assured conviction of the truth of the construction which achieves the same therapeutic result as a recaptured memory.

Despite this abiding conviction that the curative factor in psychoanalysis is the recall of the past, the bringing into consciousness of hitherto repressed unconscious material, Freud nevertheless, with his formulations of transference, laid the foundations for the subsequent ahistoric focus. By 1912,[33] Freud had come to a full appreciation of the concept of transference and realized that the transference phenomenon represented at once both a potential impediment in the analysis and a major "vehicle in the healing process." He suggested constant vigilance by the analyst for transference phenomena; attention must be focused upon what is happening between patient and analyst. For example (1912):

Experience shows and a test will always confirm it, that when the patient's free associations fail the obstacle can be removed every time by the assurance that he is now possessed by a thought which concerns the person of the physician or something relating to him. No sooner is this explanation given than the obstacle is removed or at least the absence of thoughts has been transformed into a refusal to speak.

Note, though, that in this example Freud suggests attending to the patient-therapist relationship not as an end in itself but so that obstacles to the real task, the recall of the past, can be continued.

In 1917 in *Introductory Lectures on Psychoanalysis*[34] and in 1920 in *Beyond the Pleasure Principle*[35] Freud extended his observations on transference. Soon the investigation and analysis of the transference became the major task of analysis. Strachey says, "It was found that as work proceeded the transference tended, as it were, to eat up the entire analysis."[15] Furthermore, it was found that the patient, instead of recollecting the repressed material, repeated it as a current experience in his relationship with the analyst. "When this point in therapy is reached, it may be said that the earlier neurosis is now replaced by a fresh one, *viz.* the transference neurosis."[35] The solution of the transference neurosis then becomes the decisive part of the analysis and "implies the simultaneous solution of the infantile conflict of which it is a new edition."[35] This procedure was therapeutically effective because it offered "a path back to the point at which they [the symptoms] originated" and a method of reviewing "the conflict from which they proceeded and, with the aid of propelling forces which at that time were not available, to guide it towards a new solution."[34]

Taking this emphasis on the transference situation as their starting point, two of Freud's most productive students, Wilhelm Reich and Sandor Ferenczi, devoted considerable energy to increasing the therapeutic effectiveness of psychoanalysis; each, in a different manner, laid the foundations for a here-and-now approach. Reich clarified the patient's here-and-now presentation of himself, Ferenczi the here-and-now aspects of the therapist-patient relationship.

WILHELM REICH

Clearly the most extraordinary and influential pioneer after Freud of modern dynamic psychotherapy was Wilhelm Reich, Freud's most brilliant student. He is a curious figure. Director of Training at the prestigious Psychoanalytic Institute of Vienna, lionized in his heyday, Reich engaged ceaselessly in a restless search for methods of augmenting the therapeutic value of analysis, only to adopt an increasingly incredible and concrete theory of libido displacement and eventually to die, an abject figure, in a United States federal prison, convicted of illegally selling Orgone boxes for their medicinal value. It is a credit to the analytic establishment as well as a testimony to the intrinsic power of his work that Reich's early work was valued for its substantive value and not discarded with his later bizarre orgone therapy concepts.

A perusal of the first half of Reich's book, *Character Analysis*,[36] will reveal Reich's foresight and his anticipation of what we have come to consider as hypermodern therapeutic practices. Basically Reich called attention to character resistance, the resistance to the analytic process via the patient's character traits—i.e., his manifest interpersonal characteristics. Reich realized that the then current distinction between the symptom neurosis and the character neurosis was invalid and that every neurotic patient had a neurotic character. Furthermore, every analysis must be a character analysis; character traits, like symptoms, can be fully understood and altered. Thus, in the therapy situation, the therapist must attend to far more than the content of the patient's statement. In 1927 Reich said:[37]

> The manner in which the patient talks, in which he greets the analyst or looks at him, the way he lies on the couch, the inflection of the voice, the degree of conventional politeness, all these things are valuable criteria for judging the latent resistances against the fundamental role, and understanding them makes it possible to alter or eliminate them by interpretation.

It will be noted that at this stage of his thinking Reich's primary interest was to remove the character resistance so that the real analysis—the recapture and working through of repressed infantile material—could then proceed.

Reich continues, presenting a clear definition of a process orientation:

"The *how* of saying things is as important 'material' for interpretation as is *what* the patient says. . . . What is specific of the character resistance is not what the patient says or does but how he talks and acts." [38] Interpret character resistance, Reich taught, and the rest of the analysis would take care of itself; the infantile source material would spontaneously emerge and become accessible for working through.

SANDOR FERENCZI

Like Reich, Ferenczi continuously sought methods to enhance and accelerate therapy. According to his students,[39, 40] much of his work in this area was unpublished because of his disinclination to oppose Freud publicly. He objected to the cold, depersonalized analytic role in the 1920's and emphasized the importance of the current real (not transference) aspects of the therapeutic relationship. Unlike many of his contemporaries, he maintained an abiding faith and belief in his patients and, unlike Freud who emphasized a child's struggles with his instincts, he believed that the etiology of neurosis lay in the transmission of parental problems. "There are no bad children. There are only bad parents." [39] He felt the child especially suffered as a result of insincerity and underscored the ensuing confusion which occurred when verbal messages of, for example, love or acceptance conflicted with nonverbal contrary messages.* Since the analytic situation was a repetition of the childhood experience, Ferenczi reasoned that to undo, as it were, the past it was essential not to reproduce the same types of trauma; the cold, impassive, aloof analyst recreated a sterility and rejection with which the patient was only far too familiar.

Also the pose of infallibility repeats all too well the childhood situation when mother is only right, although the child often has good evidence that she is wrong. Repeating this experience in the analysis only maintains the neurotic status quo. The patient's defenses were originally developed to cope with the insincerity of the parent—they will continue to cope with the insincerity of the analyst.[39]

Ferenczi therefore undertook to transform the therapeutic situation into a sincere, honest human relationship in which the therapist must be free to

---

* These formulations are clearly adumbrative of the "double bind" phenomenon observed thirty years later in families of schizophrenic patients by Bateson, Jackson, *et al.*[41]

admit that which the patients know anyway—his blind spots, annoyances, his fallibility. Furthermore, he attempted to supply the patient with the love he needed. Thompson [39] points out that in part this doctrine is accepted today; it is well recognized, for example, that without an atmosphere of positive feelings, good therapeutic results are unlikely. However, Ferenczi sometimes mistook the love demanded for the love needed and failed to take into consideration "the complications in the neurotic's character structure which prevent the patient's making use of love when it is available. He sought through dramatic reliving, through being a loving parent, to re-create a better childhood and used techniques to increase the vividness of the re-creation." [42]

From his earliest years in the field, Ferenczi was extraordinarily sensitive to the subtleties of the here-and-now; in 1912, for example, he underscored the importance of the immediate investigation of symptoms which arose abruptly during the analytic session. However, Ferenczi, like Freud, never abandoned his conviction that the reconstruction of the past was indispensable for successful therapy.[40] Thus, for Ferenczi, the here-and-now focus served two functions: first, an optimal therapist-patient relationship facilitates the recall of past traumatic events; secondly, with the help of an accepting, approving therapist the patient re-experiences, in a corrective manner, the original trauma.* During the last seven years of his life, Ferenczi moved further from classic psychoanalytic methods until Freud openly disapproved and labeled many of Ferenczi's techniques "not psychoanalysis"; in 1932, a year before Ferenczi's death, a complete break occurred between the two.

Although Ferenczi's ideas about therapeutic techniques influenced his students, it is doubtful whether they heavily influenced the main stream of analytic thought at the time. However, it is clear that, beginning around 1925, an increasing amount of attention was given to the current therapist-patient relationship.

JAMES STRACHEY

In 1934, James Strachey, a British analyst, published an extremely influential paper [15] which synthesized and clarified the then current analytic technique. Strachey advocated a here-and-now approach to the patient as he stated that the "ultimate instrument of psychoanalytic therapy," the only form of interpretation which was "mutative" (capable of producing

---

* There is, of course, a close similarity between this formulation and Alexander's later "corrective emotional experience."

change in the patient), was an interpretation which clarified a patient's immediate unconscious feelings toward the therapist. Strachey described a two-phase process: "First, then, there is the phase in which the patient becomes conscious of a particular quantity of id energy as being directed toward the analyst; and secondly there is the phase in which the patient becomes aware that this id energy is directed towards an archaic fantasy object and not towards a real one." [43] Strachey stressed that the interpretation must be timely and be directed toward what is immediately current in the patient's feelings toward the therapist. "Every mutative interpretation must be emotionally immediate; the patient must experience it as something actual . . . interpretations must always be directed to 'the point of urgency.'" He also clearly stated that no interpretations save those directed toward the transference had mutative value. "Is it to be understood that no extra-transference interpretation can set into motion the chain of events which I have suggested as being the essence of psychoanalytical therapy? This is indeed my opinion . . . extra transference interpretations tend to be concerned with impulses which are distant both in time and are thus likely to be devoid of immediate energy."

Although Stachey proposed a here-and-now approach, it was an incomplete one. He stressed that an important purpose of the mutative interpretation was to allow the patient to recapture the past. In speaking of the working through by the patient of the mutative interpretation he states, "As a further corollary to these events and simultaneously with them, the patient will obtain access to the infantile material which is being re-experienced by him in his relation to the analyst." Furthermore, the therapist-patient relationship continued to be viewed as an unreal one, rooted entirely in the past. Strachey's second phase of the mutative interpretative process, the stage of reality testing, in which the patient becomes aware that his impulses toward the therapist are inappropriate, became an apologia for the "blank screen" therapist.

The patient's sense of reality is an essential, but a very feeble ally; indeed an improvement in it is one of the things that we hope the analysis will bring about. It is important, therefore, not to submit it to any unnecessary strain; and that is the fundamental reason why the analyst must avoid any real behavior that is likely to confirm the patient's view of him as a "bad" or a "good" fantasy object.

And further on:

. . . the patient's sense of reality has the narrowest limits. It is a paradoxical fact that the best way of ensuring that his ego shall be able to distinguish between fantasy and reality is to withhold reality from him as much as possible. But it is true. His ego is so weak—so much at the mercy of his id and super ego—that he can only cope with reality if it is administered in minimal doses.[44]

I cite the latter quotations because of their bearing on the issue of therapist transparency. In my opinion Strachey overestimates the tenuousness and fragility of the patient's sense of reality and erroneously assumes that the analyst can, if he chooses, *not* communicate to the patient when, in fact, as Ferenczi knew, every action, every posture communicates some relationship message.

MELANIE KLEIN

Klein, a student of Ferenczi who was to exert a profound influence on British psychoanalytic thought, had begun to formulate her ideas about psychosexual development and therapeutic technique in the 1920's. Klein has had comparatively little impact on American psychiatric thought; and to the extent that she is known, it is for her speculations about pregenital stages of personality development and not for her innovations in psychotherapeutic technique, which are less clearly explicated in the literature. It is paradoxical that Klein, intensely interested in the psychological events of very early life, nevertheless maintained a here-and-now focus throughout the analytic process.* The present fantasy system of the patient, particularly as it involved the therapist, was investigated in detail. Although Klein felt that the therapist should be thoroughly familiar with psychological events of early life in order to discern and understand the patient's current feelings, these origins need not be shared with the patient. In fact no reconstruction of the past was considered necessary in the task of exploring the current unconscious motivations of behavior. Klein directly influenced the therapeutic technique of an entire generation of British analysts and indirectly through one of her students and analysands— Wilfred Bion—influenced the practice of group therapy. Bion, as we have already seen, employed a thoroughgoing here-and-now approach in his approach to small groups.

---

* No doubt many of Klein's views about here-and-now therapeutic technique derived from her pioneering analytic work with children, in whom there is, of course, little or no historical material.

KURT LEWIN

Lewin, whose work we shall discuss in Chapter 14, was an enormously influential psychologist who must be considered the founder of the T-group movement. In writings dating back to the late 1920's and early thirties, he had already called attention to the error in psychology of attributing systematic causation to past events. He differentiated between this mode of concept formation (Aristotelian thinking) and a systematic mode (Galilean thinking) which considers all the dynamic characteristics of the momentary situation.[45]

It was typical of the Aristotelian way of thinking not to distinguish sufficiently between historical and systematic questions. The result was that one took past or future facts as causes of present events. In opposition to this assumption we shall here strongly defend the thesis that neither past nor future psychological facts but only the present situation can influence present events.[46]

In other words, Lewin emphasized that psychological events have to be examined and explained in terms of the properties of the social system which exists at the time the events occur. The past may only indirectly have a position in the causal chains whose interweaving creates the present situation. Past events cannot directly influence present events. Understanding past historical events, therefore, sheds little light on causality, has little predictive value, and is of little value in the planning of change.

Lewin applied this principle of contemporaneity in his group work, in which he was most interested in the effects of social systems on behavior and especially in the change of behavior through changes in social structure. Although Lewin was not a psychotherapist, his impact on psychotherapeutic practice should not be underestimated. In addition to therapists who were more formally his students, he spoke frequently at meetings of psychotherapists and his work was well known by the British and American psychiatric community.

HENRY EZRIEL

An explicit, systematic ahistoric approach was developed by Rickman*
and Ezriel at the Tavistock Clinic in London in the late 1940's; in fact in

---

* Rickman, who influenced both Ezriel and Bion (he was Bion's analyst prior to World War II—later, as I have mentioned, Bion was Klein's analysand) was quite familiar with Lewin's works.[25]

1947 they jokingly suggested that a new sign, "The Here-and-Now Clinic," be posted over the front door of the Tavistock Clinic.[25] Aside from a 1922 statement by Moreno,* who used the term in a somewhat different manner, the term "here-and-now" first appeared in the psychiatric literature (to the best of my knowledge) in Ezriel's 1950 article "A Psycho-Analytic Approach to Group Treatment."[26] In this and subsequent works,[27, 28] Ezriel extends and enriches, I think, Strachey's concept of the mutative here-and-now interpretation. He states, as we have already indicated, that the therapist must do more than clarify the existence and nature of strong, unrecognized feelings toward the therapists; he must also point out that the patient is required (by his defense system) to behave overtly toward the therapist in such a way as to avoid acting out his unrecognized feelings toward him. Furthermore, the therapist should also point out the existence and nature of the calamity that the patient fears will occur if he acts upon his impulses toward the doctor. The purpose of such an interpretation should be to help the patient realize the unreal nature of the feared calamity and thereby to effect a change in his behavior and attitude toward the therapist.

The metaphor of the analyst as archeologist, still quite evident in Strachey's work, is completely abandoned by Ezriel. Past material may be valuable in two ways: (1) some discussion of the past may provide the therapist with data which will help him formulate the correct interpretation, and (2) subsequent to the interpretation, the patient may produce past material (for example, previously repressed memories or feelings toward a parent) which may help to corroborate the interpretation. However, the method may proceed perfectly well without these references to the past; they are illuminating or perhaps reassuring to the therapist but by no means essential.[25]

KAREN HORNEY

Horney, one of the most influential of the "neo-Freudians," conducted psychotherapy predominately within an ahistoric framework. Transference was important to her, not because it illuminated the past as a manifestation of the repetition compulsion, but because it illuminated the pre-

---

* "How does a moment emerge? A feeling must be related to the object of the feelings, a thought must be related to the object of thoughts, a perception must be related to the object of the perceptions, a touch must be related to the object of touching, You are the object of my feelings, the object of my thoughts, the object of my perceptions, the object of my touch. Such is an encounter in the *Here and Now*."[47]

sent. Through an examination of the patient's relationship to the therapist, Horney assisted the patient to understand his internal dynamic structure, especially insofar as it bore on his current style of interpersonal relationships. In her characteristically lucid style she stated in 1939, "Were someone to ask me which of Freud's discoveries I value most highly, I should say without any hesitation: it is his finding that one can utilize for therapy the patient's emotional reactions to the analyst and to the analytical situation." [48] Later in the essay she continues:

I differ from Freud in that, after recognition of the neurotic trends, while he primarily investigates their genesis, I primarily investigate their actual functions and their consequences. . . .

My contention is that by working through the consequences the patient's anxiety is so much lessened, and his relation to self and others so much improved, that he can dispense with the neurotic trends. Their development was necessitated by the child's hostile and apprehensive attitude toward the world. If analysis of the consequences, that is, analysis of the actual neurotic structure, helps the individual to become discriminately friendly toward others instead of indiscriminately hostile, if his anxieties are considerably diminished, if he gains in inner strength and inner activity, he no longer needs his safety devices, but can deal with the difficulties of life according to his judgment.

It is not always the analyst who suggests to the patient that he search for causes in his childhood; often the patient spontaneously offers genetic material. In so far as he offers data relevant to his development this tendency is constructive. But in so far as he unconsciously uses these data to establish a quick causal connection the tendency is evasive in character. More often than not he hopes thereby to avoid facing trends which actually exist within him. The patient has an understandable interest in not realizing either the incompatibility of such trends or the price he pays for them: up to the time of analysis both his safety and his expectations of satisfaction rested on the pursuit of these strivings.

. . . As soon as the patient himself is able to realize that his genetic endeavors lead to a dead-end, it is best to interfere actively and to point out that even though the experiences he recalls may have a bearing on the actual trend, they do not explain why the trend is maintained today; it should be explained to him that it is usually more profitable to postpone curiosity as to causation and study first the consequences which the particular trend entails for his character and for his life.[49]

Horney viewed the therapist as a facilitator whose task was to remove the obstacles which impede the autonomous process of self-realization. These obstacles consist of unrealistic demands placed on the self and others which result in a vicious sequence of distorted perceptions and relationships with others and a growing alienation from one's real self. In therapy the patient must become aware of these currently active trends; the past is useful only insofar as it clarifies the present.

Our historical excursion demonstrates that the "here-and-now" approach in psychotherapy is a venerable concept; it is also a diverse concept—a type of final common pathway of technique arrived at from many different conceptual starting points and used for widely varying purposes. Reich used a here-and-now approach to facilitate a character analysis which in turn would facilitate an analytic process rooted in the past; Ferenczi focused on the here-and-now because of his views about the importance of the realistic current therapist-patient relationship; Strachey, to facilitate the evocation of past repressed material as well as to allow the therapist to remain a constructive guide for the patient rather than being introjected as a harsh superego image; Ezriel to clarify and remove the patient's unrealistic attitudes towards the therapist; Bion, to help the group members explore their unconscious; Horney, to help her patients become aware of their current internal dynamic structure insofar as it poisoned relationships with others and oneself. In interactional group therapy we focus on the here-and-now for a number of reasons, some similar to those cited, some different: to focus the members' attention upon the group, thereby increasing involvement and cohesiveness; to increase affect by dealing with issues of immediate and common concern to the members; to help train the members in a style of direct interpersonal communication which will increase their social adaptability; and to turn the groups' scrutiny upon interpersonal behavior, encouraging feedback and testing so as to maximize opportunities for interpersonal learning and change.

REFERENCES

1. E. Berne, *Games People Play* (New York: Grove Press, 1964).
2. D. Stock and R. W. Whitman, "Patients' and Therapists' Apperceptions of an Episode in Group Therapy," *Human Relations, 10:* 367–383, 1957.
3. I. D. Yalom and J. Handlon, "The Use of Multiple Therapists in the Teaching of Psychiatric Residents," *J. Nerv. Ment. Dis., 114:* 684–692, 1966.
4. Milton Berger, "Nonverbal Communications in Group Psychotherapy," *Int. J. Group Psychother., 8:* 161–178, 1958.
5. G. Bach, *Intensive Group Therapy* (New York: Ronald Press, 1954), p. 25.
6. W. F. Murphy and F. Deutsch, *The Clinical Interview* (New York: International Universities Press, 1955).

7. J. Frank, *Persuasion and Healing* (New York: Schocken Books, 1963), p. 161.
8. E. Goffman, "The Moral Career of the Mental Patient," *Psychiatry, 22:* 123–142, 1959.
9. C. Rycroft, *Psychoanalysis Observed* (London: Constable, 1966), p. 18.
10. S. H. Foulkes and E. J. Anthony, *Group Psychotherapy: The Psychoanalytic Approach* (Harmondsworth, Middlesex: Penguin Books, 1957).
11. H. Spotnitz, "A Psychoanalytic View of Resistance in Groups," *Int. J. Group Psychother, 2:* 3–9, 1952.
12. M. B. Parloff, "Advances in Analytic Group Therapy," in J. Marmor (ed.), *Frontiers of Psychoanalysis* (New York: Basic Books, 1967).
13. Foulkes and Anthony, *op. cit.*, p. 29.
14. *Ibid.*, p. 238.
15. J. Strachey, "The Nature of the Therapeutic Action of Psycho-Analysis," *Int. J. Psychoanal., 15:* 127–159, 1934.
16. W. Bion and J. Rickman, "Intra-Group Tensions in Therapy," *Lancet,* November 27, 1943.
17. S. H. Foulkes, "A Memorandum on Group Therapy," British Military Memorandum ADM 11, BM (mimeographed), July 1945.
18. S. H. Foulkes, personal communication, April 1968.
19. M. Sherwood, "Bion's Experiences in Groups: A Critical Evaluation," *Human Relations,* 17: 113–130, 1964.
20. W. R. Bion, *Experiences in Groups and Other Papers* (New York: Basic Books, 1959).
21. *Ibid.*, p. 94.
22. Parloff, *op. cit.*
23. J. Sutherland, personal communication, 1968.
24. D. Stock and H. Thelen, *Emotional Dynamics and Group Culture* (New York: New York University Press, 1958).
25. H. Ezriel, personal communication, 1968.
26. H. Ezriel, "A Psycho-Analytic Approach to Group Treatment," *Brit. J. Med. Psychol., 23:* 59–74, 1950.
27. H. Ezriel, "Notes on Psycho-Analytic Group Therapy: Interpretation and Research," *Psychiatry, 15:* 119–126, 1952.
28. H. Ezriel, "Experimentation Within the Psycho-Analytic Session," *Brit. J. Philos. Sci., 7:* 29–48, 1956.
29. H. Ezriel, "The First Session in Psycho-Analytic Group Treatment," *Nederlands Tydskrift voor Geneeskunde, 111:* 711–716.
30. H. Ezriel, "The Role of Transference in Psychoanalytic and Other Approaches to Group Treatment," *ACTA Psychotherapeutica, Supplementum, Vol. 7,* 1957.
31. D. S. Whitaker and M. Lieberman, *Psychotherapy through the Group Process* (New York: Atherton Press, 1964).
32. S. Freud, "Constructions in Analysis," *Int. J. Psychoanal.* 19: 377–387, 1938.
33. S. Freud, *Collected Papers, Vol. 2—The Dynamics of Transference* (London: Hogarth Press, 1933), pp. 312–322.
34. S. Freud, *Introductory Lectures on Psychoanalysis* (London: George Allen and Unwin, 1922), p. 381.
35. S. Freud, *Beyond the Pleasure Principle* (London: Hogarth Press International Psychoanalytic Library, 1920).
36. W. Reich, *Character Analysis* (3rd ed.; New York: Orgone Institute Press, 1949).
37. *Ibid.*, p. 45.
38. *Ibid.*, pp. 46–47.
39. M. R. Green (ed.), *Interpersonal Analysis: The Selected Papers of Clara M. Thompson* (New York: Basic Books, 1964).

40. M. Balint, personal communication, July 1968.
41. G. Bateson, D. Jackson, J. Haley, and J. Weakland, "Toward a Theory of Schizophrenia, *Behav. Sci.*, *1:* 251–264, 1956.
42. I. de Forest, "The Therapeutic Technique of Sandor Ferenczi," *Int. J. Psychoanal.*, *23:* 120–140, 1942.
43. Strachey, *op. cit.*, p. 143.
44. *Ibid.*, pp. 146–147.
45. K. Lewin, *A Dynamic Theory of Personality* (New York: McGraw-Hill, 1935), pp. 1–42.
46. K. Lewin, *Principles of Topological Psychology* (New York: McGraw-Hill, 1936), pp. 34–35.
47. J. Moreno (ed.), *The International Handbook of Group Psychotherapy* (New York: Philosophical Library, 1966).
48. K. Horney, *New Ways in Psychoanalysis* (New York: W. W. Norton, 1939), p. 154.
49. *Ibid.*, pp. 282–283.

7

THE SELECTION
OF PATIENTS

❧

The fate of a group therapy patient and of a therapy group may, in large measure, be determined before the first group therapy session. Unless careful selection criteria are used, the majority of patients assigned to group therapy will terminate treatment discouraged and without benefit. Research on small groups, to be described in Chapter 8, suggests that the initial composition of the group has a powerful influence on the ultimate outcome of the entire group.

In this chapter I will consider the clinical consensus and research evidence bearing upon the selection of group therapy patients. How can the therapist determine whether a given patient is a suitable candidate for group therapy? The following chapter considers the task of group composition. Once it has been decided that the patient is a suitable group therapy candidate, then into which specific group shall he go? Some of the research cited in Chapters 7 and 8 has little immediate clinical relevance; nor is it definitive work. Instead, I describe the research because selection and composition are areas in which research can make a significant contribution, and the sophisticated research methodology used in laboratory and T-group work is clearly applicable to the study of therapy groups.

The first consideration in the determination of group therapy suitability is the type of group therapy available. Selection criteria vary widely depending upon the structure, procedure, and goals of the therapy group. In most inpatient settings, in which small groups are an important treatment modality, all patients are assigned (often at random) to small groups. Grossly disturbed patients are usually excluded until their behavior has been modified to the point where it will no longer disrupt group integrity. For therapy groups with specialized goals, patient selection is relatively uncomplicated; the admission criteria may be simply the existence of the target symptom—obesity, alcoholism, or addiction, for example.

The question is more difficult for the doctor dealing with intensive, dynamic outpatient group therapy, and his selection criteria will be less obvious. Some of the complications become apparent merely through an examination of the selection criteria cited in the clinical literature. We will note first that the colorful descriptive terminology is so highly individualized that it is difficult to establish any consensus. Patients deemed undesirable candidates have been called schizoid personalities, chaotic and inchoate egos, emotional illiterates, monopolists, depressives, true hysterics, and psychopaths. This potpourri of symptomatic, characterologic, behavioral, and folk nomenclature is evidence of the need for a system of classification which can convey relevant, predictive information about interpersonal behavior.

Secondly we will be struck by the contradictions which abound in the clinical literature. There a few conditions cited as contraindications for group therapy for which an opposing opinion or anecdotal report cannot be found. Homosexuality or psychosomatic conditions, for example, which are anathema to some experienced group therapists, have been successfully treated in group therapy by others. Such contradictions are not surprising considering the diversity in training, professional background, and theoretical orientation of therapists; all these factors would, of course, lead to great variations in diagnostic and therapeutic style. With these opposing clinical opinions and a paucity of relevant, controlled research, the neophyte group therapist, especially the professionally agnostic one, will have few firm guidelines for his patient selection.

Finally, one notes that, with a few exceptions, the emphasis in selection criteria is on excluding unsuitable patients from group therapy. It would seem that it is easier to identify characteristics which weigh against the admission of a patient to a therapy group than to establish clear indications for such treatment.

Exclusion Criteria

CLINICAL CONSENSUS

There is considerable clinical consensus that patients are poor candidates for outpatient intensive group therapy if they are: brain damaged,[1,2] paranoid,[3] extremely narcissistic,[4] hypochondriacal,[5] suicidal,[5,4] addicted to drugs or alcohol,[1,2] acutely psychotic,[5,6,7] or sociopathic.[8,9]

These patients seem destined to fail because of their inability to participate in the primary task of the group; they soon construct an interpersonal role which proves to be detrimental to themselves as well as to the group. Consider the sociopathic patient, an exceptionally poor risk for outpatient, interactional group therapy. Characteristically these patients are destructive in the group. Although early in therapy they may become important and active members, they will eventually manifest their basic inability to relate, often with considerable dramatic and destructive impact. To cite a clinical example:

Mr. Glebe, a thirty-five-year-old highly intelligent patient with a history of alcoholism, great mobility, and impoverished interpersonal relationships, was added with two other new patients to an ongoing group, which had been reduced to three by the recent graduation of members. The co-therapists sensed that he was a poor risk, but because the group was an observed teaching group, they were anxious to re-establish its size; he was one of the few potential patients available. In addition, they were somewhat intrigued by his alleged determination to change his life style. The classic sociopath is forever reaching a turning point in his life. Mr. Glebe, by the third meeting, had clearly become the social-emotional leader of the group—seemingly able to feel more acutely and suffer more deeply than the other members. He presented the group, as he had the therapists, with a largely fabricated account of his background and current life situation. By the fourth meeting, as the therapists learned later, he had seduced one of the female members, and by the fifth meeting spearheaded a discussion of the group's dissatisfaction with the brevity of the meetings. He proposed that the group, with or without the permission of the therapist, meet more often, perhaps at one of the members' homes, without the therapist. By the sixth meeting he had vanished, without prior notification to the group. The therapists learned later that he had suddenly decided to take a two-thousand-mile bicycle trip, hoping to sell the trip journal to a magazine.

This rather extreme example demonstrates many of the reasons why inclusion of a sociopathic individual in a heterogeneous outpatient group is ill-advised: his social "front" [10] is deceptive; he often consumes such an inordinate amount of group energy that his departure leaves the group bereft, puzzled, and discouraged; he rarely assimilates the group therapeutic norms and instead often exploits other members and the group as a whole for his more immediate gratification. This does not mean that group therapy is contraindicated for these patients. In fact, a specialized form of group therapy [11] with a more homogeneous population and a sagacious utilization of strong group and institutional pressure may well be the treatment of choice. This principle also applies to some of the other contraindications listed above—for example, alcoholics [12] and mental defectives.[13]

SYSTEMATIC STUDIES—REASON FOR FAILURE IN GROUP THERAPY

Almost all the systematic studies of group therapy selection have attempted to elaborate exclusion criteria; they have focused on the failures in group therapy rather than the successes. From the standpoint of research methodology, it is more feasible to establish failure criteria than success criteria.

The study of one obvious failure criterion, premature termination from therapy, has been a rich source of information bearing on the selection process. There is evidence that early terminators do not benefit from their brief stay in the group. In a study of thirty-five patients who dropped out in twelve or fewer meetings, only three reported themselves as improved;[14] moreover, even these three patients were adjudged to have made marginal symptomatic improvement only. In each instance therapy was discontinued because the patient sought to flee from group stress and not because of the natural conclusion of successful therapy. Most clinicians would agree that group therapy is seldom an effective form of brief therapy. Premature group terminators have, in addition, an adverse effect on the remaining members of the group, who are threatened and demoralized by the early dropouts. The work phase of the group which requires membership stability may be delayed for months.

Early group termination is thus a failure for the patient and a detriment to the therapy of the remainder of the group. It is also a very common phenomenon. Dropout rates reported in the literature are: 57 per cent (three or fewer meetings—university outpatient clinic);[1] 51 per cent (nine or fewer meetings—Veterans Administration outpatient clinic);[15] 35 per cent (twelve or fewer meetings—university outpatient clinic);[14] 30 per cent (three or fewer meetings—clinic and private outpatient groups);[16] 25 per cent (twenty or fewer meetings—inpatient and outpatient groups).[17]

To summarize, a large percentage of patients discontinue group therapy at an early stage; not only are these patients not helped (in fact often harmed) but their departure is often injurious to the remaining patients. A study of these early dropouts may help to establish sound exclusion criteria and furthermore may provide an important goal for the selection process. The refinement of the selection process, if only to reduce the early dropout rate, will be a significant achievement. Note that although the early terminators are not the only failures in group therapy, they are unequivocal failures (we may, I think, dismiss as unlikely the contingency that they have gained something positive which will manifest itself later). The study of group dropouts tells us nothing about the group continuers; group continuation is a necessary but not sufficient factor in successful therapy. However, this research strategy circumvents some taxing problems of methodology, especially the critical problem of defining and measuring success in psychotherapy. Let us now consider some of the reasons that patients prematurely terminate therapy which have relevance for the selection process.

Kotkov[18] compared twenty-eight continuers and twenty-eight dropouts (seven meetings or less) in a Veterans Administration outpatient clinic on the basis of data collected at the initial interview. The dropouts significantly differed from those who continued in several respects. The former, at their initial interview, were either more "spontaneous-composed," more hostile, or on the other hand were more placid and needed prodding. They complained less frequently of tension and more often demonstrated somatization of conflicts rather than "emotional reactivity." They complained of headaches, severe insomnia, and demonstrated motor restlessness. Often they appeared to be less motivated toward treatment and were less psychologically minded.

In other studies[19] also in Veterans Administration outpatient clinics, dropouts (as determined from Rorschach testing*) had less capacity to withstand stress, less desire for empathy, and less ability to achieve emotional rapport. However, the discriminating power of the Rorschach in the task was modest, scarcely better than the crudest interview screening. (To the best of my knowledge no predictive Rorschach studies have been done.) The dropouts had a lower Wechsler verbal scale I.Q. and came from a lower socioeconomic class.†

Nash and his co-workers[1] studied a group of forty-eight patients in a university outpatient clinic; the patients had been randomly assigned to individual therapy (N = 18) or to one of three therapy groups (total N = 30). Considerable pretherapy data was collected.‡ The seventeen

---

* The form-color/color-form ratio contributed most to this differentiation.

† That dropouts (from any psychotherapeutic format) are disproportionately high amongst the lower socioeconomic class is a finding corroborated by many other studies.[20, 21, 22]

‡ A social ineffectiveness inventory, a prognostic inventory (including attitudes toward therapy, social history, group experiences, etc.), and psychological testing including a comprehensive symptom check list.

dropouts (three or fewer meetings) differed significantly from the thirteen continuers in several respects. Dropouts were more socially ineffective than continuers and the few continuers who were socially ineffective scored exceptionally high on discomfort; the continuers had a history of fluctuating illness (which implies that the dropouts more likely experienced their illness as progressive and urgent); the dropouts were high deniers and often terminated therapy as the denial crumbled in the face of confrontation by the group.

I shall discuss one final study [14] in greater detail since it has considerable relevance for the selection process. I studied the first six months of life of nine therapy groups in a university outpatient clinic and investigated all patients who terminated in twelve or fewer meetings. A total of 97 patients were involved in these groups (71 original members and 26 later additions); of these, 35 were early dropouts. Considerable data was generated from interviews and questionnaire studies of the dropouts and their therapists, as well as from the records and observations of the group sessions and historical and demographic data from the case records.

Reasons for Premature Termination. An analysis of the data suggested nine major reasons for the patients' dropout from therapy:

1. External factors
2. Group deviancy
3. Problems of intimacy
4. The fear of emotional contagion
5. Inability to share the doctor
6. Complications of concurrent individual and group therapy
7. Early provocateurs
8. Inadequate orientation to therapy
9. Complications arising from subgrouping

Usually more than one factor is involved in the decision to terminate. Some factors are more closely related to external circumstances or to enduring character traits which the patient brings with him to the group (and thus relevant to the selective process), while others are related to problems arising within the group; these latter are more relevant to the discussion of therapist technique in Chapters 9 and 10. Most relevant to the establishment of selection criteria are the patients who dropped out because of external factors, group deviancy, and problems of intimacy.

EXTERNAL FACTORS. 1. Physical reasons for terminating therapy (e.g., irreconcilable scheduling conflicts, moving out of the geographic area) played a negligible role in decisions to terminate. When this reason was offered by the patient, closer study usually demonstrated the presence of group-related stress more pertinent to his departure. Nevertheless, in the initial screening session the therapist should always inquire about any such pending major life changes. There is considerable evidence to suggest that dynamic group therapy is not a brief form of therapy and that patients should not be accepted into a group if there is a considerable likelihood of forced termination within the next several months.

2. External stress was considered a factor in the premature dropout of several patients who were so disturbed by external events in their lives that it was difficult for them to expend the energy for involvement in the group. They could not explore their relationships with other group members while they were consumed with the threat of disruption of relationships with other significant people in their lives. It seemed especially pointless and frustrating to these patients to hear other group members discuss their problems when their own problems seemed so compelling. Among the external stresses were: severe marital discord with impending divorce, initial heterosexual exploration, impending academic failure, and disruptive relationship with parents.

The importance of external stress as a factor in premature group termination was difficult to gauge, since often it appeared secondary to internal forces. A patient's psychic turmoil may cause disruption of his life situation so that secondary external stress occurs; or a patient may focus on an external problem, magnifying it as a means of escaping anxiety originating from the group therapy. Several patients considered external stress as the chief reason for termination, but in each instance careful study indicated that external stress seemed at best a contributory but not sufficient cause for the dropout. Undue focusing on external events often seemed to be one manifestation of a denial mechanism which was helping the patient to avoid something he perceived as dangerous in the group. The patients use the external stress as a rationalization for termination in order to avoid the anticipated dangers of self-disclosure, aggression, intimacy, or facing unknown aspects of themselves.

In the selection process, therefore, an unwarranted focusing on external stress may be an unfavorable sign, whether it represents an extraordinary amount of stress or whether it is a manifestation of denial. A related problem is involved for the patient who has been propelled into therapy by an external crisis and has well-delineated goals: for example, a person distressed by a recent major loss through death or rejection. If an individual has a recurrent problem—for example, a severe reaction to a heterosexual rejection—and has had successful brief individual therapy in a similar instance in the past and seeks similar therapy again, he is in my experience a poor candidate for group therapy.

GROUP DEVIANCY. The study of patients who drop out of therapy because they are group deviants offers a rich supply of information relevant to the selection process; but first the term "deviant" must be carefully defined. Almost each group patient represents an extreme in at least one variable— i.e., he is the youngest, the only unmarried, the sickest, the only Oriental, the only nonstudent, the angriest, or the quietest. However, there were a large number of patients (33 per cent of the dropouts) who deviated significantly from the rest of the group in several areas crucial to their group participation, and this deviancy and the consequent repercussions were considered as the primary reason for their premature termination. The patients' roles varied from those who were silent nonparticipators to those who were loud, angry, group disruptors, but always they were isolates and were perceived by the therapists and by the other members as retarding group locomotion.

It was said of all these patients by the group, by the therapists, and sometimes by the patients themselves that they just "didn't fit in." This distinction is difficult to translate into objectively measurable factors. The most commonly described characteristics are: a lack of psychological sophistication, a lack of interpersonal sensitivity, and a lack of personal psychological insight manifested in part by the common utilization of denial. The patients were usually of a lower socioeconomic status and educational level than the rest of the group. The therapists, when describing their group behavior, emphasized that these patients retarded the group by functioning on a different level of communication from that of the rest of the group. They tended to remain at the symptom-describing, advice-giving and seeking, or judgmental level and avoided discussion of immediate feelings and here-and-now interaction.

There was an important subcategory of five patients who were chronic schizophrenics and, after individual treatment, were making a borderline adjustment. They had "sealed over" and were utilizing much denial and suppression. Their peculiarity was quite obvious to the other group members by their bizarre dress, mannerisms, and verbal content.

Two other patients in the study differed from the other members of their group in their style of life. One had a history of prostitution and had an illegitimate child; another had a history of narcotic addiction—with the inevitable underworld contacts. However, these two patients did *not* differ from the others in ways that impeded group locomotion (psychological insight, interpersonal sensitivity, and effective communication) and never became group deviants.

One other patient became an extreme deviant in his group because of his moral and religious norms. His therapy group was one of young college students who spoke freely of intimate areas and often acted out sexual concerns. The patient was a Quaker and was currently a conscientious objector serving a term of two years as a hospital orderly. His moral views differed so extremely from those of the other group members that he became an isolate and terminated. The therapists stated that the group felt relieved when he left because he had "put a clamp on the group's feelings."

There is considerable social psychological data from research with laboratory groups which helps us to understand the fate of the deviant in the therapy group. Group members who are unable to participate in the group task and who impede group locomotion toward completing the task are much less attracted to the group and are motivated to terminate membership.[23] Individuals whose contributions fail to match presumably unreasonably high group standards have a high rate of group dropout,[24] and this is particularly marked when the individuals have a lower level of self-esteem.[25] The task of these therapy groups is to engage in meaningful communication with the other group members, to reveal oneself, to give valid feedback, and to examine the hidden and unconscious aspects of one's feelings, behavior, and motivation. The individuals who fail at this task are those who lack the requisite skills or motivation. They lack the required amount of psychological-mindedness, are less introspective, less inquisitive, and more apt to utilize self-deceptive defense mechanisms. Lundgren and Miller [26] have shown in research upon Bethel T-groups that the individuals who are most satisfied with themselves and who are inclined to overestimate others' opinion of them tend to profit less from the group experience. The ability to face one's deficiencies, even to the point of undue self-criticism, and a degree of sensitivity to the feelings of others seem to be requisite skills for successful group membership. Similarly in group therapy, members who on post-group questionnaires cannot accurately perceive how others view them are more likely to remain, at best, peripheral members.[27]

What happens to individuals who are unable to perform the task which would elicit positive feedback from the leader and other members and are perceived by the group and, at some level of awareness, by themselves as impeding the group? Schachter [28] has demonstrated that, in a small group, communication toward a deviant is very great initially and then drops off sharply as the group rejects the deviant. The rejection (on sociometric measures) was proportional to the extent to which the deviancy was relevant to the purpose of the group. Much research has demonstrated that one's position in the group communication network significantly influences his satisfaction with the group.[29] Jackson [30] has shown also that an individual's attraction to a group is directly proportional to the extent to which this individual is considered valuable by the other members of the group. Also it has been shown [31] that the ability of the group to influence an individual is dependent partly on the attractiveness of the group for that member and partly on the degree to which the member communicates with the others in the group. It is also well known from the work of Sherif[32] and Asch[33] that an individual will often be made exceedingly uncomfortable by a deviant group role, and there is recent evidence [34] that individuals in a deviant or isolate group role, who cannot or do not verbally express anxiety, may experience physiological anxiety correlates.

There is experimental evidence, then, that the group deviant derives less satisfaction from the group, experiences anxiety, is less valued by the group, is less prone to be influenced by the group, and is far more prone than nondeviants to terminate membership.

These experimental findings coincide notably with the experience of deviants in the therapy groups studied. Moreover, of the eleven deviants, there was only one who did not terminate prematurely. This patient managed to continue in the group because of massive support he received in concurrent individual therapy. However, he not only remained an isolate in the group but, in the opinion of the therapists and other members, he impeded the progress of the group. What happened in that group was remarkably similar to the phenomena described above by Schachter [28] in experimental groups: at first considerable group energy was expended on the deviant, then the group gave up; he became excluded from the communicational network, but the group never entirely forgot him. An axiom of group process is, I believe, that if there is something important going on in the group that cannot be talked about, then there is a degree of generalized communicative inhibition. With a disenfranchised member the group is never really free; in a sense it cannot move much faster than its slowest member.

These findings bear heavily upon the selection process. The patients who achieve a deviant role in therapy groups are relatively easy to identify in screening interviews. The denial, the de-emphasis of the intrapsychic and interpersonal factors, the tendency to attribute dysphoria to somatic and external environmental factors are often quite evident.

The sample of chronic "sealed over" schizophrenic patients is particularly recognizable. These patients had been maintaining a precarious adjustment and could not intimately involve themselves in a rapidly moving interactional group without seriously threatening this adjustment. The chronic schizophrenic patients were all introduced into the group for similar reasons: their individual therapists had felt that they had probably reached a plateau in treatment and that they now needed to develop socializing skills; in some instances a transfer to group therapy was utilized as a method of gradual termination without arousal of guilt in the therapist. The error occurs then not in the identification of these patients but in the assumption that, even if they will not "click" with the rest of the group, nevertheless they will still benefit from the overall group support and the opportunity to improve their socializing techniques. In our experience this expectation is not realized. The referral is a poor one, with neither the patient nor the group profiting.

Rigid attitudes coupled with proselytizing desires may rapidly propel an individual into a deviant position. One of the most difficult patients for me to work with in groups is the individual who employs fundamentalist religious views in the service of denial. The defenses of these patients are often impervious to the ordinarily potent group pressures because they are bolstered, in his self system, by the norms of another anchor group—his particular sect. The interpretation that he is employing certain basic tenets with unrealistic literalness is often not effective, and a frontal assault on these defenses merely rigidifies them.

It is important that the therapist should attempt to screen out patients who will become marked deviants relative to the goals of the particular group for which they are being considered. As I have suggested, other forms of deviancy, unrelated to the group task, are irrelevant. The homosexual, a sexual deviant, is a case in point. Some homosexuals do very poorly in therapy groups composed of heterosexual males and females. They do poorly, however, not because of their deviant sexual style, but because of interpersonal behavior in the group which is counter to the group task. They may be so guarded and secretive that they cannot establish even minimal reciprocity of trust with other members; they may be militant homosexuals and through this denial mechanism refrain from looking inward and sharing personal concerns; or they may be so sexually driven and their drive so egosyntonic that they can only use their interpersonal contact for overt or thinly sublimated sexual purposes. However, I have found that the majority of homosexuals who seek treatment voluntarily (rather than through legal pressures) respond very well in group therapy. It does not matter whether the patient initially seeks treatment to change his sexual orientation to a heterosexual one or whether he wishes to acquire greater comfort and self-understanding within his homosexual orientation. Either goal is an entirely appropriate one in a therapy group, provided that a group climate of respect for individual differences has been established. (See Chapter 12 for a more complete discussion of the homosexual in group therapy.)

Patients, then, become deviants because of their interpersonal behavior in the group sessions and not because of a deviant life style or past history. There is no topic, no form of past behavior, too intimate or too hot for a group to accept once therapeutic group norms are established. I have seen individuals with life styles including prostitution, exhibitionism, voyeurism, kleptomania, and histories of various heinous criminal offenses accepted by a group. Alcoholics, to cite another example, do poorly in mixed intensive outpatient groups, not because of their drinking, but because of their interpersonal behavior. Generally an individual with a serious drinking problem manifests oral character traits which in the group setting take the form of insatiable demands for support, confirmation, and reassurance. He often is fixed upon receiving nurturant supplies from the therapist, whom he is unable to share with the other members. Frustration tolerance is low and when his threshhold is reached, the alcoholic responds in ways that are inaccessible to group influence, usually through some type of motoric expression—for example, by increased drinking, absenteeism, tardiness, and drunken arrivals at meetings.

Although the dropout category of "group deviancy" is the most significant one from the standpoint of the initial selection procedure, some of the other categories are also relevant.

PROBLEMS OF INTIMACY.* Conflicted feelings about intimacy represent a common reason for premature termination. The dropouts manifested their intimacy conflicts in various ways: (1) schizoid withdrawal, (2) maladaptive self-disclosure (promiscuous self-discolsures or pervasive dread of self-disclosure), and (3) unrealistic demands for instant intimacy.

Several patients diagnosed as schizoid personality pattern disturbances, because of their interpersonal coldness, aloofness, introversion, and tendency toward autistic preoccupation, experienced considerable difficulty relating and communicating in the group. Each had begun the group with a resolution to express his feelings and to correct previous maladaptive patterns of relating. They failed to accomplish this and experienced frustra-

---

* The dropout categories are heavily overlapping. For example, the sample of chronic schizophrenic "group deviants" were also, undoubtedly, heavily conflicted in the area of intimacy and would have encountered considerable difficulty in this area in the group had not their deviant group role forced their dropout earlier. Conversely many of the patients who dropped out because of problems of intimacy began to occupy a deviant role because of the behavioral manifestations of their problems in intimacy. Had not the stress of the intimacy conflict forced them to terminate, then undoubtedly the deviant role and its own idiosyncratic stresses would have created pressures leading to termination.

tion and anxiety, which in turn further blocked their efforts to speak. Their therapists described their group role as: "schizoid-isolate," "silent member," "nonentity," "peripheral," "nonrevealer," "doctor's helper." Attributing the cause of the failure to themselves, most of these patients terminated treatment thoroughly discouraged as to the possibility of ever obtaining help from group therapy.

Another schizoid patient, whose diagnosis lay closer to the nebulous boundary between schizophrenia and schizoid personality, dropped out for different reasons—his fears of his own aggression against other group members. He originally applied for treatment because "of a feeling of wanting to explode . . . a fear of killing someone when I explode . . . which results in my staying far away from people." He participated intellectually in the first four meetings he attended but was frightened by the other members' expression of emotion. In the fifth meting one patient monopolized the entire meeting with a repetitive, tangential discourse. The patient became extremely angry with the monopolizer and with the rest of the group members for their complacency in allowing this to happen; with no previous communication to the therapists, he abruptly terminated.

Other patients manifested their problems with intimacy in other ways: some experienced a constant, pervasive dread of self-disclosure which precluded their participation in the group and ultimately resulted in their dropping out; others engaged in premature, promiscuous self-disclosure and abruptly terminated, while still others made such inordinate demands on the other group members for immediate, prefabricated intimacy that they created an inviable group role for themselves.

This entire category of patients with severe problems in the area of intimacy presents a particular challenge to the group therapist both in the area of selection and in the area of therapeutic management (to be considered in Chapter 12). The irony is that these patients whose attrition rate is so high are the very ones for whom a successful group experience could be particularly rewarding. Harrison and Lubin [35] recently reported that, in a human relations laboratory (see Chapter 14), individuals designated as "work-oriented" (as opposed to "person-oriented") learn more and change more as a result of their group experience even though they are significantly more uncomfortable in the group. Harrison and Lubin do not use the label "schizoid," but their description of "work-oriented" individuals suggests a strong overlap: ". . . constriction of emotionality . . . threatened by expression of feelings by others . . . hard for them to experience and express their own emotional reactions." Therefore, these patients, whose life histories are characterized by ungratifying interpersonal relationships, stand to profit much from successfully negotiating an intimate group experience; and yet if their past interpersonal history has been too deprived, the group will prove too threatening for them and they will drop out of therapy more demoralized than before.

Thus this general category represents at the same time a specific indication and counterindication for group therapy. The problem, of course, is one of early identification and screening out of those who will be overwhelmed in the group. If only we could, with accuracy, quantify this critical cut-off point! The prediction of group behavior from pretherapy screening sessions is quite a complex task which I will discuss in detail in the next chapter. However, it may be noted here that an individual who, in the screening procedure, is a severely schizoid, isolated individual with a pervasive dread of self-disclosure is an unfavorable candidate for interactional group therapy. Even greater caution should be exercised when the therapist is seeking a replacement member for an already established, fast-moving group. If the therapist decides on a therapeutic trial, then he should adequately prepare the schizoid patient for the group (see Chapter 9) and consider also the possibility of short-term individual therapy conducted concurrently with the early phases of group therapy.

THE FEAR OF EMOTIONAL CONTAGION. Several patients who dropped out of group therapy reported that they had been extremely adversely affected by hearing the problems of the other group members. One patient stated that during his three weeks in the group, he was very upset by the others' problems, dreamed about them every night, and relived their problems during the day. Others reported being upset by one particularly disturbed patient in each of their groups; they were all frightened by seeing aspects of the other patient in themselves, fearing that they too might become as mentally ill as the severely disturbed patient or that continued exposure to this patient would evoke a personal regression. Another patient in this category experienced a severe revulsion toward the other group members, stating, "I couldn't stand the people in the group. They were repulsive. I got upset seeing them trying to heap their problems on top of mine. I didn't want to hear their problems. I felt no sympathy for them and couldn't bear to look at them. They were all ugly, fat, and unattractive." She bolted the first group meeting thirty minutes early and never returned. She had a lifelong history of being upset by other people's illnesses and avoiding sick people; once when her mother fainted, she "stepped over her" to get away rather than trying to help. Others also, as Nash et al.[1] reported in an earlier study, had a long term proclivity to avoid sick people. They reported a lack of curiosity about others and, if they had been present at an accident, were "the first to leave" or tended to "look the other way." Most of them report being very upset at the sight of blood. They became especially disturbed if another person discussed problems which were similar to their own.

A fear of emotional contagion, unless it is extremely marked and very clearly manifest in the pretherapy screening procedure, is not a terribly useful index for group inclusion or exclusion. Generally it is difficult to predict this behavior from screening interviews; furthermore a fear of emotional contagion was not, in itself, sufficient cause for failure. If the therapist is sensitive to the problem he can deal with it effectively in the therapeutic process. Occasionally patients must gradually desensitize themselves; I have known patients who dropped out of several therapy groups before finally persevering.

The other reasons for group therapy dropouts—"inability to share the doctor," "complications of concurrent individual and group therapy," "early provocateurs," "problems in orientation to therapy," and "complications arising from subgrouping"—are generally a result not so much of faulty selection but of faulty therapeutic technique and will be discussed in later chapters. None of these categories, though, belong purely to the "selection" or "therapy technique" rubric. For example, some patients terminated because of an inability to share the therapist. They never relinquished the notion that progress in therapy was dependent solely upon the amount of goods (time, attention, etc.) they received from the group therapist. While it may have been true that these patients tended to be excessively dependent and authority-oriented, it was also true that they had been incorrectly referred and prepared for group therapy. They had all been in individual therapy, and the group was considered as a method of therapy-weaning. Obviously group therapy is not a modality to be used in the termination phase of individual therapy, and the therapist, in his pretherapy screening, should be alert to the rationale behind the referral of the patient to group therapy.

Inclusion Criteria

Inclusion criteria play little role in the selection process for group therapy; most group therapists adhere to the dictum that all patients, aside from the specific exceptions enumerated above, are suitable for group therapy. In other words, if none of the exclusion criteria apply to the patient, then he may be started in group therapy.

Although this policy is not satisfactory, its source is obvious: inclusion criteria are far more difficult to elaborate. For one thing inclusion criteria must be more comprehensive; one striking feature can point to exclusion, whereas many factors must be considered in reaching a decision about suitability. Any systematic approach to the definition of inclusion criteria must issue from the study of successful group therapy patients, who theoretically should offer valuable information for the selection process. Imagine a rigorously controlled study in which a large number of patients are systematically studied before entering therapy and then followed and evaluated after a year or two of group therapy. There should, of course, be a differential rate of success, and, by correlating the pretherapy data with outcome, we should be able to determine those patient characteristics predictive of favorable outcome. Unfortunately there are extreme difficulties inherent in such a study: patients drop out of therapy, many obtain ancillary individual therapy, group therapists vary in competence and techniques, and initial diagnostic technique is unreliable and often idiosyncratic.

A team of researchers (Houts, Zimerberg, Rand, and myself) attempted, nonetheless, in 1965, to study factors which are evident pretherapy which might predict successful outcome in group therapy.[36] Forty patients* (in five outpatient therapy groups) were followed through one year of group therapy. Outcome was evaluated† and correlated with many variables studied before the onset of therapy. The results indicated that a large number of factors were *not* predictive of success in group therapy, including: level of psychological sophistication,‡ the therapists' prediction of outcome,§ previous self-disclosure,‖ and demographic data. In fact, the only variables predictive of success were the patients' attraction to the group# and the patients' general popularity** in the group (both measured at the sixth and twelfth meetings). The finding that popularity correlated highly with successful outcome has some implications for

* The patients studied were adult, middle-class, well-educated, psychologically sophisticated outpatients who suffered from neurotic or characterologic problems.

† By a team of raters who, on the basis of a structured interview, evaluated (with excellent reliability) change in symptoms, functioning, and relationships. The patients also independently rated their own outcome, using the same scales.

‡ Measured by the psychological-mindedness subscale of the California Personality Inventory and by the therapists after an initial screening interview. These measures were probably too insensitive for a population already screened clinically for this variable.

§ The therapist rated each patient on a 7-point scale after the initial interview for how well he thought the patient would do in therapy.

‖ Measured by a modification of the Jourard Self-Disclosure Questionnaire.[37]

Measured by a group cohesiveness questionnaire[36] (see Chapter 3).

** Measured by a sociometric questionnaire.[36]

selection, in that the researchers found that high previous self-disclosure, activity in the group, and the ability to introspect were some of the prerequisites for group popularity.

No other systematic outcome studies exist which bear on inclusion criteria—a glaring defect and one that must be corrected before a sound scientific base for group therapy can be established.

There are in the clinical literature numerous anecdotal reports about ideal group therapy candidates. Slavson,[5] for example, reports that group methods are expecially effective with patients who project, who persistently blame others for their inadequacies and failures. The group members deal with this trend with instantaneous, firm responses, and their clarifications are more easily accepted by the patient than would be the interpretations of the therapists. With increasing frequency patients today may, as a result of individual or some other therapy experience, come to an appreciation of their interpersonal difficulties and specifically request group therapy. Their positive expectations [38, 39] and their interpersonal set are propitious signs; generally they will profit from the group and furthermore be helpful to the group.

Other inclusion criteria become evident when we also consider the members of the group into which the patient will be placed. Thus far, for pedagogical clarity, I have oversimplified the problem by attempting to identify only absolute criteria for inclusion or exclusion. Unlike individual therapy recruitment, where we need only consider the question of whether or not the patient will profit from therapy, recruitment for group therapy cannot in practice ignore the remainder of the group members. It is conceivable, for example, that a patient such as the dependent alcoholic, the compulsive talker, or the sociopath might derive some benefit from a group but also that his presence would render the group less effective for several other members. Conversely, there are patients who would do well in a variety of treatment modalities but are placed in a slowly moving group because of their catalytic qualities or because of some specific need of a group. For example, some groups at times seem to need an aggressive member or a strong male, or a soft feminine member. Borderline schizophrenic patients,* despite their stormy course of therapy and the absence of outcome studies validating the efficacy of group therapy for them, very often find their way into therapy groups. In fact, I have often searched for them because of their beneficial influence on the therapy process. These patients have a greater awareness of their unconscious, less dedication to

---

* To be distinguished from the chronic schizophrenic patient in partial remission using repressive and suppressive defenses who was described as a poor candidate in the section on deviants.

formal social inhibitory techniques, and very often lead the group into a more candid and eventually intimate culture.

One final, and important, criterion for inclusion is the therapist's personal feeling toward the patient. Regardless of the source, if the therapist experiences a strong dislike or disinterest for the patient then he should refer the patient elsewhere. This caveat is obviously a relative one and each therapist must establish for himself the intensity of such feelings which would preclude effective therapy. It is my impression that the issue is a somewhat less crucial one for group therapists than for individual therapists; with the consensual validation available in the group from the other patients and from the co-therapist, many therapists find that they are more often able to work through initial negative feelings toward patients in group therapy than in individual therapy.

An Overview of the Selection Procedure

The material thus far presented about selection of patients has a disturbingly disjunctive nature. We can, I believe, introduce some order by applying to this material a central organizing principle—a simple punishment-reward system. Members are prone to terminate membership in a therapy group and are thereby poor candidates when the punishments or disadvantages of group membership outweigh the rewards or anticipated rewards. When speaking of punishments or disadvantages of group membership, I refer to the price the patient must pay for group membership. This includes an investment of time, money, energy, as well as a variety of dysphorias arising from the group experience, including anxiety, frustration, discouragement, and rejection.

The rewards of therapy group membership consist of the various types of satisfactions members obtain from the group. Let us consider here those rewards, or determinants of group cohesiveness, that are relevant to the selection of patients for group therapy.[40]

Members are satisfied with their groups (attracted to their groups—prone to continue membership in their groups) if:

1. They view the group as meeting their personal needs.
2. They derive satisfaction from their relationships with the other members.
3. They derive satisfaction from their participation in the group task.
4. They derive satisfaction from group membership vis-à-vis the outside world.

173

Each of these factors, if absent or of negative valence, may outweigh the positive valence of the others and result in group termination. The factors are closely interconnected; and were it possible from a literary standpoint, I should greatly prefer to discuss them simultaneously.

DOES THE GROUP SATISFY PERSONAL NEEDS?

The explicit personal needs of group therapy members are at first expressed in their "chief complaint"—their purpose for seeking therapy. These personal needs are usually couched in terms of relief of suffering, less frequently in terms of self-understanding. Several factors are important here: there must be a significant personal need; the group must be viewed as an agent with the potential of meeting that need; and the group must be seen in time as making progress toward meeting that need. There must be a reasonable degree of discomfort, of course, to provide the required motivation for change. The relationship between discomfort and suitability for group therapy is not a linear one but a curvilinear one. Patients with too little discomfort (coupled with only a modest amount of curiosity about groups or themselves) are usually unwilling to pay the price for group membership.

Patients with considerable discomfort may, on the other hand, be willing to pay a high price provided that they have faith or evidence that the group can and will help. This faith may derive from a number of sources:

1. Endorsement of group therapy by the mass media, by friends who have had a successful group therapy experience, or by a previous individual therapist
2. Explicit preparation by the group therapist (see Chapter 9)
3. Unquestioned belief in the omniscience of authority figures
4. Observing or being told about improvement of other group members
5. Observing small changes in himself occurring early in group therapy

Patients with exceedingly high discomfort stemming from either extraordinary environmental stress, inadequate ego strength, or some combination of these, may be so oriented toward a realistic management of the external stress that the group goals and activities seem utterly irrelevant. Initially the group is unable to meet highly pressing personal needs. Greatly disturbed patients may be unable to tolerate the frustration which occurs as the group gradually evolves into an effective therapeutic instrument. They may demand instant relief which the group cannot supply, or they may develop anxiety-binding defenses which are so interpersonally maladaptive (for example, extreme projection or somatization) as to make the group socially nonviable for them. Individuals who are acutely psychotic are, as we have indicated, generally to be excluded from outpatient interactional group therapy. I refer to the initial selection criteria; established group members who become psychotic during the course of treatment may often be well managed in the group setting (see Chapter 12).

Individuals who have been described as being "psychologically insensitive," "nonpsychologically minded," "nonintrospective," "high deniers," "psychological illiterates," "psychologically insensitive," may be unable to perceive the group as meeting their personal needs. In fact they may perceive an incompatibility between their personal needs and the group goals. How can the exploration of the interpersonal relations of the group members help them with their "bad nerves"? These individuals, too, may have few sources of group satisfaction available to them. Not only does the group not satisfy their personal needs, but they cannot satisfactorily engage in the group activities (which require the very abilities they lack—introspection, sensitivity, etc.), and they eventually are further burdened with the anxiety inherent in the group deviant role. Although some therapists have suggested that these patients may be quickly taught to be psychiatric patients by the other group members, this has not been my experience. While it is true that peers may function admirably as teachers, I have found that patients who utilize denial or other self-deceptive defense mechanisms, who tend to somatize psychological conflicts, or to deal with them in a nonpsychological mode, are usually poor group referrals. The benefits derived from their learning the patient role are outweighed by the negative balance of the group reward-punishment system, and they terminate group membership.

SATISFACTION FROM INTERMEMBER RELATIONSHIPS

Group members derive satisfaction from their relationship with other group members, and often this source of attraction to the group may dwarf the others. The importance of intermember relationships both as a source of cohesiveness and as a curative factor was fully discussed in Chapter 3, and we need only pause here to reflect that it is rare for a member to continue membership in the prolonged absence of interpersonal satisfaction.

The development of interpersonal satisfaction may be a slow process. Frank [40] has pointed out that mentally ill patients are often contemptuous of themselves and therefore are prone to be initially contemptuous of their fellow patients. They have had, for the most part, few gratifying interpersonal relationships in the past and have little trust or expectancy of gaining anything from close relationships with the other group members. Often the patients may use the therapist as a transitional object. By relating positively to him at first, they may more easily grow closer with each other. Parloff [41] has demonstrated that group patients who established closer relationships with the group therapist were significantly more inclined to perceive other group members as socially attractive.

SATISFACTION FROM PARTICIPATION
IN THE GROUP ACTIVITIES

The satisfaction that patients derive from participation in the group task is largely inseparable from the satisfaction derived from the relationship with the other group members. The group task (to achieve a group culture of intimacy, acceptance, introspection, understanding, and interpersonal honesty) is, in essence, an interpersonal one. However, research with a wide variety of groups has demonstrated that satisfactory participation in the group task, *regardless of its nature,* is an important source of satisfaction from group membership.[42] Therapy group members who cannot introspect, reveal themselves, care for others, or manifest their feelings will derive little gratification from their participation in the group activities. These include many of the types of individuals discussed earlier, for example, the schizoid personality, those patients with other types of overriding intimacy problems, the deniers, the somatizers, and the mentally retarded.

SATISFACTION FROM PRIDE IN GROUP MEMBERSHIP

Members of many groups derive satisfaction from membership because the outside world regards that group as highly valued or prestigious. Therapy groups obviously are at a disadvantage in this regard,[43] and generally this source of attraction to the group is unavailable. If patients manifest extraordinary shame at membership and are reluctant to reveal their membership to intimate friends or even spouses, then obviously therapy group membership must appear to them dissonant with the values of other important anchor groups; it is not likely that the patients will develop a high attraction to the group. Occasionally, as Frank [40] and Ends[12] point out, outside groups (for example, family, military, or, increasingly commonly, industry) will exert pressure on the individual to seek therapy group membership. Groups held together only by this coercion are tenuous but not infrequently, as the group process evolves, other sources of cohesiveness are generated.

In summary, the guidelines for selection stem primarily from the study of group therapy failures. If followed, these guidelines will improve our selection criteria by screening out (and assigning to another therapy modality) patients destined to fail early in the course of group therapy. The group therapy dropout rate at the Stanford Psychiatric Outpatient Clinic has gradually fallen from 35 per cent in 1964 [14] to 27.5 per cent (1965) [36] to 14 per cent (1966) [44] to 10 per cent (1967). [45] Although part of this reduction may have been due to improvement in therapist technique, the major reason for the reductions was a refinement in selection criteria. Nevertheless, this approach to selection is a distinctly limited one. For purposes of exposition we have approached the problem, thus far, in a unidimensional manner. We have attempted to delineate selection criteria for patients posited in absolute terms or, if the rest of the group has been considered, it has been a phantom anonymous group with a narrowly limited range of members' traits and behavior. In practice, of course, the members of the group into which the patient may go must be reckoned with *in vivo;* and it is not a matter of "Shall the patient enter group therapy?" but instead, "Shall he enter therapy in that particular group?" This problem, one of a higher order of complexity, is one to which we shall now turn our attention.

REFERENCES

1. E. Nash, J. Frank, L. Gliedman, S. Imber, and A. Stone, "Some Factors Related to Patients Remaining in Group Psychotherapy," *Int. J. Group Psychother.*, 7: 264–275, 1957.
2. J. A. Johnson, *Group Psychotherapy: A Practical Approach* (New York: McGraw-Hill, 1963).
3. I. W. Graham, "Observations on Analytic Group Therapy," *Int. J. Group Psychother.*, 9: 150–157, 1959.
   tional Universities Press, 1964).
4. S. R. Slavson, *A Textbook in Analytic Group Psychotherapy* (New York: Interna-
5. S. R. Slavson, "Criteria for Selection and Rejection of Patients for Various Kinds of Group Therapy," *Int. J. Group Psychother.*, 5: 3–30, 1955.
6. R. Corsini and W. Lundin, "Group Psychotherapy in the Mid West," *Group Psychother.*, 8: 316–320, 1955.

7. M. Rosenbaum and E. Hartley, "A Summary Review of Current Practices of Ninety-Two Group Therapists," *Int. J. Group Psychother., 12:* 194–198, 1962.
8. J. Abrahams and L. W. McCorkle, "Group Psychotherapy at an Army Rehabilitation Center," *Dis. Nerv. Sys., 8:* 50–62, 1947.
9. G. Bach, *Intensive Group Therapy* (New York: Ronald Press, 1954).
10. E. Goffman, *The Presentation of Self in Everyday Life* (Garden City, N.Y.: Doubleday Anchor Books, 1959).
11. I. D. Yalom, "Group Therapy of Incarcerated Sexual Deviants," *J. Nerv. Ment. Dis., 132:* 158–170, 1961.
12. E. J. Ends and C. W. Page, "Group Psychotherapy and Psychological Change," *Psychol. Monogr., 73,* No. 480, 1959.
13. R. Kaldeck, "Group Psychotherapy with Mentally Defective Adolescents and Adults," *Int. J. Group Psychother., 8:* 185–192, 1958.
14. I. D. Yalom, "A Study of Group Therapy Dropouts," *Arch. Gen. Psychiat., 14:* 393–414, 1966.
15. B. Kotkov, "The Effect of Individual Psychotherapy on Group Attendance," *Int. J. Group Psychother., 5:* 280–285, 1955.
16. E. Berne, "Group Attendance: Clinical and Theoretical Considerations," *Int. J. Group Psychother., 5:* 392–403, 1955.
17. Johnson, *op. cit.,* p. 144.
18. B. Kotkov, "Favorable Clinical Indications for Group Attendance," *Int. J. Group Psychother., 8:* 419–427, 1958.
19. B. Kotkov and A. Meadow, "Rorschach Criteria for Continuing Group Psychotherapy," *Int. J. Group Psychother., 2:* 324–331, 1952.
20. L. H. Gliedman, A. Stone, J. Frank, E. Nash, and S. Imber, "Incentives for Treatment Related to Remaining or Improving in Psychotherapy," *Am. J. Psychother., 11:* 589–598, 1957.
21. J. Frank, L. H. Gliedman, S. Imber, E. Nash, and A. Stone, "Why Patients Leave Psychotherapy," *Arch. Neurol. Psychiat., 77:* 283–299, 1957.
22. D. Rosenthal and J. Frank, "The Fate of Psychiatric Clinic Outpatients Assigned to Psychotherapy," *J. Nerv. Ment. Dis., 127:* 330–343, 1958.
23. M. Horwitz, "The Recall of Interrupted Group Tasks: An Experimental Study of Individual Motivation in Relation to Group Goals," in D. Cartwright and A. Zander (eds.), *Group Dynamics: Research and Theory* (New York: Row, Peterson, 1962), pp. 370–394.
24. L. Coch and J. R. French, Jr., "Overcoming Resistance to Change," in Cartwright and Zander, *op. cit.,* pp. 319–341.
25. E. Stotland, "Determinants of Attraction to Groups," *J. Soc. Psychol., 49:* 71–80, 1959.
26. D. Lundgren and D. Miller, "Identity and Behavioral Changes in Training Groups," *Human Relations Training News,* Spring 1965.
27. I. D. Yalom and P. Houts, unpublished data, 1966.
28. S. Schachter, "Deviation, Rejection, and Communication," in Cartwright and Zander, *op. cit.,* pp. 260–285.
29. H. F. Leavitt, "Group Structure and Process: Some Effects of Certain Communication Patterns on Group Performance," in E. E. Maccoby, T. M. Newcomb, and E. L. Hartley (eds.), *Readings in Social Psychology* (New York: Holt, Rinehart and Winston, 1958), pp. 175–183.
30. J. M. Jackson, "Reference Group Processes in a Formal Organization," in Cartwright and Zander, *op. cit.,* pp. 120–140.
31. L. Festinger, S. Schachter, and K. Back, "The Operation of Group Standards," in Cartwright and Zander, *op. cit.,* pp. 241–259.
32. M. Sherif, "Group Influences upon the Formation of Norms and Attitudes," in Maccoby, Newcomb, and Hartley, *op. cit.,* pp. 219–232.

33. S. E. Asch, "Interpersonal Influence: Effects of Group Pressure upon the Modification and Distortion of Judgments" in Maccoby, Newcomb, and Hartley, *op. cit.*, pp. 175–183.
34. P. H. Leiderman, personal communication, 1965.
35. R. Harrison and B. Lubin, "Personal Style, Group Composition and Learning—Part I," *J. Appl. Behav. Sci.*, 1: 286–294, 1965.
36. I. D. Yalom, P. S. Houts, S. M. Zimerberg, and K. H. Rand, "Prediction of Improvement in Group Therapy," *Arch. Gen. Psychiat.*, 17: 159–168, 1967.
37. S. Jourard, "Self-Disclosure Patterns in British and American College Females," *J. Soc. Psychol.*, 54: 315–320, 1961.
38. A. Goldstein and W. Shipman, "Patient Expectancies, Symptom Reduction and Aspects of the Initial Psychotherapeutic Interview," *J. Clin. Psychol.*, 17: 129–133, 1961.
39. A. P. Goldstein, *Therapist Patient Expectancies in Psychotherapy* (New York: Pergamon Press, 1962).
40. J. D. Frank, "Some Determinants, Manifestations, and Effects of Cohesiveness in Therapy Groups," *Int. J. Group Psychother.*, 7: 53–63, 1957.
41. M. B. Parloff, "Therapist-Patient Relationships and Outcome of Psychotherapy," *J. Consult. Psychol.*, 25: 29–38, 1961.
42. R. Heslin and D. Dunphy, "Three Dimensions of Member Satisfaction in Small Groups," *Human Relations*, 17: 99–112, 1964.
43. R. Harrison, "Group Composition Models for Laboratory Design," *J. Appl. Behav. Sci.*, 1: 409–432, 1965.
44. I. D. Yalom, P. S. Houts, G. Newell, and K. H. Rand, "Preparation of Patients for Group Therapy," *Arch. Gen. Psychiat.*, 17: 416–427, 1967.
45. A. Sklar, I. D. Yalom, S. Zimerberg, and G. Newell, "Time Extended Group Therapy: A Controlled Study," *Comparative Group Studies*, in press.

8

COMPOSITION OF THERAPY GROUPS

✵

Imagine the following situation: a psychiatric outpatient clinic with ten group therapists ready to form groups and seventy patients who, on the basis of the selection criteria outlined thus far, are suitable group therapy candidates. How should the triage proceed and what bearing will it have on the outcome of treatment? Are there guidelines available to assist the therapist to form, insofar as circumstances permit, the "ideal" group?

A second, more common clinical problem is closely related. Assume that there is one patient who has been deemed a suitable group therapy candidate and that there are several therapy groups each with one vacancy. Into which group should the patient go? The solution to this problem is to be found in the solution to the first. If valid principles about the effective total composition of a group can be established, then the corollaries of these principles will provide the guidelines for adding new members or replacing members who leave the group. We grope in the dark if we try to replace a missing unit without any knowledge of the organization of the total social organism.

The clinical observations and research evidence considered in this chapter attest that there are principles of group composition, which, if applied, may enhance the effectiveness of therapy groups. The evidence suggests that the right blend of individuals may form the ideal therapy group; the wrong blend may never coalesce into a group. Every group therapist has had a group that, despite his heroic efforts, never jells, never evolves into a working group until some change occurs in the membership. But what are we blending? What human characteristics are we attempting to match?

The essence of the therapy group is interaction; each member must continually communicate and interact with the other members. Regardless of any other consideration, it is the actual behavior of the members of the group that dictates the fate of the group. Therefore, if we are to talk intelligently about group composition, we must speak of composing the group in such a way that the members will interact in some desired manner. The entire procedure of group composition and selection of group patients is thus based on a very important assumption. That assumption is that we can, with some degree of accuracy, predict the group behavior of an individual from our pretherapy screening. If we cannot predict group behavior from our screening procedure, then all of our preceding pronouncements about group selection and our subsequent remarks about group composition will have little meaning.

The Prediction of Group Behavior

The previous chapter advises against the inclusion of certain patients in the group because they behave in a manner which has undesirable effects on themselves and the group. For example, alcoholic, sociopathic, and floridly psychotic individuals are, it is suggested, best excluded from an outpatient interactional group. Generally predictions limited to individuals with such extreme, fixed, maladaptive interpersonal behavior are reasonably accurate; the grosser the pathology, the greater the predictive accuracy. There is scarcely any room for error when considering a paranoid schizophrenic with an active, expanding, persecutory delusional system. He will soon grow to distrust the group members, become secretive, suspicious, perhaps openly accusatory, and then, as the delusional system generalizes, will ultimately regard the group members as inimical. Ordinarily in clinical practice the problem is a far more subtle one; most patients who apply for treatment have a wide repertoire of behavior, and their ultimate group behavior is far less predictable.

A number of pretherapy screening procedures have been employed to predict future behavior in group therapy. Before discussing the behavior variables which are most salient to group composition, let us examine existing screening practices to determine whether they predict anything at all about the future group behavior of patients.

THE PREDICTIVE VALUE OF THE
STANDARD DIAGNOSTIC INTERVIEW

The most common method of screening patients is the individual interview. Quite often the interview is the routine one used at intake with all patients applying for treatment to a practitioner or clinic. The interviewer, in addition to acquiring information about such topics as motivation for treatment, ego strength, environmental stresses, past history, etc., attempts to make predictions as to how the patient may behave in the group. These predictions are often highly remote inferences stemming from objective information about the patients' behavior in the dyadic situation.

One of the traditional end products of the mental health interview is a diagnosis which, in capsule form, is meant to summarize the patient's condition and convey useful information to another practitioner. The psychiatric diagnosis based on the American Psychiatric Association official manual [1] is, as most group therapists will attest, spectacularly useless as an indicator of interpersonal behavior. It was never meant for this purpose; it stemmed from a disease-oriented medical discipline and is basically an etiologic and symptomatic scheme.

Although a disease-oriented classification system serves many purposes, it has serious shortcomings which are especially evident to those practitioners who work primarily with individuals with relatively minor maladjustments. The typical clinician in an outpatient clinic or the private practitioner finds that the great majority of his patients have some characterologic disturbance classifiable only in some vague way in the official nomenclature. A few, but only a few, of the categories or subcategories are useful in predicting interpersonal behavior. A person labeled as a schizoid personality will most likely behave in a roughly predictable manner: he will probably remain detached, perhaps intellectualizing, be unable to reach and share his feelings with others, and be perceived by others as cold, uncaring, and distant. However, what can be predicted about the group behavior of an individual labeled as "psychoneurotic reaction, anxiety type" or "phobic type" or, for that matter, "personality disorder, sexual deviation" or "emotionally unstable personality"? Two individuals with an anxiety reaction can manifest entirely different interpersonal styles. Expanding their diagnosis to include their personality type is of little help because of the inadequacy of the available personality description labels.

Even if the American Psychiatric Association classificatory system were useful in predicting the group behavior of an individual, its value would still be limited because of its poor reliability, as attested by two controlled studies of the diagnostic procedure. Ash [2] studied the agreement between pairs of psychiatrists who examined fifty-two outpatients and found that a pair of psychiatrists tended to agree about the diagnostic subcategory (i.e., type of neurosis, psychosis, or personality disorder) in approximately 40 per cent of the cases. There was only 64 per cent agreement about the major divisions (psychotic reactions, neurotic reactions, personality disorders). Beck,[3] studying the diagnostic agreement between six pairs of senior clinicians, found a concordance rate which ranged from 33.3 per cent to 61.4 per cent. When the diagnostic categories were analyzed separately, the researchers found a higher rate of agreement for some than for others. For example, there was a rate of agreement of 63 per cent for neurotic depression, 55 per cent for anxiety reaction, 53 per cent for schizophrenia, and only 38 per cent for personality trait disturbance. When we place this final figure in juxtaposition with the fact that a large percentage of our outpatients fall into the personality trait category, and consider also that the category has little predictive value, we begin to appreciate the magnitude of the diagnostic folly.

Diagnostic formulations which require even greater inference than the standard nosological categories are even less useful. Exclusion criteria cited in the clinical literature,[4] such as "inadequate ego strength" or "sexual life deviant or charged with anxiety or guilt" or "inability to relinquish egocentricity," lack clear definitions; furthermore, interclinician reliability would no doubt be so low as to invalidate their general usefulness.

PREDICTIVE VALUE OF STANDARD PSYCHOLOGICAL TESTING

Several investigators have sought to use standard psychological diagnostic tests as predictors of group behavior. These have most prominently included the Rorschach, the MMPI, the TAT, the Sentence Completion, and Draw-a-Person tests.[5, 6, 7] All these tests failed to yield valid predictions, with the single exception [6] that individuals using considerable denial (as evidenced by the Rorschach and TAT) more often made positive, agreeing statements in group therapy.

PREDICTIVE VALUE OF SPECIALIZED DIAGNOSTIC PROCEDURES

The lack of success that these standard diagnostic procedures have demonstrated in predicting group behavior suggest that new procedures which focus primarily on interpersonal behavior must be developed. Recent clinical observations and research have suggested several promising directions. For purposes of clarity, I will discuss these under two arbitrary headings:

1. A formulation of an interpersonal nosological system
2. New diagnostic procedures which directly sample group-relevant behavior

An Interpersonal Nosological System.   The first known attempt to classify mental illness dates back to 1700 B.C.,[8, 9] and the intervening years have seen a bewildering number of systems advanced, each unacceptable, each beset with its own form of internal inconsistency. The central plan in the great majority of systems has been disease-based: either etiological, descriptive, or some combination of the two. With the advent of the object relations and the interpersonal systems of conceptualizing psychopathology, as well as an increased exposure to individuals seeking treatment for less severe problems in living, have come rudimentary attempts to classify individuals according to interpersonal styles of relating.

For example, Karen Horney [10] views troubled individuals as moving exaggeratedly and maladaptively toward, against, or away from other people and has advanced elaborate interpersonal profiles of these types and various subtypes. Individuals who chiefly move toward others invoke the "self-effacing solution" and deal with others in a currency of love. Those who move against others (the "expansive solutions") engage in an interpersonal search for mastery and are subdivided into three subgroups: the narcissistic, the perfectionistic, and the arrogant vindictive. The third maneuver, moving away from people, is labeled "resignation," and individuals so designated handle interpersonal relationships by withdrawal, by "a search for freedom." Horney's formulations have been influential and valuable for a large number of American clinicians. It is always a singularly rewarding experience to encounter a stereotyped patient who fits flush into one of Horney's character types. One has a keen sense of recognition as well as a firm conviction that, with rather great accuracy, one shall be able to predict much of the course of therapy. Unfortunately these stereotypes appear uncommonly, and Horney's nosological types are, as she recognized, highly caricaturized and composite profiles; there has been, to my knowledge, no attempt to systematize and quantify this approach to diagnosis. Much the same can be said for Erich Fromm's [11, 12] attempts to formulate nosological categories on the basis of the individual's basic interpersonal orientation (the marketing, receptive, hoarding, and exploitative personalities). These and other classificatory systems developed by interpersonally oriented clinicians may provide a philosophical background for the study of personality but have not been organized and systematized with the precision necessary for the development of a methodology for the scientific study of personality.

There have been two recent noteworthy attempts to arrive at a comprehensive, quantified interpersonal diagnostic system; the interpersonal circular grid of Timothy Leary [13] and the FIRO-B system of William Schutz.[14] Of these two the FIRO-B system has been more influential in stimulating group therapy relevant research.

THE INTERPERSONAL CIRCULAR GRID OF LEARY. Leary and his collaborators (Coffey, Freedman, and Ossorio)[15] developed a system of describing personality based on the theoretical formulations of Harry Stack Sullivan. The total personality is considered to consist of three levels: the public, the conscious, the private. These levels are defined by the sources of data which contributed to each level: the public level is derived from objective ratings of the person's behavior (e.g., his statements during group therapy sessions about himself and others); the conscious level is derived from self-descriptions; the private level from ratings of projective material of his views of himself and of others. The data on the public level, for example, are then categorized into one of sixteen interpersonal mechanisms (Table 8-1) which Leary considered sufficient for systematizing all interpersonal behavior. The raters also rated each act on a three-point scale for intensity. The sixteen interpersonal mechanisms were arranged in a circular grid with the two primary axes of love-hate and domination-submission.[15] By applying trigonometric formulas one can represent the interpersonal behavior of the individual as a point in the circle. Similar principles apply to the other levels: level—conscious, and level—private.*

Although there were some early attempts to use this system for prediction of group behavior and for group composition (which will be described shortly), these have remained rudimentary [16] and the system, perhaps because it is so complex and cumbersome, has not been widely used by other workers for this purpose.

FIRO. The FIRO ("Fundamental Interpersonal Relations Orientation") system[14] was first described by Schutz in 1958. Schutz reviewed a large number of studies of interpersonal behavior from the child development field, social psychological research, and the clinical field and concluded that control, inclusion, and affection are the three basic interpersonal needs and that others described could be reasonably considered within the framework of these three. Using these three needs, an interpersonal profile of an indi-

---

* Later Leary [13] expanded the system to five levels: (1) public communication, (2) conscious descriptions, (3) preconscious symbolizations, (4) unexpressed unconscious, and (5) ego ideal.

TABLE 8-1[13]

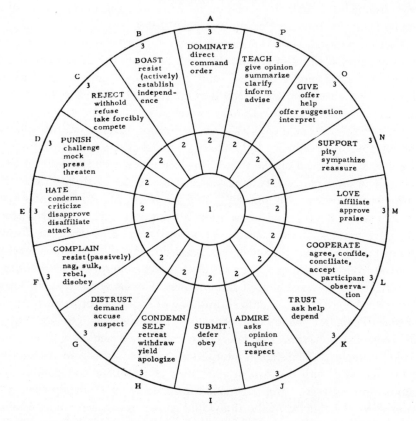

Level I variables: interpersonal mechanisms with illustrative verbs. Intensity ratings: 3, intense or extreme; 2, average or appropriate; 1, mild intensity.

vidual may be constructed. The profile attempts to describe the valence of the individual toward each of these needs. Does he very much wish to control others, to be controlled, or is he relatively unconflicted in this area? Does he wish to be included in social activities or excluded? Does he very much desire intimacy or desire to avoid intimacy? The data is derived from a self-administered questionnaire, the FIRO-B (the B stands for behavior), which consists of fifty-four items, each one answered on a six-point scale, and which takes approximately fifteen to twenty minutes to complete. The questions are so superficial and repetitious that it is not uncommon for sophisticated patients to be irritated and insulted by the questionaire.* The test seems to tap such superficial aspects of a human being that

* For example, four typical questions among the fifty-four are: (1) I like people to invite me to things: usually—often—sometimes—occasionally—rarely—never. (2) I like

one is inclined to dismiss it;* yet there are a large number and variety of studies attesting to its validity.

One such study examined the selection of roommates among college fraternity members. The FIRO theory allows one to predict the amount of attraction between two individuals. For example, one individual who wishes very much to control and another who wishes very much to be controlled would be highly compatible (if their other two need areas also intermeshed). The selection of roommates by the college students was significantly predicted by this compatibility score.

There is evidence suggesting that the FIRO-B predicts interpersonal behavior on a psychiatric ward. Gard and Bendig [17] explored the relationship between the FIRO-B score (what patients say about their interpersonal behavior) and their actual behavior. In a well-designed project, they studied 112 male Veterans Administration patients who were hospitalized for a psychotic or neurotic illness or some orthopedic disorder. Behavior ratings along a specially designed scale relevant to inclusive, affectionate, and control behavior were made by nursing personnel over a five-day period. They found that the "traits measured by Schutz's self-report questionnaire are expressed in the behavior of psychiatric subjects and can be objectively reported by observers." [17]

There are, however, no direct studies, to my knowledge, of the ability of the FIRO-B to predict interpersonal behavior in small groups. A relevant study,[18] however, demonstrated that when four groups (at a human relations laboratory) were deliberately composed from FIRO scores of individuals with similar interpersonal needs, they were able to identify significantly better than chance their own groups from the description of what these groups should be like from their FIRO composition. Descriptions of the course of the groups suggested that each group focused on particular areas which were predictable by FIRO-B measurements.† The FIRO-B has been used in a considerable amount of small group research and not only has proved useful in its present form but suggests that, as more re-

---

people to include me in their activities: usually—often—sometimes—occasionally—rarely —never. (3) I like people to invite me to things: most people—many people—some people—a few people—one or two people—nobody. (4) I like people to invite me to join their activities: most people—many people—some people—a few people—one or two people—nobody.

* Indeed Schutz in the preface to the 1966 edition stated, "My feelings about the material in this book range from thinking it is not only a remarkable system, but a way of life, to wondering how anyone can take it seriously." [14]

† These descriptions may have been biased, however, in that they were obtained months later from the leaders, who by then had been informed about the design of the experiment.

fined tools become available, an interpersonal classificatory system is a feasible as well as a highly necessary development in the field.

New Diagnostic Procedures Which Directly Sample Group Relevant Behavior. Goldstein, Heller, and Sechrest [19] in their scholarly consideration of this topic suggest that the prediction of within-group behavior will be most accurate when it is based on direct behavioral measurement of the individual when he is engaged in a task closely related to the group therapy situation. In other words, the closer we can approximate actual observation of the individual in his subsequent therapy group, the more accurate will be our prediction of his behavior. There is abundant research evidence to support this thesis. If an individual is kept in the same interpersonal format, his behavior will show a consistency over time even though the individuals with whom he must interact are rotated. Research demonstrating this has used children-adult interaction,[20] therapist-patient interaction,[21] and small group interaction.[7, 22] For example, Moos and Clemes [21] have demonstrated that a patient seen by several individual therapists in rotation will not only be consistent in his behavior but will change the behavior of each of the therapists!

The implications of these findings are that, since we cannot accurately predict group behavior from behavior in an individual interview, we should consider obtaining data about the patient's behavior in a group setting. Indeed there has been some practical application of this principle. For example, in screening applicants for positions which require group-related skills, a procedure for observing their behavior in related group situations has been used. Thus a group interview test has been used to select officers for the German Air Force,[23] shipyard foremen,[24] Public Health Officers,[25] as well as many types of public and business executives.[26]

This general principle can be refined further, however, since there is additional research which demonstrates that behavior in one group is especially consistent with behavior in previous groups if the groups are similar with regard to composition,[27] group task,[28, 29] group norms,[30] expected role behavior,[30] or global group characteristics (e.g., climate, cohesiveness).[31] In other words, although an individual's behavior is broadly consistent from one group to the next, nevertheless there is still a wide range of behavior at his disposal. The individual's specific behavior in the new group is influenced by the task and the structural properties of the group and by the specific interpersonal styles of the other group members. The further implication, then, is that we can obtain the most relevant data for prediction of subsequent group behavior by observing an individual behave in a group which is as similar as possible to the one for which he is being screened. The most literal application of this principle is to predict the behavior of the applicant by arranging for him to meet with the therapy group for which he is being considered and to observe his behavior in this setting. In fact, Foulkes [32] and Bach [33] suggest the selection technique of having prospective members visit the group and letting the group carry out its own selection. Clinically, however, this procedure is inefficient: there is considerable disruption to the group; the members are disinclined to reject a prospective member unless there is some glaring incompatibility; furthermore, the prospective member is "on trial," as it were, and a representative sample of his behavior may not be obtained.

A promising development with implications for both research and clinical practice is the test group or waiting list group, a temporary group constituted from a clinic waiting list. The prospective group therapy patient is placed in the test group, his behavior is observed, and on the basis of this data he is then referred to a specific therapy or research group. In an exploratory study Stone, Parloff, and Frank [34] formed four groups of fifteen patients each from the group therapy waiting list which met weekly from four to eight times. Observers noted that the waiting group behavior of the patients was predictive of their behavior in their subsequent long-term therapy group.* These workers found, as did Abrahams and Enright,[35] who used a group diagnostic procedure for all patients applying for treatment, that the waiting procedure is clinically benign; patients did not react adversely to the group. Malamud and Machover [36] organized large groups of approximately thirty patients from the clinic waiting list. These groups were seen for fifteen sessions of highly structured workshops designed to prepare them for therapy. This waiting list group proved very successful; not only were the patients tided over the waiting period, but many reported significant benefit from the experience.

The definitive clinical research study demonstrating that patient behavior in waiting groups will be the same as later behavior in therapy groups has yet to be done. There is, however, so much corroborating evidence from human relations group research† that we can accept this hypothesis with a reasonable degree of certainty.[37, 38]

---

* Waiting group behavior was rated by independent observers, with high inter-rater reliability, on a dependence-dominance scale. Therapy group behavior, however, was sampled by unsystematic clinical observation.

† Generally, the research procedure is to assign subjects to groups meeting for a predetermined number of meetings and to systematically observe their behavior. At this point the researchers re-group the members into new groups according to the particular aspect of behavior under the study. Since the bulk of the research has been done by non-clinicians, the attitudes and behaviors are described in non-clinical but nevertheless clinically relevant terms. Subjects may thus be placed in groups according to whether

For practitioners or clinics with limited waiting lists and facilities, the concept of trial groups may be only an intriguing, perhaps fanciful, research idea. A less accurate but more accessible method of obtaining similar data is an interpersonally oriented initial interview. Instead of conducting the traditional psychiatric diagnostic interview, the therapist shifts his focus to an interpersonal history when examining prospective group patients. Detailed inquiry should be made into the patient's interpersonal and group relationships, his relationships with early chums, closest prolonged friendships, and degree of intimacy with members of both sexes. Many of Sullivan's interview techniques [39] are of great value in this task. It is informative, for example, when inquiring about friendships to ask for the names of best friends and what has become of them. A detailed history of formal and informal groups is valuable, of childhood and adult cliques, of fraternities, of club memberships, of gangs, of teams, of elected offices, and informal roles and status positions. The validity of this type of interview is yet to be determined but, to my mind, it seems far more relevant to subsequent group behavior than an intrapsychically focused interview.

Powdermaker and Frank [40] described an interpersonal relations interview which, along with a standard psychiatric interview and psychological testing, comprised the pretherapy diagnostic workup. From this information conjectures about the patients' subsequent in-group behavior were made, many of which were correct. Examples of accurate predictions were: "will dominate the group by a flood of speech and advice" or "will have considerable difficulty in showing feelings but will have compulsion to please the doctor and other members," will be "bland and socially skillful, tending to seek the doctor's attention while ignoring the other members," "will have a wait-and-see attitude," "will have a sarcastic, superior 'show-me' attitude and be reluctant to discuss his problems."

There have been several attempts to design new psychological tests to predict subsequent group behavior. Variants of the Thematic Apperception Test,[41] Sentence Association Test,[42] Sentence Completion Test,[43] and a sixty-item, self-report Q-sort [44] have all been used for this purpose with only equivocal results.

Psychological tests which measure traits or personality needs invariably yield only low level correlations with subsequent group behavior; obviously behavior is multidetermined and is heavily influenced by social as

---

they prefer high or low structure, or positive or negative affect, or whether they are active or passive or high or low participators, or assume or shun leadership.[37, 38] The trial groups may be discontinued at this point or they may serve as a control group against which to compare the experimentally composed group.

well as personality factors. A comprehensive predictive system which attempted to take into consideration several salient determinants was used by Couch [45, 46] to demonstrate the predictability of the individual's behavior in laboratory task groups.* Couch studied four determinants of interpersonal behavior:

1. The personality needs †
2. The concealment defenses‡—a measure of the degree to which an individual would tend to conceal his underlying needs from overt manifestation
3. The apperceived press§—the individual's perception of the attitude and emotional feelings toward him
4. The behavioral press ‖—the overt behavioral acts directed toward the individual

These four determinants were then correlated with the individual's actual behavior.# Each of the determinants separately showed a positive correlation with the individual's group behavior,** and summed together they have an impressively high correlation coefficient. The research illustrates, in the author's words, "that individual behavior is multiply determined and can be explained with considerable completeness if the several psychological determinants are considered in combination with one another in an integrated explanatory framework."[45]

Another possible approach to initial screening may be through the use of a simulated group test. A simulated group has been used in social psychological research design to establish unity of environment. For example, a subject is told that he is listening through earphones to a group discussion in the adjoining room and asked for his reactions to the group. The "group" is a tape-recorded simulation of a group. This approach has also been used to test the effects of group pressure on the autokinetic estimation task.[47] Clinicians, to the best of my knowledge, have not employed

---

* These task groups were five-member Harvard University undergraduate volunteer leaderless groups which were asked to discuss and solve some problem in human relations.

† Obtained from a battery of psychological assessment questionnaires.

‡ Obtained from clinical assessment in combination with objective psychological tests.

§ Obtained from a self-administered questionnaire.

‖ Obtained from objective ratings of behavior.

Rated by objective raters along the dimensions of interpersonal dominance, affect, involvement, and hostility.

** Of the four, "behavioral press" showed by far the highest correlation with the patient's behavior; this is further evidence for the general principle that the closer the testing situation is to the subsequent clinical situation, the more accurately can subsequent behavior be predicted.

this technique. However, it may not be utterly fantastic to use as a diagnostic tool a movie or a videotape of a therapy group of patients (with proper permission, of course) or a simulated therapy group of actors following a script. At various points the film could be stopped and the patient queried about his emotional response, his ideas about what's happening, or what he might say or do if he were in the group. Strupp and Jenkins [48] have used films of simulated individual interviews as a teaching technique and as an examination for students of psychiatry.

In summary, the prediction of subsequent group behavior from a pretherapy diagnostic procedure seems completely feasible. Of all the prediction methods, the traditional intake individual interview appears the least accurate and yet the most commonly used. An individual's group behavior will vary depending on his internal psychological needs, his manner of expressing them and the task, interpersonal composition and norms of his social environment. A general principle, however, is that the more similar the intake procedure is to the actual group situation, the more accurate will be the prediction of his behavior. The most promising single clinical method may be the observation of the patient's behavior in an intake or waiting list group.

Principles of Group Composition

To return now to the central question: given the most ideal circumstances —a large number of patient applicants and a wealth of information by which we can predict behavior—how shall we compose our therapy group?

Perhaps the reason for the scarcity of interest in the prediction of subsequent group behavior is that the amount of information about group composition is even more rudimentary. Why, indeed, bother refining tools to predict group behavior if we lack the knowledge of how to use this information? Although most clinicians sense that the composition of a group profoundly influences its future course, the actual mechanism of influence has eluded clarification. I have had the opportunity to study closely the conception, birth, and development of approximately fifty therapy groups —my own and others'—and have been struck repeatedly by the fact that some groups seem to "jell" immediately, some more slowly, while other groups founder painfully, spinning off members, and only emerge as working groups after several cycles of attrition and addition of members. It has been my impression that whether or not the group "jells" is only in part related to the competence or efforts of the therapist or to the number of "good" patients in the group; in large part the critical variable is some, as yet unclear, blending of the members.

If we are to discuss group composition meaningfully, we must hope to arrive eventually at the conclusion that Method X, as compared to Method Y, is a more effective way to compose therapy groups. Yet there is no satisfactory gauge of effectiveness; group outcome studies are crude, and no rigorous study exists which investigates the relationship between group composition and the ultimate criterion—therapy outcome. We must therefore rely on nonsystematic clinical observations and studies which, though relevant to composition, stem from nontherapy settings.

CLINICAL OBSERVATIONS ABOUT GROUP COMPOSITION

The impressions of individual clinicians regarding the effects of group composition must be evaluated with caution. The lack of a common language describing behavior, the problems of outcome evaluation, the theoretical biases of the therapist, and the limited number of groups that any one clinician may treat, all limit the validity of clinical impressions in this area.

There appears to be a general clinical sentiment that heterogeneous groups have advantages over homogeneous groups for intensive interactional group therapy.[33, 49, 50, 51] Homogeneous groups are believed to "jell" more quickly, to become more cohesive, to offer more immediate support to the group members, to have better attendance, less conflict, and to provide more rapid symptomatic relief. On the other hand, however, the homogeneous group, in contrast to the heterogeneous group, is widely believed to tend to remain at superficial levels and to be an ineffective medium for the altering of character structure.

The issue becomes clouded when we ask, "Homogeneous for what?" "Heterogeneous for what?" For age? Sex? Symptom complex? Marital Status? Education? Socioeconomic status? Verbal skills? Psychosexual development? Psychiatric diagnostic categories? Interpersonal needs? Which are the critical variables? Is a group composed of mothers with infanticidal obsessions[52] a homogeneous group because of the shared symptom, or a heterogeneous group because of the wide range of personality traits of the members?

Whitaker and Lieberman[53] help to clarify the issue by suggesting that the group therapist strive for maximum heterogeneity in the patients' conflict areas and patterns of coping, and at the same time strive for homogeneity of the patients' degree of vulnerability and capacity to tolerate anxiety. For example, they state that a homogeneous group of individuals, all with major conflicts about hostility which were dealt with through denial, could hardly offer therapeutic benefit to its members. However, a group with a wide range of vulnerability (loosely defined as ego strength) will, for different reasons, also be retarded; the most vulnerable patient will place limits on the group, which will become highly restrictive to the less vulnerable ones. In the same vein, Foulkes and Anthony [54] suggest blending together a "mixed bag of diagnoses and disturbances" to form a therapeutically effective group. "The greater the span between the polar types, the higher the therapeutic potential, *if the group can stand it.*"

Unfolding from these clinical observations, is the rule that a degree of incompatibility must exist between the patient and the interpersonal need culture of the group if change is to occur. This principle—that change is preceded by a state of dissonance or incongruity—has considerable social psychological research backing and is a concept to which we will return later.

However, heterogeneity must not proceed at the price of creating a group isolate. Consider the age variable; if there is one fifty-year-old member in a group of very young adults, he may choose or be forced to assume the role of the personified older generation. Stereotyping of his role (and of those of the younger patients) occurs, and the required interpersonal honesty and intimacy fails to materialize. A similar process may occur in an adult group with a lone late adolescent who assumes the unruly teenager role. Yet there are advantages to having an age spread in the group: patients, through working out their intermember relationships, will come to understand their past, present, and future relationships with a wider range of significant people—parents, peers, and children.

The solution of the problem of how to maintain heterogeneity without creating isolates may be to provide some pairing for each patient. One group therapist [55] suggested the "Noah's Ark" principle of group composition in which each member should have his compeer. Similarly Samuels suggests a composition technique of "group balance,"[56] in which the therapist attempts to balance the group for these seven factors: transference toward the therapist, countertransference, passive-aggressivity, ability to express affect, insight or introspective ability, homosexuality-heterosexuality, ego strength. Samuels states that group movement may be curtailed in the presence of unanimous positive or negative transference toward the therapist. Too few members who are unable to express affect would result in a group's "resembling a graduate seminar composed of students not even particularly interested in the subject"; too much affect expression could lead to an "unendurably explosive" group. Similar considerations may be stated for the other categories. The problem of such an approach, recognized by the author, is the size of the universe from which these inexact seven characteristics are arbitrarily selected. The author selected those which appeared most important to him on the basis of his clinical experience; others might select considerably different factors or define the same ones differently. Although the article ends with the familiar statement that work to objectify and validate these characteristics is in progress, no refinement has appeared in the subsequent five years. The methodological problems are insurmountable unless we have a firm conceptual basis from which to operate.

The concept of heterogeneity even with pairing or balance is not without its limitations. For example, if the group has too extreme an age range, the life-stage problems of some members may be so alien to others that cohesiveness is seriously impaired. Aged individuals concerned about subsistence and the process of disengagement [57] are perhaps irreconcilably distant from late adolescents and young adults dealing urgently with identity diffusion problems.

Bach [58] employs the concept of role heterogeneity in his approach to composition. In adding a new member, his primary consideration is, "What role is open in the group?" The therapist should strive to increase the group's "role repertoire, in order to obtain better complementation between roles." Theoretically such an orientation seems quite desirable. Practically, however, it suffers from a lack of clarity. What are the roles in a therapy group? Bach [59] mentions the "guardian of democracy," the time keeper, the aggressive male, the leader, and the individual who provides humorous tension release. We might add: the provocateur, the scapegoat, the doctor's helper,[60] the help-rejecting complainer,[60] the self-righteous moralist,[61] the "star," the fight, flight, dependency, or pairing leaders, the group hysteric, the technical executive leader, the social emotional leader, the great man, etc., etc.

Can we expand the list arbitrarily and indefinitely by listing behavior trait constellations, or are there fixed roles, constant from group to group, which members are forced to fill?* Until these problems are answered by

---

* Bavelas, working with nonclinical groups, reports an interesting approach to the elucidation of roles.[62] He organized groups of eight students with the task of discussing and reaching a decision about a human relations problem. The meetings were tape recorded and then transcribed without any notation about who said what. Consultants were then asked to read the transcript and to guess the number of members in each group. The results were that, with great consistency, the consultants guessed that there were three people (roles) in the groups: two advocates of opposing viewpoints and a conciliator.

well-designed systematic research the question, "What role is open in the group?" will contribute little toward an effective approach to group composition.

Leary [63] describes a method of group composition using his interpersonal diagnostic nosology; an eight-member therapy group is formed by including two patients whose level I (public) profiles fall in each quadrant of his interpersonal circular grid, (see Table 8–1). His clinical impression was that groups composed in this manner proved to be effective and fast-moving groups. However, no systematic evaluative studies have validated this procedure,[64] and Leary himself has since pursued other interests.

To these clinical observations I shall add one of my own. As a supervisor and researcher, I had an opportunity to study closely the entire thirty-month course of an outpatient group led by Dr. R. and Dr. M., two psychiatric residents of average competence. The group consisted of seven members, all in their twenties; six of whom could be classified as schizoid personalities. The one patient who was considerably different, a passive-aggressive woman, was also frightened by the prospects of intimacy and dropped out of the group after five months. Another patient was called for military duty at the end of a year, and a third was lost to the San Francisco hippie movement at the end of two years. Two new patients were brought in to replace the losses.

The most striking feature of this homogeneous schizoid group was that it was extraordinarily dull. Everything associated with the group, the meetings, the tape recordings, the written summaries, the supervisory sessions, were low-keyed, affectless, plodding, and dull. Nothing seemed to be happening; there was no discernible movement individually among the patients or in the group as a whole. And yet the attendance was near perfect and the group cohesiveness extraordinarily high.* Since all the group patients in the Stanford clinic over this period of time were subjects in outcome research,[65, 69] thorough evaluations of clinical progress were available both at the end of one year and at the end of thirty months. The patients in this group, both the original four and the replacements, had done extraordinarily well and had undergone substantial characterologic changes as well as complete symptomatic remission. In fact, very few other groups I have studied have had comparably good results. My views about group composition were influenced by this group, and I have come

* Many of the outpatient groups in the Stanford outpatient clinic were involved in research involving the measurement of group cohesiveness (using a patient-administered cohesiveness questionnaire).[65, 66, 67, 68] The group led by Dr. R. and Dr. M. scored higher on these questionnaires than any other group.

to attach great importance to group stability, attendance, and cohesiveness. Group cohesiveness, it must be noted, is not synonymous with in-group comfort, or social ease. Often quite the reverse occurs; only in a cohesive group can a patient experience and tolerate extreme discomfort or discouragement.

While, in theory, I agree with the concept of composing a group of individuals with varied interpersonal stresses and needs, I feel that in practice it may represent a spurious issue. Only when clinical practice begins to take advantage of some of the more sophisticated diagnostic techniques which we have described can we really scientifically compose a group. Given the limited predictive value of our traditional screening interview, it is probable that we delude ourselves if we think we can achieve the type of subtle balance and personality interlocking necessary to make a real difference in group functioning. For example, although six of the seven patients in Dr. R. and Dr. M.'s group were diagnosed as schizoid personalities, they differed far more than they resembled one another. This apparently "homogeneous" group, contrary to the clinical dictum, did not remain at a superficial level and effected very significant personality changes in its members. Although I have studied many so-called homogeneous groups (e.g., ulcer patients, dermatological patients, obese women, parents of delinquent children) which have remained superficial, I felt that this was the effect, not of homogeneity, but of the set of the therapist and the restricted culture which he helped fashion. The organization of a group of individuals around a common symptom or around their children's problems may convey powerful implicit culture-relevant messages which operate toward group norms of restriction, a search for similarities, a submergence of individuality, and a discouragement of self-disclosure and interpersonal honesty. Norms, as we elaborated in Chapter 5, once set into motion, may become self-perpetuating and difficult to change.

A SYSTEMATIC STUDY OF GROUP COMPOSITION

As I have already discussed, there are no research studies which directly investigate the effect of group composition on group therapy outcome. However, there is one slightly peripheral study which is relevant to group composition. In this study Yalom and Rand [68] demonstrated the effect of group composition on group cohesiveness. Although group cohesiveness is by no means synonymous with therapy outcome, there is considerable evidence (summarized in Chapter 3) that cohesiveness is positively related to outcome and may be considered a way station or an intervening variable.* The Yalom-Rand project studied forty outpatients shortly before they began therapy in five newly forming therapy groups. The FIRO-B test was administered and the interpersonal compatibility of each member vis-à-vis each other member of his group was calculated. Furthermore, by summating all the dyads of the group, a total group compatibility [14] score was obtained for each group. These group and individual compatibility scores were then correlated with individual and total group cohesiveness scores obtained at the sixth and twelfth meetings. The results demonstrated that:

1. FIRO-B compatibility of the group correlated significantly with group cohesiveness.†
2. The patients who dropped out of therapy early in the course of the group had lower FIRO-B compatibility than the group continuers.
3. Any two members who showed extreme incompatibility with each other were significantly less satisfied with the group.

In other words, by giving a rather superficial interpersonal inventory questionnaire to a group of patients before their first contact with each other, one is able to say something, quite accurately, about the cohesiveness of their therapy group six weeks and twelve weeks later. Clinically this study suggests that a certain type of homogeneity‡ enhances the formation of group cohesiveness and that patients who are markedly dissonant with the rest of the group in that regard tend to be dissatisfied with the group and to leave therapy prematurely.

STUDIES OF COMPOSITION AND OUTCOME IN NONTHERAPY GROUPS

There have been several attempts to study the relationship between composition and outcome in human relations groups. I shall merely sum-

* From the standpoint of research methodology, an intervening variable is a simplifying device; it may be measured soon after the beginning of the group and many of the problems of long-term follow-up circumvented.

† This finding must be interpreted with caution; it has not yet been replicated, and Koran [70] working with a similar patient population failed to demonstrate a correlation between FIRO-B compatibility and group cohesiveness.

‡ Several types of compatibility may be computed from the FIRO-B profiles. This study used "interchange compatibility"—the type postulated by Schutz as most relevant for small groups—and is a measure of how much intermember agreement there is about the amount of interchange that should occur in each of the interpersonal need areas (affection, control, exclusion).[14]

marize the finding of these studies here; interested readers should refer to the articles cited for details of the study. First, let us examine the general research procedure of these studies in order to determine their relevance to group therapy.

The subjects are usually participants in a human relations laboratory (generally from the fields of education, industry, or behavioral science) or college student volunteers; they may be broadly considered "normals," although no psychiatric screening is performed. Usually homogeneous or heterogeneous groups are formed on the basis of some cluster of personality variables which are obtained from psychological tests or from behavioral observations of the subjects in trial groups. The groups are short-term, meeting for six to fifteen sessions, generally over a short period (one to two weeks) of time. Outcome of the groups and of the individuals is assessed by some observational method and/or by subject-administered questionnaires. The personality variables most often used are:

1. "Person-oriented" individuals or "task-oriented" individuals. "Person-oriented" individuals value such characteristics as warmth, openness, sympathy, and genuineness; "task-oriented" individuals value competence, ability, responsibility, initiative, and energy. A similar, overlapping dichotomy used in other studies is the "low structure" versus the "high structure" individual [38, 71]—"high structure" characteristics include a preference for clarity and order with less interest in personal feelings and a tendency to defer to authority figures; "low structure" characteristics include a readiness to recognize and examine positive and negative feelings and interpersonal relationships.
2. FIRO-B characteristics.
3. Group culture preference (Bionic basic assumption cultures of dependency, flight, fight, pairing) obtained from a self-administered questionnaire.[72]

In general the group composition experimental work is of poor quality, the highly sophisticated statistical technique and conclusive findings reported by several reviews [38, 71, 73, 74] notwithstanding. Observer bias is often uncontrolled; subjects are often asked to compare experimental groups with a previous group without controls for the length of time in each group or the sequence of the two experiences; in addition the experimental groups are often very short-term, and the effects of the developmental stage of the group may have been overlooked. The most serious shortcoming is in the measurement of individual outcome. Often the measures consist only of a few questions, the reliability and validity of which were unevaluated, asked of the subjects or other group members. The follow-up interval is, with one exception,[75] quite brief, and evaluation of change usually immediately follows the group experience (always a questionable procedure since the wave of positive sentiment at the termination of the group often obviates individual objectivity). With these reservations let us consider the research findings:

1. Homogeneous groups of task-oriented, high structure, impersonal individuals function as effective human relations groups which produce change in the members. Apparently these groups offer a combination of support and challenge. The members are supported by their perceived similarity and challenged by the task of the group, which demands that they interact more intensively and intimately than is their wont. The groups tend to be highly cohesive.[37, 76, 77]

2. Homogeneous groups of person-oriented, low structure individuals do *not* function as effective human relations groups, although the groups are interactive and initially stimulating. Apparently these groups offer too little challenge to the members, who are comfortable with the group task and with the other members.[37, 78]

3. Homogeneous groups of individuals with the same attitudes toward dominance produce less change than groups which are heterogeneously composed for the same variable.[79]

4. There is a lack of consensus about mixed half-and-half (person-oriented and task-oriented) groups. They have been generally found to be ineffective, incompatible, poorly cohesive groups, which do not move toward the goals of exploration, sharing, and intimate interaction.[38, 80] On the other hand, there is some modest evidence from one study that they induce greater change in the members.[71]

5. Task groups which are homogeneous (FIRO-B compatibility) are more productive and more cohesive than heterogeneous groups.[81]

6. Task groups which are homogeneous for culture preference (flight or pairing) [76] are more efficient than mixed groups. There is a suggestion that the mixed groups suffer from the lack of a liaison person to bridge the two subgroups.

7. In general the atmosphere of groups is predictable from the composition.[18, 82]

Overview of Group Composition

It would be most gratifying at this point to integrate these clinical and experimental findings, to point out hitherto unseen lines of cleavage and coalescence, and to emerge with a crisp theory of group composition which had not only firm experimental foundations but also immediate practical applicability. Unfortunately the insubstantial nature of the data does not permit such a synthesis.

Let us consider, however, the most unequivocal findings. The composition of the group makes a difference; it influences many aspects of group function. A group can be composed which will have certain predictable short-term characteristics: for example, high cohesion, high conflict, high flight, high dependency. Furthermore we can, if we choose to use available procedures, predict the group behavior of the individual, along a variety of parameters.

What we do *not* know, however, is the relationship between any of these group characteristics and the ultimate therapy outcome of the group members. Furthermore, we lack knowledge of the effect of the group leader's behavior on the characteristics of the group, and we do not know how long the ongoing group will manifest these characteristics. A consideration of the theoretical underpinning of the two general approaches to group composition may help clarify the issue. Underlying the heterogeneous approach to composition are two theoretical rationales which may be labeled the "social microcosm theory" and the "dissonance theory." Underlying the homogeneous group composition approach is the "group cohesiveness" theory.

The *"social microcosm" theory* postulates that since the group is regarded as a miniaturized social universe in which patients are urged to develop new methods of interpersonal interaction, then the group should be a heterogeneous one to maximize learning opportunities. It should resemble the real social universe by being composed of individuals of different sexes, professions, ages, socioeconomic and educational levels; in other words, it should be a demographic heterodox.

The *dissonance theory*, as applied to group therapy, also suggests a heterogeneous compositional approach but for a somewhat different reason. Learning or change is likely to occur when the individual, in a state of dissonance, acts to reduce that dissonance. Dissonance creates a state of psychological discomfort and propels the individual to attempt to achieve a more consonant state. If individuals find themselves in a group in which membership has many desirable features (for example, hopes of alleviation of suffering, attraction toward the leader and other members) but at the same time makes tension-producing demands (for example, self-disclosure or interpersonal confrontation), then they will experience a state of cognitive imbalance, or to use Newcomb's term, "asymmetry."[83] Similarly a state of discomfort occurs when the individual, in a valued group, finds that his interpersonal needs are unfulfilled, or when his customary style of interpersonal behavior produces discordant effects. The individual in these circumstances will search for ways to reduce his discomfort. For example, he may leave the group or, preferably, he may begin to experiment with new forms of behavior. To maximize these developments, the heterogeneous argument suggests that the patient be exposed to other individuals in the group who will not fulfill his interpersonal needs (and thus reinforce his neurotic position) but will frustrate him, challenge him, make him aware of different conflict areas, and who will also demonstrate alternative interpersonal modes. Therefore, it is argued, members with varying interpersonal styles and conflicts should be included in a group. If the frustration and challenge is too great, however, and the staying forces (the attraction to the group) too small, no real asymmetry or dissonance occurs; the individual does not change but instead physically or psychologically leaves the group. (Here we see the interface between the dissonance theory and the next model, the cohesiveness theory.) If the challenge is too small, however, no learning occurs either; members will collude, and exploration will be inhibited. The dissonance theory thus argues for a broad personality heterodox.

The *cohesiveness theory,* underlying the homogeneous approach to group composition, posits, quite simply, that attraction to the group is the critical intervening variable to outcome and that composition should proceed along the lines of assembling a cohesive, compatible group.

How can we reconcile or judge these approaches? First, let me point out that I have focused sharply on the differences between them for purposes of clarity; in fact, however, there is a permeable interface between each of the three. Thus the "social microcosm" model may demand personality heterogeneity as well as demographic heterogeneity, if the group is to be, in fact, a simulated social universe; the "dissonance" model demands a degree of cohesiveness and may automatically include demographic heterogeneity in its search for personality heterogeneity.

Second, there is no group therapy research support for the dissonance model. There is great clinical consensus (my own included) that group therapy patients should be exposed to a variety of conflict areas, coping methods, and conflicting interpersonal styles, and that conflict in general is essential to the therapeutic process;[84] however, there is no evidence that deliberately heterogeneously composed groups facilitate therapy and, as cited above, there is some modest evidence to the contrary.

On the other hand, there is a body of small group research evidence which supports the cohesiveness concept. Interpersonally compatible therapy groups (homogeneous for FIRO interchange compatibility) will develop greater cohesiveness; members of cohesive groups have better attendance, are more able to express and tolerate hostility, are more apt to attempt to influence others, and are in turn themselves more influenceable; members with greater attraction to their group have better therapeutic outcome; patients who are less compatible with the other members tend to drop out of the therapy group as do any two members with marked mutual incompatibility; members with the greatest interpersonal compatibility become the most popular group members, and group popularity is highly correlated with successful outcome.

The fear that a homogeneous group will be unproductive, constricted, or conflict-free or will deal with a narrow range of interpersonal concerns is unfounded for several reasons. First, there are few individuals whose pathology is indeed monolithic; few individuals who, despite their chief conflict area, do not also encounter conflicts in intimacy or authority, for example. Secondly, the group developmental process may demand certain role assumption. For example, the laws of group development (see Chapter 10) demand that the group deal with issues of control, authority, and the hierarchy of dominance. In a group with several control-conflicted individuals, this phase may appear early or very sharply. In a group with an absence of these individuals, other members who are less conflicted in the area of dependency and authority may be forced to deal with this area as the group inevitably moves into this phase of development. If certain roles are not filled in the group, most leaders, consciously or unconsciously,* alter their behavior to fill the void.

We must also keep in mind that the group experience is a subjective and individualized one. Patients according to their assumptive worlds, may experience the same incident in different, highly personalized ways. A therapist or an observer often fails to appreciate the personal salience of certain issues for some patients. I have on many occasions been impressed, when interviewing patients about their course of therapy, by how events that were cited by some as critical incidents in therapy appeared trivial or inconsequential to others.

Furthermore, no therapy group with proper leadership can be too comfortable or fail to provide dissonance for its members because the members must invariably clash with the group task. To develop trust, to disclose oneself, to develop intimacy, to examine oneself, to confront others, are all discordant tasks to individuals who have chronically encountered problems in interpersonal relationships. Members of impersonal, schizoid groups (recall the group of Dr. R. and Dr. M.) appear to provide so much mutual support that they can gradually engage in the group task which the therapist has kept before the group. The nonproduc-

* Lieberman demonstrated that in experimentally composed groups which have an artificially induced imbalance of emotionality, the group leader will unconsciously fill the void.[82]

tive homogeneous group of person-oriented individuals reported in T-group research is not relevant to group therapy because of the exceedingly low probability that such a group of individuals would seek psychiatric aid. It is my impression that the homogeneous group of individuals, placed together because of a common symptom or problem, which remains on a shallow, restricted level is entirely an iatrogenic phenomenon—a self-fulfilling prophecy on the part of the therapist.

On the basis of our present state of knowledge, therefore, I propose that cohesiveness be our primary guideline in the composition of therapy groups. The hoped-for dissonance will unfold in the group, provided the therapist functions effectively in the pretherapy orientation of patients and during the early group meetings. Group integrity should be a primary concern, and we must select patients with the lowest possible likelihood of premature termination. Patients with a high likelihood of being incompatible with the prevailing group culture or of being markedly incompatible with at least one other member should not be included in the group. The time and energy of the therapist which is often invested in the elusive task of balancing or casting a group can be better spent in the pretherapy preparation of the group patients (to be discussed in the next chapter).

A cohesiveness frame of reference for group composition is by no means inconsistent with the notion of demographic heterogeneity; however, it does set limits for the degree of heterogeneity. Group therapy clarifies interpersonal relationships within the group and provides the members with carryover into their external lives. It makes eminently good sense to suppose that the greater the range of interpersonal relationships clarified within the group, the more universal the carryover will be. Some patients, with restricted social environments, derive great benefit from interacting with individuals from different cultural, economic, or educational strata. Knowing and accepting an individual previously deemed alien or unacceptable is a source of great therapeutic benefit. However, the demographic variation must be conceived within the general rubric of cohesiveness; too extreme a variation breeds deviancy and undermines cohesiveness.

The available data on group composition do not permit more precise clinical guidelines to be formulated. Perhaps in no area of group therapy is there a greater need and potential for clinical research. This chapter has attempted to describe the more promising directions for research as well as available methodology.

REFERENCES

1. *Diagnostic and Statistical Manual of Mental Disorders,* (2nd ed.; Washington, D.C.: American Psychiatric Association, 1968).
2. P. Ash, "The Reliability of Psychiatric Diagnosis," *J. Abnorm. Soc. Psychol., 44:* 272–276, 1949.
3. A. T. Beck, C. H. Ward, M. Mendelson, J. E. Mock, and J. R. Erbaugh, "Reliability of Psychiatric Diagnoses: 2. A Study of Consistency of Clinical Judgments and Ratings," *Am. J. Psychiat., 119:* 351–357, 1962.
4. S. R. Slavson, "Criteria for Selection and Rejection of Patients for Various Kinds of Group Therapy," *Int. J. Group Psychother., 5:* 3–30, 1955.
5. J. Deer and A. W. Silver, "Predicting Participation and Behavior in Group Therapy from Test Protocols," *J. Clin. Psychol., 18:* 322–325, 1962.
6. C. Zimet, "Character Defense Preference and Group Therapy Interaction," *Arch. Gen. Psychiat., 3:* 168–175, 1960.
7. E. F. Borgatta and A. E. Esclenbach, "Factor Analysis of Rorschach Variable and Behavior Observation," *Psychol. Rep., 3:* 129–136, 1955.
8. W. Riese, "History and Principles of Classification of Nervous Diseases," *Bull. Hist. Med., 18:* 465–512, 1945.
9. K. Menninger, M. Mayman, and P. Pruyser, *The Vital Balance* (New York: Viking Press, 1963).
10. K. Horney, *Neurosis and Human Growth* (New York: W. W. Norton, 1950).
11. E. Fromm, *Man for Himself* (New York: Rinehart, 1947).
12. E. Fromm, *Escape from Freedom* (New York: Farrar and Rinehart, 1941).
13. T. Leary, *Interpersonal Diagnosis of Personality* (New York: Ronald Press, 1957).
14. W. Schutz, *The Interpersonal Underworld* (Palo Alto, Calif.: Science and Behavior Books, 1966).
15. M. Freedman, T. Leary, A. Ossorio, and H. Coffey, "The Interpersonal Dimension of Personality," *J. Personal., 20:* 143–161, 1951.
16. H. Coffey, personal communication, 1967.
17. J. G. Gard and A. W. Bendig, "A Factor Analytic Study of Eysenck's and Schutz's Personality Dimensions and Psychiatric Groups," *J. Consult. Psychol., 28:* 252–258, 1964.
18. W. Schutz, "On Group Composition," *J. Abnorm. Soc. Psychol., 62:* 275–281, 1961.
19. A. Goldstein, K. Heller, and L. Sechrest, *Psychotherapy and the Psychology of Behavior Change* (New York: John Wiley and Sons, 1966), p. 329.
20. B. M. Bishop, "Mother-Child Interaction and the Social Behavior of Children," *Psychol. Monogr., 65:* No. 11, 1, 1951.
21. R. H. Moos and S. R. Clemes, "A Multivariate Study of the Patient-Therapist System," *J. Consult. Psychol., 31:* 119–130, 1967.
22. G. B. Bell and R. L. French, "Consistency of Individual Leadership Position in Small Groups of Varying Membership," in A. P. Hare, E. F. Borgatta, and R. F. Bales (eds.), *Small Groups* (New York: Knopf, 1955), pp. 275–280.
23. P. M. Fitts, "German Applied Psychology During World War II," *Am. Psychol., 1:* 151–161, 1946.
24. M. Mandell, "Validation of Group Oral Performance Test," *Personnel Psychol., 3:* 179–185, 1950.
25. B. M. Bass, "The Leaderless Group Discussion Technique," *Personnel Psychol., 3:* 17–32, 1950.
    139–146, 1950.
26. H. Fields, "The Group Interview Test: Its Strength," *Publ. Personnel Review, 11:*

27. E. F. Borgatta and R. F. Bales, "Interaction of Individuals in Reconstituted Groups," *Sociometry, 16:* 302–320, 1953.
28. E. F. Borgatta and R. F. Bales, "Task and Accumulation of Experience as Factors in the Interaction of Small Groups," *Sociometry, 16:* 239–252, 1953.
29. B. M. Bass, "Leadership," in *Psychology and Organizational Behavior* (New York: Harper, 1960).
30. V. Cervin, "Individual Behavior in Social Situations: Its Relation to Anxiety, Neuroticism and Group Solidarity," *J. Exper. Psychol., 51:* 161–168, 1956.
31. R. B. Cattell, D. R. Saunders, and G. F. Stice, "The Dimensions of Syntality in Small Groups," *J. Soc. Psychol., 28:* 57–78, 1948.
32. S. H. Foulkes and E. J. Anthony, *Group Psychotherapy—The Psychoanalytic Approach* (Harmondsworth, Middlesex: Penguin Books, 1957).
33. G. Bach, *Intensive Group Therapy* (New York: Ronald Press, 1954).
34. A. Stone, M. Parloff, and J. Frank, "The Use of Diagnostic Groups in a Group Therapy Program," *Int. J. Group Psychother., 4:* 274–284, 1954.
35. D. Abrahams and J. Enright, "Psychiatric Intake in Groups: A Pilot Study of Procedures, Problems and Prospects," *Am. J. Psychiat., 122:* 170–174, 1965.
36. D. Malamud and S. Machover, *Toward Self-Understanding* (Springfield, Ill.: Charles C. Thomas, 1965).
37. H. Baumgartel, unpublished research report (Washington, D.C.: National Training Laboratories, 1961).
38. R. Harrison, "Group Composition Models for Laboratory Design," *J. Appl. Behav. Sci., 1:* 409–432, 1965.
39. H. S. Sullivan, *The Psychiatric Interview* (New York: W. W. Norton, 1954).
40. F. Powdermaker and J. Frank, *Group Psychotherapy* (Cambridge, Mass.: Harvard University Press, 1953), pp. 553–564.
41. P. J. Aston, "Behavioral Correlates of Thematic Apperception Responses," unpublished manuscript, 1966.
42. J. Sutherland, H. S. Gill, and H. Phillipson, "Psychodiagnostic Appraisal in the Light of Recent Theoretical Developments," *Brit. J. Med. Psychol., 40:* 299–315, 1967.
43. S. Ben-Zeev, "Sociometric Choice and Patterns of Member Participation," in D. Stock and H. A. Thelen (eds.), *Emotional Dynamics and Group Culture* (New York: New York University Press, 1958), pp. 84–91.
44. W. F. Hill, "The Influence of Subgroups on Participation in Human Relations Training Groups," unpublished doctoral dissertation, University of Chicago, 1955.
45. A. Couch, "The Psychological Determinants of Interpersonal Behavior," Proceedings of the XIV International Congress of Applied Psychology, Copenhagen, August 13–19, 1961.
46. A. Couch, "Psychological Determinants of Interpersonal Behavior," unpublished doctoral dissertation, Harvard University, 1959–1960.
47. R. R. Blake and J. W. Brehm, "The Use of Tape Recording to Simulate a Group Atmosphere," *J. Abnorm. Soc. Psychol., 49:* 311–313, 1954.
48. H. Strupp and J. Jenkins, "The Development of Six Sound Motion Pictures Simulating Psychotherapeutic Situations," *J. Nerv. Ment. Dis., 136:* 317–328, 1963.
49. H. D. Mullan and M. Rosenbaum, *Group Psychotherapy* (New York: Free Press of Glencoe, 1962).
50. N. Locke, *Group Psychoanalysis* (New York: New York University Press, 1961).
51. Powdermaker and Frank, *op. cit.*, pp. 66–112.
52. H. M. Feinstein, N. Paul, and P. Esmiol, "Group Therapy for Mothers with Infanticidal Impulses," *Am. J. Psychiat., 120:* 882–886, 1964.
53. D. Whitaker and M. Lieberman, *Psychotherapy Through the Group Process* (New York: Atherton Press, 1964).
54. Foulkes and Anthony, *op. cit.*, p. 94.

55. F. K. Taylor, *The Analysis of Therapeutic Groups* (London: Oxford University Press, 1961).
56. A. S. Samuels, "The Use of Group Balance as a Therapeutic Technique," *Arch. Gen. Psychiat.*, *11:* 411–420, 1964.
57. E. Cummings and W. Henry, *Growing Old: The Process of Disengagement* (New York: Basic Books, 1961).
58. Bach, *op. cit.*, p. 25.
59. *Ibid.*, pp. 331–332.
60. J. Frank *et al.*, "Behavioral Patterns in Early Meetings of Therapeutic Groups," *Am. J. Psychiat.*, *108:* 771–778, 1952.
61. D. Rosenthal, J. Frank, and E. Nash, "The Self-Righteous Moralist in Early Meetings of Therapeutic Groups," *Psychiatry*, *17:* 215–223, 1954.
62. A. O. Bavelas, personal communication, 1968.
63. Leary, *op. cit.*, p. 428.
64. H. Coffey, personal communication, 1967.
65. I. D. Yalom, P. S. Houts, S. M. Zimerberg, and K. H. Rand, "Prediction of Improvement in Group Therapy," *Arch. Gen. Psychiat.*, *17:* 159–168, 1967.
66. I. D. Yalom, P. S. Houts, G. Newell, and K. H. Rand, "Preparation of Patients for Group Therapy: A Controlled Study," *Arch. Gen. Psychiat.*, *17:* 416–427, 1967.
67. A. D. Sklar, I. D. Yalom, S. M. Zimerberg, and G. Newell, "Time Extended Group Therapy: A Controlled Study," *Comparative Group Studies*, in press.
68. I. D. Yalom and K. H. Rand, "Compatibility and Cohesiveness in Therapy Groups," *Arch. Gen. Psychiat.*, *13:* 267–276, 1966.
69. I. D. Yalom, J. Tinklenberg, and M. Gilula, "Curative Factors in Group Therapy." Unpublished study.
70. L. Koran, unpublished data, 1969.
71. R. Harrison and B. Lubin, "Personal Style, Group Composition and Learning—Part 2," *J. Appl. Behav. Sci.*, *1:* 294–301, 1965.
72. Stock and Thelen, *op. cit.*, pp. 50–64.
73. R. Harrison and B. Lubin, "Personal Style, Group Composition and Learning—Part 1," *J. Appl. Behav. Sci.*, *1:* 286–294, 1965.
74. D. Stock, "A Survey of Research on T-Groups," in L. P. Bradford, J. R. Gibb, and K. D. Benne (eds.), *T-Group Theory and Laboratory Method* (New York: John Wiley and Sons, 1964), pp. 401–406.
75. M. A. Lieberman, "The Influence of Group Composition on Changes in Affective Approach," in Stock and Thelen, *op. cit.*, pp. 131–139.
76. I. Gradolph, "The Task Approach of Groups of Single-Type and Mixed-Type Valency Compositions," in Stock and Thelen, *op. cit.*, pp. 127–130.
77. T. C. Greening and H. Coffey, "Working with an 'Impersonal' T-Group," *J. Appl. Behav. Sci.*, *2:* 401–411, 1966.
78. D. Stock and J. Luft, "The T-E-T Design," unpublished manuscript (Washington, D.C.: National Training Laboratories, 1960).
79. H. Pollack, "Change in Homogeneous and Heterogeneous Sensitivity Training Groups," unpublished doctoral dissertation, University of California at Berkeley, 1966.
80. D. Stock and W. F. Hill, "Intersubgroup Dynamics as a Factor in Group Growth," in Stock and Thelen, *op. cit.*, pp. 207–221.
81. W. Schutz, *Interpersonal Underworld*, pp. 120–143.
82. M. A. Lieberman, "The Relationship of Group Climate to Individual Change," unpublished doctoral dissertation, University of Chicago, 1958.
83. T. M. Newcomb, "The Prediction of Interpersonal Attraction," *Am. Psychol.*, *11:* 575–586, 1956.
84. J. Frank, "Some Values of Conflict in Therapeutic Groups," *Group Psychother.*, *8:* 142–151, 1955.

9

CREATION OF THE GROUP: PLACE, TIME, SIZE, PREPARATION

✣

The Physical Setting

Prior to convening the group, the therapist must make some important decisions about the setting. He must secure an appropriate meeting place and establish policy about the life span of the group, admission of new members, the duration of each session, and the size of the group.

Group meetings may be held in any setting, provided that the room affords privacy and freedom from distraction. Some therapists prefer to have the members seated about a large circular table (a rectangular table is unwieldy since members on one side may be unable to see each other). Others prefer to have nothing in the center so that the patient's entire body is visible and his nonverbal or postural responses are more readily discernible.

If the group session is to be tape recorded or viewed through a viewing screen by students, the group's permission must be obtained in advance and ample opportunity provided for discussion of the procedure. A group which is to be observed continuously appears to forget about the viewing screen after a few weeks, but often in the context of working through authority issues with the leader members return to it months later with renewed interest. If there are to be only one or two student observers, they are best seated in the room, though out of the group circle; this proves, in the long run, less distracting than the viewing screen and allows the students to sample more of the group affect which in some inexplicable manner is often filtered out by the screen. The observers, if they are to be silent, should be cautioned to remain so; the group often attempts to draw them in and once they have spoken they find it increasingly difficult to be silent therafter.

Occasionally the group may ask to listen to a taped segment of a meeting on the tape recorder in order to clarify a particular issue, but as a regular procedure, relistening is too time-consuming to be practical.* Closed-circuit television and videotape have been used in group therapy for the past few years and will undoubtedly become an increasingly common adjunct to therapy. Although many therapists are convinced that their group would either refuse to be videotaped or else would be disrupted by the procedure, experience has shown that the group is far less concerned about the matter than the therapist. Videotapes, as we will show in Chapter 13, may be used in several ways in the group therapeutic work.

Open and Closed Groups

At their inception groups are designated by their leader as open or closed: a closed group, once begun, closes its gates, accepts no new members, and meets usually for a predetermined number of sessions; an open group maintains a consistent size by replacing members as they leave the group. An open group, too, may have a predetermined life span; for example, groups in a university student health service may plan to meet only for the nine-month academic year. Usually open groups continue indefinitely, even though every couple of years there may be a complete turnover of group membership and even of leadership. I have known of therapy groups in psychiatric training centers which have endured for twenty years, being bequeathed every two to three years by a graduating resident to an incoming junior resident. Though a closed group with total stability of membership has much to recommend it, the exigencies of outpatient practice diminish its feasibility. Invariably members will drop out, move away, or face an unexpected scheduling incompatibility; and new mem-

---

* For many years I have tape recorded, with the patient's consent, the initial psychiatric interview with patients and later near the conclusion of therapy (individual or group) asked the patient to listen to this initial interview. Often it proves to be an illuminating experience which consolidates gains and occasionally opens up new areas of work. Therapeutic change is often so gradual as to be imperceptible to the patient—hence the value of a living reminder of his initial condition.

bers must be added lest the group perish from attrition. A closed group format may, however, be practical in a setting in which one is assured of considerable stability, such as a prison, a military base, a long-term psychiatric hospital, or occasionally an outpatient analytic group in which all members are concurrently in individual analysis with the group leader. Ordinarily the great majority of outpatient groups are conducted as open groups.

Duration of the Meeting

Until the mid-1960's the length of the session seemed fixed in psychotherapy; the fifty-minute individual hour and the eighty-to-ninety-minute group therapy session were part of the entrenched folk wisdom of the field. Most group therapists agree that, even in well-established groups, a period of at least sixty minutes is required for the warm-up interval and for the unfolding and working through of the major themes of the session. There is some consensus among therapists also that after about two hours a point of diminishing returns is reached; the group becomes weary, repetitious, and inefficient. Furthermore, many therapists appear to function best in segments of eighty to ninety minutes; longer sessions often result in fatigue, which renders the therapist less effective in his remaining therapy sessions that day. Although some intensive analytic groups meet two to five times weekly, the great majority of outpatient groups meet once a week.

Recently there has been considerable experimentation with the time variable. This experimentation or reaction to conventional modes of therapy has at times been so extreme as to border on procedural anarchy. Groups are reported which meet regularly for four-, six- or eight-hour sessions; some therapists choose to meet less frequently but for longer periods—for example, a six-hour meeting every other week; some psychiatric wards have instituted an intensive group therapy week during which the patients meet in small groups for eight hours a day for five consecutive days.

The most widely publicized new format has been the "marathon" group which has been described in many widely distributed American popular magazines, newspapers, and fictionalized accounts.[1, 2, 3] The marathon group, so christened by Bach,[4] has prolonged meetings, each twenty-four to forty-eight hours, with little or no time permitted for sleep. The participants are required to remain together for the entire designated time;

meals are served in the room, and sleep, if required, comes during short naps in the session or in short scheduled sleep breaks. The emphasis of the group is on total self-disclosure, intensive interpersonal confrontation, and affective involvement and participation.

The time-extended therapy session has several roots. Undoubtedly psychotherapy has been influenced by the sensitivity training field and by the frequent use of intensive seven-to-fourteen-day residential workshops in which the participants live together and meet in groups for several hours a day (see Chapter 14). Another impetus derives from recent developments in the therapeutic use of the inpatient psychiatric community. Clinicians have increasingly come to regard the psychiatric ward as a potential twenty-four-hour-a-day therapy group and have sought ways to harness the powerful interpersonal forces for therapeutic gain. Newer techniques of intensive family therapy may also have helped set the stage; Mac-Gregor, in 1962, described a mode of multiple impact therapy [5] in which a psychiatric team devoted its total attention to one family for two to three full days.

Time-extended group therapy has been used in clinical practice in several different formats. Patients who may or may not be in other therapy spend a weekend in a marathon group with a leader about whom they first learned from a friend or professional advertisement. If they are in therapy, occasionally their individual therapist may recommend such a group. Some group therapists refer their entire group for a weekend with another therapist or, more commonly, may themselves conduct a marathon meeting with their own group some time during the course of therapy.

Proponents of the time-extended group claim that the procedure has several advantages: [4, 6, 7, 8, 9, 10] the development of the small group is greatly accelerated; members undergo a more intense emotional experience; the entire course of therapy may take only twenty-four to forty-eight hours. The social microcosm of the group is said to unfold more quickly; if patients are in the group as they are in the world, then the group will replicate the real world more rapidly, with patients eating, sleeping, crying, and living together continuously in a setting in which there is no place to hide. The fatigue resulting from lack of sleep doubtlessly contributes to the abandonment of social façades. (As one marathon group leader stated, "Tired people are truthful; they do not have the energy to play games." A ninety-minute session is not long enough to compel people to "take off their masks.")[9]

The results of marathon group therapy reported in the mass media and in scientific journals have been so extraordinary that they boggle the mind. Eighty per cent of the participants undergo significant change as the result of a single meeting;[10] thirty-six hours of therapy have proved comparable to several years of conventional ninety-minute weekly group therapy sessions;[8] the marathon group has become a singular agent of change which allows rapidity of learning and adaptation to new patterns of behavior not likely to occur under traditional arrangements, etc.[4] This lack of objectivity and the indiscriminating embrace of the latest therapeutic fad are characteristics of the field of psychotherapy in general and of group therapy in particular. Parloff, discussing the claims of marathon group therapists, states, "No sooner does a new group therapy Tinker Bell appear on the scene than a number of practitioners will offer to sustain its weak and flickering light by life-supporting shouts of 'I believe! I believe!'" [7]

The results, to date, are entirely based on anecdotal reports of various participants or questionnaires distributed shortly after the end of the meeting, an exceedingly unreliable research approach. In fact, any outcome study based on interviews, testimonials, or patient self-administered questionnaires obtained at the end of the group is of little value. At no other time is the patient more loyal, more grateful, and less objective about his group than at the point of termination; at this juncture there is a powerful tendency to recall and to express only the positive, tender feelings. Experiencing and expressing negative feelings about the group at this point would be unlikely for at least two reasons: (1) there is strong group pressure at termination to participate in positive testimonials; few individuals, as Asch has shown, can maintain their objectivity in the face of apparent group unanimity; and (2) the individual rejects critical feelings toward the group at this time to avoid a state of cognitive dissonance. He has chosen to invest considerable emotion and time in the group; he has often developed strong positive feelings toward other members. To question the value or activities of the group would be to thrust himself into a state of dissonance.

Although time-extended group therapy has emerged too recently for much systematic research inquiry of the process and results to have been undertaken, undoubtedly such research will be attempted because the format of the marathon group—a short, circumscribed period of therapy —is especially well suited to a controlled research investigation. The one reported research project does not support some of the claims described above. In 1967 my co-workers and I [11] tested the hypothesis that a time-extended group session accelerates the life cycle of the group. Specifically we explored the effect of a six-hour time-extended meeting* on the devel-

---

* It is possible that a six-hour meeting may have an entirely different effect from a twenty-four-hour meeting. However, many of the claims cited above are reported also by clinicians using an eight-hour group session in outpatient clinics.[8]

opment of cohesiveness (operationally defined as member-member and member-group involvement) and on the development of a here-and-now, interactive communicational mode.

Six newly formed groups in a psychiatric outpatient department were studied for their first sixteen sessions. Three of these groups held a six-hour first session, while the other three held a six-hour eleventh session. During the period of their first sixteen meetings, each group thus had a six-hour session and fifteen meetings of conventional length (ninety minutes). Tape recordings of the second, sixth, tenth, twelfth, and sixteenth meetings were analyzed to classify the verbal interaction.* (The six-hour meeting itself was not analyzed, since we were primarily interested in studying its effect on the subsequent course of therapy.) Post-group questionnaires measuring group involvement and member-member involvement were obtained at these same meetings.

The results show that the time-extended meeting did *not* influence the communicational patterns in a favorable direction in meetings subsequent to the marathon session. In fact, there was a trend in the opposite direction—i.e., the groups, following the six-hour meetings, appeared to engage in *less* here-and-now interaction. The influence of the six-hour meeting on cohesiveness was quite interesting. In the three groups which held a six-hour initial meeting there was a trend toward *decreased* cohesiveness in subsequent meetings. However, in the three groups which held a six-hour eleventh meeting, there was a significant *increase* in cohesiveness in the subsequent meetings.

The implication of these results is that timing must be taken into consideration. It is entirely possible that, at the correct juncture in the course of the group, a time-extended session may help increase member involvement in the group. The therapists of the six groups, when questioned, were not impressed by any significant changes in the development of the group that may have been attributable to the time-extended meeting.

It would be naïve to assume, however, that forthcoming research will greatly influence the tide of interest in the marathon group: I believe that the marathon will be an important part of the American scene for quite some time to come. With continued publicity, the hope of instant therapy will continue to flourish, and group therapists will, no doubt, be pressured by many of their groups for a marathon experience. The lure of accelerated therapy and instant intimacy is highly resonant with the American penchant for prefabrication. Today in our culture instant, foundationless

---

* The Hill Interaction Matrix[12] method of scoring interaction was used. The middle thirty minutes of the meeting was systematically evaluated by two trained raters who were naïve about the design of the study.

homes and cities arise *de novo;* romances and marriages issue from the matchmaker computer; the timeless truths of religion are dispersed at a drive-in church service or via dial-a-prayer phone service; even tradition is born fully formed, fully clothed, and fully pedigreed in the guise of the London Bridge bought and transported brick by brick by an American real estate developer to span an artificial waterway in a newly constructed resort city.

Objective appraisal of the time-extended format has been confounded by the tendency of many workers to equate emotional impact and therapeutic effectiveness. My own experience as a participant and leader of marathon groups has taught me that the experience can be a powerful and moving one. There are very few other settings in our culture in which individuals can publically release pent-up emotion, reveal themselves, cry, and openly express love and hate. At the termination of the session there is no end to such testimonials as "Walking on clouds," "Never felt closer to myself and to others," "People are so beautiful," "Feel stronger than I have ever felt," "My life has been changed," etc.

And yet we must ask, what does this have to do with therapy? We must again be mindful of the difference between an emotional experience and a *corrective* emotional experience. Most of all we must consider questions of temporality in therapy: does a change in one's behavior in the group invariably and simultaneously betoken a change in one's outside life? How enduring is change which occurs in a short-term experience? Clinicians have long known that change in the therapy session is *not* tantamount to therapeutic success; carryover into important outside interpersonal relationships and endeavors is required. Despite our impatience, the laborious process of carryover cannot be hurried and instead demands a certain irreducible temporal segment of life.*

Consider the patient who, because of his early experience with an authoritarian, distant, and harsh father, tends to see all other males, especially those in a position of authority, as having similar qualities. In the group he may have an entirely different emotional experience with a male therapist and perhaps one of the male members. What has he learned? Well, for one thing he has learned that not all men are frightening bastards; at least there are one or two who are not. Of what lasting value

---

* Lorr [13] reviewed the pertinent clinical research on intensity and duration of treatment and concluded that "duration of treatment is a more influential parameter than the number of treatments . . . change would appear to require the passage of time. Insights are put into practice in daily living. New ways of reacting interpersonally must be tested again and again in natural settings before what has been learned becomes consolidated. Trial and error testing seems a prerequisite for the process of growth and change."

is this experience to the patient? Probably very little unless the experience is generalizable for future situations! As a result of the group, the individual learns that at least some men in authority positions can be trusted. But which ones? He must learn how to differentiate between people so as not to perceive all men in a pre-set manner. A new repertoire of perceptual skills is needed. Once he is able to make the necessary discriminations, he must learn how to go about making relationships on an egalitarian, distortion-free basis. For the individual whose interpersonal relationships have been impoverished and maladaptive, these are formidable and lengthy tasks, which often require the continual testing and reinforcement available in the therapeutic relationship.

Thus we question whether the marathon group precludes the use of long-term therapy; we do not deny its impact. It is an engrossing human experience—perhaps the most sophisticated and compelling of all adult games. Its psychotherapeutic potential is still unknown; clearly it cannot be dismissed summarily on the basis of any of the objections I have raised. One must somehow heed the patients who claim, months after the single extended session, that they experienced an important and durable therapeutic change; one must also heed the psychiatrists who report that some of their long-term patients who engaged in a time-extended group session suddenly became mobilized and their subsequent psychotherapy vastly augmented. Undoubtedly, as our experience increases and as research is undertaken and evaluated, the time-extended meeting will be allocated an appropriate position in our therapeutic armamentorium. As we learn more about optimal timing, the time-extended meeting may, I believe, have considerable potential as a facilitating procedure in the course of ongoing therapy rather than as an isolated procedure. The danger at present is, as with any new technique, the tendency to consider it a panacea—effective for all patients at all times.

Size of the Group

My own experience and a consensus of the clinical literature suggest that the ideal size of an interactional therapy group is approximately seven, with an acceptable range of five to ten members. The lower limit of the group is determined by the fact that a critical mass is required for an aggregation of individuals to become an interacting group. When a group is reduced to a size of four or three, it often ceases to operate as a group;

member interaction diminishes, and therapists often find themselves engaged in individual therapy within the group. Many of the advantages of a group—the opportunity for broad consensual validation, the opportunity to interact and to analyze one's interaction with a large variety of individuals—are compromised as the group size diminishes.

The upper limit is determined by sheer economic principles; as the group increases in size, less and less time is available for the working through of any individual's problems. Although most outpatient therapists set an upper limit of nine or ten on their groups, sensitivity training groups generally include more members—usually twelve to sixteen. It is possible to conduct a face-to-face group with this number—each member may interact in a meaningful way with each of the other members—however, there will be insufficient time to work through with any thoroughness the problem areas which are identified. Still larger groups ranging from twenty to eighty are conducted by Alcoholic Anonymous, Recovery, Inc., and therapeutic communities. However, these groups rely on different curative factors: the AA and Recovery, Inc., groups use inspiration, guidance, and suppression, while the large therapeutic community relies on group pressure and interdependence to encourage reality testing, to combat regression, and to instill a sense of individual responsibility toward the social community.

To some extent the optimal group size is a function of the duration of the meeting: the longer the meeting, the larger the number of patients who can profitably engage in the group. Thus, many of the "marathon" therapy groups include up to sixteen members. Innumerable variations in terms of group size and duration of meetings are currently being explored; one therapist in California, for example, has adopted the procedure of seeing all of his individual patients (and their spouses) in a fifty-member, six-hour weekly meeting.

Little highly relevant research exists on the size variable. Bales and Borgatta,[14] studying laboratory task groups, reported that the size (which was varied from two to seven members) influenced the communication network of the group. They noted, for example, that even-numbered groups (four or six members) exhibited significantly more disagreement, antagonism, inability to reach a decision, and significantly less expression of positive affect than odd-numbered groups (three, five, or seven members). The relevance of these findings to therapy groups has, however, yet to be determined.

An observation by Asch [15] is noteworthy. Group pressure, as we have noted, may be harnessed in the service of therapy. Long-cherished but self-defeating beliefs and attitudes may waver and decompose in the face of a dissenting majority. Asch investigated the influence of the size of the majority on group pressure and found a major gradient between a majority of two and three (i.e., a four-member group is significantly more powerful than a three-member group); but an increase of the majority to four, eight, and even sixteen did not produce effects greater than a majority of three.

Several studies suggest that, from the perspective of the group member, five-member groups are the most harmonious problem-solving groups.[16] Other studies show that as the size of the group increases there is a corresponding tendency for cliques and disruptive subgroups to form.[17] A comparison between twelve-member and five-member problem-solving groups indicates that the larger groups are more dissatisfied and show less consensus.[18] As the group increases in size, research demonstrates too that only the more forceful and aggressive members are able to express themselves, while the less forceful members are unable to express their ideas or abilities.[19]

Castore [20] investigated the relationship between the size of the group and the number of different member-to-member verbal relationships initiated (i.e., the number of other members to whom each individual directed at least one remark—a measure of the spread of interpersonal interaction in the group) in fifty-five inpatient therapy groups with a range in size from five to twenty patients. The results indicated a marked reduction in interactions between members when the group's size reached nine members and a second marked reduction when seventeen or more members were present. The implication of the research is that, in inpatient settings, groups of five to eight offer a greater opportunity for total patient participation.

Since one must anticipate that one or two patients will drop out of the group in the course of the initial meetings, it is advisable to start with a group slightly larger than one's preferred size; thus to obtain a seven-member group many therapists start a new group with eight or nine members.

Preparation for Group Therapy

There is great variation in clinical practice regarding the interviewing of patients prior to group therapy. Some therapists, after seeing the patient once or twice in selection interviews, do not meet with the patient individually again, whereas other therapists continue individual sessions with the patient until he starts in the group. The chief purpose of the post-selection, pregroup interviews is to prepare patients for the impending group experience. I would agree with Foulkes[21] that there is little purpose in pretherapy anamnestic interviews since any truly relevant material will be forthcoming in the group setting. There is some value in considering the pregroup individual sessions as an opportunity to build rapport with the patient, which may prove helpful in keeping him in the group during periods of discouragement and disenchantment early in the course of group therapy. Although there is no research-supporting evidence, my hunch is that the more often a patient is seen pretherapy, the less likely he is to terminate prematurely from the group. Often the first step in the development of intermember bonds is their mutual identification with a common shared object—the therapist. I would recommend, incidentally, if the group is to be led by two therapists, that the co-therapists jointly conduct these interviews. Otherwise patients come to regard, often for many months or even years, the original interviewer as their primary therapist, which results in chronic splits in the group.

The most effective use of pretherapy interviews is to help patients recognize and work through misconceptions and unrealistic fears and expectations of group therapy and, in addition, to provide patients with some cognitive structure which will enable them to participate more effectively in the group.

MISCONCEPTIONS ABOUT GROUP THERAPY

Certain misconceptions and fears about group therapy occur with such great regularity that the therapist can, with a reasonable degree of certainty, take their presence for granted; and if they go unmentioned by the patient, he should introduce them as potential problems. Despite recent sympathetic presentation by the mass media, there is still a widespread belief among prospective patients that group therapy is second-rate therapy—i.e., that it is cheap therapy for those who cannot afford individual therapy; that it is diluted therapy because each patient has only twelve to fifteen minutes of the therapist's time each week; that it exists only because the number of patients greatly exceeds the supply of therapists.

These misconceptions may produce a set of expectations so unfavorable to group therapy that successful outcome becomes unlikely. Many researchers have demonstrated that the patent's initial expectations and faith in therapy and in the therapist are positively and significantly related to his remaining in treatment and to an ultimate favorable outcome.[22, 23, 24]

In addition to evaluative misconceptions, patients are usually encumbered with a burden of procedural misconceptions and unrealistic interpersonal fears. Many of these are evident in the following dream which a patient reported at her second pregroup individual session shortly before she was to attend her first group meeting:

I dreamed that each member of the group was required to bring cookies to the meeting. I went with my mother to buy the cookies that I was to take to the meeting. We had great difficulty deciding which cookies would be appropriate to take. In the meantime, I was aware that I was going to be very late to the meeting and I was becoming more and more anxious about getting there on time. We finally decided on the cookies and proceeded to go to the group. I asked directions to the room where the group was to meet and was told that it was meeting in Room 129A. I wandered up and down a long hall in which the rooms were not numbered consecutively and in which I couldn't find a room with a number A. I finally discovered that 129A was located behind another room and went into the group. When I had been looking for the room I had encountered many people from my past, many people whom I had gone to school with and many people whom I had known for a number of years. The group was very large and about forty or fifty people were milling around the room. The members of the group included members of my family: most specifically, two of my brothers. Each member of the group was required to stand in front of a large audience and say what they thought was their difficulty and why they were there and what their problems were, etc. The whole dream was very anxiety-provoking and the business of being late and the business of having a large number of people was very distracting.

Although time did not permit intensive analysis of the dream, several themes were abundantly clear. The patient anticipated the first group meeting with considerable dread. Her concern about being late reflected a fear of being excluded or rejected by the group. Furthermore, since she was starting in an ongoing group—one which had already met for several weeks—she feared that she would be left behind, the others having progressed far past her position. (Recall that she could not find a room with an "A" marked on it.) She dreamt that the group would number forty or fifty. Concerns about the size of the group are common; patients fear that their unique individuality will be lost as they become one of the mass. Moreover, patients erroneously apply the model of the economic distribution of goods to the group therapeutic experience, assuming that the size of the crowd is inversely proportional to the goods received by each individual.

The dream image of each member confessing his problems to the group audience reflects one of the most basic and pervasive fears of individuals entering a therapy group: the anticipation of having to reveal oneself and to confess shameful transgressions and fantasies to an alien audience. Further inquiry reveals the expectation of a critical, scornful, ridiculing, or humiliating response from the other members. The experience is fantasied as an apocalyptic trial before an unsympathetic tribunal. The dream also suggests that pregroup anticipation resulted in a recrudescence of anxiety linked to a number of early group experiences in the patient's life, including those of school, family, and play groups. It is as if her entire social network, all the significant people and groups she has encountered in her life, will be present in this group. In a sense this is true, since the patient has been shaped by her experiences with these groups and individuals and will, through the suggestibility of her perceptual apparatus, re-create them in the therapy group.

It is clear from the reference to Room 129 (an early schoolroom) that the patient associates her impending group experience with a time in her life when few things were more crucial than the acceptance and approval of a peer group. Her expectation of the therapist is that he, like her early teachers, will be an aloof evaluator.

Closely related to the dread of forced confession is the concern about confidentiality. The patient anticipated that there would be no group boundaries, that every intimacy she disclosed would be known by every significant person in her life.

Other common concerns, not evident in this dream, include a fear of mental contagion and fear of losing control over one's own hostility.[25, 26] Fear of contagion, of being made sicker through association with other psychiatric patients, is often, but not exclusively, a preoccupation of schizophrenic or borderline patients. In part this concern is a reflection of the self-contempt of psychiatric patients who project onto others their feelings of worthlessness and their imagined proclivity to besmirch others with whom they relate. Such dynamics underlie the frequently posed query, "How can the blind lead the blind?" Convinced that they themselves have nothing of value to offer, patients find inconceivable the notion that they might profit from others like themselves.

The unrealistic expectations which, unchecked, would lead to a rejection or a blighting of group therapy can be allayed by an adequate preparation of the candidate. Before outlining a preparation procedure, we shall consider some problems commonly encountered in the course of the group which may also be ameliorated by pretherapy preparation.

THE ANTICIPATION OF GROUP PROBLEMS

One important source of perplexity and discouragement for patients early in the course of therapy is a *perceived goal incompatibility;* they will often be unable to discern the congruence between group goals (e.g., group integrity, construction of an atmosphere of trust, and an interactional confrontive focus) and their individual goals (relief of suffering). What bearing, they wonder, does a discussion of their interpersonal reactions to other members have on their symptoms of anxiety, depression, phobias, impotence, or social inhibition?

A *high turnover* in the early stages of the group is, as we have already shown, a major impediment to the development of an effective group. The therapist, from his very first contacts with the patient, should discourage irregular attendance and premature termination. The issue is a more pressing one than in individual therapy, where absences and tardiness can be profitably investigated and worked through. In the initial stages of the group, irregular attendance results in a discouraged and disjunctive group; the group as a whole must do so much pressing business that resistance expressed through physical absence is especially destructive.

Subgrouping and extragroup socializing, which has been referred to as the "Achilles heel of group therapy," is a problem that may be encountered at any stage of the group. The issue is a complex one which we shall consider later in detail in Chapter 11. For the present, it is sufficient to point out that the therapist may begin to shape the group norms regarding subgrouping in his very first contacts with the patients.

A SYSTEM OF PREPARATION

I have come to prefer a procedure of systematic preparation of group therapy patients which is designed to resolve each of the foregoing misconceptions, erroneous expectations, and initial problems of group therapy. The misconceptions and expectations should be explored in detail with the patients and corrected not by empty exclamation but by an accurate and complete discussion of each. Early problems in therapy may be predicted by the therapist in the preparatory session and a conceptual framework and clear guidelines to effective behavior presented to the patients. Although each patient's preparation must be individualized according to the concerns expressed and the amount of prior knowledge and sophistication about the therapy process, I have found that a preparatory interview, as outlined below, is of considerable value.

Patients are presented with a brief explanation of the interpersonal theory of psychiatry, beginning with the statement that although each manifests his problems differently, all who seek help from psychotherapy have in common the basic problem of difficulty in establishing and maintaining close and gratifying relationships with others. They are reminded of the many times in their lives that undoubtedly they have wished to clarify a relationship, to be really honest about their positive and negative feelings with someone and get reciprocally honest feedback. The general structure of society, however, does not often permit totally open communication. The therapy group is described as a special microcosm in which this type of honest interpersonal exploration vis-à-vis the other members is not only permitted but encouraged. If people are conflicted in their methods of relating to others, then obviously a social situation which encourages honest interpersonal explorations can provide them with a clear opportunity to learn many valuable things about themselves. It is emphasized that working on their relationships directly with other group members will not be easy; in fact, it may be very stressful, but it is crucial because if one can completely understand and work out one's relationships with the other group members, there will be an enormous carryover. They will then find pathways to more rewarding relationships with significant people in their lives now and with people they have yet to meet.

The patients are advised that the way in which they can help themselves most of all is to be honest and direct with their feelings in the group *at* that moment, especially their feelings toward the other group members and the therapists. This point is emphasized many times and is referred to as the "core of group therapy." They are told that they may, as they develop trust in the group, reveal intimate aspects of themselves, but that the group is not a forced confessional and that people have different rates of developing trust and revealing themselves. It is suggested that the group be seen as a forum for risk taking and that, as learning progresses, new types of behavior may be tried in the group setting.

Certain stumbling blocks are predicted. Patients are forewarned about a feeling of puzzlement and discouragement in the early meetings. It will, at times, not be apparent how working on group problems and intragroup relationships can be of value in solving the problems which brought them to therapy. This puzzlement, they are told, is to be expected in the typical therapy process, and they are strongly urged to stay with the group and not to heed their inclinations to give up therapy. It is almost impossible to evaluate the eventual usefulness of the group during the first dozen meetings, and they are asked to make a commitment of at least twelve meetings before even attempting to evaluate the group. They are told that many patients find it painfully difficult to reveal themselves or to express directly positive or negative feelings. The tendencies of some to withdraw emotionally, to hide their feelings, to let others express feelings for them, to form concealing alliances with others, are discussed. The therapeutic goals of group therapy are ambitious because we desire to change behavior and attitudes many years in the making; treatment is therefore gradual and long. I discuss with them the likely development of feelings of frustration or annoyance with the therapist, and how they will expect answers from him but in vain. The source of help will be primarily the other patients, although it is difficult for them to accept this fact.

Next they are told about the history and development of group therapy —how group therapy passed from a stage during World War II, when it was valued because of its economic features and allowed psychiatry to reach a large number of patients, to its present position in the field where it is clearly seen as having something unique to offer and is often the treatment of choice. Results of psychotherapy outcome studies are cited in which group therapy is shown to be as efficacious as any mode of individual therapy.[27, 28, 29] My remarks in this area are focused toward instilling faith in group therapy and dispelling the false notion that group therapy is "second-class therapy."

Confidentiality, patients are told, is as essential in group therapy as it is in any form of doctor-patient relationship; for the members to feel free they must have confidence that their statements will remain within the group. In my group therapy experience I can scarcely recall a single serious breach of confidence and can therefore reassure patients on this matter with considerable conviction.

The issue of extragroup socializing may be tactfully and effectively approached in preparatory sessions from two standpoints:

1. The group provides an opportunity for learning about one's problems in social relationships; it is not an assembly for meeting and making social friends, and it is the experience of therapists that if used in this manner the group loses its therapeutic effectiveness.
2. However, if by chance or design, members do meet outside the group, then it is their responsibility to discuss the salient aspects of the meeting inside the group.

It is particularly useless for the therapists to lay down rules prohibiting extragroup socializing; almost invariably during the course of the therapy, group members will engage in some extragroup socializing and, in the face of prohibitions, may be reluctant to disclose this in the group. As we shall elaborate further in the next chapter, the extragroup relationships are not harmful per se; what impedes therapy is the conspiracy of silence which often surrounds such meetings. Furthermore, such rules may involve patients in a nonproductive discussion of rule breaking, whereas the statement that it is the therapist's experience that such activity impedes therapy may, with greater profit, confront patients with the issue of why they act to sabotage their own therapy.

RESEARCH EVIDENCE

In 1966, my co-workers and I [30] tested the effectiveness of such a preparatory session in a controlled experiment. Of a sample of sixty patients awaiting group therapy, half were seen in a thirty-minute preparatory session, while the other half were seen for an equal period of time in a conventional interview. Six therapy groups (three of prepared patients, three of unprepared patients) were organized and led by group therapists unaware that there had been an experimental manipulation. A study of the first twelve meetings demonstrated that the prepared groups had more faith in therapy (which in turn positively influences outcome) and engaged in significantly more group and interpersonal interaction than the nonprepared groups,* and that this difference was as marked in the twelfth meeting as in the second. The research design demanded that identical preparation be given to each patient; we may surmise that if the preparation were individualized for each patient, then the effectiveness might have been further enhanced. Although the information imparted may appear elaborate, the procedure of preparation, be it noted, is a simple one and can easily be accomplished in a single interview.

THE RATIONALE OF GROUP THERAPY PREPARATION

I have deliberately devoted considerable space to the preparation of the patient because I believe it is a crucial but oft neglected function of the therapist. Let us consider briefly the rationale for a preparatory process. The first dozen meetings of the therapy group are precarious and at

---

* The interaction of the groups was measured by scoring each statement during the meeting on a sixteen-cell matrix (Hill Interaction Matrix [12]). Scoring was performed by a team of raters naïve to the experimental design. Faith in therapy was tested by postgroup patient-administered questionnaires.

the same time vitally important: many members are unnecessarily discouraged and terminate therapy; the group is in a highly fluid state and maximally responsive to the influence of the therapist who, if he is sensitive, can take giant strides in influencing the group to elaborate therapeutic norms. The early meetings are a time of considerable patient anxiety, both intrinsic, unavoidable anxiety and extrinsic, unnecessary anxiety.

The intrinsic anxiety issues from the very nature of the group; individuals who have encountered lifelong disabling difficulties in their interpersonal relationships will invariably be stressed when they come face to face with their social anxiety in a group of individuals. In fact, as we have noted from group research cited in Chapter 8,[31, 32, 33] the dissonance, which arises from a desire to remain in the group and, on the other hand, an incompatibility with the group task, seems to be vital for the initiation of change. There is an imposing body of evidence,[34, 35, 36] however, which demonstrates that, although anxiety with accompanying hypervigilance may be adaptive, an excessive degree of anxiety will obstruct one's ability to cope with stress. White notes in his masterful review of the evidence supporting the concept of an exploratory drive [36] that anxiety and fear are the enemies of environmental exploration; they retard learning and result in decreased exploratory behavior to an extent correlated with the intensity of the fear. In group therapy crippling amounts of anxiety may prevent the introspection, interpersonal exploration, and testing of new behavior so essential to the process of change.

Much of the anxiety experienced by patients early in the group is not anxiety intrinsic to the group task but is unnecessary, extrinsic, and sometimes iatrogenic. This anxiety is a natural consequence of being placed in a group situation in which one's expected behavior, the group goals, and the relevance to one's personal goals are exceedingly unclear. Research with laboratory groups demonstrates that if the group's goals, the methods of goal attainment, and expected role behavior are ambiguous, then the group will be less cohesive, less productive, and its members will be more defensive, anxious, frustrated, and prone to terminate membership.[37, 38, 39, 40, 41] An effective preparation for the group will reduce the extrinsic anxiety which stems from uncertainty. By clarifying the group goals and the confluence of group and personal goals, by presenting unambiguous guidelines for effective behavior, by providing the patient with an accurate formulation of the group process, one reduces uncertainty and extrinsic anxiety.

A systematic preparation for group therapy by no means implies a structuring of the group experience. I do not espouse didactic or directive group therapy, but, on the contrary, suggest a technique which will enhance the formation of a freely interacting, autonomous group. By averting lengthy ritualistic behavior in the initial sessions and by diminishing initial anxiety stemming from unclarity, the group is enabled to plunge into group work more quickly. In my view, anxiety caused by deliberate unclarity is not necessary in order to prevent the group from becoming too socially comfortable. Patients are highly conflicted about their interpersonal relationships, and groups which have an increased rate of interpersonal interaction will continually present challenging and anxiety-provoking interpersonal confrontations. Therapy groups which are too comfortable are groups which flee the task of direct interpersonal confrontation.

Although a systematic consideration of the preparatory process is rare (most group therapy texts omit any mention of it), nevertheless all group therapists do attempt to clarify the therapeutic process and expected role behavior; the difference between therapists or between therapeutic schools is largely a difference in timing and style of preparation. Some group therapists initially prepare the new patient by providing him with written material about group therapy,[42] or by having him hear a tape of a model group therapy work meeting,[43] or by having him attend a trial meeting,[44] or by a long series of individual introductory lectures or an instrumented program of therapy and insight aids.[45, 46] However, even the therapists who deliberately avoid initial preparation and orientation of the patient, nevertheless have in mind goals and preferred modes of group procedure which eventually are transmitted to the patient. By subtle or even subliminal verbal and nonverbal reinforcement, even the most nondirective therapist structures his group so that inevitably they adopt his values as to what is important and what is unimportant in the group process.[47, 48] To cite a clinical example, consider this transcribed statement made in the second meeting by a nondirective British group analyst* who engages in no pretherapy preparation.

Isn't there something noteworthy in what you have done in the last thirty or forty minutes? Because having had this uneasy silence at first, and then my having commented on that, you began looking at some of the ways that you were facing the problems here . . . it was almost as though you had looked and seen the situation in a more realistic way after that, because since that time you might say you have been exploring each other. You see, Miss H. started to ask Miss A. a lot about herself and this started to show that perhaps you can say something about yourself and people won't be hostile about it. So you could explore each other's attitudes in a way that might even be helpful. But it was quite

* Courtesy of Dr. John Sutherland, Tavistock Clinic, London.

a striking change from what you had done in the first few minutes, as though you had started a process of, well, perhaps you can feel about each other, perhaps you can think about each other, perhaps you can even look inside each other's thoughts and feelings in a way that might lead to something. Certainly quite a lot of exploration is going on of your own attitudes. This is done in a conventional way up to a point, but perhaps also for the purpose of indicating where you stood with each other, so that you might be more personal about your difficulties.

The group therapist here does a great deal more than merely summarize the events of the previous thirty minutes. He expresses his approval of certain types of activities and suggests future desirable behavior.

Some therapists staunchly oppose preparation of the patient, and hold that ambiguity of both patient and therapist role expectation is a desirable condition of the early phases of therapy.[49, 50] If one accepts the premise that the development and eventual resolution of patient-therapist transference distortions is a key curative factor in therapy, then it follows that one should seek, in the early stages of therapy, to enhance the development of transference. Enigma, ambiguity, absence of cognitive anchoring, and frustration of conscious and unconscius wishes all facilitate a regressive reaction to the therapist and help create an atmosphere favorable to the development of transference. These therapists wish to encourage such regressive phenomena and the emergence of unconscious impulses so that they may be identified and worked through in therapy.[51]

Such controversies cannot be settled definitively because of the dearth of evidence bearing on the curative process in the transference-based analytic group. From my observations of these groups, I believe that, despite the therapist's intentions, the major curative factors are the same as those described in the first four chapters and that interpersonal interaction in these groups, as in more overtly labeled interactional therapy groups, is crucial to the operation of effective therapy. The research cited above demonstrates that a systematic preparatory interview will facilitate the appearance of such interaction.

Two practical observations about preparation: first, the therapist should deliberately repeat and emphasize the essential points of the preparation. Patients, in part because of high anxiety levels immediately before therapy, have an unbelievable tendency to inattend selectively, or to misunderstand key aspects of the therapist's initial comments. Some of my patients have forgotten they were told that observers would be viewing the group through a one-way mirror screen; others who were asked to remain in the group for at least twelve sessions before attempting to evaluate group therapy understood the therapist to say that the group's entire life span would be twelve meetings. Therapists doing time-limited individual therapy often encounter the patient who, toward the end of therapy, denies that the therapist had predetermined a limited number of sessions.

The second observation is that group therapists often find themselves pressed to find group members. A sudden loss of members may provoke therapists into hasty activity to rebuild the group, often resulting in the selection of unsuitable members, inadequately prepared. The therapist then has to assume the position of selling the group to the patient—a position generally obvious to the patient. The therapist does better to continue the group with reduced membership, to select his additions very carefully, and then to present the group in such a way as to maximize the patient's desire to join the group. In fact, research [52] indicates that the more difficult the entrance procedure and the greater an individual's desire to join, the greater his subsequent attraction to the group.

REFERENCES

1. R. Adler, "Reporter at Large," *New Yorker*, April 15, 1967, pp. 55–58.
2. *Palo Alto Times*, January 3, 1967.
3. J. Sohl, *The Lemon Eaters* (New York: Simon and Schuster, 1967).
4. F. Stoller, "Marathon Group Therapy," in G. M. Gazda (ed.), *Innovations to Group Psychotherapy* (Springfield, Ill.: Charles C. Thomas, 1968).
5. R. MacGregor, "Multiple Impact Therapy with Families," *Family Process, 1:* 15–29, 1962.
6. E. Mintz, "Time-Extended Marathon Groups," *Psychother. Res. and Practice, 4:* 65–70, 1967.
7. M. Parloff, "Discussion of F. Stoller's Paper," *Int. J. Group Psychother., 18:* 239–244, 1968.
8. B. Navidzadeh, "The Application of Marathon Group Psychotherapy in Outpatient Clinic Settings," paper presented at American Group Psychotherapy Association Convention, Chicago, January 1968.
9. S. B. Lawrence, cited in *Palo Alto Times,* January 3, 1967.
10. F. Stoller, "Accelerated Interaction: A Time-Limited Approach Based on the Brief Intensive Group," *Int. J. Group Psychother., 18:* 220–235, 1968.
11. A. D. Sklar, I. D. Yalom, S. M. Zimerberg, and G. L. Newell, "Time-Extended Group Therapy: A Controlled Study," *Comparative Group Studies,* in press.
12. W. F. Hill, *HIM: Hill Interaction Matrix* (Los Angeles: Youth Study Center, University of Southern California, 1965).
13. M. Lorr, "Relation of Treatment Frequency and Duration to Psychotherapeutic Outcome," in H. Strupp and L. Luborsky (eds.), *Conference on Research in Psychotherapy* (Washington, D.C.: American Psychological Association, 1962), pp. 134–141.

14. R. Bales and E. Borgatta, "Size of Group as a Factor in the Interaction Profile," in P. Hare, E. Borgatta, and R. Bales (eds.), *Small Groups* (New York: Alfred Knopf, 1962), pp. 369–413.
15. S. E. Asch, "Effects of Group Pressure upon the Modification and Distortion of Judgments," in D. Cartwright and A. Zander (eds.), *Group Dynamics: Research and Theory* (Evanston, Ill.: Row, Peterson, 1962).
16. A. Goldstein, K. Heller, and L. Sechrest, *Psychotherapy and the Psychology of Behavior Change* (New York: John Wiley and Sons, 1966), p. 341.
17. A. P. Hare, *Handbook of Small Group Research* (New York: Free Press of Glencoe, 1962), pp. 224–245.
18. A. P. Hare, "A Study of Interaction and Consensus in Different Sized Groups," *Am. Soc. Rev.*, 17: 261–267, 1952.
19. L. F. Carter *et al.*, "The Behavior of Leaders and Other Group Members," *J. Abnorm. Soc. Psychol.*, 46: 256–260, 1958.
20. G. F. Castore, "Number of Verbal Interrelationships as a Determinant of Group Size," *J. Abnorm. Soc. Psychol.*, 64: 456–457, 1962.
21. S. H. Foulkes, oral communication, April 1968.
22. A. P. Goldstein, *Therapist/Patient Expectancies in Psychotherapy* (New York: Pergamon Press, 1962).
23. S. Lipkin, "Clients' Feelings and Attitudes in Relation to the Outcome of Client-Centered Therapy," *Psychol. Monogr.*, 68: No. 374, 1954.
24. H. L. Lennard and A. Bernstein, *The Anatomy of Psychotherapy* (New York: Columbia University Press, 1960).
25. I. D. Yalom, "A Study of Group Therapy Dropouts," *Arch. Gen. Psychiat.*, 14: 393–414, 1966.
26. M. A. Lieberman, "The Implications of a Total Group Phenomena Analysis for Patients and Therapists," *Int. J. Group Psychother.*, 17: 71–81, 1967.
27. M. Pattison, "Evaluation Studies of Group Therapy," *Int. J. Group Psychother.*, 15: 382–397, 1965.
28. J. Mann, "Evaluation of Group Psychotherapy," in J. L. Moreno (ed.), *The International Handbook of Group Psychotherapy* (New York: Philosophical Library, 1966), pp. 129–148.
29. A. Bergin, "The Implications of Psychotherapy Research for Therapeutic Practice," *J. Abnorm. Psychol.*, 71: 235–246, 1966.
30. I. D. Yalom, P. S. Houts, G. Newell, and K. H. Rand, "Preparation of Patients for Group Therapy," *Arch. Gen. Psychiat.*, 17: 416–427, 1967.
31. I. Gradolph, "The Task-Approach of Groups of Single-Type and Mixed-Type Valency Compositions," in D. Stock and H. Thelen (eds.), *Emotional Dynamics and Group Culture* (New York: New York University Press, 1958).
32. D. Stock and J. Luft, "The T-E-T Design," unpublished manuscript (Washington, D.C.: National Training Laboratories, 1960).
33. D. Stock and W. F. Hill, "Intersubgroup Dynamics as a Factor in Group Growth," in Stock and Thelen, *op. cit.*, pp. 207–221.
34. I. L. Janis, *Psychological Stress: Psychoanalytic and Behavioral Studies of Surgical Patients* (New York: John Wiley and Sons, 1958).
35. H. Basowitz *et al.*, *Anxiety and Stress* (New York: McGraw-Hill, 1955).
36. R. W. White, "Motivation Reconsidered: The Concept of Competence," *Psychol. Rev.*, 66: 297–333, 1959.
37. B. H. Rauer and J. Reitsema, "The Effects of Varied Clarity of Group Goal and Group Path Upon the Individual and His Relation to His Group," *Human Relations*, 10: 29–45, 1957.
38. D. M. Wolfe, J. D. Snock, and R. A. Rosenthal, *Report to Company Participants at 1960 University of Michigan Research Project* (Ann Arbor, Mich.: Institute of Social Research, 1961).

39. A. R. Cohen, E. Stotland, and D. M. Wolfe, "An Experimental Investigation of Need for Cognition," *J. Abnorm. Soc. Psychol.*, *51:* 291–294, 1955.
40. A. R. Cohen, "Situational Structure, Self-Esteem and Threat-Oriented Reactions to Power," in D. Cartwright (ed.), *Studies in Social Power* (Ann Arbor, Mich.: Research Center for Group Dynamics, 1959), pp. 35–52.
41. Goldstein, Heller, and Sechrest, *op. cit.*, p. 405.
42. H. Martin and K. Shewmaker, "Written Instructions in Group Therapy," *Group Psychother.*, *15:* 24, 1962.
43. B. Berzon and L. Solomon, "Research Frontiers: The Self-Directed Group," *J. Counsel. Psychol.*, *13:* 491–497, 1966.
44. G. Bach, *Intensive Group Therapy* (New York: Ronald Press, 1954).
45. D. I. Malamud and S. Machover, *Toward Self-Understanding: Group Techniques in Self-Confrontation* (Springfield, Ill.: Charles C. Thomas, 1965).
46. M. D. Bettis, D. Malamud, and R. F. Malamud, "Deepening a Group's Insight into Human Relations," *J. Clin. Psychol.*, *5:* 114–122, 1949.
47. Goldstein, Heller, and Sechrest, *op. cit.*, p. 329.
48. E. J. Murray, "A Content Analysis for Study in Psychotherapy," *Psychol. Monogr.*, *70:* No. 13, 1956.
49. L. Horwitz, "Transference in Training Groups and Therapy Groups," *Int. J. Group Psychother.*, *14:* 202–213, 1964.
50. A. Wolf, "The Psychoanalysis of Groups," in M. Rosenbaum and M. Berger (eds.), *Group Psychotherapy and Group Function* (New York: Basic Books, 1963), pp. 273–328.
51. S. Schiedlinger, "The Concept of Repression in Group Psychotherapy," paper presented at American Group Psychotherapy Association Conference, New York, January 1967.
52. E. Aronson and J. Mills, "The Effect of Severity of Initiation on Liking for a Group," *J. Abnorm. Soc. Psychol.*, *59:* 177–181, 1959.

10

IN THE BEGINNING

❧

The work of the group therapist begins long before the first group meeting; indeed, as we have already emphasized, successful group outcome depends largely on the therapist's effective performance of his pretherapy tasks. In previous chapters I have discussed the crucial importance of proper group selection, composition, setting, and preparation. In this chapter I will consider the birth and development of the group: first I will describe the natural history of the therapy group and then problems of attendance and punctuality–important issues in the life of the developing group.

Formative Stages of the Group

INTRODUCTION

Every group with its unique cast of characters, all interacting complexly with one another, undergoes a highly individualized development. Each member begins to manifest himself interpersonally and to create his own social microcosm; in time each will begin to analyze his interpersonal style and eventually to experiment with new behavior. Considering the complexity and richness of human interaction compounded further by the grouping of several individuals with maladaptive styles, it is obvious that the course of the group, over many months or years, will be complex and, to a great degree, unpredictable. Nevertheless, there are mass forces operating in all groups which broadly influence their course of development and which provide us with a crude but nonetheless useful schema of developmental phases.

There are compelling reasons for the therapist to familiarize himself with the developmental sequence of groups. If he is to perform his task of assisting the group to form therapeutic norms and to prevent the establishment of norms which hinder therapy, then obviously the therapist must have a clear conception of the natural, optimal development of the therapy group. If he is to diagnose group blockage and to intervene in such a way as to allow the group to proceed, he must have a sense of favorable and of flawed development. Furthermore, a knowledge of broad developmental sequence will provide the therapist with a sense of mastery and direction in the group, and prevent a feeling of confusion and anxiety, which would only compound similar feelings in the patients.*

Our knowledge of group development stems from a few systematic research inquiries with laboratory task groups and many observational studies of sensitivity and therapy groups. Although the descriptive language, of course, varies, there is considerable consistency regarding the basic phases of early group development. Broadly, groups go through an initial stage of orientation, characterized by a search for structure and goals, a great dependency on the leader, and a concern about the group boundaries. Next they encounter a stage of conflict, as the group deals with issues of interpersonal dominance. Following this, the group becomes increasinglly concerned with intermember harmony and affection, while intermember differences are often submerged in the service of group cohesiveness. Much later the fully developed work group emerges, which is characterized by high cohesiveness, considerable inter- and intrapersonal investigation, and full commitment to the primary task.

THE FIRST MEETING

The first group therapy session is invariably a success! Patients (and neophyte therapists) anticipate the initial meeting with a degree of dread so unrealistic that it is always allayed by the actual event. Some therapists choose to begin the meeting with a brief introductory statement about the purpose and method of the group (especially if they have not prepared the patients beforehand); others may simply mention one or two basic ground rules—for example, honesty and confidentiality. The therapist may suggest that the members introduce themselves, or he may remain silent.

* An analogy may be made to the practice of psychoanalysis. There are many reasons for the analyst to be thoroughly familiar with the developmental phases of the analytic process; perhaps one of the more important reasons is that the knowledge forestalls such incapacitating feelings in the analyst as frustration, discouragement, rage, and bewilderment.

Invariably some member will suggest that they introduce themselves and usually within minutes, in American groups, the norm of using first names is established. Following this, a very loud silence ensues, which, like most psychotherapy silences, seems eternal but in actuality lasts only a few seconds. Usually the silence is broken by the patient destined to dominate the early stages of the group, who will say, "I guess I'll get the ball rolling," or words to that effect. He then frequently recounts his reasons for seeking therapy, which often elicit similar descriptions from other patients. An alternative course of events occurs when a member (perhaps spurred by the therapist's remark about the tension of the group during the initial silence) comments on his social discomfort or fear of groups. This often stimulates similar comments from other patients about first-level interpersonal pathology.

THE INITIAL STAGE—ORIENTATION, HESITANT PARTICIPATION, SEARCH FOR MEANING

Two tasks confront members of any newly formed group: first they must determine a method of achieving their primary task—the purpose for which they joined the group; second they must attend to their social relationships in the group, lest these interfere with the attainment of the primary task and also so that each member may receive additional gratifications from his group membership. In many groups, such as athletic teams, college classrooms, and work details, the primary task and the social task are well differentiated; in therapy groups, although this is not often appreciated at first by members, the tasks are confluent—a fact vastly complicating the group experience of socially ineffective individuals.

Several simultaneous concerns are present in the initial meetings. Members, especially unprepared members, search for the meaning of therapy; they may be quite confused about the relevance of the group's activities to their personal goals in therapy. The initial meetings are often peppered with questions reflecting this confusion, and even months later members wonder aloud: "How is this going to help?"

At the same time, the members are sizing up one another and the group. They search for a viable role for themselves and wonder whether they will be liked and respected or ignored and rejected. Although patients ostensibly come to a therapy group for treatment, social forces are such that they invest most of their energy in a search for approval and acceptance. To some, acceptance and approval appear so unlikely that they defensively reject or depreciate the group by silently derogating the other members and by reminding themselves that the group is an unreal artificial one, or that they are too special to care about a group membership which requires sacrificing even one particle of their prized individuality. Members wonder what membership entails. What are the admission requirements? How much must one reveal himself or give of himself? What type of commitment must one make? At a conscious or near conscious level they seek the answers to questions such as these and maintain a vigilant search for the types of behavior which the group expects and approves.

If the early group is a puzzled, testing, hesitant group, so too is it a dependent one. Overtly and covertly members look to the leader for structure and answers, as well as for approval and acceptance. Many of the comments in the group are directed at or through the therapists; surreptitious reward-seeking glances are cast at him, as members demonstrate behavior which in the past has gained approval from authority. The leader's early comments are carefully examined for directives about desirable and undesirable behavior. Patients appear to behave as if salvation emanates solely or primarily from the therapist, if only they can discover what he wants them to do. There is considerable realistic evidence for this belief; the therapist's professional identity as a healer, his host role in providing a room for the group, his preparing the patients and charging a fee for his services—all reinforce the patients' expectations that the therapist will care for them. Some therapists unwittingly compound this belief by behavior which offers unfulfillable promise of succor.

However, the existence of initial dependency cannot be totally accounted for by the situation, by the therapist's behavior, or by a morbid dependency state on the part of the patient. Man's omnipresent need for an all-caring parent and his infinite capacity for self-deception create a belief in the superbeing, which is relinquished only with great difficulty. In Freud's terms, the group wishes, at one level, "to be governed by unrestricted force; it has an extreme passion for authority . . . a thirst for obedience." [1] (I have often wondered whether the inordinately high suicide rate among psychiatrists [2] issues from their awareness that they must be their own superbeing. At times of depression and futility, when confidence in themselves wanes, they abandon all hope for the future. If they, in their shriveled state, embody for themselves intercession and salvation, how then can they not despair?)

The content and communicational style of the initial phase is relatively stereotyped and restricted. The social code is consistent with that of a cocktail party or similar transient social encounters. Problems are approached rationally; the irrational aspects of the patient who presents a problem are suppressed in the service of support, etiquette, and group tranquillity. Semrad [3] suggests the phrase "goblet issues" to refer to early group communication. The analogy refers to the process of picking up a cocktail goblet at a party and figuratively using it to peer at and size up the other guests. Thus, at first groups may endlessly discuss topics of apparently little substantive interest to any of the participants; these "goblet issues," however, serve as vehicles for the first interpersonal exploratory forays. A member discovers who responds favorably to him, who sees things the way he does, whom to fear, whom to respect; gradually he begins to formulate a picture of the role he will play in the group. These "goblet issues" in social settings include such burning subjects as the weather, "Do you know what's-his-name?" and "Where are you from?" In therapy groups symptom description is a favorite early issue, along with previous therapy experience, medications, and the like.

One common process of early groups is the search for similarities. Patients are intrigued by the notion that they are not unique in their misery, and most groups invest considerable energy in demonstrating how the members are similar. This process often offers considerable relief to members (see the discussion of "universality," Chapter 1) and provides part of the foundation on which group cohesiveness will be erected.

Giving and seeking advice is another characteristic of the early group; patients present the group with the problems of dealing with their spouses, children, employers, etc.; the group then attempts to provide some type of practical solution. As we discussed it in Chapter 1, this guidance rarely is of any functional value but serves as a vehicle through which members can express mutual interest and caring.

Many of these concerns are so characteristic of the initial stage of therapy that their presence can be used to estimate the age of a group. If, for example, one hears a tape recording of a group in which there is considerable advice giving and seeking, a search for similarities, symptom description, the meaning of therapy, and "goblet issues," then one may conclude that the group is either a very young one or an older group with a serious maturational block.

SECOND STAGE—CONFLICT, DOMINANCE, REBELLION

If the first core concern of the group is with "in or out," then the next is with "top or bottom."[4] The group shifts from preoccupation with acceptance, approval, commitment to the group, definitions of accepted behavior, and the search for orientation, structure, and meaning to a preoccupation with dominance, control, and power. The conflict characteristic of this phase is between members or between members and the leader. Each member attempts to establish for himself his preferred amount of initiative and power, and gradually a control hierarchy, a social pecking order, is established.

Negative comments and intermember criticism are more frequent; members often appear to feel entitled to a one-way analysis and judgment of others.[5] As in the first stage, advice is given but in the context of a different social code; social conventions are abandoned and members feel free to make personal criticism about the complainant's behavior or attitudes. Judgments are made of past and present life experiences and styles; it is a time of "oughts" and "shoulds" in the group, a time when the "peer-court," as Bach[5] phrased it, is in session. Members make suggestions or give advice, not as a manifestation of acceptance and understanding—norms yet to be established—but as part of the process of jockeying for position in the group.

The emergence of hostility toward the therapist is an inevitable occurrence in the life sequence of the group. A large number of observers have emphasized an early stage of ambivalence to the therapist coupled with a resistance to self-examination and self-disclosure.[5, 6, 7] In a research project previously described (Chapter 5), Liberman[8] attempted, through social reinforcement, to hasten therapeutic group development. He chose to reinforce two types of behavior, each of which reflects a "widely accepted" task of the early group. The "expression of hostility toward the leader" was one of the two behaviors chosen for reinforcement. (The other was the expression of intermember concern and acceptance which will be discussed in our consideration of the next phase.)

The sources of hostility toward the leader are obvious when we recall the unrealistic, indeed magical, attributes with which patients secretly imbue the therapist. Their expectations are so limitless that, regardless of the therapist's competence, he will disappoint them; gradually, as the recognition of his limitations becomes apparent, the process of disenthrallment commences. By no means is this a clearly conscious process; the members may intellectually advocate a democratic group which draws on its own resources but nevertheless may, on a deeper level, crave dependency and attempt first to create and then to destroy an authority figure. For many individuals there is no more vivid manner of experiencing their own integrity and potency than to assail the mighty. Group therapists attempt to reject this expected role by refusing to lead in the traditional manner, by not providing answers and solutions, by redirecting the group to explore its own resources. The members' wish lingers, however, and it is usually only after several sessions that the group comes to realize that the therapist will frustrate their secret plans for him.

Yet another source of resentment toward the leader derives from the gradual recognition by each member that he will not be the favored one. During the pretherapy session, each member comes to harbor the fantasy that the therapist is his very own therapist, preciously interested in fine details of his past, present, and fantasy world. In the early meetings of the group, however, each member begins to realize that the therapist is no more interested in him than in the others; seeds are sown for the emergence of rivalrous, hostile feelings toward the other members. The therapist, in some unclear manner, is thought to have been deceitful.

These unrealistic expectations of the leader and consequent disenchantment are by no means a function of childlike mentality or psychological naïvete; the same phenomenon occurs, for example, in groups of psychiatric residents. In fact, there is no better way for the trainee to appreciate the group's proclivity both to deify and to attack the leader than to experience the feelings as a group member.

Some workers[9] who have taken Freud's *Totem and Taboo* [10] extremely literally regard the group's pattern of relationship with the leader as a recapitulation of the primal horde patricide. Freud does indeed suggest at one point that modern group phenomena have their prehistoric analogues in the misty events of the primal horde: "Thus the group appears to us as a revival of the primal horde. Just as primitive man survives potentially in every individual, so the primal horde may arise once more out of any random collection; in so far as men are habitually under the sway of group formation, we recognize in it the survival of the primal horde." [10] The primal horde, not unlike the chorus in Sophocles' *Oedipus Tyrannus*, is able to free itself from restrictive growth-inhibiting bonds and progress to a more satisfying existence only after the awesome leader has been removed.[11, 12]

The patients are never unanimous in their attack upon the therapist; invariably some champions for the therapist will emerge from the group. The line-up of attackers and defenders may serve as a valuable guide for the understanding of characterologic trends useful for future work in the group. Generally the leaders of this phase, those members who are earliest and most vociferous in their attack, are heavily conflicted in the area of dependency and have dealt with intolerable dependency yearnings by reaction formation. These individuals, sometimes labeled counterdependents,[13] are inclined to reject *prima facie* all statements by the therapist and to entertain the fantasy of unseating and replacing the leader. Thus in the third session one patient proposed a group barbecue (from which the leader would be excluded) and later, when the therapist declined to hold a weekend "marathon" session, suggested the group hold such a meeting without him. At some point in therapy, these individuals must recognize and work through their dependency cravings. Other members invariably side with the therapist; these members too must be helped to investigate their need to defend him at all costs, regardless of the issue involved. Occasionally patients defend the therapist because they have encountered a series of unreliable objects and misperceive him as extraordinarily frail; others need to preserve him because they fantasy an eventual alliance with him against other powerful members of the group. The therapist must beware lest he, in fact, transmit covert signals of personal distress to which the rescuers appropriately respond.

Although we have posited disenchantment and anger with the leader as an ubiquitous feature of small groups, by no means is the process constant across groups in form or degree. The therapist's behavior may potentiate or mitigate both the experience and the expression of rebellion. Thus one prominent sociologist who has for many years led sensitivity training groups of college students reports that inevitably there is a powerful insurrection against the leader, culminating in his being removed bodily by the members from the group room.[14] I, on the other hand, have led more than twenty similar groups over the past several years and have never encountered a reaction of this magnitude. Such a difference can only be due to differences in leader styles and behavior. Invoking greater negative response are those therapists who are ambiguous or deliberately enigmatic, who offer no structure or guidelines for patients, and who covertly make unfulfillable promises to the group early in therapy.

This stage is often difficult and personally unpleasant for group therapists. The neophyte therapist should be reminded, however, that he is essential to the survival of the group; the members cannot afford to liquidate him and he will always be defended. Moreover, for his own comfort, he must learn to discriminate between an attack on his person and an attack on his role in the group. The group's response to the leader is similar to a transference distortion in individual therapy in that it is inappropriate to his behavior, but its source in the group must be understood both from an individual psychodynamic and from a group dynamic viewpoint.

Therapists who are particularly threatened by a group attack protect themselves in a variety of ways. Recently I was asked to act as a consultant for two therapy groups, each approximately twenty-five sessions old, which had developed similar problems: both groups appeared to have reached a plateau, no new ground appeared to have been broken for several weeks, and the patients seemed to have withdrawn interest in the groups. A study of current meetings and past protocols revealed that neither group had yet directly dealt with any negative feelings toward the therapists. However, the reason for this inhibition was quite different in the two groups. In the first group, the two co-therapists (who were leading their first group) had rather clearly shown their throats, as it were, to the group and through their obvious anxiety, uncertainty, and avoidance of hostility-laden issues had pleaded frailty. In addition, they both desired to be loved by all the members and had been at all times so benevolent and so solicitous that an attack by the patients would have appeared ungrateful.

The therapists of the second group had forestalled an attack in quite a different fashion: they remained aloof Olympian figures whose infrequent interventions were oracular in their ambiguity and ostensible profundity. At the end of each meeting they summarized the predominant themes and each member's contributions. To attack them would have been perilous as well as impious and futile. In the words of one patient, "It would have resembled shaking one's fist at a lofty mountain peak."

These developments are inhibitory for the group; suppression of important ambivalent feelings about the therapist results in covert sponsoring of taboo norms which run counter to the overt therapist-proclaimed norm of complete honesty of expression. Furthermore, an important model-setting opportunity is lost; the therapist who withstands an attack without being either destroyed or destructive in retaliation but instead responds by attempting to understand and work through the sources and effects of the attack demonstrates to the group that aggression need not be lethal and that it can be expressed and understood in the group.

One of the consequences of suppression for the two groups in question, and for most groups, is the emergence of displaced, off-target attacks on the therapist. For example, one group persisted for several weeks in attacking "doctors." Previous unfortunate experiences with doctors, hospitals, and individual therapists were described in detail, often with considerable uncritical group consensus on the injustices and inhumanity of the medical profession. In one group, a member attacked the field of psychotherapy by bringing in an article by Eysenck which purported to prove that psychotherapy is ineffective. At other times, police, teachers, and other representatives of authority are awarded similar treatment.

Scapegoating is another "off-target" manifestation and may reach such proportions that unless the therapist intervenes to direct the attack onto himself, the sacrificial patient may be driven from the group. Other groups covertly appoint a leader from their ranks to replace the therapist—always an unsatisfactory process which leaves the group and the patient-leader discouraged and confused. I agree with Bach [15] who states that a group therapist has launched the group on its way once it has passed the twentieth meeting, approximately, without either having been forced to lead in an authoritarian fashion or having appointed a patient to assume this role. Sensitivity training groups usually resolve the issue by defining the leader's role as that of a specialized member with certain technical skills. The mature group learns to evaluate his contributions for their intrinsic value rather than to accept them because of the authority behind them. Therapy groups do not resolve the problem for many months or years; again and again the group returns to the issue, as members at a differential rate, according to their degree of dependency conflict, gradually work through their attitudes toward the therapist. What is essential, however, is that the group feel free to confront the therapist, who must not only permit, but encourage, such confrontation.

THIRD STAGE—DEVELOPMENT OF COHESIVENESS

The third (and last) widely recognized phase of the early formative group is the development of group cohesiveness. Following the previous period of conflict, the group gradually develops into a cohesive unit. Many varied phrases with similar connotations have been used to describe this phase: in-group consciousness;[13, 16] common goal and group spirit;[17, 18] consensual group action, cooperation, and mutual support;[7, 19] group integration and mutuality;[20, 21, 22, 23] we-consciousness unity;[24] and support and freedom of communication.[25] During this phase there is an increase of morale, mutual trust, and self-disclosure. Some members reveal the "real" reason why they have come for treatment; sexual secrets may be shared, long-buried past transgressions are publically unearthed. Post-group coffee meetings may be arranged; attendance improves and patients evince considerable concern about missing members.

The chief concern of the group is with intimacy and closeness. Schutz,[4] who characterizes patients' concerns in the first phase as "in or out" and in the second as "top or bottom," characterizes the third phase as "near or far"; the primary anxieties have to do with not being liked or close enough to people, or with being too intimate.

Although there may be greater freedom of self-disclosure in this phase, there may also be communicational restrictions of another sort: often the group suppresses all expression of negative affect in the service of cohesion. Compared with the previous stage of group conflict, all is sweetness and light, the group basking in the glow of its newly discovered unity. Eventually, however, the glow pales and the group embrace seems ritualistic and futile unless the hostility in the group is permitted to emerge. Only when all affects can be expressed and constructively worked through in a cohesive group does the group become a mature work group—a state lasting for the remainder of the group's life, with periodic short-lived recrudescences of each of the earlier phases.

DEVELOPMENTAL STAGES—OVERVIEW

Now that we have outlined the early stages of group development, let us consider a series of qualifying conditions lest the novice take the proposed developmental sequence too literally. The developmental phases are rarely well demarcated; there is considerable overlap and the boundaries between them are, at best, dim. The evidence for the developmental sequence stems from nonsystematic clinical observational studies—virtually no controlled research exists which clarifies the development of therapy groups. Group developmental research in sensitivity groups has been rudimentary and inconclusive. For example, Bennis et al.[26] in a study of six sensitivity groups, tested the hypothesis that the groups would move through two developmental phases: a primary concern with authority and then a primary concern with intimacy. Of these six groups studied, only one showed such a sequence; the other five showed a continuous dealing and redealing with the two problems.* In therapy groups, too, rarely does the group permanently graduate from one phase. In describing group development, Schutz [4] uses the apt metaphor of tightening the bolts one after another just enough so that the wheel is in place; then the process is repeated, each bolt tightened in turn, until the wheel is entirely secure.† In a similar way, phases of a group emerge, become dominant, and then recede, only to have the group return again later to deal with the same issues with greater thoroughness. Perhaps, given these considerations, it would be more accurate to speak of developmental tasks rather than developmental phases or developmental sequence.

Impact of the Leader on Group Development. The determination of the natural history of the therapy group is made even more complex when

* The research data was derived from multiple-choice questionnaires filled out after each meeting by the leaders and trainees. The questions focused on the existence and amount of power struggle, preoccupation with the leader, self-disclosure, and intimacy.

† Hamburg [27] suggests the term "cyclotherapy" to refer to this process of returning to the same issues but each time from a different perspective and each time in greater depth.

one considers that leaders may anticipate a certain development phase and, unbeknown to themselves, firmly guide the group through the predicted stages. Lieberman [28] demonstrated that the leader, unknowingly, fills a gap in the group. He systematically composed a T-group from which were excluded all individuals with a need for pairing behavior, and compared its development during a three-week human relations laboratory with a control group, a naturally composed group. He found that the leaders of the control group expressed the same amount of pairing behavior throughout the course of the group; however, the leader of the experimental group expressed five times more pairing in the third week than in the first. Apparently he was attempting to fill the need for warmth which had developed in the experimental group. With no control over the highly influential behavior of the leader the determination of the "natural" developmental sequence becomes very difficult indeed.

A study by Psathas and Hardert [29] is illustrative of the quandary posed for researchers. They collected the group leaders' statements which the members had considered most significant in the initial, middle, and late stages of a sensitivity group and found that statements concerned with acceptance were far more frequent in the final stages than in earlier stages.*
However, the interpretation of these results is problematic. It is possible that the members were indeed intrinsically more concerned with affection late in the course of the group and that the leaders' statements were merely a reflection of the group trend; furthermore, the members were so attuned to this phase that they considered the leaders' intimacy statements as most significant. However, it is also possible that the leaders had predetermined that intimacy should be dealt with in the last part of the group and thus influenced the group by making a large number of statements to that effect.

Impact of the Patients on Group Development. The developmental sequence I have proposed perhaps accurately describes the unfolding of events in a theoretical, unpeopled therapy group. This developmental scheme is much like the major theme of an ultramodern symphony which is all but obscured by shrill notes and discordant chords. In the group, the obfuscation derives from the richness and unpredictability of human interaction, which complicates the course of treatment and yet contributes to the excitement and challenge of the therapy group.

* Seven two-week training groups at the human relations laboratory were studied, all sessions were recorded, members at the end of each session were asked to recall the leaders' statements which seemed most significant. The verbatim statement was then transcribed from the tape and categorized according to a list of twelve norm categories selected from the literature. In the early and middle stages "acceptance" was ranked fourth while in the final stage it was ranked first of the twelve categories.

Generally the course of events in the early meetings is heavily influenced by the group member with the "loudest" interpersonal pathology. By "loudest" I refer not to severity of pathology but to pathology which is most immediately manifest in the group: for example, monopolistic proclivities, exhibitionism, promiscuous self-disclosure, easily expressed anger or judgmentalism, or an unbridled inclination to exert control. Not infrequently these patients receive covert encouragement from the therapist and the other group members. The therapists value these patients because they provide a focus of irritation in the group, stimulate the expression of affect, and enhance the interest and excitement of the meeting. The other patients initially often welcome the opportunity to hide behind the protagonist as they hesitantly test out the group.

In a study of the therapy dropouts of nine outpatient groups,[30] I found that in five groups a patient labeled as an "early provocateur" fled the therapy group within the first dozen meetings. These patients, though differing from one another dynamically, assumed a similar role in the group: they stormed in, furiously activated the group, and then vanished. They were alternately referred to by their therapists and by themselves as "catalysts," "targets," "hostile interpreters," "the only honest ones," etc. Some of these early provocateurs were active counterdependents and challenged the therapist early in the group. One, for example, who asked in the third meeting why the session has to end when the therapist decrees, attempted to rally interest in a leaderless meeting or, only half-jokingly, in an investigation of the leader's personal problems. Others prided themselves on their honesty and bluntness, mincing no words in giving the other members candid feedback; while others, heavily conflicted in intimacy, both seeking it and fearing it, engaged in considerable self-disclosure and exhorted the group to reciprocate. Although the early provocateurs usually claimed that they were impervious to the opinions and evaluations of others, in fact they cared very much, and in each instance created a nonvariable role for themselves in the group. The therapist must recognize this phenomenon early in the group and, through clarification and interpretation of their role, help prevent them from commiting social suicide. Perhaps, even more important, he must recognize and discontinue his own covert encouragement of their behavior. It is not uncommon for the therapist to be stunned and alarmed at the early provocateur's dropping out; he so welcomed the behavior of these patients that he failed to appreciate both their distress and his own dependence on them for keeping the group alive.

The development of a group may also be heavily influenced by the presence of members who are experienced therapy group patients. For example, one group which had shrunk to a size of three members was rebuilt after a three-month summer vacation by adding four new members (none of whom had ever been in a group before) and a new therapist. The three members were powerful culture bearers and the group moved very quickly by passing such early developmental stages as symptom description, suggestions and advice, and search for structure.

Despite these shortcomings, the proposed developmental sequence has much to recommend it. Common sense decrees that a group first deal with its *raison d'être* and boundaries, then with dominance and submission, and later, as shared experience increases, with issues of intimacy and closeness. Recently at a two-week group workshop I took part in an intergroup exercise in which the sixty participants were asked to form four groups in any manner they wished and then to study the ongoing relationships between groups. The sixty participants, in near panic,* stampeded from the large room toward the four rooms designated for the four small groups. In the group in which I participated, the first words spoken after approximately sixteen members had entered the room were, "Close the door. Don't let anyone else in!" The first act of the group was to appoint an official doorkeeper. Once the group's boundaries were defined and its identity vis-à-vis the outside world established, the group turned its attention to regulating the distribution of power by speedily, before multiple bids for power could immobilize the group, electing a chairman. Only much later was intimacy fully experienced and discussed in the group.

Once the therapist has a concept of the developmental sequence, he is more easily able to maintain his objectivity and to appreciate the course the group pursues despite considerably yawing. He may note that the group never progresses past a certain stage or may omit others. At times, therapists may demand something for which the group is not yet ready. For example, some neophyte therapists express impatience at the group members' seeming lack of concern for each other. One student therapist compared the members to the thirty-eight silent witnesses [32] who, several years ago in New York City, remained uninvolved as they heard a young woman being murdered. What he did not appreciate is that mutual caring and concern develops late in the group; in the beginning, members are more apt to view each other as interlopers or rivals for the royal touch of the therapist.

---

* The panic is an inevitable part of this exercise,[31] probably stemming from a primitive fear of being excluded from the primary group.

Membership: Dropouts, Absences, Tardiness, Addition of New Members

The early developmental sequence of the therapy group is heavily influenced by membership problems. Turnover in membership, tardiness, and absence are facts of life in the developing group and often threaten its stability and integrity. Although the therapist starts the group with seven members, temporary or permanent attrition occurs when members miss meetings or drop out; the group's attention and energy is directed then from the developmental tasks to the problem of maintaining membership. The therapist must intercede to discourage irregular attendance and, when necessary, to replace dropouts by adding new members.

MEMBERSHIP TURNOVER

In the normal course of events, 10 to 35 per cent of the members drop out of the group in the first twelve to twenty meetings; new members are added and often a similar percentage of these additions drop out in their first dozen or so meetings. Only after this does the group solidify and begin to engage in matters other than those which concern group stability. Generally by the time patients have remained in the group for approximately twenty meetings they have made the necessary long-term commitment. In one attendance study [33] of five outpatient groups, there was considerable turnover in membership over the first twelve meetings, a settling-in between the twelfth and twentieth, and near perfect attendance, with excellent punctuality and no dropouts, between the twentieth and forty-fifth meeting (the end of the study).

ATTENDANCE AND PUNCTUALITY

Although therapists initially encourage regular attendance and punctuality, difficulties invariably arise in the early stages of the group. The therapist must not accept fatalistically the impossibility of seven individuals' synchronizing busy schedules and transportation so as to attend punctually and regularly. Tardiness and irregular attendance usually signify resistance to therapy and should be regarded in the same way in which one regards these phenomena in individual therapy. When several members are often late or absent, one must look for the source of the group resistance; for some reason, cohesiveness is limited and the group is floundering. When a group has solidified into a hard-working cohesive group, many months may go by with perfect attendance and punctuality.

At other times, the resistance is individual rather than group based. I am continually amazed by the transformation which occurs in some patients who for long periods of time are tardy because of absolutely unavoidable contingencies—for example, periodic business conferences, classroom rescheduling, babysitter emergencies. These patients, after recognizing and working through the resistance, may become the most punctual members for months on end. Thus one periodically late member hesitated to involve himself in the group because of his shame about his impotence and homosexual fantasies. After he disclosed himself and worked through his shame, he found that the crucial high-priority business commitments responsible for his lateness (commitments which he later disclosed consisted of perusing his afternoon mail) suddenly ceased to exist.

Occasionally a problem in attendance is inextricably linked with the patient's psychopathology. For example, one patient who sought therapy because of a crippling fear of authority figures and a pervasive inability to assert himself in interpersonal situations was frequently late because he was unable to muster the courage to interrupt a conversation or conference with a business associate.

Whatever the basis for resistance, it is behavior which must, for several reasons, be modified *before* it can be understood and worked through. For one thing irregular attendance is destructive to the group; it is, in a sense, contagious and begets group demoralization and further absences. Obviously it is impossible to work on an issue in the absence of the relevant patients; there are few exercises more futile than addressing the wrong audience and discussing and deploring irregular attendance with the group members who are present—the regular, punctual patients.

Various methods of influencing the attendance rate have been adopted by various therapists. Many stress the importance of regular attendance during pretherapy interviews. Patients who appear likely to have scheduling or transportation problems are best referred for individual therapy, as are patients who must be out of town every four weeks or who, a few weeks after the group begins, plan an extended out-of-town vacation. Charging full fees for missed sessions is standard practice unless there is an extraordinary excuse for absence explained to the therapist well in advance. Many group therapists charge patients a set fee per month; the fee remains constant whether there are four or five meetings a month or whether the patient misses a meeting for any reason. Other therapists attempt to harness group pressure by, for example, refusing to hold the meeting until a predetermined number of members (usually three or four) are present. Even if not formalized in this manner, the pressure exerted by the other members is the most effective lever brought to bear on errant members. The group is often frustrated and angered by the repetitions and false starts necessitated by irregular attendance; the therapist should encourage the members to express their reactions to late or absent members. At times, though, one must keep in mind that the immature group often welcomes the small meeting, regarding it as an opportunity for more individualized attention from the leader; at those times the therapist's anxiety and concern about attendance is not shared by the group.

It is helpful to the group for the therapist to request that patients phone in advance should they find that they must miss or arrive late at a meeting so that he may announce this in the session; without this notification the group may spend considerable time expressing their curiosity or concern about the missing member. Often, in advanced groups, the fantasies of the patients about why a member is absent provide the group with valuable material for the therapeutic process; however, in early groups the speculations are often superficial and unfruitful. Occasionally, though, the absence of members may result in certain important shifts of behavior and in the emergence and expression of feelings which facilitate therapy.

For example, one two-month-old group composed of four women and three men met one day when two of the men were unable to attend. Albert, the remaining male, had previously been withdrawn and submissive in the group. In the meeting in which he was alone with the four women, a dramatic transformation occurred: Albert suddenly erupted into activity, talked about himself, questioned the other members, spoke loudly and forcefully, and on a couple of occasions challenged the therapist. His nonverbal behavior was saturated with quasi-courtship bids [34] directed at the women members—for example, frequent adjustment of his necktie knot and preening of the hair at his temples. Later in the course of the meeting the group focused on Albert's change, and he realized and expressed his fear and envy of the two missing males, both of whom were aggressive, assertive men. He had long experienced a pervasive sense of social and sexual impotence which had been reinforced by his feeling that he had never made a significant impact on a group of people and especially a group of women. In subsequent weeks Albert did much valuable work on these issues—issues which might not have become accessible for many months without the adventitious absence of other members.

My clinical preference is to encourage attendance in most of these ways but never, regardless of how small the group, to cancel a session. There is considerable therapeutic value in the patients' knowing that the group is always there, stable and reliable; its constancy will in time beget constancy of attendance. Furthermore, I have had many group sessions with small membership, even at times with a single member, that have proven to be critical meetings for the patients involved. The technical problem with small meetings, especially of three or fewer members, is that the therapist may revert to focusing on intrapsychic processes in a manner characteristic of individual therapy and abandon his focus on group and interpersonal issues. It is far more therapeutically consistent and technically undemanding to focus in depth on group and interpersonal processes even in the smallest of sessions. Consider the following clinical example from a ten-month-old group:

For various reasons—vacations, illnesses, and resistance—only two members (and the therapist) attended: Mary, a thirty-eight-year-old depressed borderline schizophrenic, who on two previous occasions had required hospitalization; and Edward, a twenty-three-year-old schizoid, psychosexually immature individual with moderately severe ulcerative colitis.

Mary spent much of the early part of the meeting describing the depth of her despair, which during the past week had reached such proportions that she had been preoccupied with suicide and, since the group therapist had been out of town, had visited the emergency room at the hospital. While there, she had surreptitiously read her medical chart and seen a consultation note written a year previously by the group therapist in which he had diagnosed her as borderline schizophrenic. She said that she had been anticipating this diagnosis and now wished the therapist to hospitalize her. Edward then recalled a fragment of a dream which he had dreamt several weeks before but had not discussed: the therapist was sitting at a large desk interviewing him; he, Edward, stood up and looked at the paper on which the therapist was writing. There he saw in huge letters one word which covered the entire page: IMPOTENT. The therapist helped them to discuss their feelings of awe, helpless dependence, and resentment toward him, as well as their inclination to shift responsibility and project their bad feelings about themselves onto him.

Mary proceeded to underscore her helplessness by describing her inability to cook for herself and her delinquence in paying her bills, which was so extreme that she now feared police action against her. The therapist and Edward both commented on her persistent reluctance to comment on her positive accomplishments—for example, her continued high-level performance in her teaching profession. The therapist wondered if her presentation of herself as helpless was not designed to elicit responses of caring and concern from the other members and the therapist, which she felt would not be forthcoming in any other way.

Edward then mentioned that he had gone to the medical library the previous day to read some of the therapist's professional articles. In response to the therapist's question about what he really wanted to find out, Edward answered that he guessed he really wanted to know how the therapist felt about him and later described, for the first time, his longing for the therapist's sole attention and love.

Later the therapist expressed his dismay at Mary's reading his note in her medical record. Since there is a realistic component to a patient's anxiety upon learning that her therapist has diagnosed her as "borderline schizophrenic," the therapist discussed, quite candidly, his own discomfort at having to use diagnostic labels for hospital records and conveyed to the patient the confusion surrounding psychiatric nosological terminology; he recalled as best he could his reasons for using that particular label and its implications.

Mary then commented upon the absent members and wondered if she had driven them from the group (a common reaction to the absence of members). She dwelled on her unworthiness and, at the therapist's suggestion, made an inventory of her baleful characteristics, citing her slovenliness, selfishness, greed, envy, and hostile feelings toward all those in her social environment. Edward both supported Mary and resonated with her by identifying many of these feelings in himself. He discussed how difficult it was for him to reveal himself in the group (Edward had discussed very little of himself previously in the group). Later he discussed his fear of getting drunk or losing control in other ways; for one thing he might become indiscreet sexually. Edward then discussed, for the first time, his fear of sex, his impotence, his inability to maintain an erection, and his last-minute refusals to take advantage of sexual opportunities. Mary empathized deeply with Edward and, although she had for some time regarded sex as abhorrent, expressed the strong feeling that she would like to help him by offering herself to him sexually. Edward then described his strong sexual attraction to Mary, and later both he and Mary discussed their sexual feelings toward the other members of the group. The therapist made the observation, one which proved subsequently to be of great therapeutic importance to Mary, that her interest in Edward and her desire to offer herself to him sexually belied many of the items in her inventory: her selfishness, greed, and ubiquitous hostility to others.

The aspects of this meeting relevant to the present discussion are self-evident. Although only two members were present, they met as a group and not as two individual patients. The other members were discussed *in absentia*, and previously undisclosed interpersonal feelings between the two patients and toward the therapist were expressed and analyzed. It was a valuable session, deeply meaningful to both participants.

THE ADDITION OF NEW MEMBERS

There are two major junctures in the group when new patients are often added: during the first twelve to twenty meetings (to replace early dropouts) and after approximately one and a half years (to replace improved, graduating members).

Timing. The success of this operation depends, in part, upon proper timing; there are favorable and unfavorable times to introduce new members into a group. Generally a group which is in crisis, or is actively engaged in an internecine struggle, or has suddenly entered into a new phase of development, is an unfavorable group for the addition of new members; often it will reject the newcomers or else will evade confrontation with the pressing group issue and instead redirect its energy toward the incoming members. An example might be a group which is, for the first time, dealing with hostile feelings toward a controlling, monopolistic patient or a group which has recently developed such cohesiveness and trust that a member has, for the first time, shared the secret of his homosexuality with the group.

The most auspicious period for adding new members is during a phase of stagnation in the group. Many groups, especially older ones, sensing the need for new blood, actively encourage the therapist to add members.

Response of the Group. A Punch cartoon, cited by Foulkes,[35] portrays a harassed woman and her child trying to push their way into a crowded train compartment. The child looks up at his mother and says, "Don't worry mother, at the next stop it will be our turn to hate!" The parallel to new patients entering the group is trenchant. Hostility to the newcomer is evident even in the group which has beseeched the therapist to add new members. A content analysis of the session in which a new member or members are introduced reveals several themes which are hardly consonant with benevolent hospitality. The group suddenly spends far more time than in previous meetings discussing "the good old days." Long-departed group members and events of bygone meetings are avidly recalled, as new members are guilelessly reminded, lest they have forgotten, of their novitiate status.

Similarly members may express resemblances they perceive between the new member and some member no longer present in the group. Recently I observed a meeting in which two new members were introduced; the group noted a similarity between one of them and Matthew, a patient who (the newcomer shortly learned) had committed suicide a year before; the other patient was compared with Roger, a patient who had dropped out, discouraged and unimproved after three months of therapy. These groups, be it noted, were unaware of the acerbity of their greetings and consciously felt that they were extending a welcome to the newcomers. The group may also express its ambivalence by discussing in the newcomers' first meeting threatening, confidence-shaking issues. For example, in the seventeenth session (one in which two new members entered) one group discussed for the first time the co-therapists' competence. The members brought up the fact that the therapists were listed in the hospital catalogue as resident-students and that they might be leading their first group. This issue, a valid and important one which must be discussed, was nonetheless highly threatening to new members. It is of interest that the information was already known to several group members but until that meeting had never been broached in the group.

There are, of course, simultaneous evidences of welcome and support for new members, which are particularly marked if the group has been searching for new members. The members may exercise great gentleness and patience in dealing with new members' initial fear or defensiveness. The group, in fact, may collude in many ways to increase the attractiveness of the group for the newcomer. Often patients may gratuitously offer testimonials and describe the various improvements they have experienced. In one such group, the newcomer asked a disgruntled, resistive member about her progress; and, before she could reply, two other members, sensing that she would devaluate the group, interrupted and described their own progress. Although groups may unconsciously wish to discourage newcomers, they would seem to prefer to do so by threatening the new member or by severe initiation rites; the group is not willing to deter new members by so devaluating the group that the candidates choose not to join it.

Reasons for the Group's Response. There are several reasons for the group's ambivalent response to new members. Some members who highly prize the solidarity and cohesiveness of the group may consider any proposed change as a threat to the status quo. Others may envision the new members as potential rivals for the therapist's and the group's attention; they perceive their own fantasied role as favored child to be in jeopardy. Still other members, particularly those conflicted in the area of control and dominance, may regard the new member as a threat to their position in the hierarchy of power or influence. In one group, in which a new female patient was being introduced, the two incumbent female members, desperately protecting their stake, employed many prestige-enhancing devices, including the recitation of poetry. When John Donne is quoted in a therapy group as part of the incoming ritual, it is hardly for an aesthetic end.

251

A common concern of the group is that, even though new members are needed, they will nonetheless slow up the group. The group fears that familiar material will have to be repeated for the newcomers and that the group must recycle, as it were, and relive the stages of gradual social introduction and ritualistic etiquette. This expectation proves to be unrealistic; new patients introduced into an ongoing group generally move quickly into the prevailing level of group communication and bypass the early testing phases characteristic of the members in a newly formed group. One additional but less frequent source of the ambivalent welcome to the newcomer is that group patients who have improved are occasionally threatened by contrast with individuals in whom they see themselves as they were at the beginning of their own therapy. In order to avoid re-exposure to painful, past periods of life, they will frequently shun new patients who appear as reincarnations of their earlier selves.

Therapeutic Guidelines. New members entering an ongoing group need to be prepared by the therapist for the therapy experience. In addition to preparing these patients in the standard manner (see Chapter 9), the therapist should also attempt to help them deal with the unique stresses accompanying entry into an established group. I prefer to anticipate for patients their feelings of exclusion and of bewilderment at entering an unusual culture which they have not helped to build. They may be reassured that they will be allowed to enter and participate at their own rate. New patients entering established groups are especially prone to fears of contagion, since they are immediately confronted with patients revealing "sicker" sides of themselves than are revealed in the first meetings of a new group; this contingency should therefore be discussed with the patient. It is rarely necessary to describe the group to the new patient or to recount the past history of the group unless the group is a peculiarly hostile, threatening one for the new members. Many therapists prefer to introduce two new members at a time. Such a practice may have advantages both for the group and for the new members. The group conserves energy and time by assimilating two patients at once; the new patients may ally with each other and thereby feel less alien. Although introduction in pairs does not result in a statistically lower dropout rate [30] and occasionally, if one patient integrates himself into the group with much greater facility than the other, may backfire and create even greater discomfort for a newcomer, nevertheless introduction in pairs has much to recommend it.

Occasionally clinics attempt to amalgamate nuclei of two groups which have been reduced in number. It is my clinical impression that this procedure is unsound; too often a culture clash and clique formation along lines of the previous groups may persist for a remarkably long period of time.

The introduction of new patients may, if properly considered, enhance the therapeutic process of the old members who may respond to a new-comer in highly idiosyncratic styles. An important principle of group therapy that we have discussed on several previous occasions is that every major stimulus presented to the group elicits a variety of responses by the group members. The investigation of the reasons behind these differential responses is generally a rewarding pursuit which clarifies aspects of character structure. To observe that other patients respond to a situation in a manner markedly different from one's own is an arresting experience which, if exploited, can provide considerable insight into one's behavior. Such an opportunity is unavailable in individual therapy and constitutes one of the chief strengths of the group therapeutic format. An illustrative clinical example may clarify this point.

A new member, Alice—a forty-year-old divorcee—was introduced at a group's eighteenth meeting. The three men in the group greeted her in striking-ly different fashions. Peter arrived fifteen minutes late and thereby missed the introduction. For the next hour Peter was active in the group, discussing issues left over from the previous meeting as well as events occurring in his life during the past week. He totally ignored Alice, avoiding even glancing at her—a formidable feat in a group of six people in close physical proximity. Later in the evening, as others attempted to help Alice participate, he, still without introduc-ing himself, fired questions at her in a prosecuting, attorney-like fashion. Peter, a twenty-eight-year-old devout Catholic father of four, had sought therapy be-cause he, as he phrased it, loved women too much and had had a series of extramarital love affairs. In subsequent meetings the group used the events of Alice's first meeting to help Paul investigate the nature of his "love" for women. Gradually he came to recognize how he used women, including his wife, as part objects, valuing them for their genitals only and disregarding their personal integ-rity and experiential world.

The two other men in the group, Brian and Arthur, on the other hand, were preoccupied with Alice during her first meeting. Arthur, a twenty-four-year-old homosexual who sought therapy in order to change his sexual orientation, react-ed strongly to Alice and found that he could not look at her without experienc-ing the strongest sense of embarrassment. His discomfort and blushing were ap-parent to the other members, who helped him explore far more deeply than he had previously his relationship with the women in the group. Arthur had desex-ualized the other two women in the group by establishing in his fantasy a brother-sister relationship with them. Alice, who was sexually attractive, divorced, and "available" and at the same time old enough to evoke in him

253

affect-laden feelings about his mother, presented a special problem for Arthur, who had previously been settling down into a too comfortable niche in the group.

Brian, on the other hand, transfixed Alice with his gaze and delivered an unwavering broad smile to her throughout the meeting. An extraordinarily dependent twenty-three-year-old, Brian had sought therapy for depression following the breakup of a love affair. Having lost his mother in infancy, he had been raised by a succession of governesses and had had only occasional contact with an aloof, powerful father of whom he was terrified. His romantic affairs, always with considerably older women, had invariably collapsed because of the insatiable demands he made on the relationship. The other women in the group in the past few meetings had similarly withdrawn from him, and with progressive candor had confronted him with, as they termed it, his puppy-dog presentation of self. Brian thus welcomed Alice, hoping to find in her a new source of succor. Alice in subsequent meetings proved to be quite helpful to Brian, as she revealed her feeling during her first meeting of extreme discomfort at his beseeching smile and her persistent feeling that a relationship with Brian would totally empty her.

In the next three chapters we will discuss later stages of therapy. Freud once compared psychotherapy to chess in that far more is known and written about the opening and the end game than the middle game. Accordingly the opening stages of therapy and termination may be discussed with some degree of exactness, but the vast bulk of therapy cannot be systematically described. Instead the following chapters deal with general issues, problems, and techniques of therapy.

REFERENCES

1. S. Freud, *Group Psychology and the Analysis of the Ego* (New York: Bantam Books, 1960), p. 76.
2. P. Blachly, paper presented at National Conference of Suicidology, Chicago, 1968.
3. E. Semrad, cited by W. Schutz, *The Interpersonal Underworld*, (Palo Alto: Science and Behavior Books, 1966), p. 170.
4. Schutz, *op. cit.*, p. 24.
5. G. Bach, *Intensive Group Therapy* (New York: Ronald Press, 1954).
6. B. Tuckman, "Developmental Sequence in Small Groups," *Psychol. Bull., 63:* 384–399, 1965.
7. S. Parker, "Leadership Patterns in a Psychiatric Ward," *Human Relations, 11:* 287–301, 1958.
8. R. Liberman, "Social Reinforcement of Group Dynamics," paper delivered at American Group Psychotherapy Association Convention, Chicago, January 1968.

9. P. Slater, *Microcosm* (New York: John Wiley and Sons, 1966).
10. S. Freud, *Totem and Taboo,* trans. J. Strachey (London: Routledge and Kegan Paul, 1950).
11. J. Friedman and S. Gassel, "The Chorus in Sophocles' *Oedipus Tyrannus,*" *Psychoanal. Quart., 19:* 213–226, 1950.
12. S. H. Foulkes and E. J. Anthony, *Group Psychotherapy—the Psychoanalytic Approach* (Harmondsworth, Middlesex: Penguin Books, 1957).
13. W. G. Bennis, "Patterns and Vicissitudes in T-Group Development," in L. P. Bradford, J. R. Gibb, and K. D. Benne, *T-Group Theory and Laboratory Method: Innovation in Re-education* (New York: John Wiley and Sons, 1964), pp. 248–278.
14. T. Mills, personal communication, April 1968.
15. Bach, *op. cit.,* p. 42.
16. H. I. Clapham and A. B. Sclare, "Group Psychotherapy with Asthmatic Patients," *Int. J. Group Psychother., 8:* 44–54, 1958.
17. F. K. Taylor, "The Therapeutic Factors of Group-Analytic Treatment," *J. Ment. Sci., 96:* 976–997, 1950.
18. H. Coffey, M. Freedman, T. Leary, and A. Ossorio, "Community Service and Social Research—Group Psychotherapy in a Church Program," *J. Soc. Iss., 6:* 14–61, 1950.
19. R. S. Shellow, J. L. Ward, and S. Rubenfeld, "Group Therapy and the Institutionalized Delinquent," *Int. J. Group Psychother., 8:* 265–275, 1958.
20. D. Whitaker and M. A. Lieberman, *Psychotherapy Through the Group Process* (New York: Atherton Press, 1964).
21. J. Mann and E. V. Semrad, "The Use of Group Therapy in Psychoses," *J. Soc. Casework, 29:* 176–181, 1948.
22. M. Grotjahn, "The Process of Maturation in Group Psychotherapy and in the Group Therapist," *Psychiatry, 13:* 63–67, 1950.
23. A. P. Noyes, *Modern Clinical Psychiatry* (4th ed.; Philadelphia: Saunders, 1953), pp. 589–591.
24. J. Abrahams, "Group Psychotherapy: Implications for Direction and Supervision of Mentally Ill Patients," in T. Muller (ed.), *Mental Health in Nursing* (Washington, D.C.: Catholic University Press, 1949), pp. 77–83.
25. J. J. Thorpe and B. Smith, "Phases in Group Development in Treatment of Drug Addicts," *Int. J. Group Psychother., 3:* 66–78, 1953.
26. W. Bennis, R. Burke, H. Cutter, H. Harrington, and J. Hoffman, "A Note on Some Problems of Measurement and Prediction in a Training Group," *Group Psychother., 10:* 328–341, 1957.
27. D. A. Hamburg, personal communication, 1968.
28. M. A. Lieberman, "The Relationship of Group Climate to Individual Change," unpublished doctoral dissertation, University of Chicago, 1958.
29. G. Psathas and R. Hardert, "Trainer Interventions and Normative Patterns in the T-Group," *J. Appl. Behav. Sci., 2:* 149–169, 1966.
30. I. D. Yalom, "A Study of Group Therapy Dropouts," *Arch. Gen. Psychiat., 14:* 393–414, 1966.
31. K. Rice, *Learning for Leadership* (London: Tavistock Publications, 1965).
32. A. M. Rosenthal, *Thirty-Eight Witnesses* (New York: McGraw-Hill, 1964).
33. I. D. Yalom, P. S. Houts, S. M. Zimerberg, and K. H. Rand, "Prediction of Improvement in Group Therapy: An Exploratory Study," *Arch. Gen. Psychiat., 17:* 159–168, 1967.
34. A. Sheflin, "Quasi-Courtship Behavior in Psychotherapy," *Psychiatry, 28:* 245–257, 1965.
35. Foulkes and Anthony, *op. cit.,* p. 137.

255

11

THE ADVANCED
GROUP

❧

Once the group has survived its first few months, it is no longer possible to describe discrete stages of development. When a group achieves a degree of stability, the long working-through process begins: the major curative factors described in the earlier chapters operate with increasing force and effectiveness. Each member, as he engages more deeply in the group, reveals to others and to himself his problems in living, and there is no limit to the richness and complexity which may characterize the sessions of the group.

No one, therefore, can offer specific procedural guidelines for each contingency. In general, the therapist must maximize the development and operation of the curative factors. The application of the basic principles of the therapist's role and technique to specific group events and to each patient's therapy (as discussed in Chapters 5 and 6) constitutes the art of psychotherapy, and for this there is no substitute for experience, supervision, and intuition.

Certain issues and problems occur, however, with sufficient regularity to warrant discussion. This chapter considers the phenomena of subgrouping, self-disclosure, conflict, and termination of therapy. Chapter 12, "The Problem Patient," deals with certain recurrent behavioral configurations which present a challenge to the therapist and to the group, and Chapter 13 describes some specialized techniques of therapy.

Subgrouping

Fractionalization—the splitting off of sub-units—occurs in every social organization. The process may be transient or enduring, helpful or harmful, for the parent organization. Therapy groups are no exception; subgroup formation is an inevitable and usually disruptive feature in the life of the group; and yet there, too, the process, if understood and harnessed properly, may further the therapeutic work.

Subgroup formation in the therapy group arises from the belief of two or more members that they can derive more gratification from a relationship with each other than from a relationship with the entire group. Subgroups often arise from extragroup socializing. A clique of three or four members may begin to visit each others' homes, to have lengthy telephone conversations, or to engage in business ventures with one another. Occasionally two members will become sexually involved. Subgroup formation may occur, however, completely within the confines of the group therapy room, as members who perceive themselves to be similar form coalitions. There may be any number of common bonds: a comparable educational level, similar values, similar age, marital status, or group status (e.g., the "old-timer" original members), etc. Social organizations, especially those larger than a therapy group, will characteristically develop opposing factions—two or more conflicting subgroups—but such is not the case in therapy groups. Here usually one clique of members forms, while the remaining patients, exluded from the clique, do not coalesce into a second subgroup.

The members of the subgroup may be identified by a general code of behavior: they agree with one another regardless of the issue and avoid confrontations among their own membership; they may exchange knowing glances when a non-clique member speaks; they may arrive and depart from the meeting together.

EFFECTS OF SUBGROUPING

Subgrouping can have an extraordinarily disruptive effect on the course of the therapy group. In a study[1] of thirty-five patients who prematurely dropped out from group therapy, I found that eleven (31 per cent) dropped out largely because of problems arising from subgrouping. Complications arise whether the patient is included or excluded from a subgroup.

257

Inclusion. Those included in a dyadic or larger subgroup often find that group life is vastly more complicated and less rewarding. As a patient transfers his allegiance from the group goals to the subgroup goals, loyalty becomes a major issue. Should he abide by the group procedural rules of free and honest discussion of feelings if, in so doing, he would be breaking a confidence established secretly with another member? For example, two group members, Christine and Jerry, often met after a therapy session to have long, intense conversations. Jerry had remained withdrawn in the group and had sought out Christine because, as he informed her, he felt that she alone could understand him. After obtaining her promise of confidentiality, he soon was able to reveal to her his homosexual obsessions and occasional pedophilic involvements. Back in the group, Christine felt restrained by her promise and avoided interaction with Jerry, who eventually dropped out unimproved. Ironically Christine was an exceptionally sensitive member of the group, who might have been particularly useful to Jerry by encouraging him to participate in the group had she not been restrained by the antitherapeutic subgroup norms (i.e., her promise of confidentiality). Another example of the conflict between group and subgroup norms is cited by Lindt and Sherman:[2]

An older, paternal man had been giving two other patients a ride home and had invited them to see television at his house. The visitors witnessed an argument between the older patient and his wife, and at a subsequent group session told him that they felt he was mistreating his wife. The older patient, evidently feeling betrayed, and considering the group his enemy rather than his friend, seemed to develop feelings of rejection and dropped out of treatment.

Similar problems occur when group members engage in sexual relations; they often hesitate to "besmirch" (as one patient phrased it) an intimate relationship by giving it a public airing. But, as a consequence, the two participants sacrifice their value for each other as helpmates in the group; lest they betray private confidences, they will frequently become impersonal to each other during the group session. Often the other group members are dimly aware that something unusual is occurring that is being actively avoided in the group discussion—a state of affairs which usually results in a global group inhibition.

A group in which some preliminary research was being conducted provides some evidence for these comments.[3] Several observers (as well as the patients themselves in post-group questionnaires) rated each meeting along a seven-point scale for: amount of affect expressed, amount of self-disclosure, and general value of the session. In addition, the communication flow system was recorded with the number and direction of each patient's statements charted on a who-to-whom matrix. In the observed group, Bruce and Geraldine had developed a sexual relationship which was kept secret from the therapist and the group for three weeks. During these three weeks there was a steep downward gradient in the scoring of the quality of the meetings, with particularly limited expression of affect and diminished self-disclosure. Moreover, the overall verbal activity of the group decreased and scarcely a single verbal exchange between Geraldine and Bruce was recorded! The couple resolved the problem by means of a pact according to which Geraldine dropped out of the group (not an uncommon form of resolution); Bruce then discussed the entire incident in the next meeting, which the ratings revealed as a valuable and intense meeting.

Exclusion: Exclusion from the subgroup also complicates group life. Anxiety associated with earlier exclusion experiences is evoked which, if not discharged by working through, may reach disabling levels. Often it is exceptionally difficult for members to comment on their feelings of exclusion; they may be disinclined to intrude into a relationship or to risk incurring the wrath of the involved members by discussion of the subgroup in the session.

Nor are therapists immune to this problem. Recently one of my supervisees observed two of his group patients who were both married walking arm in arm along the street. The therapist found himself unable to comment on this and supplied a number of rationalizations: the therapist should not place himself in the position of spy or disapproving parent in the eyes of the group; the therapist is not free to bring up nongroup material; the involved members will, when they are psychologically ready, discuss the problem. However, these are rationalizations; there is no more important issue than the interrelationship of the group members. If the therapist feels extremely uncomfortable in bringing up outside material, then often the best approach is to share both facts with the group—his observations and his reluctance to discuss them.

One college student group had a disproportionately high number of dropouts. Through a variety of factors, including poor selection and subgrouping complications, five of the original eight members dropped out. The remaining members, badly shaken by the threat to the existence of the group, banded tightly together and excluded several newcomers, each of whom dropped out after a few meetings. As Frank [4] has pointed out, this is a form of group suicide since, if continued, the group will perish from attrition. Most groups at this juncture will elaborate initiation rites. In this group the rites were particularly severe; the new members felt excluded and attacked. As one patient put it, "The group received me like,

'Who the heck are you?' I felt it was a closed corporation and I was an interloper." The culture that the original group had established was a playfully hostile one with much bantering, sarcasm, and little expression of support or positive feelings. To new members who had had no share in the creation of the culture, the atmosphere seemed exceedingly threatening and destructive. Their fears and feelings of isolation were greatly accentuated by the knowledge that the core members met socially at informal meetings to which the new members were not welcome.

CAUSES OF SUBGROUPING

Subgrouping is caused by both group and individual forces. Some groups (and some therapists) have a disproportionately high incidence of subgrouping; some individuals will invariably become involved in subgrouping in whatever group they are placed.

Subgrouping may be a manifestation of a considerable degree of undischarged hostility in the group, especially toward the leader. In their classic research on three different styles of leadership, White and Lippit [5] noted that the group was more likely to develop disruptive in-group and out-group factions under an authoritarian, restrictive style of leadership. The members, unable to express their anger and frustration directly to the leader, released these feelings by making a scapegoat of one or more members.

Whenever members decide that a subgroup offers more satisfaction than the parent group, fractionalization is likely. For example, patients with strong needs for intimacy, dependency, sexual conquests, or dominance sense the impossibility of gratifying these needs in the group and often attempt to gratify them outside of the formal group. In one sense, these patients are "acting out," in that, outside the therapy setting, they engage in an organized, symbolically determined form of behavior which relieves inner tensions. It is exceptionally difficult to discriminate, except in retrospect, "acting out" from acting or participation in the therapy group. The course of the therapy group is a continual cycle of action ("cathartic free play")[6] and analysis of this action. The social microcosm concept depends on patients engaging in their habitual patterns of behavior, which are then examined by the patient and the group. "Acting out" as a form of resistance to therapy occurs when the patient refuses to examine and to allow the group to examine his behavior. Extragroup behavior which is *not* examined in the group becomes then a particularly potent form of resistance, whereas extragroup behavior which is subsequently brought back into the group and worked through may prove to be of considerable therapeutic import.

THERAPEUTIC CONSIDERATIONS

By no means, then, is subgrouping, with or without extragroup socializing, invariably disruptive. If the goals of the subgroup are identical with the goals of the parent group, then subgrouping may ultimately enhance group cohesiveness; for example, a coffee group or a bowling league may operate successfully within a larger social organization. In one group, a dramatic example of effective subgrouping occurred when members became concerned about one of their therapy group who felt so lonely and discouraged that she considered suicide. Several group members maintained a week-long telephone vigil, which proved to be beneficial both to the patient and to the cohesiveness of the entire group.

Meetings of the entire group without the leader—for example, the post-group coffee session or the scheduled leaderless group meeting (to be discussed in Chapter 13)—also prove helpful in the therapeutic work; aspects of members' behavior not evident during the therapy sessions may become apparent in a more traditional social setting without the inhibiting presence of the therapist.

Extragroup social meetings of dyads or cliques may also prove quite useful, provided that the goals of the parent group are not relinquished. If such meetings are viewed as part of the group rhythm of behaving and understanding this behavior, much valuable information can be made available to the group. For this to occur, the involved members must inform the group of all extragroup events. If they do not, the disruptive effects on cohesiveness we have described will take place. It is not the subgrouping per se that is destructive to the group but the conspiracy of silence that generally surrounds it.

In reality, once-weekly groups generally experience all the disruptive effects of subgrouping and few of the potentially beneficial ones. A large proportion of extragroup socializing never comes directly to the group's attention, and the behavior of the involved members is never made available for analysis in the group. For example, the extragroup relationship described earlier between Christine and Jerry, in which Jerry revealed in confidence his homosexual behavior, never was made known to the group. Christine disclosed the incident over a year later to a research psychiatrist who interviewed her in a psychotherapy outcome study!

The therapist should, then, encourage open discussion and analysis of all extragroup contacts and all in-group coalitions. It may be emphasized in the pregroup preparation that it is the patient's responsibility to report extragroup contacts to the group. If the therapist surmises from glances between two members in the group or from their appearance together outside the group that a special relationship exists between them, he should not hesitate to present his feeling to the group. No criticism or accusation is implied, since the investigation and understanding of a possible affectionate relationship between two members may be as therapeutically rewarding as the exploration of a hostile impasse. Furthermore, other members must be encouraged to discuss their reaction to the relationship, whether it be one of envy, jealousy, rejection, or vicarious satisfaction.

One practical caveat: patients engaged in some extragroup relationship which they are not prepared to discuss in the therapy group may request the therapist for an individual session and ask that the material discussed not be divulged to the rest of the group. The therapist who gives such a promise of confidentiality soon finds that he is in an untenable collusion from which it is difficult to extricate himself. I would suggest that the group therapist *never* offer a promise of confidentiality; instead he should only assure the patients that he will be guided by his professional judgment and act in their therapeutic behalf.

Therapy group members may develop sexual relationships with one another but not with any great frequency. The therapy group is not a prurient group; patients have severe sexual conflicts resulting in such problems as impotence, frigidity, social alienation, and sexual guilt. Probably far less sexual involvement occurs in a therapy group than in a social or professional group with a similar longevity.

The therapist cannot, by edict, prevent the formation of sexual relations or any other form of subgrouping. I agree with Wolf who states:

. . . men and women who become so engaged do so compulsively and generally drift into physical familiarity whether the physician forbids it or not. Then the therapist is faced with their sense of guilt, a tendency to hide aspects and a secret defiance that complicates and obscures the significance of the act. Furthermore, patients who leap into bed with one another do so rather extensively with people outside the group. In the therapeutic setting, the repetition of the sexual act has the advantage of subjecting compulsive promiscuity to examination under the microscope.[7]

Consider the clinical example (described in Chapter 2) of Mrs. Cape, Charles, and Louis. Recall that Mrs. Cape seduced Charles and Louis as part of her struggle for power with the group therapist. The episode was, in one sense, disruptive for the group; Mrs. Cape's husband learned of the incident and threatened Charles and Louis, who, along with other members, grew so distrustful of Mrs. Cape that dissolution of the group appeared imminent. The crisis was resolved by the group's expelling Mrs. Cape (who continued therapy in another group). Despite these complications, some benefits occurred. The episode was thoroughly explored within the group and the participants obtained considerable help with their sexual pathology. For example, Charles, who had a history of a Don Juan style of relationships with women, at first disclaimed all responsibility in the matter. He washed his hands of the incident by pointing out that Mrs. Cape had asked him to go to bed, and, as he phrased it, "I don't turn down a piece of candy when it's offered." Louis also tended to disclaim responsibility for his relationships with women and customarily regarded them as objects or "pieces of tail." Both Charles and Louis were presented with powerful evidence of the implications of their act—the effects on Mrs. Cape's marriage and the effects on their own group—and so came to appreciate their personal responsibility for their acts. Mrs. Cape, for the first time, realized the sadistic nature of her sexuality; not only did she employ sex as a weapon against the therapist but, as we have already described, as a means of depreciating and humiliating Charles and Louis.

If the therapist cannot forbid subgrouping, neither should he encourage it. I have found it most helpful to make my position on this problem explicit to patients in the preparatory or initial sessions; I tell them that it has been my experience that extragroup activity impedes therapy and, if necessary, I describe to the patient some of the complications we have discussed. The therapist must help the patient understand that the group therapy experience will provide him with the skills necessary to establish durable relationships but will not provide him with the relationships. If patients do not transfer their learning, they derive social gratification exclusively from the therapy group and therapy becomes interminable.

In inpatient psychotherapy groups, the problem is even more complex since the group members spend their entire day in close association with one another. For example, in a group in a psychiatric hospital for criminal offenders, a subgrouping problem had created great divisiveness. Two members, who were by far the most intelligent, articulate, and best educated members of the group, had formed a close friendship and spent much of every day together. The group sessions were characterized by an inordinate amount of tension and hostile bickering, much of it directed at these two men, who by this time had lost their separate identities and were primarily regarded, and regarded themselves, as a dyad. Much of the attacking was off-target, and the therapeutic work of the group had become overshadowed by the attempt to destroy the dyad. As the situation progressed, the therapist, with good effect, helped the group explore several themes. First the group had to consider that the two members could scarcely be punished for their subgrouping since everyone had an equal opportunity to form such a relationship. The issue of envy was thus introduced, and gradually the members discussed their own longing and inability to establish a friendship. Furthermore, they discussed their feelings of intellectual inferiority to the dyad, as well as their sense of exclusion and rejection by them. The two members had, however, augmented these reponses by their actions; both had, for years, maintained their self-esteem by demonstrating their intellectual superiority whenever possible. With other members they deliberately used polysyllabic words and maintained a conspiratorial attitude which accentuated the others' feelings of inferiority and rejection. Both profited from the group's description of the subtle rebuffs and taunts they had meted out and came to realize that others had suffered painful effects from their behavior.

In outpatient groups such an approach is not possible because the members do not have an equal opportunity for forming extragroup relationships. It has been my experience that the inclusion of two members with a special relationship—be they roommates, husband and wife, or business associates—is inevitably disruptive to the group.

Conflict in the Therapy Group*

Conflict cannot be eliminated from human society, whether we consider dyads, small groups, macrogroups, or such megagroups as nations and blocs of nations. If conflict is denied or suppressed, invariably it will manifest itself in oblique, corrosive, and often ugly ways. Although our immediate association with conflict is negative—destruction, bitterness, war, violence—a moment of reflection brings to mind positive associations; conflict brings drama, excitement, change, and development to human life and societies. Therapy groups are no exception. Conflict is inevitable in the course of the group's development; its absence, in fact, suggests some impairment of the developmental sequence. Furthermore, conflict can be harnessed in the service of the group; the group members can, in a variety of ways, profit from conflict, provided its intensity does not exceed their

* This discussion draws heavily from essays by Jerome Frank [8] and Carl Rogers.[9]

tolerance and provided that proper group norms have been established. This section will consider conflict in the therapy group—its sources, its meaning, and its value in therapy.

There are many sources of hostility in the therapy group. Initially there are antagonisms based on mutual contempt, a contempt which arises from the patient's own self-contempt. Indeed often months pass before some patients really begin to hear and respect the opinions of other members; they have so little self-regard that it is at first inconceivable that others, similar to themselves, have something valuable to offer.

Transference or parataxic distortions often generate hostility in the therapy group. A patient may respond to others, not on the basis of reality, but on the basis of an image of the other distorted by his own past relationships and his current interpersonal needs and fears. Patients may see in others aspects of significant individuals in their lives. Should the distortion be a negatively charged one, then a mutual antagonism may be easily initiated.

The "mirror reaction"[10] is a form of parataxic distortion and a particularly common source of hostility in the therapy group. Individuals may have suppressed, for years or their entire lives, some traits or desires of which they are much ashamed; when they encounter another person who embodies these very traits, they generally shun him or experience a strong but inexplicable antagonism toward him. The process may be close to consciousness and recognized easily with guidance by others, or it may be deeply buried and understood only after many months of investigation. For example:

One patient, Vincent, a second-generation Italian-American, who had grown up in the Boston slums and obtained a good education with great difficulty, had long since dissociated himself from his roots. Having invested his intellect with considerable pride, he spoke with care to avoid any nuance of his background. In fact, he abhorred the thought of his lowly past and feared that he would be found out—that others would see through his front to his real core, which he regarded as ugly, dirty, and repugnant. In the group Vincent experienced extreme antagonism for another member, also of Italian descent, who had, in his values and in his facial and hand gestures, retained his identification with his ethnic group. It was through his investigation of his antagonism toward the other that Vincent arrived at many important insights about himself.

Frank [8] described a similar, double mirror reaction:

. . . in one group a prolonged feud developed between two Jews, one of whom flaunted his Jewishness while the other tried to conceal it. Each finally realized that he was combatting in the other an attitude he repressed in himself. The militant Jew finally admitted that he was disturbed by the many disadvantages of being Jewish, and the man who hid his background confessed that he secretly nurtured a certain pride in it.

Rivalry may be yet another source of conflict, as patients compete with one another in the group. They may vie for the largest share of the therapist's attention or for some particular role; patients may wish to be the most powerful, most respected, most sensitive, most disturbed or needy person in the group.

In the fiftieth meeting of one group, a new member, Grace, was added. In many aspects she was quite similar to Douglas, one of the original members: they were both artists, mystical in their approach to life, often steeped in fantasy, and both too familiar with their unconscious. It was not an affinity, however, but an antagonism which developed between the two. Grace immediately established the role she invariably assumed with others: she behaved in a spirit-like, irrational, and disorganized fashion in the group. Douglas, who saw his role as the sickest and most disorganized member being usurped, reacted to her with less tolerance and understanding than to any of the "squarer" members of the group. Only after active interpretation of the role conflict and Douglas's assumption of a new role ("most improved member") was an entente between the two members achieved.

Occasionally antagonisms may also develop on the basis of differences in outlook based on differing life experiences. Members of different generations may dispute the drug issue or the new sexual code. Liberals and conservatives may develop considerable heat around civil rights or political issues.

As the group progresses, the members may grow increasingly impatient and angry at patients who have not adopted the group's norms of behavior. If one member, for example, continues to hide behind a façade, the group may coax him, attempt to persuade him, and finally angrily demand that he be honest with himself and the others in the group.

Chapter 10 discusses another source of hostility in the group: the growing disenchantment and disappointment with the therapist for frustrating the patients' unrealistic expectations of him. If the group is unable to confront the therapist directly, it may create a scapegoat, which further increases the general level of conflict in the group.

Regardless of its source, the discord, once begun, follows a predictable sequence. The antagonists develop the belief that they are right and the others are wrong, that they are good and the others bad. Moreover, although it is not recognized at the time, these beliefs are characteristically held with equal conviction and certitude by each of the two opposing parties. Where such a situation of opposing beliefs exists, we have all the ingredients for a deep and continuing tension.

Generally a breakdown in communication ensues. The two parties cease to listen to each other with any degree of understanding. Often, if the social situation permits, the two opponents completely rupture their relationship at this point and the correction of misunderstandings is thus permanently prevented. The analogy to international relations is all too obvious.

Not only do the opponents stop listening, but they also may unwittingly distort their perceptions of one another. Perceptions are filtered through a screen of stereotypy. The opponent's words and behavior are shaped to fit a preconceived view of him. Contrary evidence is ignored or distorted; conciliatory gestures may be perceived as deceitful tricks.

Distrust is the basis for this sequence; opponents view their actions as honorable and reasonable and the behavior of others as scheming and evil. If this sequence, so common in human events, were permitted to unfold in therapy groups, little opportunity for change or learning would be available to the group members. A group climate and group norms which can preclude such a sequence must be established early in the life of the group.

Cohesiveness is the prime prerequiste for the successful management of conflict. Members must develop a feeling of mutual trust and respect and must come to value the group as an important means of meeting their personal needs. The patients must understand that communication must be maintained if the group is to survive; all parties must continue to deal directly with one another, no matter how angry they become. Furthermore, everyone is to be taken seriously; when a group treats one patient as a mascot whose opinions and anger are lightly regarded, the hope of effective treatment for that patient has all but officially been abandoned. Moreover, group cohesiveness will have been seriously compromised, since the next most peripheral member will have reason to fear similar treatment. The cohesive group in which everyone is taken seriously soon elaborates norms which obligate members to go beyond name calling. Each member must pursue and explore derogatory labels; he must be willing to search more deeply within himself to understand his antagonism and to make explicit those aspects of others which anger him. Norms must be established which make it clear that group members are there to understand themselves, not to defeat or ridicule others.

Once a member realizes that others accept him and are trying to understand him, then he finds it less necessary to hold rigidly to his own beliefs, and he may be willing to explore previously denied aspects of himself. Gradually he may develop motivational insight. He "comes to recognize that not all of his motives are those he has proclaimed and that some of his attitudes and behaviors are not so fully justified as he has been maintaining to his opponent and to the world." [9] When this step has been achieved, a breakthrough may occur, in which the individual changes his perception of the situation and realizes that the problem can be viewed in more than one way.

Empathy is an important element in conflict resolution and facilitates a humanization of the struggle. Often the understanding of the past plays an important role in the development of empathy; once an individual understands his opponent's earlier life which has resulted in his current stance, the position of the other not only makes sense but may even appear right for him. *Tout comprendre, c'est tout pardonner.*

Conflict resolution is often impossible in the presence of off-target or oblique hostility. For example:

In one group a patient began the session by requesting and obtaining the therapist's permission to read a letter she was writing in conjunction with a court hearing on her impending divorce, which involved considerable property settlement and custodianship of children. The letter reading consumed considerable time and was eventually interrupted by the therapist and then the patients, who disputed the content of the letter. The sniping by the group and defensive counterattacks by the protagonist continued until the group atmosphere was crackling with irritability. The group made no constructive headway until the therapist explored with the patients the process of the meeting. The therapist was annoyed with himself for having permitted the letter to be read and with the patient for having put him in that position. The group members were angry at the therapist for having given permission and at the patient both for consuming so much time and for relating to them in the frustrating impersonal manner of letter reading. Once the anger had been directed away from the oblique target of the letter's contents onto the appropriate targets of the therapist and the letter reader, steps toward conflict resolution could begin.

Permanent conflict abolition, let me note, is not the final goal of the therapy group; conflict will continuously recur in the group despite successful resolution of past conflicts and despite the presence of considerable mutual respect and warmth. The point of constructive conflict resolution in the group is, therefore, not to abolish it but to allow it to occur and to be harnessed in the service of therapy.

Many different benefits may accrue from experiencing and exploring hostility in the group. The self-esteem of the antagonists may be increased by the conflict; when patients become angry at one another, this in itself may be taken as an indication that they are important to one another and take each other quite seriously. At other times patients learn that although others may respond negatively to some trait, mannerism, or attitude, they themselves are valued; indeed members often become angry at someone who refuses to let others experience any personal emotion toward him. The knowledge that others care is often ego-enhancing.

For some patients who have been able to experience and express anger, the group may serve as a testing ground for taking risks and learning that such behavior is neither dangerous nor necessarily destructive. Chapter 2 described a number of incidents cited by patients as turning points in their therapy; a majority of these critical incidents involved the expression, for the first time, of strong negative affect. It is also important for patients to learn that they can withstand attacks and pressure from others. Overly aggressive patients may learn some of the interpersonal consequences of blind self-assertion. They may be held in check initially by having to take on many group patients at once; later the therapist may help them examine some of the motivations underlying their behavior. Furthermore, angry confrontations may provide valuable learning opportunities, for patients learn to remain in mutually useful contact despite their anger.

In the process of disagreeing, each patient may learn more about the reasons for his position and may, in fact, discover new and more valid reasons. He may also understand that, despite the sources of his anger, he expresses himself in self-defeating, maladaptive ways. Some may learn from feedback that they habitually display scorn, irritation, or disapproval. Our sensitivity to facial gestures and nuances of expression far exceeds our proprioceptive sensitivity; [11] only through feedback do we learn that we communicate something which is not intended or, for that matter, even experienced.

Strong shared affect may enhance the importance of the relationship. Chapter 3 described how group cohesiveness is increased when members of a group go through intense emotional experiences together, regardless of the nature of the emotion. "In this manner," as Frank says, "members of a successful therapy group are like members of a closely knit family who may battle each other, yet derive much support from their family allegiance."[8] A dyadic relationship, too, which has weathered much stress is apt to be an especially rewarding one. An experience in which two individuals in group therapy experience an intense mutual hatred and then, through some of the mechanisms we have described, resolve the hatred and arrive at some mutual understanding and respect is always of great therapeutic import.

Self-Disclosure

Self-disclosure—both feared and valued by participants—plays an integral part in all group therapies. Culbert [12] has offered the following definition:

Self-disclosure refers to an individual's explicitly communicating to one or more others some personal information that he believes these others would be unlikely to acquire unless he himself discloses it. Moreover, this information must be "personally private"; that is, it must be of such a nature that it is not something the individual would disclose to everyone who might inquire about it.

RISK

Obviously self-disclosure requires the presence of at least one other person and must be examined within the context of that relationship. Every self-disclosure involves some risk on the part of the discloser. The degree of rish depends on several factors: [12]

1. The nature and intensity of the disclosed material. If the disclosure is of a highly personal nature, emotionally charged and previously undisclosed, then obviously the risk is greater. First-time disclosures (i.e., the first time the individual has shared this information with anyone) are especially charged.
2. The probability that the receiver will receive the disclosure as the communicator intends. The risk is diminished if the discloser is certain that the receiver shares similar concerns and that he is sensitive to the communicator's needs.
3. The probability that the receiver will react as the communicator intended. The self-discloser always has some hopes and expectations of a specific type of response from the receiver. The more familiar the receiver, the more frequently they have had similar transactions in the past, the less the risk. If the receiver is vulnerable with respect to the discloser, then too the risk is less. For example, the receiver may have previously disclosed himself to the communicator; in such an instance the communicator has a degree of leverage and may, with little risk, reciprocate.

SEQUENCE OF SELF-DISCLOSURE

In conventional social relationships, in which one participant has an inclination for self-disclosure, a predictable sequence usually occurs. The discloser begins by making low level disclosures. The receiver who is involved in a lasting relationship with the discloser (and not merely a casual acquaintance at a cocktail party) is likely to consider himself charged with certain responsibilities or obligations to the discloser. He generally responds to the disclosure by some appropriate comment, depending on the nature of the disclosure, and then reciprocates with some disclosure of his own. The receiver now, as well as the original discloser, is vulnerable, and a deepening relationship usually continues, with the participants making slightly more open and intimate disclosures in turn until some optimal level for that relationship is reached.

ADAPTIVE FUNCTIONS OF SELF-DISCLOSURE

Self-disclosure is a prerequisite for the formation of meaningful interpersonal relationships in a dyadic or in a group situation. As disclosures proceed in the group, the entire membership gradually increases its level of involvement, responsibility and obligation to one another. If the timing is right, there is nothing which will commit an individual to a group more than to receive or to reveal some intimate secret material. There is nothing more exhilarating than for a member to disclose, for the first time, some material which has burdened him for years and to be understood and fully accepted. If, as interpersonalists such as Sullivan and Rogers have maintained, self-acceptance must be preceded by acceptance by others, the individual must gradually permit others to see and to accept his real self.

Research evidence validates the importance of self-disclosure in group therapy. Chapter 3 described the relationship between self-disclosure and popularity in the group. Popularity (determined from sociometrics) correlates positively with the therapy outcome;[13] patients who are high disclosers in the early meetings often assume high popularity in their groups.[14] Peres [15] demonstrated that successfully treated patients in group therapy had made almost twice as many self-disclosing personal statements during the course of therapy as did unsuccessfully treated patients. Truax and Carkhuff [16] also found that patients' success in group therapy correlated with their transparency during the course of the group.

The concept of carry-over is vital here; not only are patients rewarded by the other group members for self-disclosure, but the behavior, thus reinforced, is integrated into the individual's relationships outside the group, where it is similarly rewarded. Often the first step in revealing to a spouse or a potential close friend is the "first-time" disclosure in the therapy group.

MALADAPTIVE SELF-DISCLOSURE

Self-disclosure is related to optimal psychological and social adjustment in a curvilinear fashion: too much or too little self-disclosure is both a manifestation and a cause of maladaptive interpersonal behavior.

Too little self-disclosure usually results in severely limited opportunity for reality testing. If an individual fails to disclose himself in a relationship, he generally forfeits an opportunity to obtain valid feedback. Furthermore, he prevents the relationship from developing further; without reciprocation the other party will either desist from further self-disclosure or else rupture the relationship entirely.

The individual who does not disclose himself in the group has little chance of genuine acceptance by the other members and therefore little chance of experiencing a rise in self-esteem. Vosen has demonstrated this very point experimentally. In his study "a self-perceived lack of self-disclosure resulted in reduced self-esteem." [17] Should it occur that an individual is accepted on the basis of a (false) image he attempts to project, no enduring boost in self-esteem occurs; moreover, he is even less likely at this point to engage in valid self-disclosure, since he now runs the added risk of losing the acceptance he has gained through his false presentation of self. [12]

Some individuals dread self-disclosure, not primarily because of shame or fear of nonacceptance, but because they are heavily conflicted in the area of control: to them self-disclosure is dangerous because it makes them vulnerable to the control of others. When others in the group have made themselves exceedingly vulnerable through self-disclosure, then and only then are they willing to reciprocate.

Sex is no longer the most difficult topic to discuss. Money and income have become threatening subjects. Many clinics set their fees according to a sliding fee schedule based on income. I have found that it is extremely rare for patients spontaneously to disclose their fees to the other group members. Sex, on the other hand, is often discussed with abandon in early meetings. This is consistent with data obtained from a method of inquiry described in Chapter 1, in which members are asked to write, anonymously, their top secret. Most frequently these secrets involve a sense of inadequacy and incompetence, which is, in the minds of the members, often reflected in amount of income.

One must differentate, too, between a healthy need for privacy and neurotic compulsive secrecy. There are some individuals, not often likely to find their way into groups, who are private individuals in an adaptive way; they share intimacies with only a few intimate friends and shudder at the thought of self-disclosure in a group. Moreover, they enjoy private, self-contemplative activities. This is a far different thing from privacy which is based on fear, shame, or crippling social inhibitions. In fact, as Maslow [18] suggests, the resolution of neurotic privacy may be an essential first step toward the establishment of a healthy desire for privacy. Many patients who are nondisclosers have at the same time a fear of being alone and involve themselves in many unrewarding dependent relationships; they so dread loneliness that they can no longer experience the pleasures of privacy.

Too much self-disclosure can be as maladaptive as too little. Indiscriminate self-disclosure is not a goal of mental health nor a pathway to it. Some patients make the grievous error of reasoning that if self-disclosure is good, then total and continuous self-disclosure must be a very good thing indeed. But, as Goffman [19] notes, urban life would become unbearably sticky if every contact between two individuals entailed a sharing of personal concerns and secrets. Obviously the type of relationship that exists between the discloser and the receiver should be the major factor in determining the pattern of self-disclosure. Several research investigations have demonstrated this experimentally: individuals disclose different types and amounts of material, depending on whether the receiver is a mother, father, best male friend, female friend, work associate, or spouse.[20, 21, 22]

However, some maladaptive disclosers disregard and thus jeopardize their relationship to the receiver. The individual who in his self-disclosure fails to discriminate between intimate friends and more distant acquaintances perplexes his receivers. We have all, I am certain, experienced a feeling of confusion or betrayal upon learning that supposedly intimate material confided to us has been shared with many others. Furthermore, a great deal of self-disclosure may frighten off an unprepared recipient. In a rhythmic, flowing relationship, one party leads the other in self-disclosures, but never by too great a gap. Projects, too, may be sabotaged by indiscriminate self-disclosure. For example, the general who, after having made an important tactical decision, goes around wringing his hands and verbally expressing his uncertainty, is certain to undercut the morale of his entire command.[18]

In group therapy, members who reveal early and promiscuously will often drop out early in the course of therapy. Patients should be encouraged to take risks in the group; such behavior change results in positive feedback and reinforcement and encourages further risk taking. But if they reveal too much too early, they may exceed their tolerance: they feel so much shame that any interpersonal rewards are offset; furthermore, they may threaten others willing to support them but not yet prepared to reciprocate. The discloser is then placed in a position of such great vulnerability in the group that he often chooses to flee.

Termination

Termination is more than an act signifying the end of therapy; it is an integral part of the process of therapy and, if properly understood and managed, may be an important force in the instigation of change. There are at least three common forms of termination in the therapy group: (1) the termination of the unsuccessful patient, (2) the termination of the successful patient, and (3) the termination of the entire group.

THE UNSUCCESSFUL PATIENT

Generally, unsuccessful patients who drop out of group therapy prematurely leave the group within the first twenty meetings; research [13] has indicated that there are extremely few dropouts between the twentieth and fiftieth meetings and furthermore that patients who remain in the group for as long as fifty meetings have a high likelihood of improvement (85 per cent in one study).[13]

The reasons for premature termination have been discussed elsewhere in this book. The general reasons stem from problems caused by deviancy, subgrouping, conflicts in intimacy and disclosure, the role of the early provocateur, external stress, concurrent individual and group therapy, inability to share the doctor, inadequate preparation, and emotional contagion. Underlying all these reasons is the fact that there is considerable stress early in the group; patients who have maladaptive interpersonal patterns are exposed to unaccustomed demands for candor and intimacy, they are often confused about procedure, they suspect that the group activities bear little relevance to their problem, and, finally, too little support occurs for them in the early meetings to sustain their hope.

The general principles of preventing dropouts have been discussed in Chapters 9 and 10. One important approach to decreasing the dropout rate is to provide a thorough pretherapy preparation, which serves to reduce initial anxiety stemming from uncertainty and confusion. The anticipation of group concerns and problems makes it clear to the patient that therapy is a process and that periods of discouragement are expected parts of that process. Furthermore, patients are less prone to lose confidence in a therapist who appears to have a long-term perspective.

Some groups contain experienced group members who assume some of this predictive function. For example:

One group which graduated several members but which contained three old members was reconstituted with five new members. In the first two meetings the old members briefed the new ones and, among other information, told them that by the sixth or seventh meeting some patient would decide to drop out and then the group "would have to drop everything for a couple of meetings to persuade him to stay." The old members went on to predict which of the new members would be the first to decide to terminate. This form of prediction is the most effective manner of insuring that the prediction does not come to pass.

Even despite painstaking preparation, however, many patients will consider dropping out. When a patient informs a therapist that he wishes to leave the group, the traditional approach is to urge him to return to the group to discuss it with the other group members. Underlying this practice is the assumption that the group will help the patient work through his resistance and thereby dissuade him from terminating. This approach, however, is rarely successful. In one study[1] of thirty-five dropouts from nine therapy groups (with an original membership of ninety-seven patients) I found that every one of the dropouts was urged to return for another meeting; not once was this effective in averting the premature termination. (Furthermore, none of the group continuers who at some point threatened to drop out were saved by this technique.) When the patient did return to a final meeting, he did not amplify his reasons for leaving the group because in each instance he was no longer committed to the group or to the group norms; generally he communicated in a defensive, guarded manner, and neither he nor the group benefited from the exchange.

Generally the therapist is well advised to see a potential dropout for a short series of individual interviews in which the sources of group stress are discussed. An accurate penetrating interpretation by the therapist may be extremely effective in keeping the patient in therapy.

For example, one schizoid, alienated patient announced in the eighth meeting that he felt he was getting nowhere in the group and had decided to terminate. In an individual session the patient stated something he had never been able to say in the group: namely that he had many positive feelings toward a couple of the group members. Nevertheless, he insisted that the therapy was ineffective and that he desired a more accelerated and more relevant form of therapy. The therapist correctly interpreted the patient's intellectual assessment of the group therapy format as a rationalization; he was, in fact, fleeing from the closeness he had felt in the group. The therapist again explained the social microcosm phenomenon and clarified for the patient that in the group he was repeating his lifelong style of relating to others; he had always avoided or fled from intimacy and no doubt would always do so in the future unless he stopped running and allowed himself the opportunity to explore his interpersonal problems *in vivo*. The patient returned to the group and eventually made considerable gains in therapy.

The inexperienced group therapist is often highly threatened by the patient who threatens to drop out. Often during the second or third month of therapy several patients simultaneously consider termination; at this point the neophyte therapist may suffer considerable discomfort and experience the fantasy of "standing all alone in the group with everything crumbling away underneath." [23] In time he will learn that early dropouts are inevitable in the group* and that they do not signify a personal failure on his part. If the therapist panics and puts undue pressure on the patient to continue in the group, the patient will generally perceive that he is being asked to do something, not for himself, but for the therapist or for the group, and will almost certainly leave therapy.

When a patient, despite the therapist's best efforts, does choose to leave the group, then it is up to the therapist to make the experience as constructive as possible; patients ordinarily are considerably demoralized and tend to view the group experience as "one more failure." Even if the patient denies this feeling, the therapist should still assume that it is present and in a private discussion with the patient should advance alternative methods of viewing the experience. For example, he may present the notion of "readiness" or "group fit." Some patients are able to profit from

---

* In fact, an escape hatch is essential to the group process; its presence allows some patients to make their first tentative commitments to the group. The group must have some decompression mechanism; mistakes in the selection process are inevitable, unexpected events in the lives of the new members occur, unanticipated group incompatibilities develop. Some intensive week-long human relations laboratories meeting at a geographically isolated locale lack such an escape hatch, and on several occasions I have observed psychotic reactions stemming from the forced continuation in an incompatible group.

group therapy only after a period of individual therapy; others, for reasons unclear to us, are never able to work effectively in therapy groups. Research [24] has shown that by chance some patients have interpersonal styles (measured by the FIRO-B) which do not blend well with those of the other members in a particular group; these patients are less attracted to that group and tend to terminate therapy prematurely. It is entirely possible that they may have a successful course of therapy in another group and this possibility should be explored. In any case, the patient should be helped to understand that it is not *he* who has failed but that, due to a number of possible reasons, a form of therapy has failed.

The therapist may use the final interview to review in detail the patient's experience in the group in a manner useful for the patient. Occasionally the therapist is uncertain about the usefulness or advisability of confronting patients who are terminating therapy. Should he, for example, confront a denying patient who attributes his dropping out of the group to his hearing difficulties when in fact he had been an extreme deviant and was clearly rejected by the group? As a general principle it is useful to view the patient from the perspective of his entire career in therapy. If he is very likely to re-enter therapy, a constructive confrontation will, in the long run, enable him to use his next therapy more effectively. If, on the other hand, there is little likelihood that the patient will pursue a dynamically oriented therapy, there is little point in presenting a final interpretation which the patient will never be able to use or to extend; there is little point in undermining defenses, even self-deceptive ones, if one cannot provide a satisfactory substitute.

TERMINATION OF THE SUCCESSFUL PATIENT

Throughout, this book has empahasized that group therapy is a highly individualized process. Each patient will enter, participate in, use, and experience the group in a highly personal manner. The end of therapy is, no less, an individualized matter. Only very general assumptions about the length and overall goals of therapy may be made. Most patients require approximately eighteen to twenty-four months to undergo substantial and durable change, although it is possible to resolve crises and achieve symptomatic relief in far briefer periods of time. The goals of therapy have never been stated more succinctly than in Freud's "to be able to love and to work." Some would, today, add a third, "to play," while others would hope too that the patient would be able to love himself, to allow others to love him, to be more flexible and to search for and trust his own values.

Nevertheless, these are vague guideposts. Some patients may achieve a great deal in a few months, whereas others require years of group therapy. Some patients have far more ambitious goals than others; it would not be an exaggeration to state that some patients terminate therapy, satisfied, in approximately the same state in which others may begin therapy. Some patients—for example, some homosexual patients—may have highly specific goals in therapy and, because much of their psychopathology is ego-syntonic, choose to limit the amount of change they are willing to undertake. Others may be hampered by important external circumstances in their lives. All therapists have had the experience of helping a patient improve to a point at which further change would make him worse. For example, a patient may, with further change, outgrow, as it were, his spouse; continued therapy would result in the rupture of an irreplaceable relationship unless concomitant changes occur in the spouse. If that contingency is not available, the therapist may be well advised to settle for the positive changes that have occurred, even though the personal potential for greater growth is clearly evident.

Termination of professional treatment is but a stage in the individual's career of growth; termination is not tantamount to graduation. Patients continue to change, and one important effect of successful therapy is to enable patients to use constructively the resources in their personal environment. I have seen many successful patients in long-term follow-up interviews who have not only continued to change post-termination but who, even many months after they have left the group, recall an observation or interpretation made by another member or the therapist which suddenly becomes meaningful to them. Not only growth but setbacks occur following termination; many successfully treated patients will encounter stress in excess of their coping ability and need temporary help. In addition, all patients experience anxiety and depression following departure from the group; a period of mourning is an inevitable part of the termination process.

The timing of termination is as inexact and as individualized a matter as the criteria for termination. Some therapists find that termination from group therapy is less problematic than termination from long-term individual therapy, in which patients often become so dependent on the therapeutic situation that they are loath to part with it. (Freud once said that "for many patients the wish to be treated outweighs the wish to be cured.") Group therapy patients are usually more aware that therapy is not a way of life but a process with a beginning, middle, and end. In the therapy group there are many living reminders of the therapeutic sequence. Patients see new members enter therapy and improved members terminate; they observe the therapist beginning the process over and over again as he helps the beginners over difficult phases of therapy. Through this they realize the bittersweet fact that though the therapist is a person with whom they have had a real and meaningful relationship, he is also a professional; he must shift his attention to others, he will not remain as a permanent and bottomless source of gratification for them. Occasionally patients may delay their termination because they sense that the group or the therapist needs them; they may respond to subtle group pressures by remaining in treatment far longer than is necessary. There is no justification for this, and the therapist should explore this openly as soon as he becomes aware of it. Some socially isolated patients may postpone termination because they use the therapy group as a social group rather than as a means for developing the skills to create a social life for themselves in their home environment. The therapist must in this instance focus on transfer of learning and encourage risk taking outside the group.

The group members are an invaluable resource in helping one another decide about termination, and a unilateral decision made by a patient without consulting the other members is often a premature one. Generally a well-timed termination decision will be discussed for a few weeks in the group, during which time the patient works through his feelings about leaving the group. Not infrequently patients make an abrupt decision to terminate their membership in the group immediately; I have found that these patients find it difficult to express gratitude and positive feeling, hence they attempt to abbreviate the separation process as much as possible. These patients must be helped to understand and correct their jarring, unsatisfying method of ending relationships. To ignore this phase of interpersonal relationships is to neglect an important area of human relations. Termination is, after all, a part of almost every relationship, and throughout one's life one must, on many occasions, say goodbye to important people.

I have made a practice of recording the first pretherapy interview with the patient. Not infrequently these tapes are useful in arriving at the termination decision. By listening, many months later, to their initial session, patients can obtain a clearer perspective of what they have accomplished and what remains to be done. Therapists who use alternate sessions report that when a patient's behavior in the leaderless meeting is identical to his behavior in the presence of a therapist, the optimal time for termination may be at hand.

The therapist must also look to his own feelings during the termination process because occasionally he unaccountably and unnecessarily delays the patient's termination. Some perfectionistic therapists may unrealis-

279

tically expect too much change in their patients and refuse to accept anything less than total recovery; moreover, they lack faith in the patient's ability to continue growth following the termination of formal therapy. Other patients bring out Pygmalion pride in us; we find it difficult to part with someone who is, in part, our own creation: saying goodbye to some patients is saying goodbye to a part of ourselves. Furthermore, it is a permanent goodbye;* if the therapist has done his job properly, the patient no longer needs him and breaks all contact. It is difficult at times to part with all the former immature, but often endearing, roles the patient has played; gone forever, for example, is the coquettish, moist-lipped, ingenuous co-ed. In her place is a mature integrated woman. We welcome her, we have helped her emerge, but what therapist does not at times find the farewell to her earlier self a poignant affair?

THE TERMINATION OF THE GROUP

Groups terminate for various reasons. Some therapists set a time limit at the beginning of the group. Often external circumstances dictate the end of the group; for example, groups in a university mental health clinic usually run for eight to nine months and disband at the beginning of the summer vacation.† Other groups end when the therapist leaves the area, although this is not inevitable since the co-therapist, if present, may continue the group, or the group may be transferred to another therapist (who should, incidentally, attend the original therapist's last few meetings to aid in the transition). Occasionally a therapist may decide to end a group because the great majority of patients all are ready to terminate at approximately the same time.

Often the group avoids the difficult and unpleasant work of termination by ignoring or denying their concerns, and it is the therapist who must keep the task in focus for them. The end of the group is a real loss; patients gradually come to realize that it can never be reconvened, that even if they continue a relationship with a member or a fragment of the group, nevertheless the entire group will be gone forever. It is entirely analogous to the death of a loved one and may evoke memories of past losses.

* A weaning process, common in individual therapy termination, in which the patient gradually decreases the frequency of his visits, is not feasible in group therapy. A patient attending every second or third meeting would be disruptive to the group.

† These groups, meeting twice a week, may often accomplish a great deal in the short space of eight months. The students are often in crisis and not yet so fixed in character structure as older patients.

The therapist must often repeatedly call the members' attention to the impending termination. If avoidance is extreme—manifested, for example, by an increased absence rate—the therapist must confront the group with their behavior. Usually with a mature group the best approach is a direct approach; the members can be reminded that it is their group and they must decide how they want to end it. Irregularly attending members must be helped to understand their behavior. Do they feel their absence makes no difference to the others or do they so dread expressing positive feelings toward the group or perhaps negative feelings to the therapist for ending it that they avoid a confrontation? Pain over the loss of the group is, in part, dealt with by a sharing of past experiences; exciting and meaningful past group events are remembered, patients remind each other of "the way you were then"; personal testimonials are invariably heard in the final meetings.

Throughout, the therapist facilitates the group work by disclosing his own feelings about separation. The therapist, no less than the patients, will miss the group. For him, too, it has been a place of anguish, conflict, fear, and also of great beauty; some of life's truest and most poignant moments occur in the small and yet limitless microcosm of the therapy group.

REFERENCES

1. I. D. Yalom, "A Study of Group Therapy Dropouts," *Arch. Gen. Psychiat.*, 14: 393–414, 1966.
2. H. Lindt and M. Sherman, "Social Incognito," in "Analytically Oriented Group Psychotherapy," *Int. J. Group Psychother.*, 2: 209–220, 1952.
3. I. D. Yalom and P. Houts, unpublished data, 1965.
4. J. D. Frank, "Some Determinants, Manifestations, and Effects of Cohesiveness in Therapy Groups," *Int. J. Group Psychother.*, 7: 53–63, 1957.
5. R. White and R. Lippit, "Leader Behavior and Member Reaction in Three 'Social Climates,' " in D. Cartwright and A. Zander (eds.), *Group Dynamics: Research and Theory* (New York: Row, Peterson, 1962), pp. 527–553.
6. G. Bach, *Intensive Group Therapy* (New York: Ronald Press, 1954).
7. A. Wolf, "The Psychoanalysis of Groups," in M. Rosenbaum and M. Berger (eds.), *Group Psychotherapy and Group Function* (New York: Basic Books, 1963), p. 320.
8. J. D. Frank, "Some Values of Conflict in Therapeutic Groups," *Group Psychother.*, 8: 142–151, 1955.
9. C. Rogers, "Dealing with Psychological Tensions," *J. Appl. Behav. Sci.*, 1: 6–24, 1965.

10. S. H. Foulkes, *Therapeutic Group Analysis* (New York: International Universities Press, 1964), p. 81.
11. E. Berne, *Games People Play* (New York: Grove Press, 1964).
12. S. A. Culbert, *The Interpersonal Process of Self-Disclosure: It Takes Two to See One* ("Explorations in Applied Behavioral Science," No. 3 [New York: Renaissance Editors, 1967]).
13. I. D. Yalom, P. S. Houts, S. M. Zimerberg, and K. H. Rand, "Prediction of Improvement in Group Therapy: An Exploratory Study," *Arch. Gen. Psychiat.*, *17*: 159–168, 1967.
14. S. Hurley, "Self-Disclosure in Small Counseling Groups," unpublished Ph.D. dissertation, Michigan State University, 1967.
15. H. Peres, "An Investigation of Non-Directive Group Therapy," *J. Consult. Psychol.*, *11*: 159–172, 1947.
16. C. Truax and R. Carkhuff, "Client and Therapist Transparency in the Psychotherapeutic Encounter," *J. Couns. Psychol.*, *12*: 3–9, 1965.
17. L. M. Vosen, "The Relationship Between Self-Disclosure and Self-Esteem," unpublished Ph.D. dissertation, University of California at Los Angeles, 1966; cited by Culbert, *op. cit.*
18. A. H. Maslow, unpublished mimeographed material, 1962.
19. E. Goffman, *The Presentation of Self in Everyday Life* (Garden City, N.Y.: Doubleday Anchor Books, 1959).
20. M. Rickers-Ouiankina, "Social Accessibility in Three Age Groups," *Psychol. Rep.*, *2*: 283–294, 1956.
21. S. M. Jourard and P. Lasakow, "Some Factors in Self-Disclosure," *J. Abnorm. Soc. Psychol.*, *56*: 91–98, 1950.
22. D. E. Bugenthal, R. Tannenbaum, and H. Bobele, unpublished manuscript cited by Culbert, *op. cit.*
23. I. D. Yalom, "Problems of Neophyte Group Therapists," *Int. J. Soc. Psychiat.*, *12*: 29–52, 1966.
24. I. D. Yalom and K. Rand, "Compatibility and Cohesiveness in Therapy Groups," *Arch. Gen. Psychiat.*, *13*: 267–276, 1966.

12

PROBLEM
PATIENTS

❧

The Monopolist

The habitual monopolist is surely one of the most common and frustrating problems for the therapy group. The individual who seems compelled to chatter on incessantly taxes the patience of group members and therapists alike. These patients are anxious if they are silent; if others get the floor they reinsert themselves with a variety of techniques: they rush in indecently to fill the briefest silence, they respond to every statement in the group, they continually note similarities between the problems of the speaker and their own, with the recurring refrain, "I'm like that too." The monopolist may persist in describing, in endless detail, conversations with others (often taking several parts in the conversation) or in presenting accounts of newspaper or magazine stories which may be only slightly relevant to some group issue. Some hold the floor by assuming the role of the interrogator, while still others capture the members' attention by enticing them with bizarre or sexually piquant material. I have known some patients who monopolized by puzzling the others: they described rare, "out of the blue" *déjà vu* or depersonalization episodes, often omitting mention of important clarifying details such as severe precipitating stress. Grand hysterics may monopolize the group by means of the crisis method: they regularly present the group with major life upheavals, which always seem to demand urgent and lengthy attention.

EFFECTS ON GROUPS

Although the group may in the initial meeting or two welcome and perhaps encourage the monopolist, the mood rapidly turns to one of frustration and anger. New group members are often disinclined to silence a member for fear that they will thus incur an obligation to fill the silence. If the group does not contain a particularly assertive member, it may not deal directly with the monopolist for some time; instead it may smolder quietly or make indirect hostile forays. Generally, indirect attacks on the monopolist will only aggravate the problem. The monopolist's compulsive speech is an attempt to deal with anxiety; as he senses the rising group tension and resentment, his anxiety rises also; his tendency to speak compulsively is thereby augmented and a vicious circle is established. Some monopolists have perceived that their drive to speak is increased at this point in order to divert the group from making a direct attack.

Eventually this source of unresolved tension will have a detrimental effect on cohesiveness, manifested by such signs of group disruption as indirect, off-target fighting, absenteeism, dropouts, and subgrouping. When the group does confront the monopolist, it is often in an explosive, brutal style; the spokesman for the group usually receives unanimous support, sometimes, literally, by a round of applause. The monopolist may then sulk, enforce complete silence on himself for a meeting or two ("See what they do without me"), or leave the group. In any event, little that is therapeutic has been accomplished.

THERAPEUTIC CONSIDERATIONS

The overall task of the therapist is to interrupt the behavioral pattern of the monopolist in a therapeutically effective fashion. Despite the strongest provocation and temptation to shout the patient down or to silence him by edict, such an assault has little value except as a temporary catharsis for the therapist. The patient is not helped: no learning has accrued; the anxiety underlying the monopolist's compulsive speech persists and will erupt again in further monopolistic volleys or, if no outlet is available, will force the patient to drop out of the group. Neither is the group helped; regardless of the circumstances, the others are threatened by the therapist's silencing, in a heavy-handed manner, one of the members. Therapy is perceived as potentially dangerous, and a crystal of caution and fear is implanted in the mind of each member lest a similar fate befall him.

Nevertheless, the monopolistic behavior must be checked, and generally it is the therapist's task to do this. Often, with good reason, the therapist does well to wait for the group to handle a group problem; however, the monopolistic patient is one problem that the group, and especially a young group, often cannot handle. The therapist must prevent the emergence of certain irreversible group trends, such as dropping out, or the elaboration of therapy-obstructing norms; in addition, he must intervene to prevent the monopolistic patient from committing social suicide. A two-pronged approach is most effective: the therapist must consider both the monopolizing patient and the group which has allowed itself to be monopolized.

From the standpoint of the group, the therapist should bear in mind the principle that, by definition, no monopolistic patient may exist in a vacuum; he always abides in a dynamic equilibrium with a group which permits or encourages his behavior. The therapist may thus inquire why the group permits or encourages one member to carry the burden of the entire meeting. Such an inquiry may startle the members, who had only perceived themselves as passive victims of the monopolist. After the initial protestations are worked through, the group may then, with profit, examine their exploitation of the monopolist; for example, they may have been relieved by not having to participate verbally in the group. They may have permitted the patient to do all the self-disclosure, or to make a fool of himself, or to act as a lightning rod for the group's anger, while they assumed little responsibility for the therapeutic goals of the group. When the members once disclose and discuss their reasons for inactivity, their personal commitment to the therapeutic process is augmented. They may, for example, discuss their fears of assertiveness, or of harming the monopolist, or of a retaliatory attack by some specific member or by the therapist; they may wish to avoid seeking the group's attention lest their greed be exposed; they may secretly revel in the monopolist's plight and enjoy being a member of the victimized and disapproving majority. A disclosure of any of these issues by a hitherto uninvolved patient signifies progress and greater engagement in therapy.

The group approach to this problem must be complemented by work with the monopolistic patient. The basic principle is a simple one: the therapist does not want to silence the monopolist; he does not want to hear less from the patient but instead wants to hear more. The seeming contradiction is resolved when we consider that the monopolist conceals himself behind his compulsive speech. Often he presents issues to the group which have been selected, not because they deal with a deeply felt personal concern, but because they have a high attention-gaining power. The monopolist sacrifices himself and his chance of relief to his insatiable need for attention and control. Although each therapist will fashion his intervention according to his own style, the essential message to the monopolist must be that, through his compulsive speech, he holds the group at arm's length and prevents others from relating meaningfully to him. He is offered not rejection but an invitation to engage more fully in the group. If the therapist harbors only the singular goal of silencing the patient, then he has, in effect, abandoned the therapeutic goal and may as well remove the patient from the group.

In addition to his grossly deviant behavior, the monopolist has a major impairment of his social sensory system. He seems peculiarly unaware both of his interpersonal impact and of the response of others to him; moreover, he lacks the capacity or inclination to empathize with others in his social setting. Data from an exploratory research endeavor [1] supports this conclusion. Patients and student observers were asked to fill out questionnaires at the end of each group meeting. One of the areas explored was activity; the participants were asked to rank the group members, including themselves, for the total number of words uttered during the meeting. There was excellent reliability in the activity ratings among patients and observers, with two exceptions: (1) the ratings of the therapist's activity by the patients showed large discrepancies (we have discussed this finding in Chapter 5), and (2) monopolistic patients placed themselves far lower on the activity rankings than did the other members, who were often unanimous in ranking the monopolist as the most active member in the meeting.

The therapist must, then, help the monopolist observe himself by encouraging the group to provide continual feedback for him; without the leader's encouragement the group may, as we have shown, provide the feedback only in a disjunctive, explosive manner, which elicits only a defensive posture. Such a sequence has little therapeutic value and merely recapitulates a drama in which the patient has performed far too often. For example, in the initial interview one male monopolist complained about his relationship with his wife who, he claimed, often abruptly resorted to such "sledgehammer tactics" as publicly humiliating him or accusing him of infidelity in front of his children. The sledgehammer accomplished nothing durable for this patient; once his bruises had healed, he and his wife began the cycle anew. Within the first few meetings of the group a similar drama unfolded: because of his monopolistic behavior, judgmentalism, and inability to hear the members' response to him, the group pounded harder and harder until finally, when he was forced to listen, the message was a cruel and destructive one.

Mere feedback is not enough; the therapist must help the group provide a steady and constructive flow of feedback for the monopolist. The therapist may have to be forceful and directive in saying, for example, "Mr. X, I think it would be best now for you to stop speaking because I sense there are some important feelings about you in the group which I think would be very helpful for you to know." The therapist should also help the group disclose their responses to Mr. X rather than their interpretations of his motives. Far more useful and acceptable is a statement such as, "When you speak in this fashion I feel . . ." rather than, "You are behaving in this fashion because. . . ." The patient may often perceive motivational interpretations as accusatory but must accept the validity of others' subjective reponses to him.

Too often we confuse or interchange the concepts of interpersonal manifestation, response, and cause. The cause of monopolistic behavior may vary considerably from patient to patient: some individuals speak in order to control others, many so fear that they will be influenced or penetrated by others that they compulsively defend each of their statements; others so overevaluate their productions that delay is impossible and all thoughts must be immediately expressed. Generally the cause of the monopolist's behavior is not well understood until much later in therapy and interpretation of the cause offers little help in the early management of the disruptive behavior patterns. It is far more effective to concentrate on the patient's manifestation of self in the group and the other members' response to his behavior. Gently but repeatedly the patient must be confronted with the paradox that, however much he may wish to be accepted and respected by others, he persists in behavior which generates only irritation, rejection, and frustration.

A clinical illustration of many of these issues occurred in a therapy group in a psychiatric hospital in which sexual offenders were incarcerated:

Ron, who had been in the group for seven weeks, launched into a familiar lengthy tribute to the remarkable improvement he had undergone. He described in exquisite detail how his chief problem had been that he hadn't understood the damaging effects his behavior had on others, and how now, having achieved such understanding, he was able to leave the hospital. The therapist observed that some of the members were restless, one softly pounded his fist into his palm, while others slumped back in a posture of indifference and resignation. He stopped the monopolist by asking the group how many times they had heard Ron relate this account. The group members agreed that they had heard it at every meeting, in fact they had heard Ron speak this way in the first meeting he attended; furthermore, they had never heard Ron talk about anything else and knew him only as a "story." The members discussed their irritation with Ron, their reluctance to attack him for fear of seriously injuring him, of losing control of themselves, or of painful retaliation. Some spoke of their hopelessness about ever reaching Ron, and of the fact that he related to them only as a matchstick figure without flesh or depth. Still others spoke of their terror of speaking and revealing themselves in the group; therefore, they welcomed Ron's monopolization. A few members expressed their total lack of interest or faith in therapy and therefore failed to intercept Ron because of apathy.

Thus the process was overdetermined; a host of interlocking factors resulted in a dynamic equilibrium called monopolization. By halting the runaway process, uncovering and working through the factors, the therapist obtained maximum therapeutic benefit from a potentially crippling group phenomenon. Each member moved closer to group involvement; Ron was no longer permitted or encouraged to participate in a fashion that could not possibly be helpful to him or the group.

The Help-Rejecting Complainer

The help-rejecting complainer,[2, 3, 4, 5, 6] a variant of the monopolist, was first identified and christened by Frank [2] in 1952; since then the behavior pattern has been recognized by many group clinicians, and the eponym has become a common one in psychiatric literature.

DESCRIPTION

The help-rejecting complainer (hereafter HRC) has a very distinctive behavioral pattern in the group: he implicitly or explicitly requests help from the group by presenting problems or complaints and then rejects the help which is offered. He continually brings environmental or somatic problems to the group and often describes them in a manner which causes them to appear insurmountable; in fact, the HRC seems to take pride in the insolubility of his problems. Often he directs all of his attention toward the therapist in a tireless campaign to elicit medication or advice from him. Clearly his behavior indicates a need, not for approval or respect, but for help. He seems oblivious to the group's reaction to him and apparently is willing to appear ludicrous so long as he is allowed to persist in his search for help. He bases his relationship to the other members along the singular dimension of establishing that he is more needy of aid than they. The HRC rarely shows competitiveness in any area except when another member makes a bid for the therapist's or group's attention by presenting a problem; at this juncture he often attempts to belittle others' complaints by comparing them unfavorably with his own. One such patient stated quite explicitly, "It seems like such a waste to me listening to you when my problems involve life and death and yours seem so superficial."[4] The HRC seems entirely self-centered in that he speaks only of himself and his problems. In fact, however, his problems are not clearly formulated to the group or to himself; they are obscured by his propensity to exaggerate them and to affix blame on others in his environment, often on authority figures on whom he is dependent in some fashion.

When the group and the therapist respond to his plea, the entire bewildering configuration takes form, as the patient rejects the help offered him. The rejection is unmistakable, though it may assume many varied and subtle forms; sometimes the advice is rejected overtly, sometimes indirectly, sometimes it may be accepted verbally but is never acted upon or, if acted upon, inevitably fails to improve the plight of the patient.

EFFECTS ON THE GROUP

The effects on the group are obvious: the other members become bored and irritated, then frustrated and confused. The HRC appears to them as a greedy whirlpool, sucking down the group's energy. Worse yet, no deceleration of the HRC's demands is evident. Faith in the group process suffers, as members experience a sense of impotence and, further, as they despair of making their own needs appreciated by the group. Cohesiveness is undermined as absenteeism occurs or as patients subgroup in an effort to exclude the HRC.

DYNAMICS

The behavioral pattern of the HRC appears to be an attempt to resolve highly conflicted feelings about dependency. On the one hand, the patient feels helpless and insignificant and experiences himself as totally dependent on others, especially on the therapist, for a sense of personal worth. If the therapist notices and ministers to him, his sense of significance and self-acceptance is augmented. His entire identity has become inextricably interwoven with his claim for attention due him because of his suffering; he may feel alive and important only when he functions as a "crisis-creator." [4] On the other hand, however, his dependent postion is vastly confounded by a pervasive distrust and enmity of authority figures. A vicious circle results, one which has been spinning for much of the patient's life: consumed with need, he turns for help to a figure whom he anticipates as unwilling (or unable) to help him; his anticipation of refusal so colors his style of requesting help that his prophecy is fulfilled, and further evidence is accumulated for his belief in the malevolence of the potential care-giver.

The characteristic pattern of behavior in the group both expresses and attempts to resolve this predicament. The HRC manifests and at the same time denies his dependency by exaggerating his helplessness while blaming others for his difficulties; he asks for help only indirectly through an interminable presentation of problems and avoids an overt supplicant posture. He then presents these problems in such form as to preclude effective help, thus denying his helplessness by defeating the potential care-givers.[3] The victory is, of course, a Pyrrhic one since the HRC destroys others through first destroying himself.

Berger and Rosenbaum, who report several cases,[4] particularly emphasize the HRC's latent motivation to frustrate and defeat the group and the therapist. Their series of HRC's were subject to severe deprivation early in life; parents were either absent or seriously disturbed. Often marked depressive trends were evident as well as a pervasive need to deprive others of pleasure as they themselves had been deprived. Should an HRC undergo some positive change, it will often be withheld from the group until several months after the fact.

The help-rejecting complaining pattern of behavior is not an all-or-nothing distinct clinical syndrome. Patients may arrive at this style of interaction through various psychodynamic pathways and may persistently manifest this behavior in an extreme degree with no external provocation; others may demonstrate only a trace of this pattern; whereas still others may become help-rejecting complainers only at times of particular stress.

GUIDELINES FOR MANAGEMENT

A severe HRC is an exceedingly difficult clinical challenge, and many such patients have won a dubious victory over therapist and group by failing in therapy. It would be thus presumptuous and misleading to attempt to prescribe a careful therapeutic plan; however, certain generalizations may be posited. Surely it is a blunder for the therapist to confuse the help requested for the help needed. The HRC solicits advice not for its potential value but in order to reject it; ultimately the therapist's advice, guidance, and medication will be rejected, forgotten, or, if used, will prove ineffective. It is also a blunder for the therapist to unburden himself of his growing frustration and resentment to the patient. Retaliation merely completes the familiar vicious circle; the patient's anticipation of ill-treatment and abandonment is once again realized and he finds justification for his own anger. Once again he is able to affirm that no one, especially a therapist from a different background, can ever really understand him.

What course, then, is available to the therapist? One clinician suggests, perhaps in desperation, that the therapist interrupt the vicious circle by indicating that he "not only understands but shares the patient's feelings of hopelessness about his situation, thus refusing to perpetuate his part in a futile relationship." [2] Although this strategy resulted in the HRC's breaking off therapy, there was a suggestion that the patient, in an effort to prove the doctor wrong, experienced considerable improvement.

In general, however, the therapist should attempt to mobilize the major curative factors in the service of the patient. Once a cohesive group has been formed and the patient through universality, identification, and catharsis has come to value his membership in the group, then the therapist can encourage interpersonal learning by continually focusing on feedback and process in much the same manner as that described in the discussion of the monopolistic patient. Once the patient cares about his interpersonal impact on the other members, then he should be helped to recognize his characteristic pattern of relationships. One therapist, having once identified the process, called the group's attention to it by humming the tune "Nobody Knows the Trouble I've Seen . . . but Jesus" [4] when the HRC engaged in his typical behavior. Eric Berne,[7] who considers the HRC pattern as the most common of all social and psychotherapy group games, has christened it "Why don't you—yes but." The use of such easily accessible descriptive labels often makes the process more transparent and acceptable to the group members.

An example of a critical incident which initiated an adaptive spiral occurred in the sixtieth meeting of a therapy group. Mrs. Gaul, the help-rejecting complainer, was an obese, poorly groomed, thirty-seven-year-old housewife who had originally been a monopolist in the group but had gradually altered this aspect of her behavior. Her participation, though more moderate, was still HRC in style. For the two previous meetings the group had worked hard on Mrs. Gaul's disinclination to accept help—a discussion initiated by Mrs. Gaul's ambivalently declining an offer of chewing gum which one of the members passed around the group; when pressed she finally relented but insisted on accepting only half a stick. In the current meeting Mrs. Gaul began all over again, with a repetitious account of the malfeasance of her husband (now threatening to leave her again) and of her rare metabolic abnormality which made it impossible for her either to lose weight or to refrain from compulsive midnight eating. Finally Mr. Grady, an ally of hers on previous occasions and the group member whom she most liked and respected, erupted to tell her how she evoked feelings of futility and despair in him. He boomed out then in his heavy Irish brogue, "You, Mrs. Gaul, by your whole demeanor, render me impotent, and I must get away from you!" With that he strode out of the room, although the meeting was not yet over. Subsequently her demeanor, her behavior, as well as her grooming changed considerably and the single incident seemed to consolidate a great deal of previous work in the group. Certainly the social microcosm concept became abundantly clear; only too obvious was the parallel between Mr. Grady and her husband, who had also had to leave her and who, incidentally, was also impotent.

Generally, however, the treatment of a patient with an extreme HRC behavior pattern is an extraordinarily difficult and unrewarding task. If possible, such patients should not be included in a therapy group. Unfortunately the prediction of this pattern of group behavior is difficult with standard pretherapy screening techniques. Occasionally these patients can be recognized from their waiting group behavior, or from records of their experience in a previous therapy group, and at that point referred to individual therapy. If the HRC pattern is present but less extreme and fixed, the patient may well be accessible to group therapy, though, as Frank[2] suggests, he should be introduced into an ongoing rather than a beginning therapy group; the advanced group will be able to offer the patient more understanding and acceptance and at the same time be less disrupted than the young, developing group.

The Self-Righteous Moralist

The self-righteous moralist (SRM), first described by Rosenthal, Frank, and Nash,[8] evinces a pattern of behavior evident in the early group meetings. The most outstanding characteristic of the self-righteous moralist is the need to be right and to demonstrate that the other person is wrong, particularly when some moral issue is involved. His interpersonal motives differ from those of patients evincing other behavioral patterns we have discussed. The monopolist wants to control others for sundry reasons. The help-rejecting complainer wants to solicit help and then to defeat the benefactor. The self-righteous moralist, on the other hand, is relatively unconcerned about being liked or respected; above all, he wishes to be right, to be respected for his moral integrity, and to be successful in imposing his values on other people.

In the first meeting the SRM usually presents himself as calm and self-assured, demonstrating his superiority by his poise. He is often silent at first until he is clear about the group or some member's position. He then usually becomes the key figure in the discussion because of the intensity of his convictions and his propensity to belabor his viewpoint indefatigably. Characteristically he refuses to concede any points, to admit any error, or to make any modification of his original formulation.[8] When others discuss problems, he participates in a manner which will enhance his status. He may point out that he has survived greater environmental stress, that he has continued to succeed despite manifold handicaps, and that his solutions may serve as models for others. Although the group may empathize with him when he first presents his problems, the empathy is soon transformed into irritation when the members realize that his primary interest is in attaining a position of moral superiority rather than in sharing experiences. If another member attempts to assume a position of superiority in the group, the self-righteous moralist feels challenged and engages the interloper by attempting to prove him wrong. The therapist, too, is challenged, though often only obliquely; the patient may express doubts about therapy and refer to the opinions of other experts in the field or cite reputable authorities in other fields. When particularly threatened, he may challenge and attack the therapist's moral values.

Patients with this behavioral pattern are deeply troubled by feelings of shame and anger. Rosenthal et al.[8] report that their four patients all experienced an early loss of the parent of the opposite sex which resulted in deprivation and loss of social status. Blame for these events is affixed to the parent of the same sex, but the patients, for fear of retaliation, are unable to express their anger. Each responded by attempting to show up the parent of the same sex by assuming and "correctly" filling the parental role. However, instead of gratitude from the concerned parties, the patients received indifference and hostility. So gradually, as manifested in the group, they have come to experience themselves as much maligned figures who have sacrificed themselves for others. This lifetime of sacrifice accounts for the SRM's failure to achieve status and has provided him with a special understanding of life. "His attitude has become one of righteous indignation, his mien is that of one who has suffered nobly. He seeks recognition for his nobility of character rather than for his achievements." [8] The anticipated recognition, however, does not materialize, a fact which merely reinforces the patient's view of himself as long-suffering and unrewarded. His pride in his noble character, his only perceived virtue, is reinforced and more vigorously claimed in his interpersonal dealing. Thus the vicious process comes full circle.

The recognition of the role that shame and lowered self-esteem play in the dynamics of these patients is important in formulating a therapeutic plan. Unless the therapist intervenes, the self-righteous moralist mobilizes so much resentment that he is soon forced out of the group. Not only must the patient be protected but the group must be helped to deal with his provocative behavior. Shame is perhaps the key concept in the successful therapeutic approach. If the group can be helped to sense the shame which underlies the angry self-righteous polemics of the patient, their response to him will be constructive. The therapist, once attuned to the patient's deep sense of failure and shame, will respond accordingly rather than be drawn into the same catastrophic interpersonal sequence that the patient creates in his customary way of relating to the world.

Often, however, before the therapist fully recognizes the pattern, the entire malignant sequence has unfolded and reached a point of irreversibility. The group has responded to the self-righteous moralist at first with patience, then with irritation, at times with studied indifference, and finally with fury. The patient often defends himself and rationalizes the fact that he has not attained the respect he desired by devaluating the group and by convincing himself that the group's opinion is of little import. I have known two patients who were forced to leave the group and only later, in subsequent therapy, were able to integrate the course of events they experienced in the group.

Many of these principles are illustrated in this clinical vignette.

Victor, a twenty-nine-year-old male who sought therapy because of intense sexual urges toward adolescent girls, immediately slid into the self-righteous moralist pattern in the group. He attempted to establish his moral superiority by underscoring his ability to lead a good Christian life despite the handicap of ego-alien sexual impulses. His behavior in the group conformed closely to the pattern described above, and he especially berated the group and the therapists for their personal disregard of Christian ethics. The group's response to him, particularly their pointing out that his contempt and scorn for them was not only infuriating but highly un-Christian, apparently went unheeded. The feelings of the members toward him degenerated to the point of name calling, and three members expressed deep, ungovernable feelings of hatred toward Victor.

Victor expressed little concern for the opinions of pagans and, by the twentieth meeting, when the situation became unbearable, he dropped out of the group. To the casual observer, Victor's experience in the group was not only not helpful but indeed catastrophic. However, he immediately began therapy in a married couples' group and proved to be far more receptive when he received the same feedback from his wife and from other couples. Follow-up interviews confirmed that he had learned a great deal in the group but had reflexly locked himself into a relationship with the group which precluded experimentation with new behavior. His behavior, however, in the initial meetings of the second group was considerably different from his behavior in the first.

The Doctor's Assistant

The patient who assumes the role of the "Doctor's Assistant" [2,3] acts in accordance with his conception of the ideal role of the doctor, so as to gain the approval of the group leader and members. He consistently offers advice to the other members, often of a platitudinous nature, and resists admitting any personal weaknesses or needs, except those that he has handled successfully. He discourages others from offering him suggestions by behaving as though he needs no help. Generally he attempts to prove his superiority to others by demonstrating his competence. He desires the respect and approval of the doctors and defends the viewpoint of the authority when it is attacked by others.

The doctor's assistant usually generates considerable interaction in the group. The other members may react to his pose of superiority with antagonism, and indeed he is often an easy target. The therapists may welcome the support of the doctor's assistant at first; for example, his inclination to answer inquiries directed to the therapist relieves the therapist of the task at a time when he considers it ill-advised or premature. Some therapists, therefore, overprotect the "doctor's assistant" to such a degree that some other patients begin to wonder whether the "assistant" may not be a "plant" in the group.[2] Occasionally the opposite occurs:

Since the doctor's assistant tried to display complete competence, the doctor sometimes considered him less vulnerable than he actually was and might fail to protect him or even join the group members in undermining his "superior" position. With or without the doctor's support, these patients did not seem to survive many group meetings. With increasing pressure by the other patients for self-revelation, they felt that they had made or would make fools of themselves by remaining in the group and abandoned it for good at a point when their shaky position of superiority became untenable. . . .[2]

As time progresses, the doctor's assistant is placed in a position of considerable conflict. To win the therapist's approval he needs to assume the patient role and admit to problems which conflict with his need to appear superior. He grows angry at the doctor for making these implicit demands and devalues him as a leader. These feelings further jeopardize, in his mind, his ability to win the doctor's respect.

Effective intervention with these patients must occur very early before they have created a nonviable role for themselves in the group. They must be disabused of the misconception that they will earn the leader's approval by a show of competence and superiority. Self-disclosure and admission of needs must be strongly reinforced, and such patients must in a nonhumiliating way be continually reminded of the fact that they come to therapy not for acceptance but for help in dealing with their problems in living.

The Schizoid Patient

In Chapter 7 we have already described some of the problems involved with the schizoid patient in the group. Generally this category consists of affect-blocked, emotionally distant individuals who often seek group therapy because of their awareness that they cannot relate closely to others and that they cannot experience their emotions with the same intensity with which others appear to. Sartre in *The Age of Reason* vividly describes the experiential world of such an individual: [9]

. . . He closed the paper and began to read the special correspondent's dispatch on the front page. Fifty dead and three hundred wounded had already been counted, but that was not the total, there were certainly corpses under the debris. . . . There were thousands of men in France who had not been able to read their paper that morning without feeling a clot of anger rise in their throat, thousands of men who had clenched their fists and muttered: "Swine!" Mathieu clenched his fists and muttered: "Swine!" and felt himself still more guilty. If at least he had been able to discover in himself a trifling emotion that was veritably if modestly alive, conscious of its limits. But no: he was empty, he was confronted by a vast anger, a desperate anger, he saw it and could almost have touched it. But it was inert—if it were to live and find expression and suffer, he must lend it his own body. It was other people's anger. "Swine!" He clenched his fists, he strode along, but nothing came, the anger remained external to himself. . . . Something was on the threshold of existence, a timorous dawn of anger. At last! But it dwindled and collapsed, he was left in solitude, walking with the measured and decorous gait of a man in a funeral procession in Paris. . . . He wiped his forehead with his handkerchief and he thought: "One can't force one's deeper feelings." Yonder was a terrible and tragic state of affairs that ought to arouse one's deepest emotions.

. . . "It's no use, the moment will not come. . . ."

The schizoid patient often finds himself in a similar predicament in the therapy group. On many occasions other members comment on their here-and-now feelings about a patient or event in the group, and the patient gradually notes the discrepancies between his own responses and those of others to the same event.

In the second meeting of a group some of the members were discussing their reactions following the last meeting.* One patient, Mary, a terrified and obviously deeply disturbed young woman, described with great tremulousness her profound feelings of emptiness at the end of the meeting. She had wept for hours following the last meeting and seemed on the verge of tears again in the group. A wave of empathy enveloped the group until another member, Paul, a highly schizoid young man, then described his reactions to the previous meeting, which were a series of intellectual queries about the rationale of group therapy. The group listened, fidgeted, became more restless, and finally, at the first semblance of a pause, one of the members interrupted to ask Mary about her weeping and offer her support. The therapist, a few minutes later, made the first of many similar interventions to help Paul become aware of his stifled emotions. He asked the group both about their response to Mary's account of her reaction to the previous week and about their response to Paul's comments. Paul became aware that everyone but himself seemed deeply concerned about Mary at that point in the meeting.

The awareness of his emotional restriction is only the first step. Next he must be helped to find a method of engaging emotionally in the group. Often the patient must be taught to observe himself. For example, he may experience only the autonomic components of affect and complain of tightness in the stomach, sweating, or flushing; he should be encouraged to report on these phenomena immediately as a first step toward more affective participation. Gradually these autonomic responses can be translated into their psychic equivalents by the therapist's noting, for example, the timing of their appearance. Nonverbal cues emitted by the patient

* This is, incidentally, a valuable exercise for a new group. It switches them off content and helps them to focus on feelings, especially feelings about the group; many members are able, for example, in this discussion to speak about what (or whom) they fear most of all in the group.

should be attended to and dealt with in similar fashion by the therapist. Often some nonverbal techniques (to be described in Chapter 13) are valuable in increasing the patient's ability to discern nascent or repressed feelings.

The therapist should also beware of assessing events solely according to his own experiential world. As we have shown previously, patients may experience the same event in totally different manners; a seemingly trivial event to the therapist or to one patient may represent an exceedingly important experience to another. A slight show of irritation by a restricted schizoid patient may represent for him a major breakthrough; it may be the first time in adulthood that he has expressed anger and may further enable him to test out new behaviors both in and out of the group.

In the group, the schizoid patient is both a high risk and a high reward patient. If he can manage to presevere, to continue in the group and not be discouraged by his inability to change his relationship style quickly, then he stands to profit considerably from the group therapy experience.

The Silent Patient

The converse of the monopolist, the silent member, represents a less disruptive but often equally challenging problem to the therapist. A story, probably apocryphal, which has circulated among group therapists for years is the account of the patient who attended a group for a year without uttering a word. At the end of the fiftieth meeting, he announced to the group that he would not return; his problems had been resolved, he was due to get married the following day, and he wished to express his gratitude to the group for the help they had given him! Patients may profit from vicariously engaging in treatment through identifying with active patients with similar problems; it is possible that changes in behavior and risk taking can gradually occur in their relationship outside the group while they remain silent and seemingly unchanged in the group.

Generally, however, the silent patient does not profit from the group. The greater the verbal participation, the greater the sense of involvement, and the more the patient is valued by others and ultimately by himself. Lundgren and Miller [10] have demonstrated in T-groups that, regardless of what the participants said, the more words they spoke the greater was the positive change in their picture of themselves.

Patients may be silent for many reasons. Some may experience a pervasive dread of self-disclosure; every utterance, they feel, may commit them to progressively more disclosure. Others may feel so conflicted about aggression that they cannot undertake the self-assertion inherent in speaking. Others who demand nothing short of perfection of themselves never speak because they must be the greatest every time they open their mouths, whereas others keep their distance from the group or manage to control it by maintaining a lofty superior silence. Some patients are especially threatened by a particular member in the group and habitually speak only in the absence of that member, in smaller meetings or in alternate (leaderless) meetings.

Proper management depends in part on the dynamics of the silence, which the therapist ascertains from the pregroup individual interviews and from the patient's nonverbal cues, as well as from his few verbal contributions. A middle course must be steered between placing undue pressure on the patient and, on the other hand, allowing him to slide into an extreme isolate role. The therapist may still maintain an attitude of allowing each patient to modulate his own degree of participation and yet periodically including the silent patient by commenting on his nonverbal behavior, when, by gesture or demeanor, he is evincing interest, tension, sadness, boredom, or amusement. Often he may hasten the member's participation by encouraging the other members to reflect on their perceptions of him and then asking the silent member to validate these perceptions. If a patient's participation remains very limited even after three months of meetings, my experience has been that the prognosis is poor, unless active intervention is instigated. A group may be increasingly frustrated and puzzled at vainly coaxing, encouraging, or challenging a silent, blocked patient to participate. Often concurrent individual sessions may be useful in helping the patient to overcome his dread of the group.

The Psychotic Patient in the Group

The therapy group is severely challenged when a member develops a psychosis during the course of treatment. The fate of the psychotic patient, the response of the other members, and the effective options available to the therapist all depend, in part, upon when the psychosis occurs in the history of the group. In general, the older the group and the more well-established the affected member, the more tolerant and effective will the therapy group be in the crisis.

THE PSYCHOTIC PATIENT IN THE
EARLY PHASES OF THE GROUP

In Chapter 7 ("The Selection of Patients") we emphasized that the grossly psychotic patient should be excluded in the initial screening process from outpatient, interactional group therapy. If, by accident or design, such a severely ill patient is included in the group, both the group and the patient almost invariably suffer. The group is impeded in its progress in a manner which will be illustrated shortly; the patient soon slides into a deviant role in the group and eventually terminates treatment, often much the worse for his experience.

At times, despite cautious screening, a patient, because of unanticipated stress from his life circumstances or from the group, becomes psychotic in the early stages of therapy. In these instances the problems created for the newly formed group are very considerable. This book has repeatedly stressed that the early stages of the group are a time of great flux and great importance. The young group is easily influenced, and the norms which are established early are usually exceedingly durable. A rather intense sequence of events occurs as, in a few weeks, an aggregate of frightened, distrustful strangers evolves into an intimate, mutually helpful group. Any event which, in the early part of the group, consumes an inordinate amount of time and which diverts energy from the tasks of the developmental sequence is potentially destructive to the group. A number of the relevant problems are illustrated by this clinical example:

Joan, a thirty-seven-year-old housewife who had once, several years before, been hospitalized and treated with electro-convulsive therapy for depression, sought group therapy at the insistence of her individual therapist who thought that an understanding of her interpersonal relationships would help her to improve her relationship with her husband. In the early meetings of the group she was an active member who tended to reveal far more intimate details of her past history than the other members. Occasionally she expressed anger toward another member and then engaged in excessively profuse apologies coupled with self-depreciatory remarks. By the sixth meeting her behavior became still more inappropriate. For example, she discoursed at great length on her son's urinary problems and described, with intricate detail, the surgery that had been performed to relieve urethral stricture. At the following meeting she noted that the family cat had also developed a blockage of the urinary tract; she then pressed everyone in the group to describe his own pets.

In the eighth meeting, Joan disorganized completely. She behaved in a bizarre, irrational manner, insulting members of the group, openly flirting with the male members to the point of stroking their bodies, and finally lapsed into punning, klang associations, and inappropriate laughter and tears. One of the therapists then escorted her from the room, phoned her husband and arranged for immediate psychiatric hospitalization. Joan remained in the hospital in a hypomanic state for a month, during which she underwent a gradual recovery.

The members during the meeting were obviously extremely uncomfortable, their feelings ranging from bafflement and fright to annoyance. After Joan left they expressed feelings of guilt for, in some unknown manner, having triggered her behavior. Others spoke of their fear, and one recalled another person who had acted in a similar fashion but, in addition, had brandished a gun.

During the subsequent meeting, the members discussed many feelings related to the incident. One member expressed his conviction that no one could be trusted; even though he had known Joan for seven weeks, her behavior proved to be totally unpredictable. Others expressed their relief that they were, in comparison, psychologically healthy; others, in response to their fears of similarly losing control, employed considerable denial and veered away from discussing these problems. Some expressed a fear of Joan's returning and making a shambles of the group. A lack of faith in the effects of hospitalization was expressed. "What good," they asked, "could a hospital do for Joan?" Others expressed their diminished faith in group therapy; one member asked for hypnosis, while another brought to the meeting an article from a scientific journal claiming that psychotherapy was ineffective. A loss of faith in the therapists was expressed in the dream of one member, in which the therapist was in the hospital and was rescued by the patient.

In the next few meetings, all these themes went underground; the meetings became listless, shallow, and intellectualized. Attendance dwindled and the group seemed resigned to its own impotence. At the fourteenth meeting, the therapists announced that Joan was improved and would return the following week. A vigorous, heated discussion ensued. The members feared that:

1. They would upset her, that an intense meeting would make her ill again, and that therefore the group would be forced to move slowly and superficially.
2. Joan would be unpredictable; at any point she might lose control and display dangerous frightening behavior.
3. Joan would, because of her lack of control, be untrustworthy; nothing in the group would remain confidential.

At the same time, the members expressed considerable anxiety and guilt for wishing to exclude Joan from the group, and soon tension and a heavy silence prevailed. The extreme reaction of the group persuaded the therapist to delay for a few weeks the reintroduction of Joan (who was, incidentally, in concurrent individual therapy).

When Joan re-entered the group, she was treated as a fragile object, and the entire group interaction was guarded and defensive. By the twentieth meeting, five of the seven members had dropped out of the group, leaving only Joan and another peripheral member who terminated shortly afterwards.

The therapists reconstituted the group by adding five new members. It is of interest to note that, despite the fact that only two of the old members and the therapists continued in the reconstituted group, the old group culture persisted: Joan was treated so delicately and so obliquely by the new members that the group moved slowly, floundering in its own politeness and social conventionality. Only when the therapists openly confronted this issue and discussed in the group their own fears of upsetting Joan and thrusting her into another psychosis were the members able to deal with their feelings and fears about her. At that point the group moved ahead more quickly; Joan remained in the new group for a year and made decided improvements in her ability to relate with others and in her self-concept.

THE PSYCHOTIC PATIENT LATER IN THE COURSE OF THE GROUP

An entirely different situation often presents itself when a patient who has been an involved, active group member develops a sudden and severe worsening of his clinical condition. The concern of the other members may be primarily for the patient rather than for themselves or for the group. Since they had previously known and understood the now psychotic patient as a person, they often react with great concern and interest; the patient is less likely to be viewed as a strange and frightening object to be avoided. The popular stereotype of the insane person includes a strong element of strangeness; the patient's appearance and behavior seem totally dissimilar to anything the observer has experienced within himself.*

Although perceiving similarity may enhance the other members' ability to continue relating to the distressed patient, it also creates a personal upheaval in some members, for they begin to fear that they, too, can lose control and slide into a similar abyss. It is most important for the therapist to anticipate this reaction so as to enable the others to work through their dread.

When faced with a psychotic patient in a group, many psychiatrists reflexly revert back to their early medical model and symbolically "dismiss" the group by intervening forcefully in a one-to-one fashion. In effect they

---

* Moos and Yalom [11] demonstrated, for example, that medical students assigned for the first time to a psychiatric ward regarded the psychotic patients as extremely dangerous, frightening, unpredictable and dissimilar to themselves. At the end of their five weeks' assignment, these attitudes underwent considerable change; the students grew less isolated and frightened of their patients, as they learned that "psychotics" were but confused and deeply anguished human beings.

say to the group, "This is too serious a problem for you to handle"; such a maneuver, however, is often antitherapeutic: the patient is frightened and the group is emasculated.

It has been my experience that a mature group is perfectly able to deal with the psychiatric emergency and, although there may be false starts, the group will be able to consider every contingency and take every action that the therapist might have considered. Consider the following clinical example:

In the forty-fifth meeting Rhona, a forty-three-year-old divorcee, arrived a few minutes late in a disheveled, obviously disturbed state. Over the previous few weeks she had gradually been sliding into a depression, but the process had clearly suddenly accelerated. She was tearful, despondent, and evidenced a degree of psychomotor retardation. During the early part of the meeting she wept continuously and expressed feelings of great loneliness, hopelessness, and inability to love, hate, or, for that matter, to have any deeply felt emotion; she described her feeling of great detachment from everyone, including the group, and when prompted, discussed her suicidal ruminations.

The group members responded to Rhona with great empathy and concern. They inquired about events during the past week and helped her discuss two important occurrences which seemed related to the depressive crisis: (1) she had for months saved money and planned a summer trip to Europe; her seventeen-year-old son had, during the past week, decided to decline a summer camp job which had been offered him and refused to search for other jobs—a turn of events which, in Rhona's eyes, jeopardized her trip; (2) she had after months of hesitation decided to attend a dance for divorced middle-aged people which proved to be a disaster: no one had approached her to dance and she had left for home consumed with feelings of total worthlessness.

The group helped her to explore her relationship with her son: she for the first time expressed rage at him for his lack of concern for her. With the group's assistance she attempted to define the limits of her responsibility toward him. It was difficult for Rhona to discuss the dance because of the amount of shame and humiliation she felt. Two other women in the group, one single and one divorced, empathized deeply with her and shared their experiences and re-actions to the scarcity of males. Rhona was also reminded by the group of the many times she had, during sessions, interpreted every minor slight as a total rejection and condemnation of herself. Finally, after much attention, care, and warmth had been offered her, one of the members pointed out to Rhona that the experience of the dance was being disconfirmed right in the group: several people who knew her well were deeply concerned and involved with her. Rhona rejected this by claiming that the group, unlike the dance, was an artificial, unreal situation in which people followed artificial, unnatural rules of conduct. The members quickly pointed out that quite the contrary was true: the dance, the contrived congregation of strangers, was the artificial situation and the group was the real one, since it was there that she was truly and completely known.

Rhona, consumed with the conviction of her own worthlessness, then berated herself for her inability to feel reciprocal warmth and involvement with the group members. One of the members then quickly intercepted this maneuver by pointing out that this was a familiar and repetitive pattern of hers: that she experienced some feelings toward the other members which were evidenced by her facial expression and body posture, but then her "shoulds" took over and tortured her by insisting that she "should" feel more, "should" feel more warmth and love than anyone else. The net effect was that the real feeling she did have was rapidly extinguished by the winds of her impossible self-demands.

In essence, what then transpired was Rhona's gradual recognition of the discrepancy between her public and private esteem (described in Chapter 3). At the end of the meeting, Rhona responded by bursting into tears and crying for several minutes. The group was reluctant to leave but did so when they had all convinced themselves that suicide was no longer a serious consideration. Throughout the next week the members maintained an informal vigil; each phoned Rhona at least once.

Rather early in the session the therapist realized the important dynamics operating in Rhona's depression and, had he chosen, might have made the appropriate interpretations to allow the patient and the group to arrive much more quickly at a cognitive understanding of the problem—but at considerable cost to the meaningfulness and value of the meeting both to the protagonist and to the other patients. For one thing, the group would have been deprived of an opportunity to experience its own potency; every success adds to the group's cohesiveness and enhances the self-regard of each of the members.

At times, as in this clinical episode, the group chooses and performs the appropriate action; at other times the group may decide that the therapist must act. One must differentiate between a hasty decision stemming from infantile dependence and an unrealistic appraisal of the therapist's powers and, on the other hand, a decision based on a thorough investigation of the situation and a mature appraisal of the therapist's expertise.

These points lead us to an important principle of group dynamics, one which is substantiated by considerable research. A group which reaches an autonomous decision based on a thorough exploration of the pertinent problems will employ all of its resources in support of its decision; a group which has a decision thrust upon it is likely to resist and to show inadequate problem-solving ability.* A widely cited study by Coch and French [13] is relevant here. The authors studied a pajama-producing fac-

---

* This is hardly a hypermodern principle: Thomas Jefferson once stated that "that government is the strongest of which every man feels a part." [12]

tory in which periodic changes in jobs and routine were necessitated by advances in technology. For many years these changes were resisted by the employees; with each change there was an increase in absenteeism, turnover, aggression to the management, as well as decreased efficiency and output. An experiment was designed to test various methods of overcoming the employees' resistance to change. The critical variable studied was the degree of participation of the group members (the employees) in the planning of the change. The employees were divided into three groups and three variations were tested: (1) the first variation involved no participation by the employees in planning the changes, though an explanation was given to them; (2) the second variation involved participation through elected representation of the workers in designing the changes to be made in the job; (3) the third variation consisted of total participation by all the members of the group in designing the changes. The results showed conclusively that, on all measures studied (aggression toward management, absenteeism, efficiency, number of employees resigning from the job), the success of the change was directly proportional to the degree of participation of the group members.

The implications for group therapy are apparent: members of a therapy group who personally participate in the planning of a course of action will be more committed to the enactment of the plan. They will, for example, invest themselves more fully in the care of a psychotic member if they recognize that it is their problem and not the therapist's alone.

At times, as in the clinical example cited above, the entire experience is beneficial to the development of group cohesiveness; sharing intense emotional experiences usually strengthens intermember ties. The danger to the group occurs when the psychotic patient consumes a massive amount of energy for a prolonged period of time. At this point other members may drop out of the group, and the group may deal with the disturbed patient in a cautious, concealed manner or attempt to ignore him; all of these methods never fail to aggravate the problem further. In such critical situations, one important option always available to the therapist is to see the disturbed patient in individual sessions for the duration of the crisis (this will be dealt with more fully in the discussion of concurrent individual therapy). However, here too the group should explore the implications thoroughly and share in the decision.

One of the worst calamities that can befall a therapy group is the presence of a manic-depressive member. A patient in the midst of a severe hypomanic thrust is perhaps the single most disruptive problem for a group. (In contrast, a full-blown manic episode presents little problem since the decision is clear: hospitalization is required.)

One of my therapy groups attempted to deal with a manic-depressive patient for over a year. Most of the time the patient was an extraordinarily valuable member; she was fully committed to the group, insightful, sensitive, and provocative. When she became depressed, the group was deeply concerned for her, feared suicide, and devoted many hours to bolstering her self-concept and dissuading her from resignation or suicide. When she grew manic she dominated the group; she could not refrain from responding to every comment made in the meeting, she interrupted other members continuously, and she also stirred up great concern on the part of the other members, who grew alarmed at the many unwise and impulsive economic and personal life decisions she made. Gradually the depressive and manic episodes grew more severe and the lucid interval between episodes shorter. Eventually hospitalization was required and she left the group with no benefit from her experience.

There is clinical evidence to indicate that the classic manic-depressive patient is probably impervious to psychologically based treatment, even when the therapy is carried out by the most experienced clinicians.[14] It is obviously unwise, then, to allow the group to invest so much time in treatment which has such little likelihood of success. There are times when a patient, for his own sake and certainly for the other members' sakes, should be removed from the group. The problem lies, of course, in ascertaining when that time has arrived; generally we are certain only when viewing the situation retrospectively. The manic-depressive patient, however, represents a clearer indication than most. Such a decision, too, should be shared with the group, but generally the therapist must actively take the lead. It is important for the therapist to take the responsibility for arranging for the patient's future treatment. Otherwise patients may be extraordinarily threatened at the prospect of similar abandonment.

The Homosexual in the Group

There is a certain inconsistency in including a section on the homosexual as a problem patient since one of the major points I wish to make is that the homosexual can be successfully treated only when he and the group no longer consider him as a special problem. When the person emerges from "the homosexual," the special problem no longer exists. However, there are so many stereotypes about the homosexual that these patients will encounter certain predictable problems in the therapy group, problems generated by ingrained responses of other members as well as by the patient's own highly stylized self-image.

INCLUSION CRITERIA

In the chapter on selection for group therapy, I made the point that homosexuality is not a criterion for exclusion from group therapy; neither is it a criterion for inclusion. An individual is incompletely described by his sexual behavior alone, and the same criteria must be evaluated in the homosexual as with any candidate: e.g., interpersonal style, psychological sensitivity, and motivation for therapy. It has been my experience with a large number of patients that individuals with homosexual problems can be treated very effectively in an outpatient heterogeneous group. Whether or not a homosexual applying for therapy wishes to change his sexual orientation and "switch" to heterosexuality is irrelevant to the selection process. Individuals who are quite committed to a homosexual style of sexual relations can nonetheless benefit greatly from group therapy. In fact, a homosexual who is confirmed in his sexual orientation but markedly symptomatic is a more suitable candidate than a rather comfortable individual who desires to alter his sexual orientation because of intellectual, social, or legal pressures.

A particularly unsuitable candidate is an asymptomatic individual whose homosexual style of life is egosyntonic and who requests therapy in order to reassure himself of the immutability of his life patterns—i.e., he goes through the motions of obtaining therapy to satisfy his superego that no stone has been left unturned in his attempt to conform. Such a patient derives a sufficient amount of gratification from his life style so that he will thwart his own therapy. Perhaps the most unsuitable of all candidates is the individual who has been legally prosecuted for a homosexual offense and must obtain psychotherapy as a condition of his probation or parole status. Although there are exceptions, these patients generally are not helped in an outpatient heterogeneous therapy group.

Although individuals with a homosexual proclivity may come to therapy with the same broad spectrum of complaints and precipitating stress as nonhomosexual patients, there are nevertheless certain recurring configurations which stem from characteristic features of their life style. Most commonly such patients experience anxiety and depression related to a confrontation between their homosexuality and their social environment. Compulsive "cruising" which has become so indiscriminate and so flagrant that exposure and jeopardy of the patient's professional and social life are imminent is a frequent complaint. Others seek help after exposure has tumbled down their professional and, if they are married, their family lives. Others apply for treatment in an exceedingly distraught state, following a disruption or a threatened disruption of a love relationship. Middle-aged homosexuals often seek help for a pervasive sense of emptiness and futility; the chief currency in the gay world is youth, and with its passing, individuals feel bankrupt and unable to raise capital once more for an interpersonal investment. Often a "last leaf on the tree" feeling prevails, and a realization of their biological sterility adds to their despair.

As a general rule, the more acute the presenting symptoms, the more distinct the precipitating stress, and the more the patient views his salvation in the hands of others, the *less* favorable a candidate he is for group therapy. Acute stress rapidly vanishes: anxiety stemming from the disruption of a love relationship dissipates with the return of a lover or the acquisition of another; the humiliation and pain of exposure soon diminish as do family and social pressures to seek therapy. As these forces which once propelled the patient to therapy lose their vigor, so too does the patient's commitment to therapy wane. If, on the other hand, the patient's decision to enter therapy has been a more deliberate judgment, if he has a clear sense of personal responsibility for the origin and solution of his life predicament, if he experiences guilt, self-hatred, and concern that his life has escaped his conscious control, then the outlook is more favorable.

THE PATIENT IN THE GROUP

The first important task for the homosexual patient is self-disclosure. For him to become a working, engaged member of the therapy group he must disclose himself to the other members and preferably he should do so early in the course of the group. Otherwise it is very likely that the patient will drop out of the group in the early months of therapy, since he will be merely recapitulating the highly dishonest, unsatisfying social relationships which he experiences outside the group. Despite good public relations work and a growing public understanding and acceptance of homosexuality, the homosexual remains estranged from the "straight" world. So often he considers homosexuality as the matrix of his identity and yet must conceal this very aspect of himself from family, teachers, business associates, and many "front" male and female friends. He therefore has a sense of sham and deceit about his presentation of self; lest his "real self" leak out, he must maintain a constant vigilance and suppression of spontaneity. The resulting mental fatigue and tension is stoically borne by the secret homosexual until it reaches such proportions that symptomatology ensues. The open homosexual gains periodic release in the company of other homosexuals in the gay world. (The term "gay" is well chosen for it *is* a gay world in which the fetters of conventionality are cast off in a spirit of reckless abandon. One of my patients described the gay world as a "magic wonderful fairyland in which secret notes, affairs, rendezvous, and intrigues are everywhere. It is like eating forever the frothy icing of a cake; only one must never notice that there is no cake underneath.")

The therapy group offers such individuals an opportunity for rapprochement with his environment. Simply to be known fully and accepted by representatives of the straight world has great therapeutic value for many homosexuals; despite a professed, well-practiced scorn for the straight world, there is also a great longing to be accepted by it. Often the group's acceptance is a novel type of acceptance for him, based neither on his youth, physical attributes, nor on the achievements of his sham self.

One patient entered therapy because of his inability to assert himself professionally or socially; he had repeatedly found himself entrapped in a series of "sick" homosexual relationships which had generated considerable shame as well as a progressive sense of alienation from the everyday world. This individual experienced a sharp sense of liberation at his acceptance by the group. In his twenty-first meeting he reported this patently transparent dream:

It was in a dilapidated house with lots of rooms with different groups in them. I wandered about for a long time trying to find a room for myself. In one room was a bunch of faggots, in another a group of unpleasant homosexuals and addicts, and in another a group of beatniks. In the end I chose none of these but went outside, saw a group of respectable men and women, and chose to walk along with them.

The therapy group offers the homosexual patient a valuable opportunity, unavailable elsewhere, to explore his attitudes and relationships to women. Not infrequently many such patients have a heterosexual phobia of such magnitude that they have in their adult life avoided virtually all contact with women; and the therapy group, with mandatory heterosexual interaction, may appear initially threatening on this basis. A dream reported at the twelfth meeting by a homosexual patient illustrates this:

I was in a Greyhound bus with some other people. I didn't know who they were. There were two handsome male drivers. I don't know why there were two of them. We were on a trip. At first it was a trip to some place very beautiful; there was ocean on both sides and beautiful trees with Spanish moss. And then suddenly we ended up on an island on which there were a lot of trapped people. There were some vampire bats, and we had to drive them off. We even crushed them under our feet—they made a crunching sound! There was also a woman who was knitting and had a child and who was like Ann (a group member). She had leprosy, and I couldn't get too close to her.

There were many relevant associations to the dream: the two bus drivers seemed like the two (male) co-therapists, the bus of people like the therapy group, the trip like the course of therapy which at first, with the sweet taste of approval and acceptance, seemed idyllic but now grew increasingly threatening and was finally experienced as a terrifying entrapment on an island. The knitting woman was overtly a group member who often brought knitting to the group. (Knitting also culled forth the association of Mme La Farge.) The vampire bats reminded him of another woman in the group who seemed caustic and intrusive. All of these primitive phantoms—a bloodsucking vampire; a leprous, defiled, contagious hag; a guillotine-tending necrophiliac—had contributed to a phobic avoidance of women.

Often the homosexual patient must be pressed to discuss his feelings toward the women members; generally his fear of them is not conscious initially; instead he experiences revulsion, indifference, or minor irritation. Only as he relates closely to several women in the group and recognizes their individuality, their similarity to himself, their own longings to accept themselves and be accepted and approved by others, will he be able to relinquish these irrational stereotypes.

Many patients with homosexual problems may, when particularly stressed, respond by a compulsive, promiscuous sexual acting out, often cruising such familiar homosexual locales as gay bars, lavatories, or certain public parks. After repeated acting-out cycles, the therapist and the group gradually arrive at an understanding of the stress and the subsequent sequence of events; often, with forceful interpretive intervention, the group is then able to terminate such a cycle early in its development. Generally the sequence is initiated by an event which produces an intense feeling of alienation, loneliness, or self-hatred. The patient responds by seeking immediate refutation; he demonstrates to himself that, corporally, he is loved, admired, and "in touch" with others. The reassurance is short-lived, since his behavior is but a caricature of intimacy and love; presently he is flooded with even more shame and estrangement as his critical, ego-observing faculties respond to the gulf between his actual and his idealized behavior. The additional shame and estrangement cause again the same fixed acting-out patterns, thus perpetuating the vicious circle.

Jed, a twenty-two-year-old male, who had done no cruising for several months, attended a college graduation banquet the night before the group session. During the course of the evening he experienced an overwhelming desire to cruise and left the dinner early to drive about in a frenzied, aimless search for a sexual contact. As Jed described these still present feelings to the group, they helped him to explore the precipitating event—the graduation banquet. He recalled his feelings of great loneliness and unworthiness as he witnessed the "good people" of his class relating warmly to one another; he reflected on the squandered opportunities for closeness and was overcome by the abyss that he felt existed between himself, the pariah, and his classmates. The group helped Jed both cognitively and emotionally. They pointed out that his frantic search for a man, any man, was an attempted solution to his feelings of exclusion and self-hatred; he had, they recalled, gone through similar sequences previously in the group. Furthermore, Jed's picture of the entire class, save himself, as one closely bonded circle of brotherhood was illusory; the group reminded him of the universality of many of his feelings of alienation and uniqueness. The group's display of interest, affection, and respect for him during the meeting allowed him to disconfirm the very feelings which had launched the compulsion to cruise. The effect of the meeting was to de-energize the compulsion and to allow Jed to regain conscious control of his behavior.

THE RESPONSE OF THE GROUP

Patients with homosexual problems vary as widely in their presentation of self as do heterosexual individuals, and the response of the group to them is equally varied. There are, however, certain characteristic responses of the group to the issue of homosexuality. The members' initial response to the disclosure by a patient that he is a homosexual is invariably sympathetic and accepting. Very often they will attempt to put the discloser at ease by revealing their own homosexual fantasies and experiences; in fact, the group often welcomes the opportunity to unburden themselves.

De-individuation of the patient sometimes follows in which the group discusses their best friends who are homosexuals and the "homosexual problem" in society. Voyeurism is another form of de-individuation, with members delving into the patient, not because of an interest in him, but to peep into the life and the sexual practices of the homosexual. Early in the group, the presence of a homosexual often stimulates the other members to "figure him out." Homosexual symptomatology and psychodynamics seem particularly clear and enticing, and the group members launch a historical inquiry into the events of his early psychosexual development. This exploration, too, seems curiously unrelated to the patient and often represents a flight from more immediate feelings on the part of the group.

A therapy group rarely expresses moral condemnation or attempts to make normative judgments of the homosexual patient, and yet it does not easily relinquish the goal of "converting" the patient to a heterosexual pattern. Although the group appears to accept the patient's own goal of making a better homosexual adjustment, they will, often months or years later, express disappointment at anything less than a shift to a hetero-sexual orientation.

Individual members, according to their own dynamics, may have extreme responses to a homosexual patient in the group. Some male patients who have considerable doubts about their sexual adequacy may experience particular discomfort in the presence of a homosexual. They may be forced too early to look at their own secret fears that they, too, are homosexual; indeed there are few males who escape this uncertainty. Ovesey [15] in his essay on "pseudohomosexuality" has called attention to the fact that too often in our culture we erroneously equate homosexuality with nonaggressive behavior, lack of proficiency in heterosexual behavior, or the use of the genitals to satisfy nonsexual drives like dependency or power. I have seen male patients who, for months, avoided interaction with a homosexual patient as a way of avoiding confrontation with what they feared was a part of themselves. One member with doubts about his sexual identification was told by a homosexual patient that his dress and grooming were slightly feminine. The patient brooded over this for a couple of days and then dismissed the feedback by reminding himself that he must "consider the source." Subsequently in the group he found himself audibly muttering "Goddamned queer" every time the homosexual patient spoke. It is the patient with the severest, yet unrecognized, conflicts of sexual identity who responds most adversely to the overt homosexual.

One of the therapist's chief tasks is to re-individualize the homosexual patient. Patients do not seek therapy because of homosexuality; they request help instead because of profound problems in relating to others, manifested, in part, by homosexuality. As therapy proceeds and the group and the patient himself lay aside the appelate of "homosexual," the patient's manifold problems of dependency, self-contempt,* and fear of competition become evident and accessible for therapy. The same type of schematization operates as other members ruminate at length about whether they are or are not homosexuals; as they realize the universality of so-called perverse behavior, they begin to understand that labels are irrelevant

---

* The self-contempt of these patients is evident often in the scorn that two homosexuals in the same group may have for each other. They may express, for example, the feeling that only a heterosexual can help them and that *nothing* their counterpart has to offer can be of value.

and dehumanizing. In this way the patient with homosexual behavior often adds breadth and depth to the group.

REFERENCES

1. I. D. Yalom and P. Houts, unpublished data, 1965.
2. J. D. Frank *et al.*, "Behavioral Patterns in Early Meetings of Therapeutic Groups," *Am. J. Psychiat.*, 108: 771–778, 1952.
3. J. D. Frank *et al.*, "Two Behavior Patterns in Therapeutic Groups and their Apparent Motivation," *Human Relations*, 5: 289–317, 1952.
4. M. Berger and M. Rosenbaum, "Notes on Help-Rejecting Complainers," *Int. J. Group Psychother.*, 17: 357–370, 1967.
5. S. Brody, "Syndrome of the Treatment-Rejecting Patient," *Psychoanal. Rev.*, 51: 75–84, 1964.
6. Correspondence by Dr. Derbolowsky, *Group Analysis*, 1: No. 1, 13–16, 1967.
7. E. Berne, *Games People Play* (New York: Grove Press, 1964).
8. D. Rosenthal, J. Frank, and E. Nash, "The Self-Righteous Moralist in Early Meetings of Therapeutic Groups," *Psychiatry*, 17: 215–223, 1954.
9. J. Sartre, *The Age of Reason*, trans. Eric Sutton (New York: Alfred A. Knopf, 1952), p. 144. © 1947 by Eric Sutton.
10. D. Lundgren and D. Miller, "Identity and Behavioral Changes in Training Groups," *Human Relations Training News*, Spring 1965.
11. R. H. Moos and I. D. Yalom, unpublished data, 1963.
12. B. B. Wassel, *Group Analysis* (New York: Citadel Press, 1966), p. 148.
13. L. Coch and J. R. French, "Overcoming Resistance to Change," *Human Relations*, 1: 512–532, 1948.
14. M. B. Cohen *et al.*, "An Intensive Study of 12 Cases of Manic Depressive Psychosis," *Psychiatry*, 17: 103–137, 1954.
15. L. Ovesey, "The Pseudohomosexual Anxiety," *Psychiatry*, 18: 17–25, 1955.

13

TECHNIQUE
OF THE THERAPIST:
SPECIALIZED
FORMATS AND
PROCEDURAL AIDS

❧

The standard group therapy format in which one therapist meets with six to eight patients is often complicated by other factors: the patient may be in concurrent individual therapy; there may be a co-therapist in the group; occasionally the group may meet without the therapist—in fact, some groups operate completely without the presence of a therapist. This chapter will discuss these contingencies and will in addition describe some specialized therapist techniques which, though not essential, may at times accelerate the course of therapy.

Concurrent Individual and Group Therapy

Many different combinations of group and individual therapy may be practiced. There is no systematic data which permits firm conclusions about the effectiveness of any of these combinations; the relevant research has yet to be done. Until definitive studies are available, guidelines must be formulated from clinical judgment and from deductive reasoning based on the posited curative factors. My clinical experience in group therapy indicates that concurrent individual therapy is neither necessary nor helpful except in certain instances. Optimal combinations in order of my personal preference are: (1) all patients exclusively in group therapy; (2) all group members in concurrent individual therapy with the group therapist; (3) all or some members in concurrent individual therapy with other therapists; (4) some members in concurrent individual therapy with group therapist.

Occasionally individual therapy is required to keep a patient in the group: the patient may be so fragile, anxious, or threatened that the risk of dropout is very high.

For example, one young, borderline schizophrenic woman participating in her first group was considerably threatened by the first few meetings. She had felt increasingly alienated because her bizarre fantasy and dream world seemed so far from the experience of the other members. In the fourth meeting she attacked one of the members and was in turn attacked. For several nights thereafter she had terrifying nightmares, the main themes of which were: (1) her mouth turning to blood (which appeared related to her fear of aggressing verbally because of her world-destructive fantasies); (2) walking along the beach and being engulfed by a huge wave (related to her fear of losing her boundaries and identity in the group); (3) being picked up and then held down by several men while the therapist performed an operation on her brain; his hands were, however, guided by the men holding her down (obviously related to her fears of therapy and of the therapist's being overpowered by the members).

Her hold on reality grew more tenuous and it seemed unlikely that she could continue in the group without added support. Concurrent individual therapy with another therapist was arranged; it enabled her to remain in the group and ultimately to obtain considerable benefit.

Some patients may go through a severe life crisis which requires considerable individual temporary support in addition to this group therapy. Occasionally individual therapy is required in order to enable a patient to use the group; a patient may be so blocked by anxiety or fear of aggression that he is unable to participate effectively in the group therapeutic process. In fact, some studies [1,2] suggest that such patients may be worsened by the group experience.

Concurrent individual therapy can complicate the group therapy process in several ways. When there is a marked difference in the individual and the group therapist's basic approach, the two therapies can work at cross purposes. If, for example, the individual approach is oriented toward understanding genetic causality and delves deeply into past experiences while the group focuses primarily on here-and-now material, the patient is apt to become confused and to judge one approach on the basis of the other. Generally patients beginning group therapy are discouraged and frustrated by the initial group meetings, which offer less support than their individual therapy hours, where their narcissistic needs are gratified by the therapist's exclusive attention and by the exploration of the minute details of their past and present life, dreams, and fantasies. Sometimes such patients, when attacked or stressed by the group, may defend themselves by unfavorably comparing their group to their individual experience; such an attack on the group invariably results in further attacks on the individual and further deterioration of the situation. Later in the course of therapy, patients may often reverse their comparative evaluations of the two modes. Some therapists [3] have noted that, as therapy progresses, patients may terminate their individual therapy and rely solely on the group; moreover, at the conclusion of therapy, patients, when reviewing their therapy experience, may state that they wished they had begun the group earlier or that much of their individual therapy was superfluous.

Another complication of concurrent therapy occurs when patients use their individual therapy to drain off affect from the group. The patient may interact like a sponge in the group, taking in feedback and reacting to it in the safer domain of his individual therapy hour. This resistance is often reinforced by a rationalization of the patient: "I will allow the others to have the group time since I have my own hour." When this pattern is marked and very clear, the group therapist, in collaboration with the individual therapist, may insist that the individual therapy be terminated. I have known several patients who, in retrospect, described a sudden acceleration in their involvement in the group when their concurrent individual therapy was stopped.

If two conditions are met, the individual and the group therapeutic approaches may complement one another. First the individual and the group therapist must be in frequent communication with one another—a condition often recognized but rarely fulfilled because of the time pressures of clinical practice. Secondly the individual therapy must be modified to complement the group approach: the individual therapy should be group-oriented. Group patients can best use their individual hour to explore, in depth, their feelings toward the group members and toward incidents and themes of current meetings. Such an exploration can serve as a testing ground for further involvement in the life of the group. The patient is often able to examine an uncomfortable, turbulent relationship in the individual setting long before he is able to confront the issue in the group. It is obvious too that the therapists must avoid undermining one another. An effort by the individual therapist to explore the group experience in the individual therapy hour is viewed by the patient as a vote of confidence in the group.

Many of these potential complications can be avoided if the group therapist serves also as the individual therapist. Clearly he then has control over the type of individual therapy conducted. Similarly a group in which all members are in concurrent individual therapy with the group leader is generally a stable group with few dropouts from therapy. However, this format has its own inherent complications. Some therapists become confused about confidentiality: it becomes increasingly difficult to remember who said what in which setting.[4] Can the therapist repeat in the group some intimate material which was revealed in an individual session? Or must he couch his remark in vague language only identifiable by the one patient? As a general rule it is ill-advised to make any contract of confidentiality regarding the individual sessions; the therapist should retain the privilege of bringing up any individual material in the group according to his professional judgment.

At times factionalism and sibling rivalry are pronounced in a group in which the members see the leader in concurrent individual therapy; intermember resentment may be particularly extreme if some of the members are not in concurrent therapy because they cannot afford the fee. Occasionally it may be necessary for the therapist to see a group member who is in crisis for a few individual sessions. For example, patients who are severely stressed by a loss (through death, separation, or divorce) or by some other major environmental stress (academic or job failure) or are on the verge of dropping out of the group may need some temporary support, guidance, or medication. The individual attention the patient receives in this instance rarely arouses any resentment from other members, particularly if they have shared in the decision that the extra help is needed at this time.

Concurrent group and individual therapy may present some special problems for neophyte group therapists. Some find it difficult to see the same patient in two formats since they customarily assume a different role in the two types of therapy; in group they tend to be more informal, more open, more actively engaged with the patients; in individual therapy they remain more impersonal, more distant, and more sage. Often therapists in training prefer that the patients have a "pure" treatment experience—i.e., that they be solely in group therapy without concurrent individual therapy from themselves or others. This is probably a realistic concern since it

317

enables them to establish a base line of expectations about the effects of each type of therapy.

Co-Therapists

Some group therapists choose to meet alone with a group while others prefer to work with a co-therapist. No research has been conducted to determine the relative efficacy of the two methods, and clinicians differ in their opinions.[5] My clinical experience has taught me that the co-therapy approach may have some special advantages but many potential hazards as well.

A co-therapy arrangement of anything other than two therapists of completely equal status is, in my experience, inadvisable. Some training programs have utilized an apprenticeship format in which a neophyte therapist participates as a junior therapist in a group led by a senior clinician; however, the status differential often results in tension and unclarity about the leadership role for both therapists and patients. Even a partnership of nominally equal status between two therapists who are in actuality widely different in competence and sensitivity will almost invariably result in serious difficulty for the group. After a few meetings the members are clearly aware of any strain between the two leaders and this, if marked, can lead to a tense, inhibited group. It is therefore of utmost importance that the therapists feel comfortable and open with each other before deciding to lead a group together.* Some time should be reserved following each meeting for a discussion of the session as well as each other's behavior. If the group is supervised, both therapists should attend the supervisory session.

Whether or not co-therapists should openly express disagreement during the group session is an issue of some controversy. I have generally found co-therapist disagreement unhelpful to the group in the first few meetings; at that point the group is too unstable and precohesive to tolerate such a division of leadership. Later, however, therapist disagreement may contribute a great deal to therapy. In one study [7] I asked twenty patients who had concluded long-term group therapy about the effects of

---

* In Evelyn Waugh's *Brideshead Revisited* [6] the protagonist, as he departed for his first year of college, was counseled by his father that if he were not circumspect, a considerable part of his second year at college would be devoted to getting rid of undesirable friends he had made during his first year.

therapist disagreement on the course of the group and on their own therapy. The patients were unanimous in their judgment that it was beneficial. It was a model setting experience for some patients: they observed individuals whom they respected disagree openly and resolve their differences with dignity and tact. Others found it most useful in working through some of their feelings about authority figures: they witnessed the therapists make mistakes, differ with their colleagues, and experience discomfort, without permanently harming themselves. In short, the therapists are experienced as humans who, despite their imperfections, are genuinely attempting to help the patients. Such a humanization process is inimical to irrational stereotyping, and patients learn to differentiate others according to their individual attributes rather than to their roles.

Some patients were made uncomfortable by co-therapist disagreement and likened it to the witnessing of parental conflict; nonetheless, it strengthened the honesty and the potency of the group. On many occasions I have observed stagnant groups spring into life when the two therapists differentiated themselves as individuals.

Splitting is another phenomenon often occurring in groups led by co-therapists. Some patients respond to their feelings of impotence and helplessness in the presence of adults by attempting to split the therapists, in much the same way as they may have, in their primary family, attempted to split their parents. They may attempt in a variety of ways to undermine the therapists' interrelationship and to intrude between them. Such a process should be noted and interpreted; it is usually an indication of highly conflicted attitudes toward authority imagos.

Some groups become split into two factions with each co-therapist having his own "team" of patients with whom he feels a special relationship. Sometimes this split has its genesis in the relationship which the therapist and those patients established before the onset of the group, when he saw them in prior individual therapy or in consultation. (For this reason it is advisable that both therapists interview the patient, preferably simultaneously, in the pregroup screening. I have noted patients who have continued to feel a special bond throughout their entire group therapy course with the member of the co-therapy team who first interviewed them.) Other patients align themselves with one therapist because of his personal characteristics, or because they feel he is more intelligent, more senior, more sexually attractive, or more similar to them. Whatever the reasons for the subgrouping, the process should be noted and openly discussed. Transference distortions may become quite evident as several patients discuss widely varying perceptions of the two therapists.

Most co-therapy teams deliberately or, more often, unwittingly split roles: one therapist assumes a more provocative role—much like a Socratic gadfly—while the other is more supportive and serves as a harmonizer in the group.* When the co-therapists are male and female, the roles are usually assumed accordingly. A male-female co-therapist team may have some unique advantages: the image of the group as the primary family may be more strongly evoked; many fantasies and misconceptions among the group members about the relationship between the two therapists occur and may, with profit, be worked through. Many patients may benefit from the model setting of a male-female pair working together collaboratively with mutual respect without the destructive competition, mutual derogation, or exploitation or pervasive sexuality too often associated with male-female pairings by the patients.

A father-son (both psychiatrists) co-therapy team has been described with interesting results.[9] The therapists concluded that the presence of a parent and a son working together harmoniously was a living demonstration to the patients of the successful resolution of parent-child conflicts. Patients at first distorted and misperceived the relationship in several ways: they interpreted benign remarks by the father as criticism or attacks on the son; they refused to believe that the son made independent interpretations in the group; they felt that he had to "clear" them first with his father. By working through such issues, the members were helped to understand their own relationship with parents and parental imagos.

From my observations of over thirty co-therapy groups led by two neophyte therapists, I consider this format to have special advantages for the beginning therapist. For one thing, the presence of a co-therapist lessens initial anxiety and permits the therapist greater equanimity and objectivity in his efforts to understand the meeting. In the post-meeting rehash, the co-therapists can provide valuable feedback about each other's behavior. Until the therapist obtains sufficient experience to be reasonably clear of his presentation of self in the group, this co-therapist feedback is vital in enabling him to differentiate what is real and what is transference distortion in the patients' perceptions of him.

It is especially difficult for beginning therapists to maintain their objectivity in the face of massive group pressure. For example, one group unan-

* This split is consonant with findings by Robert Bales in some well-known research on group leadership.[8] Bales studied laboratory task groups of college students discussing some problem in human relations. Almost invariably two types of leaders (as determined by activity ratings and sociometric rankings) emerged from the membership: (1) a "task-executive" leader, the most active member who spurs the group on and who helps them perform the primary task and (2) a social-emotional leader who attends to the group's emotional needs and reduces tension sufficiently to allow the group to proceed.

imously prescribed for one young male member that he take advantage of several available casual sexual opportunities in an effort to work through his sexual timidity. In actuality the advice was destructive for the patient who was, with great difficulty, working on his relationship to his recently acquired wife; however, unable to oppose the group current, the therapist found himself agreeing with the group's advice to the patient—a type of advice that would have been unthinkable to him were he seeing the patient in individual therapy. In such a situation the presence of a co-therapist may be an excellent stabilizer.

One of the more unpleasant and difficult chores for the neophyte therapist is to weather a group attack upon himself and to help the group make constructive use of it. When under the gun, he may be too threatened either to clarify the attack or to encourage further attack without appearing defensive or condescending. A co-therapist may prove invaluable here; he may help the members work through their anger and at the same time encourage further exploration of all feelings toward the therapist.

The Leaderless Group

Leaderless groups have been used in group psychotherapy in two major forms: (1) the occasional or regularly scheduled leaderless meeting which serves as an adjunct to traditional therapist-led therapy groups and (2) the self-directed group—a group which meets for its entire life span without a designated leader.

THE LEADERLESS MEETING

In 1949 Alexander Wolf, a pioneer in the development of group therapy, first suggested the use of regularly scheduled "alternate" meeting without the therapist.[10] His groups, which met three times weekly, were asked to meet an additional two or three times without him at one of the members' homes. Since then other therapists have reported the use of alternate meetings in a variety of temporal arrangements: some suggest two therapist-led meetings and one alternate meeting weekly, while others, myself included, prefer only an occasional leaderless meeting. Other senior clinicians have spoken out vociferously against the leaderless meeting, describing the chaotic acting out and disruption which may ensue.[11, 12] Again, as with most specialized clinical techniques, no research evaluative studies exist; however, as we shall shortly elaborate, there is some evidence about the emotional climate of the leaderless meeting and some outcome research on the effectiveness of the self-directed group.

The alternate meeting, despite its uncertain efficacy in the overall course of therapy, nevertheless has important implications for the understanding of the dynamics of the member-leader relationship. Members generally do not initially welcome the suggestion of the leaderless meeting; many unrealistic fears and consequences of his absence are evoked. In one study[7] I asked a series of patients who had been in group therapy for at least eight months, "What would have happened in the group if the group therapists were absent?" (This is another way of asking what function the group therapists perform in the group.) The replies were varied. Although a few patients stated they would have welcomed leaderless meetings, most of the others expressed, in order of frequency, these general concerns:

1. The group would stray from the primary task. A cocktail hour atmosphere would occur, problems would be avoided, long silences would transpire, the discussions would become increasingly irrelevant. "We would end up in left field without the doctor to keep us on the track!" "I could never express my antagonisms without the therapist's encouragement." "We need him there to keep things stirred up." "Who else would bring in the silent members?" "Who would make the rules? We'd spend the entire meeting simply trying to make rules."

2. The group would lose control of its emotions. Anger would be unrestrained and there would be no one available either to rescue the damaged members or to help the aggressive ones maintain control.

3. The group would be unable to integrate its experiences and to make constructive use of them. "The therapist is the one who keeps track of loose ends and makes connections for us." "He points out the similarities between us." "He helps clear the air by pointing out where the group is at a certain time." He was viewed by the members as the "time-binder"—the one who sees patterns of behavior longitudinally and who points out that what a member did today, last week, and last month fit into an understandable pattern. The members say in effect that though they may have a great deal of action and involvement without the therapist, they will be unable to make use of it.

Many of the concerns are clearly unrealistic and reflect an infantile, dependent posture on the part of the members. It is for this very reason that a leaderless meeting may play an important role in the therapy process. The members are helped to experience themselves as autonomous, responsible, and resourceful adults who, though they may profit from the therapist's expertise, are nevertheless able to control their emotions, to pursue the primary task of the group, and to integrate their experience. In a sense the rationale is identical to that underlying the therapeutic community. Jones,[13] Daniels,[14] and many others have pointed out that the traditional authority-bound mental hospital not only failed to counteract feelings of helplessness and inadequacy on the part of hospitalized pa-patients but, by its authoritarian total-care structure, has reinforced these very features. Thus, it is reasoned, a new patient-directed intentional social system which encourages patients' personal growth and decision-making capacity must be constructed. Few would extend the analogy in group therapy to the conclusion that the therapist should be permanently excluded; the outpatient therapy group, unlike the therapeutic community, does not consider assuming responsibility to be the overriding goal in therapy. All outpatients do, to some degree, function adequately and assume responsibility for themselves; nevertheless it remains an important minor theme in the treatment of many patients—a theme which is highlighted by the patients' reactions to the absence of the therapist.

If the leaderless meeting is to be a constructive experience, then it is important that the patients' unrealistic predictions about their own helplessness are not realized. Proper timing is important in insuring that this does not occur; the therapist must be certain that the therapy group has developed cohesiveness and has established productive norms before suggesting that alternate meetings be considered.

The leaderless meeting has, in addition to fostering a group sense of autonomy and responsibility, several other advantages. Issues arise in the alternate meetings which yield important insights about patients' relations to the therapists. Some patients feel liberated and are far more active and uninhibited in the absence of the therapist; others are for the first time able to express critical feelings toward him; still others display their contempt for their peers (and thus their self-contempt) by refusing to participate, on the grounds that all benefit emanates solely from the therapist.* Often greater warmth, affection, and sexual attraction are more evident in the alternate meetings; evidently the therapist is regarded as a threatening figure who would disapprove of or condemn such sentiments. Although many therapists fear that intense sexual acting out will occur in leaderless

* Usually group pressure will ensure that all members attend alternate meetings. If one patient steadfastly refuses to attend frequently scheduled leaderless meetings, his chances for improvement in the group are poor and the therapist should consider transferring him to another group.

323

meetings, experience has shown the fear to be unfounded.* Groups generally frown on sexual relations between two members since such activity is viewed as disruptive to the entire group. (A group may be more likely to engage in some forbidden activity en masse; one group, for example, planned a beach party at a nudist colony.) In assessing the possible hazards of leaderless meetings we must keep in mind the distinction between acting and acting out. Acting out is, by definition, a resistance to therapy; patients discharge through action those impulses which should be discussed and examined in therapy. Acting is far different; as Lieberman states, "For *acting* read *trying out, reality testing, practice,* and the distinction becomes clear." [16] All change must be preceded by action and all action in therapy meetings which is available for the group's analytic scrutiny may be useful in the process of change. "Rightly understood and accepted, all experiences are good and the bitter ones best of all." [17]

How the group chooses to communicate the events of the alternate meeting to the therapist is often of great interest. Do they attempt to conceal or distort information or do they compulsively brief him on all details? Sometimes the ability of a group to withhold information from the therapist is in itself an encouraging sign of group maturation, although therapists are usually uncomfortable at being excluded. In the group, as in the family, not only must the individual strive for autonomy but the leader must be willing to allow him to do so. Often the leaderless session and subsequent events allow the therapist to experience and understand his own desires for control and his feelings of threat as his patients grow away from him.

SELF-DIRECTED GROUPS

The alternate session has two primary goals: to increase the group's and the members' sense of personal responsibility and autonomy and to hasten the emergence of several important themes for subsequent working

---

* There exists only one controlled research inquiry into the change in the emotional climate of the group caused by the therapist's absence. Harrow *et al.*[15] studied groups of five to seven hospitalized patients who met with and without a therapist. Eighteen meetings, covering a six-week period, were taped and rated according to emotional area, process of interaction, specific content, and amount of activity. Differences between the leaderless and leader-led sessions were slight: therapist-led groups showed significantly more depression and tension; there was in addition a slight trend for greater warmth in the leaderless meeting. The emotional climate of the leaderless session seemed, therefore, little different from that of the professionally led group. (Considering the number of variables studied, the number of significant findings could have resulted from chance alone.)

through with the therapist's help. The self-directed group operates on another principle: the primary healing forces are inherent in the group and may be evoked and harnessed without the presence of a formal leader. In part the self-directed group has sprung into being as a result of the shortage of professional manpower; in part it is a reflection of a humanistic trend which decries the need for an authority structure that is perceived as restrictive and growth inhibiting.

Although no formal inventory of self-directed groups exists, there is no doubt that it is a movement of considerable magnitude; Mowrer [18] in 1961 reported 265 self-directed groups in America; one such organization, the Yokefellows, is reputed to have over fifteen thousand members attending weekly sessions of their religiously based self-directed groups. Self-directed groups are a heterogeneous lot; few are, in actuality, leaderless but rely instead on leaders drawn from the ranks of former members—for example, Synanon, Alcoholics Anonymous, or Recovery, Inc. Some may remain nominally leaderless, such as a self-led group of mental health professionals, but yet be guided by a natural leader who has emerged from the ranks.

One of the more interesting ventures into the self-directed group field has been conducted by Berzon and her associates.[19] Their work has been with groups of physically or psychiatrically disabled subjects referred by the Division of Vocational Rehabilitation and with groups of subjects from the community or college campus who have volunteered for a group therapy experience. Somewhat analogous groups have been used in hospital settings [20] and in a variety of clinical and educational settings.

Berzon at first organized groups which, with no further instructions, were asked to meet for a series of twelve to eighteen meetings. (There was a buzzer placed in the center of the room which could be used to signal a group leader when the group desired help. The buzzer was not often used and was later discontinued.) It soon became clear that the leaderless group needed more direction, and a booklet of programmed instructions was prepared for the group's use. Later this was changed to a series of audio tapes. The tapes were designed to help the group members accomplish certain goals: to encourage participation, to focus attention on the here-and-now, and to encourage helping behavior.

Berzon's work clarifies the role of the leader in the group by eliminating him and then building in his functions artificially, using some rather ingenious techniques. For example, in a ten-session program [19] three basic stages were proposed: (1) group building (first four sessions); (2) intensification of feelings (fifth through ninth sessions) and (3) separation (last session). A task was designated and an exercise assigned, via an audio tape, for each session according to the principles of group development. Following each exercise the group spent the remainder of the time discussing their reactions to it.

Session 1: Activities are proposed which make the participants aware of the boundaries of the group. For example, the members of the group stand in a circle and one at a time one member steps out of the circle and then tries to break into the group.

Session 2: The basic ground rule of discussing the here-and-now is presented to the group. A tape of two groups is presented, one which is tuned in to this principle and one which is not. The group is asked to break into pairs to practice this type of participation.

Session 3: Another norm is instituted: the principles of facilitative feedback are explained and members asked to practice in a go-around.

Session 4: A review session. Members evaluate themselves about their progress in employing group principles thus far presented.

Session 5: Top secret exercise (described in Chapter 1).

Session 6: Members form a circle with a member in the center who attempts to break out. The group is to be experienced as standing between him and his freedom. Each member attempts this and then discusses his feelings about the exercise.

Session 7: Each member goes around the group and describes the other members metaphorically—as an animal, a piece of furniture, a car, etc.

Session 8: Each group member in turn spends three minutes telling the group of his strengths and five minutes listening to feedback from the others of his strengths.

Session 9: The group selects three members who have kept the others farthest away from them. They go one at a time to the center of the group and then each member expresses, nonverbally, positive feelings to him. The task is assigned as an exercise in the reception of positive feelings.

Session 10: A series of short exercises is followed by a discussion of the changes that have occurred in members. Unfinished business is attended to and the members say goodbye to one another.

Berzon has reported on several evaluative studies of versions of this program. These studies indicate that members of the self-directed groups become more interpersonally sensitive, self-accepting, and self-reliant [19] than no-treatment controls. One study [19] compared seventy-five subjects in self-directed groups to forty-four comparable subjects who had no group experience. Self-concept (measured by a semantic differential rating scale) [21] was significantly higher at the end of the ten meetings in the group members than for the controls after a comparable period of time. No change occurred on the other measure, "personal efficacy" (a five-item forced-choice instrument).[22]

In 1965 an evaluative study [19] was carried out comparing the results of professionally directed groups (N = 34), self-directed groups (N = 29), and control groups (no group experience) (N = 20). All subjects were vocational rehabilitation patients. An eighteen-session self-directed program was used which was similar in concept to the ten-session program described above. The professionally directed groups and the self-directed groups, but not the control group members, showed a significant increase in self-concept. Both professional-directed and self-directed members showed a significant increase in the ratings of vocational rehabilitation counselors; one year later the positive changes persisted for the professional-directed groups but not for the self-directed groups. On a therapeutic climate scale (measuring self-exploration and facilitative behavior) the professional-directed but not the self-directed groups showed an increase in the last nine group sessions. The dropout rate was slightly higher in the self-directed groups. It would seem then that both professional-directed and self-directed groups showed positive change but that the changes in the professional-directed groups were more marked and durable.

The ultimate relevance of the programmed self-directed group to the group therapy field remains to be seen. The programmed groups which have been evaluated have such a brief span (ten to eighteen meetings) that enduring changes can hardly be expected; perhaps, however, individuals are enabled by this learning experience to take advantage of other therapeutic resources in their environment. The theoretical implications of the endeavor are most interesting; the program presents, in unusually clear form, many of the initial tasks of the therapist in the early norm-building stage of the group.

Acceleration of Interaction: Specialized Techniques

Like a slowly descending spiral the relationship between group members gradually increases in intensity and depth; the involvement deepens from the shy, polite, cautious transactions of the first meeting to the uninhibited and meaningful exchanges of the mature group. Many group therapists have developed techniques to accelerate the process of involvement: "warm-up" procedures, fantasy, dreams, and nonverbal exercises have all been used for this purpose.

WARM-UP PROCEDURES

Some therapists structure exercises in the beginning of the group to help members engage each other more quickly in a confrontive here-and-now fashion. For example, members may be instructed to have a "go-around" [3] in which each person is asked to express his feelings toward the member on his right; following this each may express his response to the feedback he has received. Or similarly all the members may express their feelings to one member or to an event in the group. The task may be structured more by the therapist's suggesting that each patient discuss what part of the other members he finds hardest to like or to accept. (This wording may help members distinguish between rejection of themselves and rejection of personal traits or attitudes.) An accompanying task may be for each to comment on the strengths or the most attractive aspects of each member.

Other procedural aids are frequently used in T-groups (see Chapter 14) and may occasionally be useful in therapy groups. For example, the "top secret" exercise is often highly effective in accelerating interaction and development of trust. Each member realizes that his most dreaded secret concerns are shared by others and that others can understand and empathize with his feelings. Another technique[23] consists of asking each member to write, anonymously, on a slip of paper something he would like to say to some other member but, for some reason, has been unable to. The slips are collected, read by the therapist, and the group members are asked to speculate about the identity of the sender and receiver of each message.

Numerous other techniques have been used: [24, 25] milling around (the group is asked to mill around the room for a short time to observe to what position and toward which members they gravitate); centering (everyone moves his chair closer or further to the center of the circle, depending on whether they feel in or out of the group); dark meetings (some groups meet for a period of time in total darkness to evoke previously unrecognized feelings); family resemblances (members choose those group members who resemble their parent and siblings or those members whom they would prefer to have as parents and siblings); metaphors (members are asked to describe other members in terms of some animate or inanimate object). In human relations laboratories I have asked members to take a short walk and to bring back some object that reminds them of some specified person in the group.

Obviously these devices are no substitute for the long hard work of therapy. Occasionally, in the proper place, they may be of some value. Keep in mind the phrase "in the proper place"; nothing is as disconcerting as a good idea in the wrong place at the wrong time. Therapy groups for the most part do not require these techniques; occasionally, however, the therapist may diagnose a particular group problem or inhibition and through the careful selection of some accelerating technique facilitate the group work.*

FANTASY

As therapy proceeds, many therapists reinforce the use of fantasy in the group. Members are encouraged to discuss the thoughts and fantasies they have had about the group or the members during the interval since the previous meeting. They may be asked by the therapist to discuss the fantasies about the group they have had on the way to the meeting that day. Often when two members are deeply involved, the therapist may clarify the relationship by asking not for their feelings toward one another (often these are not clearly known) but for what they would like to do with one another. One twenty-eight-year-old woman was told by a male member that he would simply like to walk alone with her in the woods with his head on her shoulder. Since one of her primary problems centered about her inability to attract men to her, it proved of great benefit to her to discover how she had been manifesting herself maternally rather than sexually to the other member.

DREAMS

The number and types of dreams that patients bring to their therapy is very largely a function of the therapist's behavior. His response to the first dreams presented by patients will influence the choice of dreams subsequently presented. The intensive, detailed, personalized investigation of dreams practiced in analytically oriented individual therapy is hardly feasible in group therapy. For groups meeting once or twice weekly, such a practice would demand that a disproportionate amount of time be spent on one patient; the process would, furthermore, be minimally useful to the remaining members who would become mere bystanders.†

---

* The group therapist, in comparison to the T-group trainer, is more interested in the investigation of each member's role in the group inhibition as an aid to a fuller understanding of the member's dynamics; he is often less interested in getting the group past the inhibition. (See Chapter 14 for full discussion of this issue.)

† Some group analysts whose groups meet several times weekly attempt to involve all members by asking every member to free-associate to the dream.

What useful role, then, can dreams play in group therapy? In individual analysis or analytically oriented treatment, the therapist is usually presented with a large number of dreams and dream elements; in a variety of ways, he selects certain aspects of the dreams which he deems most pertinent to therapy. He may not pursue some dreams, he may ask for extensive associations to others, he may specifically choose a dream theme to investigate more deeply, he may establish connections with a previous dream or issue in therapy. Generally the therapist will use dreams to pursue the current theme in individual therapy; for example, if a patient, who is currently working on his concerns about his sexual identity, brings in a dream with male-female doubles as well as a heavily disguised patricidal theme, then the therapist will generally select the former theme for work and ignore or postpone the latter. The process is a self-reinforcing one, since it is well known that patients who are deeply involved in therapy will dream or remember dreams compliantly—i.e., they will produce dreams which reinforce the theoretical framework of the therapist.

The therapist can use dreams in the same fashion in group therapy. The investigation of certain types of dreams can accelerate the group therapeutic work. Most valuable are group dreams—dreams which involve the group as an entity—or dreams which reflect the dreamer's feelings toward one or more members of the group. Either of these types can be most valuable to the group; often the dream elucidates not only the dreamer's but other members' concerns which are until then not yet fully conscious. Sometimes the dream introduces, in disguised form, material which is conscious but which members have, for various reasons, been reluctant to discuss in the group. In either case the dream may be used in the service of a primary task of the group: to explore the here-and-now interpersonal relationships of the group members.

Some illustrative examples of members' dreams in group therapy may clarify these points.

In the sixth meeting of a group a patient related a dream fragment: "We [the group] were in a strange large room. We were expected to undress. Everyone else took off their clothes. I was afraid and ran out of the room."

In discussing her dream, the patient, who had until then been an almost completely silent member, spoke of her great fears of self-disclosure and her feeling that once she began to participate in the group in any manner she would be humiliated by being forced to disrobe completely. As the group encouraged her to explore her fear more deeply, she spoke of her particular dread of one of the co-therapists and one of the dominant members of the group; she dreaded, especially, their disapprobation of her current extramarital sexual activities. The dream thus enabled her both to enter the group and to forewarn the group about her great sensitivity and vulnerability to criticism.

At the twentieth meeting a patient related this dream: "I was walking with my younger sister. As we walked she grew smaller and smaller. Finally I had to carry her. We arrived at the group room where the members were sitting around drinking tea. I had to show the group my sister. By this time she was so small she was in a package. I unwrapped the package but all that was left of her was a tiny bronze head."

The investigation of this dream clarified several previously unconscious concerns of the patient. The dreamer, Miss Sands (see Chapter 2), had been extraordinarily lonely and had immediately become deeply involved in the group; in fact, it represented her only important social world. At the same time, however, she feared her intense dependence on the group; it had become too important to her. She modified herself rapidly to meet with group expectations and, in so doing, lost sight of her own needs and identity. The rapidly shrinking sister symbolized herself becoming more infantile, more undifferentiated, and finally inanimate as she sacrificed herself in a frantic quest for the group's approval. Some of the manifest content of the dream becomes clearer through a consideration of the content of the meeting preceding the dream: the group had spent considerable time discussing her body—she was moderately obese—and finally one member had offered her a diet she had recently seen in a magazine. Thus her concerns about losing her personal identity took the dream form of shrinking in size.

Shortly afterwards in the same group another patient brought in this dream fragment: "I brought my sister in to meet the group. She was beautiful and I wanted to show her off to the members."

This patient, Mr. Farr (Chapter 2), had had many dreams involving his family members, all of whom had died at Auschwitz, but he had never before had a dream involving the group. His Don Juan style of life had for many years served to bolster his self-esteem by enabling him to possess beautiful women whom other men would desire. The dream helped to uncover these dynamics as they operated in the microcosm of the group. He dreamed of eliciting respect and admiration from the members by showing off his possession, his beautiful (but dead) sister; behind this desire was the conviction that he had little intrinsic personal substance for which others would value him.

Another patient, who also valued herself very little, dreamed: "I was talking in the group and one by one everyone got up and left the room. Finally there was only the therapist left; he listened disinterestedly for a short time and then he, too, left the room."

In each of these two instances, the dream investigation enabled the patient to experience and to discuss his low self-regard and his conviction that the other members shared this opinion of him.

The following is an example of a dream which clarifies a previously undisclosed facet of a patient's interpersonal behavior. A female patient dreamed: "I went to a dance recital given by Joyce [one of the members]. Jim was there; I went over to him at intermission and asked him where he was sitting. He stammered and hesitated so that I grew uncomfortable and ran away."

Jim, a homosexual, responded to this dream by commenting that it was prophetic: if he were to see any members of the group at a social event he would be so ashamed of their meeting any of his homosexual friends that he would go to any lengths to avoid encountering the group members. The other member's dream thus enabled Jim to plunge into the crucial issue of his shame and his need to conceal himself continually from the straight world.

The following three dreams illustrate how conscious but avoided material may, through dreams, be brought into the group for examination.

"There were two rooms side by side with a mirror in my house. I felt there was a burglar in the next room. I thought I could pull the curtain back and see a person in a black mask stealing my possessions."

This dream was brought in at the twentieth meeting of a demonstration group which was observed through a one-way mirror by the therapist's students. Aside from a few comments in the first meeting the group members had never voiced and explored their feelings about the observers. A discussion of the dream led the group into a valuable discussion of the therapist's relation to the group and to his students. Were the observers "stealing" something from the group? Was the therapist's primary allegiance toward his students and were the group members merely a means of presenting a good show or demonstration for them?

332

"It was session time. The session took place in a big blue bathroom like the therapist's. We all sat down around the bathtub, in a circle, with our feet in the water. We all had our shoes on, so the water in the bathtub became very dirty. The faucet was opened to clean up the water. Someone suggested that we should take our shoes off. Some agreed with this, but others did not. I was ashamed because my feet are ugly, so I had to agree with those who wanted to keep their shoes on. To solve the problem, someone brought some wooden mats to put under our feet, but there were too few mats and we began to argue and quarrel. At this moment, I woke up full of anguish." [26]

The group listened to the dream and reported that following the previous meeting, four of the seven members had gone to a bar and formed two heterosexual couples. To them the bathtub represented the group, in which they deposited their dirty feelings (all four of the involved members had a history of homosexual difficulties). Later in the session one of the members mentioned that he could never profit from the sessions because whenever he talked, someone always interrupted him. The group then began to argue about how various members usurped the others' time, and several illustrative episodes from recent meetings were recalled. The dream image of the members fighting for the few wooden mats of the therapist brought to light long-smoldering feelings of rivalry and competition for the therapist's attention.

A patient in another group presented a similar dream fragment: "The whole group was sitting around the bathtub washing their feet. The dirt slowly went down the drain."

This was the group which two sessions previously had expelled Mrs. Cape (see Chapter 2) because she had, by breaking rules of confidentiality, become exceedingly disruptive to the group. The meeting immediately prior to the dream was a breast-beating session in which all members, including the therapists, had felt extraordinarily guilty at expelling her.* The dream, by its stark symbolism, "washing the dirt out of the group," reminded the members not to become overwhelmed by their guilt; there had been a very valid reason for their drastic action.

---

* Mrs. Cape had created even greater guilt by arriving nonetheless at the meeting and asking that she be permitted to attend as an observer for two weeks until the new therapy group to which she had been referred began meeting.

333

NONVERBAL EXERCISES

Every experienced therapist realizes the importance of nonverbal communication in psychotherapy. Body posture, bearing, demeanor, grooming, movements, and gestures may communicate some important feeling or attitude of which the expresser is largely unaware. The therapist may register what he learns and use his knowledge in the verbal, intellectual work of therapy. He may at times choose to point out aspects of the nonverbal behavior to the patient; often the awareness of his nonverbal behavior hastens the patient's cognitive understanding. Similarly the experienced therapist is aware of the importance of his own nonverbal behavior, which transmits as much information to patients as his words. Patients generally recognize a therapist's insincerity, boredom, disinterest, or despair by his nonverbal communications and will consider this information to be more valid than contrary verbal assertions.

Recently another use of nonverbal behavior has emerged in psychotherapy. Therapists have found that the deliberate performance of some appropriate nonverbal behavior may bring preconscious or unconscious thoughts and feelings into consciousness. These may be nonconscious thoughts in the mind of one individual or may, in a group, be nonconscious common concerns shared by the group members. Often conscious but ambiguous thoughts or feelings can be clarified by these procedures. In addition, nonverbal exercises in groups can help to "warm up" the group, or bring verbally reticent members into greater involvement. The overall importance of nonverbal exercises in the group therapeutic process is difficult to determine. The technique stems largely from the T-group field and from Reichian [27] and Gestalt therapists.[28] Most group therapists see little need for nonverbal exercises in their clinical work; others use them sparingly when a particular indication arises in the group; a few therapists have a large repertoire of nonverbal exercises and employ them in much the same way in which one might employ a verbal intervention.

Group workers agree that proper timing is essential in the use of these exercises; a poorly timed exercise will "bomb out," be puzzling or harmful to the group. They are best used to clarify some shared, but dimly conscious, group concern or problem. For example, if the group is concerned about the status hierarchy of the members and yet so avoids the problem that the group atmosphere is one of oblique, veiled hostility, then a nonverbal exercise, to be described shortly, which clarifies the "pecking order" may be indicated. These techniques are of little value as "emotional fillers" —i.e., something interesting to do when the group seems to be at loose ends. Furthermore, sufficient time must be available for discussion of pre-

viously little understood feelings—the sheer nonverbal experience without some accompanying cognitive integration is of little value and recalls
to mind Alexander's remarks about the corrective emotional experience
(Chapter 2): he emphasized that the purely emotional experience could
be moving or powerful but not corrective; our lives are full of emotional
experiences that do not result in significant learning.

A few illustrations of nonverbal exercises may clarify these points.

Some exercises pertaining to inclusion issues have been described elsewhere in this book: for example, the "breaking-in" exercise in which the
group forms a circle and one member tries to break into the circle. The
"centering task" consists of each member's moving his chair closer or
further from the center of the group circle. "Paper images" invite each
member to select, from a number of sheets of paper of various colors,
shapes, and sizes, one sheet that most resembles himself; he may then
modify it to make it resemble himself even more and then must place it
along with those of the other members on a large sheet of white paper
(which represents the group space) according to where he feels he fits in
the group.

Several exercises relate to the building of trust in the group, such as
"falling back," in which one participant, with eyes closed, falls backwards,
allowing himself to be caught in the arms of each of the group members in
turn. "Passing and cradling" is an analogous exercise: "One member is
encircled by the others standing shoulder to shoulder. The subject stands
in the center with his eyes closed. Trying to relax he leans in any direction.
The closest member reaches out and supports him as he leans off balance.
He is then passed from hand to hand inside the circle. The subjects tend to
loosen up, leaning more off balance, and trusting the group to keep him
from falling . . ." [29]

Other exercises deal with power, influence, and conflict. When the
group is struggling ineffectively with the question of power and influence
in the group, or when there is a total avoidance of the issue and an over-
abundance of affection, a "pecking order" exercise may be used in which
the group is simply asked to arrange itself in a line according to each
person's influence, from the most influence to the least. This may be a
rather explosive, threatening exercise which generates a great deal of data.
If two members are locked in an oblique or a seemingly unresolvable
conflict, a "put-down lift-up" exercise may be useful: each party, in turn,
puts his hands on the other's shoulders and slowly presses him to the floor,
then he reverses and places his hands under the other's arms and raises
him up again. The feelings generated in each party during this exercise
may change the destructive tone of the relationship.

335

A number of improvised exercises can be used to effect a *detente* in an unsatisfactory relationship. For example, I was once in a group in which I found it difficult to relate to another member because of his hand which had been severely deformed in a childhood accident. I was so repulsed by the deformity that I could not see or experience the person attached to the hand. The group leader suggested, with good results, that I hold and examine the deformed hand for several minutes.

This list, of course, may be extended indefinitely, as each group leader develops exercises which fit his own style or meet the needs of a particular group. In my own therapy groups (in contrast to my practice in T-groups), I use nonverbal exercises very rarely; other group therapists may find them far more useful. Until well-controlled evaluative research appears, each clinician must determine for himself the usefulness of these ancillary techniques.

The Use of Videotape in the Therapy Group

Modern scientific technology, which has so largely contributed to the dehumanization of present-day society and to the related necessity for group therapy, has at the same time created an instrument—the videotape recorder—which has considerable potential benefit for the teaching, practice, and understanding of group therapy.

There is little doubt that the videotape recording will become of increasing importance in the teaching of all forms of psychotherapy. Students and supervisors are permitted to view the session with a minimum of distortion. Important nonverbal aspects of behavior of both students and patients which may be completely missed in the traditional supervisory format become available for study. The student-therapist has a rich opportunity to observe his own presentation of self and his own body language. Confusing aspects of the meeting may be viewed several times until some order appears. Valuable teaching sessions which clearly illustrate some basic principles of therapy may be stored and a teaching videotape library created. These features suggest that videotapes are a significant advance over older methods of observation such as audiotapes, closed-circuit television, or one-way mirrors.

The opportunity to view oneself is a powerful and often important experience. No therapy group viewing a videotape of itself responds with indifference to the procedure, and at present many therapists are experimenting with methods of using the impact of videotape in the service of therapy. A common technique is to videotape a group session and to devote the following session to viewing and reacting to it. Some therapists schedule an extra playback meeting in which most of the previous tape is observed; others tape the first half of the meeting and observe the tape during the second half. Instant replay is also possible: a particularly important or affect-laden sequence can be played back immediately.

Patient response depends upon the timing of the procedure. Berger[30] notes that the patient's response to the first playback session differs from his response to later sessions. In the first playback patients attend primarily to their own image and are relatively less involved with the process of the group; later they may be more attentive to their styles of responding and relating to others.

Often a patient's long-cherished self-image is radically challenged by a first videotape playback. It is not unusual for him to recall and to accept previous feedback he had gotten from other members; often with dramatic impact he understands that the group had been honest and, if anything, overprotective in previous confrontations. The group is no longer experienced as a critical or destructive body, and the patient may become more amenable to future interpretations. Often profound self-confrontations occur; one cannot hide from oneself and patients may subsequently abandon defensive and incongruent façades. Many initial playback reactions are concerned with the presence or absence of sex appeal in women and masculinity in men.[30] In subsequent playback sessions patients note their interactions with others, their withdrawal, incongruence, self-preoccupation, hostility, or aloofness. They are far more able to be self-observant and objective than when actually involved in the group interaction.

Occasionally videotape playback may be extraordinarily useful in studying a crisis situation. Berger [30] cites two such instances: Two patients in different sessions had behaved in an extraordinarily disorganized, disruptive manner; one patient was intoxicated, the other in a manic state. Neither had ever had the opportunity to observe himself in this condition. The manic patient was especially stunned since when in the manic condition she had, of course, never felt as though she were high or behaving peculiarly. The therapist felt that in each instance the video playback had a profound and salubrious effect.

A description of the technical procedure is unwise at this juncture; the technology of the field is progressing so quickly that any description of cameras, equipment, and operating techniques will be obsolete in a matter of months. In the last three years the price of a satisfactory recording and viewing unit has fallen from $12,000 to $2,000. Size and operating convenience have improved correspondingly.

Written permission must be obtained from the patients if the tape will be viewed by anyone other than the group members. Many therapists are reluctant to inflict a TV camera on the group; they feel that it will inhibit the group's spontaneity and that the group will resent, though not necessarily overtly, the intrusion. In my opinion the situation is virtually identical to the introduction of the audio tape recorder into psychotherapy in the 1950's. The person who appears to experience the most discomfort is the therapist; generally the patients, especially if they will view the playback, are quite receptive to the suggestion of videotaping. Furthermore, recent research suggests that the presence of the TV camera does not significantly alter the affect or content of the group meeting.[31]

The technique is so new that we will for some time be unable to evaluate its overall importance in the psychotherapy process. We may expect over the next couple of years, as with any new technique, overstated claims. The process is a self-reinforcing one since the enthusiasm engendered by the innovators will itself have a salutory effect on therapy outcome. There is little doubt that self-observation plays a role in the therapy process; however, it is a precondition for therapeutic change, not synonymous with change.

REFERENCES

1. J. Frank, L. H. Gleidman, S. Imber, E. Nash, and A. Stone, "Why Patients Leave Psychotherapy," *Arch. Neurol. Psychiat.*, 77: 283–299, 1957.
2. E. Nash, J. Frank, L. Gleidman, S. Imber, and A. Stone, "Some Factors Related to Patients Remaining in Group Psychotherapy," *Int. J. Group Psychother.*, 7: 264–275, 1957.
3. G. Bach, *Intensive Group Therapy* (New York: Ronald Press, 1954).
4. B. B. Wassel, *Group Analysis* (New York: Citadel Press, 1966), pp. 282–283.
5. H. Spitz and S. Kopp, "Multiple Psychotherapy," *Psychiat. Quart. Suppl.*, 31: 295–331, 1957.
6. E. Waugh, *Brideshead Revisited* (Boston: Little, Brown, 1945).
7. I. D. Yalom, J. Tinklenberg, and M. Gilula, unpublished data, 1967.
8. R. F. Bales, "The Equilibrium Problem in Small Groups," in T. Parsons, R. F. Bales, and E. A. Shils (eds.), *Working Papers in the Theory of Action* (Glencoe, Ill.: Free Press, 1953), pp. 111–161.
9. J. Solomon and G. Solomon, "Group Therapy with Father and Son as Co-therapists: Some Dynamic Considerations," *Int. J. Group Psychother.*, 13: 133–140, 1963.
10. A. Wolf, "The Psychoanalysis of Groups," *Am. J. Psychother.*, 3: 529–557, 1949.
11. S. R. Slavson, *A Textbook in Analytic Group Psychotherapy* (New York: International Universities Press, 1964), pp. 398–399.

338

12. J. Johnson, *Group Therapy: A Practical Approach* (New York: McGraw-Hill, 1963), pp. 56–57.
13. M. Jones, *The Therapeutic Community* (New York: Basic Books, 1953).
14. D. Daniels, "Milieu Therapy of Schizophrenia," in C. P. Rosenbaum, *Perspectives on the Schizophrenias: Phenomenology, Sociology, Biology and Therapy* (New York: Science House, forthcoming).
15. M. Harrow *et al.*, "Influence of the Psychotherapist on the Emotional Climate in Group Therapy," *Human Relations, 20:* 49–64, 1967.
16. M. A. Lieberman, D. S. Whitaker, and M. Lakin, "Groups and Dyads: Never the Twain Shall Meet," unpublished mimeograph, University of Chicago, 1967.
17. Anonymous, from *Calendar of Health* (New York: League for Right Living, 1908), cited in *J. Appl. Behav. Sci., 3:* 101, 1967.
18. O. H. Mowrer, *The New Group Therapy* (Princeton, New Jersey: D. Van Nostrand Co., Inc., 1964).
19. B. Berzon, "Final Narrative Report: Self-Directed Small Group Programs," NIMH Project RD 1748, mimeographed material, Western Behavioral Science Institute, 1968.
20. R. B. Morton, "The Uses of the Laboratory Method in a Psychiatric Hospital— Section A: The Patient Training Laboratory; An Adaptation of the Instrumented Training Laboratory," in E. H. Schein and W. G. Bennis (eds.), *Personal and Organizational Change Through Group Methods: The Laboratory Approach* (New York: John Wiley and Sons, 1965), pp. 114–151.
21. E. G. Aiken, "Alternate Forms of a Semantic Differential for Measurement of Changes in Self-Description," *Psychol. Rep., 16:* 177–178, 1965.
22. G. Gevrin, "JOBS Project Report," Institute for Social Research, University of Michigan, 1967.
23. G. Higgins, personal communication, 1967.
24. D. Malamud and S. Machover, *Toward Self-Understanding: Group Techniques in Self-Confrontation* (Springfield, Ill.: Charles C. Thomas, 1965).
25. W. Schutz, *JOY: Expanding Human Awareness* (New York: Grove Press, 1967).
26. D. Zimmerman, "Some Characteristics of Dreams in Group-Analytic Psychotherapy," *Int. J. Group Psychother., 17:* 524–535, 1967.
27. A. Lowen, *The Betrayal of the Body* (New York: Macmillan, 1967).
28. F. Perls, R. Hefferline, and P. Goodman, *Gestalt Therapy* (New York: Dell Publishing Co., 1965).
29. C. Alderfer and J. C. Daniels, "A Compilation of Non-Verbal Exercises," unpublished paper, Ithaca, New York: Graduate School of Business, Cornell University, 1968.
30. M. Berger, "The Use of Video Tape with Psychotherapy Groups in a Community Mental Health Program," paper delivered at the American Group Psychotherapy Conference, Chicago, January 1968.
31. H. Langee, G. Newell, and S. MacIntosh, "Effects of Video Tape Replay on Group Process and Group Members," in preparation.

14

GROUP THERAPY
AND THE
NEW GROUPS

❧

Introduction

The classified ad section of a recent copy of a California newspaper contained the following:

Encounters

• ENCOUNTER: group forming—psychodrama, gestalt, mind-body connections, more. . . .

• ENCOUNTER: groups & seminars on self-actualization, explorations Institute. . . .

• ENCOUNTER: openings: $15/10 sessions, Mon, Thurs. . . .

• ENCOUNTER: Gestalt, meets Sun, Mon, Wed 8pm. . . .

• ENCOUNTER: openings for new members.

• PSYCHODRAMA: Sundays. 12:30pm, $1. . . .

• PSYCHODRAMA: Sundays. 12:30pm, free (or so). . . .

• PSYCHODRAMA: Encounter groups. . . .

• GROPE GROUP: Forming (Yoga, Zen, relaxation). . . .

• ENCOUNTER: New member openings. . . .

"Encounter" groups go by many names: sensitivity training groups, T-groups, human awareness groups, human relations groups, human enrichment groups, Synanon games, marathon groups, personal growth groups, sensory awareness groups, etc. Of these aliases, "T-group" is perhaps the best known and I have used this term for the entire genre throughout this book. ("T" stands for "training" as in "human relations training group" or "interpersonal sensitivity training group.") Furthermore, as we shall see, the T-group is the prototype of the many varieties of new groups.

Although there are many similarities among these groups, there are also marked procedural differences between them, and to consider them as similar or identical would be an error. However, the rapidly changing nature of the new groups makes a stable classification impossible at this time. One rudimentary distinction I would suggest is between "encounter group" and T-group. Generally encounter groups have no institutional backing, are far more unstructured, are more often led by untrained leaders, may rely more on physical contact and nonverbal exercises, and generally emphasize an experience, or getting "turned on," rather than change per se.

Although there is no accurate registry of these groups, it is clear that they are rapidly proliferating; a recent survey which two of my colleagues* and I conducted of the groups in the Palo Alto, California, area (population approximately 100,000) resulted in a list of approximately two hundred groups currently operating. One organization, Synanon (Oakland branch), conducts weekly groups ("square-games") for 1500 non-drug addicts. Scarcely a week passes without my receiving in the mail notification of some new organization offering a group experience or training in group methods. Esalen, an institute at Big Sur, California, which in 1960 offered only occasional weekend groups, has now had over 50,000 participants in various programs and has a mailing list of 21,000 individuals to whom it distributes a massive catalogue of group activities, including nonverbal groups, experiential groups, Gestalt therapy groups, body dynamic groups, breathing and awareness groups, sensory awakening groups, etc., which are held year round at the parent institute at Big Sur or at one of several new Esalen branches.[1] In 1969 at least seventy-five other growth centers, many modeled after Esalen, were operating throughout the country.

These groups cannot, I believe, be dismissed as part of the evanescent California youth culture. Although many of the participants are college students, the majority of the group-goers are middle-aged; furthermore, a large number of young mental health professionals attend these groups. Nor are the groups confined to California; like so many California-based social phenomena, there is a rapid eastward spread: already encounter groups, marathon groups, and nude weekend therapy groups are common

* Morton Lieberman, Ph.D., and Peggy Golde, Ph.D.

on the eastern seaboard. Maine, our easternmost state, is the cradle of the T-group, and in Bethel over five thousand individuals have participated in human relations training groups. Carl Rogers[2] has called the intensive group experience movement "one of the most rapidly growing social phenomena in the United States . . . perhaps the most significant social invention of this century."

This social movement has important implications for the mental health field and for many other institutions, especially organized religion, education and industry—institutions which have both embraced and attacked the new groups. To appreciate fully the shape of a social movement one must consider the negative and positive reactions of all the related institutions. I shall, however, leave this to generalists and limit myself in this chapter to a discussion of the new groups from the perspective of the mental health field.

Because of the loose, noninstitutional structure of the new groups, there is no systematic information on either the number or the motivation of the participants. Interviews with leaders and my own experience lead me to the conclusion that although many participants attend for purposes of stimulation, novelty, social and sexual contacts, a large number attend for reasons that would ordinarily have resulted in a consultation with a mental health professional. In fact, it might not be overstating the point to estimate that in California more troubled individuals seek help from these new groups than from traditional sources of psychotherapy!

The accelerated rate of growth of these new groups suggests the presence of considerable social contagion and raises the possibility that, like dianetics and dada, they will gradually fade away. Yet there are grounds for believing that the new group phenomenon will be with us for a long time. These groups are not spontaneously generated; they arise in response to a pressing need in our culture, which I shall discuss more fully later. Furthermore, T-groups will probably become an increasingly important factor in the therapeutic group field. There have been many recent signs that the group therapy field has been influenced by the T-group. In fact, ten years ago this chapter would never have been written; therapy groups and T-groups existed as parallel and separate streams. Most clinicians were totally ignorant of the existence or nature of T-groups, and when I referred to T-groups in lectures I was careful to distinguish T-groups from tea groups. At the present time the term is so well known that I feel fatuous in defining T-groups. A perusal of the titles of workshops, panels, and papers at recent American Group Psychotherapy Association conventions demonstrates also an increased familiarity and concern with T-groups. So too with group therapy journals; a recent issue of the *Interna-*

tional Journal of Group Psychotherapy [3] contained four articles on the use of T-groups in the education of group therapists. There has also been a spate of publications [4, 5, 6, 7] attempting to point out the difference between T-groups and therapy groups. The annual two-day American Group Psychotherapy Institute has gradually evolved from formal small discussion groups dealing with specific and substantive group therapy issues to an experiential group virtually identical with many brief T-group-centered human relations laboratories.

Because of the current growth and turbulence in the field, it is difficult to predict the future relationship between the T-group and the therapy group. In fact, as we shall show, even the current relationship is shrouded in uncertainty. I have found that an understanding of the origin and thrust of both the T-group and the therapy group field clarifies the current situation and enables us to make some informed predictions about the future interaction and overlap between the two fields.

Evolution of the T-Group [8, 9, 10, 11, 12]

THE FIRST T-GROUP

In 1946, Frank Simpson, the executive director of the Connecticut Interracial Commission, which had been created to implement the new Connecticut Fair Employment Practices Act, asked Kurt Lewin for help in training leaders who could deal effectively with intergroup tensions. Kurt Lewin at that time was the director of the Commission of Community Interrelations, an undertaking of the American Jewish Congress, as well as the director of the Massachusetts Institute of Technology's new Research Center for Group Dynamics. Simpson requested help in training a wide range of community leaders—businessmen, labor leaders, schoolteachers —to deal more effectively with interracial tensions, and to use their knowledge to change racial attitudes in other people.

After surmounting many financial difficulties, Lewin organized a workshop in June 1946 at New Britain, Connecticut. Three group leaders, Leland Bradford, Kenneth Benne, and Ronald Lippit—all destined to exert great influence in the nascent field of human relations training—led groups of ten members each. Kurt Lewin headed a small team of social psychologists who researched the process and outcome of the conference experience. The small groups were discussion groups which analyzed

343

"back-home" problems presented by the group members. Some role-playing techniques were used to diagnose behavioral aspects of the problems and to practice alternative approaches to solution.

A research observer who recorded and coded behavioral interactions and sequences had been assigned to each of the small groups. Evening meetings were held in which the group leaders and the research observers met and pooled their observations of leader, member, and group behavior. Soon some participants learned of these evening meetings and asked permission to attend. Lewin agreed, but the other staff members were at first reluctant to allow the members to overhear the staff's private discussion of the members' behavior; the staff feared that their own inadequacies might be revealed and, furthermore, they were extremely uncertain about the effects on the members of hearing direct observations about their behavior. The members were finally permitted to attend the open meetings on a voluntary basis and the effects on them as well as on the staff were "electric." [12] Soon the format of the evening meetings was widened to permit the participants to respond to the observations, and shortly thereafter all parties were involved in the analysis and interpretation of their own behavior. Before many evenings had passed, all the participants were attending the evening meetings, which were often continued for as long as three hours; there was widespread agreement that the meetings offered the participants a rich understanding of their own behavior. The staff immediately realized that they had, somewhat inadvertently, discovered a powerful technique of human relations education: group members may profit enormously by being confronted, in an objective manner, with observations about their own behavior and its effects on others; they may learn about their interpersonal styles, the responses of others to them, and about group behavior and development in general.

From this beginning the T-group, as a technique of education, has undergone considerable change. This development can be understood more fully if we first backtrack to consider the question of why Kurt Lewin was asked to perform this task and why he accepted.

THE INFLUENCE OF KURT LEWIN

Although he died only a few months after the Connecticut experience, Kurt Lewin, through his students and his ideas, exerted a mighty influence on the future development of the T-group and the human relations field. Lewin, a German psychologist, well known for his work in field theory, visited America on a lecture tour before World War II. Once out of Germany he appreciated the impending Nazi calamity and, after helping his family escape, took up permanent residence in the United States. Lewin accepted a visiting professorship at Harvard for a short time, and, while there, he lectured at Springfield College where he met Lawrence Hall, who was teaching a course in group work and provided Lewin with his first introduction to the small group field. (During this time Lewin also had some brief contact with Samuel Slavson, one of the early group therapists.) When, a short time later, Lewin accepted a professorship at the University of Iowa, he was accompanied by Ronald Lippit, one of Hall's students, whose major field of interest was small groups.

At the same time as Lewin was growing more interested in group dynamics (a term which he coined) he became increasingly dedicated to changing behavior. Much of the impetus for his action orientation arose from his observation of Nazi Germany, which stimulated a deep interest in such problems as the re-education of the Hitler youths and the changing of anti-Semitic attitudes. His interest in the effect of the social climate on individual attitudes led him to such research as the classic experiment with Lippit and White on the effects of three types of leadership: authoritarian, democratic, and laissez-faire.[13] During the war he explored methods of changing attitudes toward foods and attempted, through group methods, to persuade individuals to increase their intake of such available foods as brains and kidneys.[14] He became interested in retraining individuals who were, for example, ineffective authoritarian group leaders, to perform a task more effectively. Although he was aware that such retraining might result in broad characterologic change, he never researched this possibility,[9] nor did he give serious consideration to the possibility that the authoritarian characterologic traits were present from early life and impervious to change. Toward the end of his career, Lewin and his students moved to M.I.T., where he headed the research Center for Group Dynamics. After Lewin's death his students, who include many of the prominent contemporary social psychologists* moved to the Institute for the study of Group Dynamics at the University of Michigan.

Lewin's research had led him to several conclusions about changing behavior, conclusions which were instrumental in the Connecticut laboratory. He believed that long-held beliefs can be changed only when individuals are able to examine them personally and conclude that they are unsatisfactory. Methods of changing attitudes, or retraining, therefore, are effective if trainees are provided with opportunities for discovering the deleterious effects upon themselves and others of their customary behav-

* John French, Dorwin Cartwright, Alex Bavelas, Ronald Lippit, R. K. White, Leon Festinger.

ior. Thus the trainee must be helped to see himself as others see him. Only when the individual himself discovers these facts will his attitudes and subsequent behavior change. As Lewin put it, "This result occurs when the facts become really *their* facts (as against other people's facts). An individual will believe facts he himself has discovered in the same way he believes in himself." [10]

Lewin's dual dedication to action and research and his principle of "no research without action, no action without research" have left an indelible impression on the entire development of the T-group. From the very beginning, as exemplified in the Connecticut laboratory, research has been woven into the fabric of the T-group. I refer not only to formal research but to a research attitude on the part of the leader; he and the group members are collaborators in a research inquiry designed to enable each participant to experience, understand, and change his behavior. This feature, together with the concept of the T-group as a technique of education, is essential, as we shall shortly show, in the differentiation of the T-group from the therapy group.

DEVELOPMENT OF THE NATIONAL TRAINING LABORATORY

After the Connecticut workshop, Leland Bradford, Ronald Lippit, and Kenneth Benne, who fully realized the important implications of the experience, made plans for a similar three-week laboratory the following summer at the Gould Academy in Bethel, Maine. Sixty-seven participants and thirty-seven staff members participated in a heavily researched laboratory. The laboratory plan consisted of morning small discussion groups and afternoon and evening large group meetings and theory sessions. The small discussion groups, the ancestor of the encounter group, were called "basic skill training groups" (shortened in 1949 to "T-group") and met with a leader, called the trainer, and an observer; the first part of the meeting was a discussion of some substantive issue or "back-home" problem; the second part was a feedback session in which the observer reported his process observations to the group and led the ensuing discussion. The laboratory was so successful that similar laboratories were held in 1948 and 1949. The T-group soon became the central and dominant function of the laboratory. Gradually its format altered: the feedback process became less formalized and more integrated into the matrix of the T-group, and the feedback observer became, correspondingly, an assistant trainer.

By 1950 the sponsoring organization, the National Training Laboratory (NTL), was established within the National Education Association (NEA) as a year-round organization. Leland Bradford, who at that time was chief of the NEA Division of Adult and Veteran Education, became the executive director of the NTL and has guided it in its development from the fledgling institute which sponsored the 1947 summer lab for sixty-seven participants to its present mammoth stature in which it employs over sixty-five full-time professional and administrative staff, has a network of six hundred NTL trained leaders, and in 1967 alone held human relations laboratories for over 2500 participants. From his earliest student days Bradford has been deeply interested in methods of education. As a teaching assistant in the 1930's he made effective use of the informal discussion group and sought to decrease the emotional distance between teacher and student. T-groups have always been for him part of a technology of education.

In the first Bethel laboratories it soon became clear that the T-group was overloaded with tasks: it was asked not only to teach members about their interpersonal behavior but also to explicate group dynamic theory, to discuss members' problems in their home organizations, to help them develop leadership skills, and to aid in the transfer of T-group learning to the "back-home" situation. The trainer, correspondingly, was asked to assume too many disparate roles. The NTL human relations laboratories in the 1950's (and still to some extent today) were characterized by efforts to unburden the T-group so that it could fulfill its central purpose more effectively. The laboratory day was generally divided between the T-group and other functions. For example, A-groups (action groups) composed of individuals of the same occupation were sociologically oriented and focused on problems and methodologies of change in larger social systems. Often supplementary reading material was distributed to members of the A-groups, short lectures were given, and outside cases were presented for analysis. Application groups were created which attempted to build bridges between T-group learning and "back-home" settings. Very frequently T-group members experienced a sense of let-down and were disillusioned when they attempted to apply their T-group learning to their work situation; the application group dealt with the "re-entry phenomenon" and such problems as how to improve staff meetings, how to increase the influence of subordinates, and how to initiate constructive organizational change.

The problem with theory groups, A-groups, application groups, etc., is that the members attempted to turn all such sessions into additional T-

347

groups. The pull of the T-group was of such force that it tended to eat up the entire human relations laboratory, and consequently the staff was often faced with the problem of how to insure that other types of learning were not ignored.

In the early 1950's more of the training staff were clinically oriented, and the language of interpretation and clarification gradually grew less Lewinian and more Rogerian and Freudian. The founders of the field expressed some concern at this point lest the T-group turn into a therapy group. They underscored both the fact that participants had contracted for an educational experience in human relations and not for psycho-therapy and that there was not sufficient time available in a laboratory to resolve deeper therapeutic issues.[12]

Throughout, the NTL human relations laboratories have been charac-terized by their great flexibility and their willingness to research their own activities* and to use the findings of such research to modify subsequent laboratories. In 1952 sociologists were invited to study the development of the social organization of the entire laboratory community. Later a large group exercise was instituted in many labs, and the differences in dy-namics between the large group and the small T-group were thoroughly studied. In 1957 the intergroup task was introduced: a series of exercises were developed in which T-groups competed or interacted with one another; the researchers and participants studied both the intergroup rela-tionship and the intragroup repercussions of this relationship.[16]

DEVELOPMENT OF THE T-GROUP

As the nature of the entire human relations laboratory evolved, so too did the character of the T-group. As other exercises were developed to take over the cognitive and application functions, the T-group increas-ingly came to focus on interpersonal behavior. Obviously the character of the group depends greatly upon the techniques of its trainer, as well as upon situational factors. For example, beginning in the late 1950's, trainers were often asked to be change agents by organizations such as business corporations, school systems, branches of government; T-groups com-posed of work group peers or of the entire hierarchical structure of a work unit differ from a T-group of strangers.

Generally the T-group moved in the direction of ever greater emphasis on feedback, interpersonal honesty, self-disclosure, unfreezing, and ob-servant participation. Discussion of outside material ("there-and-then"),

* See Stock (1964) [15] for a summary of much of the NTL research.

including "back-home" current problems or past personal history, was discouraged, whereas here-and-now material was highly prized.

Feedback. This term, borrowed from the electrical engineers, was first applied to the behavioral sciences by Lewin (it is no accident that he was teaching at M.I.T. at the time).[17] The early trainers realized that an important flaw in society was that too little opportunity exists for individuals to obtain accurate feedback from their back-home associates: bosses, fellow employees, wives, teachers, students, etc. Feedback became an essential ingredient of all T-groups; without it the here-and-now focus has little meaning or vitality. Feedback seems most effective in the group when it stems from here-and-now observations and when it follows the generating event as closely as possible. Furthermore, the feedback should be checked out with other group members to establish its validity and reduce perceptual distortion.

Unfreezing. This term, also adopted from Lewinian change theory, refers to the process of disconfirming an individual's former belief system. The individual must be primed and his motivation for change must be generated before change can occur. He must be helped to re-examine many cherished assumptions about himself and his relations to others. The familiar must be made strange;[18] many common props, social conventions, status symbols, ordinary procedural rules are eliminated from the T-group, and the individual's values and beliefs about himself are challenged. This may create a state of considerable discomfort for the individual, a state which he is willing to tolerate only under certain conditions: he must experience the group as a refuge wherein he is safe, wherein he can entertain new beliefs and experiment with new behavior without fear of reprisal.

Observant Participation. Most trainers considered observant participation as the optimal method of involvement for all group participants. Members must both participate emotionally in the group and observe themselves and the group objectively. Often this is a difficult task to master and members chafe at the trainer's attempts to subject the group to objective analysis. Yet the dual task is essential to learning: either action or intellectual scrutiny alone produces a low yield for learning. Camus once wrote, "My greatest wish: to remain lucid in ecstasy." [19] So too the T-group (and the therapy group) is most effective when its members can couple cognitive appraisal with an emotional experience.

Cognitive Aids. Cognitive guides around which T-group participants (or delegates, as they are often called) can organize their experience are often presented in brief "lecturettes" by the T-group leader or another staff member. One example of such a cognitive guide is the Johari window, a four-celled personality paradigm which clarifies the function of feedback:*

	Known to Self	Unknown to Self
Known to Others	A	B
Unknown to Others	C	D

Cell A, Known to Self and Known to Others, is the public area of the self; Cell B, Unknown to Self and Known to Others, is the blind area; Cell C, Known to Self and Unknown to Others, is the secret area; Cell D, Unknown to Self and Unknown to Others, is the unconscious self. The goals of the T-group, the trainer suggests, are to increase the size of Cell A by decreasing Cell B (blind spots) through feedback, and Cell C (secret area) through self-disclosure.

The use of such cognitive aids, lectures, reading assignments, and theory sessions demonstrates that the basic allegiance of the T-group was to the classroom rather than to the consulting room. The participants were considered students; the task of the T-group was to facilitate learning for its members. Different trainers emphasized different types of learning: some focused primarily on group dynamics and helped the members to understand group development, group pressures, the leadership role, and common group tensions and obstacles; others emphasized personal learning and focused on the interpersonal style and communication of the members. These two emphases became more polarized until a formal distinction was made in laboratory planning between group process groups and personal development groups. I shall pursue the evolution of the personal development group, since it is this form of T-group which most closely resembles the therapy group and which has spawned the many varieties of intensive encounter groups.

Group Therapy for Normals. In the 1950's the NTL established several regional branches, and each of the various sectors gradually developed its own T-group emphasis. It was the West Coast and particularly Southern California which pursued the "personal development" model most vigorously. A 1962 article by Southern California trainers [21] which presents a model of a T-group as "group therapy for normals" clearly signals the change in emphasis from group dynamics to individual dynamics, from

---

* Named after Joe Luft and Harry Ingham, who first described the window.[20]

stress on the development of interpersonal skills to a greater concern with individual dynamics and the unfolding of the fully actualized self.

THE STRESSES OF NORMALITY. These trainers in their group work with healthy members of society, indeed with individuals who by most objective standards had achieved a considerable degree of success, came to appreciate that normality in our culture is too often linked with a fairly continuous level of tension, insecurity, and value conflict.

In most respects we seem adjusted in our day-by-day activities. We appear to behave appropriately with regard to the demands made upon us by our families, friends, and jobs. Yet this appearance is deceptive. Internal doubts and schisms persist. As no convenient learning vehicle is typically available to the "pseudo-healthy" person, tensions below the surface debilitate realization of potential capacities, stunt creativity, infuse hostility into a vast range of human contact, and frequently generate hampering psychosomatic problems.[21]

The highly competitive American culture, many behavioral scientists have noted, encourages façade building. The successful man who has had his expertise validated by his peers too often strives to protect his public image at all cost. If he has doubts about his adequacy, he swallows them and maintains constant vigilance lest any personal uncertainty or discomfort slip through. This process is an isolating and crippling one since it curtails communication not only with others but with oneself. Gradually, in order to eliminate a perpetual state of self-recrimination for personal dishonesty, the successful individual comes to believe in the reality of his façade and attempts through unconscious means to ward off internal and external attacks on his self-image. Thus a state of equilibrium is reached but at a costly price: considerable energy is invested in maintaining intra- and interpersonal separations, energy which might otherwise have been used in the service of self-actualization; creativity and self-knowledge are sacrificed as the individual turns his gaze outward in a never-ending search for peer validation; interpersonal relationships are shallow and unrewarding; he squelches spontaneity so that his studied façade remains unruffled; he avoids self-disclosure, and he refrains from confronting others lest he be similarly challenged.

THE T-GROUP AS A SOCIAL OASIS. The T-group is a respite from this "culture game." [21] It often represents an oasis in which many of the restrictive norms described above are altered. All accoutrements which in the outside world symbolize success and normality are deposited at the door of the T-group. Individuals are no longer rewarded for their material success, for their hierarchical position, for their unruffled aplomb, for their efficiency, or for their expertise in their area of specialization; instead they are exposed to the totally different values of the T-group, in which they are rewarded for interpersonal honesty and for the disclosure of self-doubts and perceived weaknesses. Gradually they discover that in the T-group the façade is not only unnecessary but an encumbrance. For years they have operated on the assumption that there is a high cost to pay if they lower their façade; the cost was envisioned as humiliation, rejection, and loss of social or professional status. Their experience in the T-group helps to challenge these assumptions and enables them to experiment with openness and to differentiate its real costs from its pseudo-costs. Obviously there are some real risks in the disclosure of all our thoughts and feelings: "The realities of living, of sensible interpersonal strategy and tactics, clearly dictate the advisability of keeping some things as part of our private selves." [21] But many of the pseudo-costs are exposed. Lowering of the façade does not result in rejection; in fact, members find themselves more completely accepted since they are accepted on the basis of a fully disclosed self rather than on the basis of a false projected image. Moreover, their deep sense of isolation is assuaged, as each becomes aware of the universality of his secret doubts and fears. These processes are self-reinforcing since the experience of universality encourages each to reveal even more of himself. Members who have previously regarded interpersonal relationships as automated or threatening are able to sample the inherent richness and depth of human intimacy.

As communication becomes more open in the group and members "level" with each other, sharing their positive and negative perceptions with each other, they become more familiar with their "blind selves," those aspects of their personality of which they were previously unaware. Generally the more an individual has disengaged himself from honest interpersonal confrontations, the grosser are his blind spots. Often this process is a painful and threatening one; but once a member realizes that others are nonjudgmental and desire reciprocal feedback, his defensiveness diminishes.

Thus the T-group seeks to reverse the restricting and alienating effects of the "culture game." Internal and external separations are removed as the individual learns to relate honestly to himself and to others. "The isolation from others and of the two selves, one from the other, now wanes as individuals learn to become aware of their true selves rather than continuing in flight towards phony fronts."[21] The goal of the T-group has been broadened until now some trainers consider their goal "the total enhancement of the individual." [21] Time in the group is set aside for reflective silences, for listening to music and poetry; individuals are encouraged to voice their deeper and more pervasive concerns; for example, they are encouraged to re-examine their basic life values and the discrepancies between these values and their life styles; they examine their many false selves; they explore the softer, long-buried, feminine parts of themselves. Obviously the boundary between a T-group with these goals and a therapy group may be very blurred indeed; both attempt to improve functioning, to enhance reality testing, to enrich interpersonal relationships, to eliminate crippling intrapsychic splits, and to strengthen the ego.

Despite these overlapping goals, there are, nonetheless, important and basic distinctions between training and therapy and it is to these distinctions that we now turn our attention.

Evolution of Group Therapy

The history of group therapy has been too thoroughly described in other texts [22, 23, 24] to warrant repetition here. A rapid sweep will reveal the basic trends. Joseph Hershey Pratt, a Boston internist, is generally acknowledged to be the father of contemporary group therapy. Pratt undertook in 1905 the treatment of a large number of patients with far-advanced tuberculosis. Recognizing the relationship between psychological health and the physical course of tuberculosis, Pratt undertook to treat the person rather than the disease. He designed a treatment regimen which included home visits, diary keeping by patients, and weekly meetings of a tuberculosis class of approximately twenty-five patients. At these classes the diaries were inspected, weight gains were recorded publicly on the blackboard, and testimonials were given by successful patients. A degree of cohesiveness and mutual support developed which appeared helpful in combating the depression and isolation so common to tubercular patients.

During the 1920's and 1930's several psychiatrists experimented with group methods. Adler employed group methods in Europe because of his awareness of the social nature of man's problems and because of a desire to provide psychotherapeutic help to the working classes.[25] Lazell [26] in 1921 met with groups of schizophrenic patients in St. Elizabeth's Hospital in Washington, D.C., and delivered lectures on schizophrenia. Marsh,[27] a few years later, used groups for a wide range of clinical problems, including psychosis, psychoneurosis, psychophysiological disorders and stammering. He employed a variety of techniques, including such didactic methods as lectures and homework assignments as well as exercises, which

353

promoted considerable interaction; for example, members were asked to "treat" one another, or all were asked to discuss such topics as one's earliest memory, ingredients of one's inferiority complex, night dreams and daydreams. Wender[28] used analytic group methods with hospitalized nonpsychotic patients in the 1930's, while Burrows [29] and Schilder [30] applied these techniques to the treatment of psychoneurotic outpatients. Slavson,[31] who worked with groups of disturbed children and young adolescents, exerted considerable influence in the field through his teaching and writing at a time when group therapy was not yet considered by most workers as an effective therapeutic approach. Moreno,[32] who first used the term group therapy, employed group methods before 1920 but has been primarily identified with psychodrama, which he introduced into America in 1925.

These tentative beginnings in the use of group therapy were vastly accelerated by World War II, when the large number of military psychiatric patients and the small number of trained psychiatric workers made individual therapy impractical and required that more economic modes of treatment be used.

The tradition from which group therapy springs is quite evident: it arose as a form of medical treatment intended to relieve suffering. The members of the groups were afflicted individuals who hoped for succor through the person of the leader. Attendance, though nominally voluntary, in one sense was forced since participants believed that membership was necessary in order to obtain relief from their suffering. The leader of the group was a healer, generally a highly prestigious individual who used his prestige in the service of healing.

The T-group derived from an educational tradition. The group participants were voluntary members who hoped to gain knowledge and skills in circumscribed areas which would increase their effectiveness at work. The leader was designated as a teacher who presented himself as an equal and sought to decrease any unrealistic expectations held of him by the group members. Although the field of education (as well as the field of psychotherapy) has undergone a redefinition, nevertheless the T-group continues to be primarily a technique of education. The National Training Laboratories frequently makes this assertion in order to clarify popular misunderstandings. For example, in May 1967, Leland Bradford, director of the National Training Laboratories, wrote the following in a letter to the editor of the *New Yorker*:

Contrary to the report carried in your April 15, 1967 issue—"The Thursday Group," by Renata Adler—the National Training Laboratories does not conduct group therapy sessions in its various educational programs. We do conduct a variety of experience-based learning programs relating to group dynamics, but these programs are not designed for or intended as psychotherapy or as substitutes for psychotherapy. We feel that this clarification is important, since persons reading the article might be misled into seeking psychiatric assistance from our programs when they are neither designed for nor intended for that purpose.[33]

The T-group and the therapy group thus arose from different disciplines and for many years the two disciplines, each generating its own store of theory and technique, continued as two parallel streams of knowledge, even though some leaders straddled both fields and in different settings led both T-groups and therapy groups. The T-group maintained a deep commitment to research and continued to identify with the fields of social psychology, education, organizational science, and industrial management. Indeed, many of the leading trainers held academic positions in graduate schools of business. The T-group literature consequently appeared in the journals of these disciplines and was relatively inaccessible to group therapy clinicians. Until the early 1960's, to the best of my knowledge, no clinical journal published material related to the practice or theory of T-groups.

During the 1950's the main thrust of the group therapy field was in a different direction: toward the application of group therapy in different clinical settings and for different types of clinical problems. Theoreticians —Freudian, Sullivanian, Horneyan, Rogerian—explored the application of their conceptual framework to group therapy theory and practice.

When the T-group field expanded to a point where it was clearly visible to clinicians, the common interests of therapists and trainers became more obvious and they were forced to interact with one another. One response by some group therapy clinicians is to view the T-group suspiciously as an unwelcome intruder. This response stems, in part, from irrational claims of territoriality clearly analogous to the past efforts on the part of the psychiatric profession to prevent social workers and psychologists from engaging in psychotherapy. (Such euphemisms as counseling and case work attest to the tenacity of these efforts.)

In part, however, the response is appropriate to certain excesses in some factions of the T-group field. These excesses issue from a crash-program mentality, successful in such ventures as space exploration and industrialization, but resulting in a *reductio ad absurdum* in human relations ventures. If something is good, more is better. If self-disclosure is good in groups, then total, immediate, indiscriminate disclosure in the nude must be better. If involvement is good, then prolonged, continuous, marathon involvement must be better. If expression of feeling is good, then hitting, touching, feeling, kissing and fornicating must be better. If human relations training is good, then it is good for everyone—in all stages of the life cycle, in all life situations. These excesses are often offensive to the public taste and may be dangerous to some participants. Recognizing that these procedures have an inherent risk, the NTL has recently adopted the practice of including a professional counselor on the staff of the summer laboratories. Unfortunately, most other growth centers generally assume little responsibility for possible adverse effects upon members. To the best of my knowledge, those growth centers espousing procedural excesses have not undertaken follow-up studies to determine the incidence of psychological casualties. Yet if we are to believe the growing number of anecdotal reports from mental health professionals, the casualty rate is noteworthy.

These excesses have resulted in a rising wave of criticism directed indiscriminately against the entire field of sensitivity training. Several important industrial corporations have abandoned their training programs, school supervisors have campaigned and won elections largely on an anti-sensitivity training platform, and the Congressional Record recently included a thirty thousand word blistering attack on sensitivity training, likening it to Bolshevistic brainwashing.[1]

It will be unfortunate if mental health professionals fail to differentiate between responsibly conducted human relations training and those segments of the field associated with these excesses. Such a failure of discrimination would jeopardize the recent constructive interchange between the group therapy and sensitivity training fields. Clinical researchers have learned a great deal from the T-group research methodology; T-groups are commonly used now in the training of group therapists;[4, 5, 34] T-groups have been used in psychiatric hospitals in the treatment program of chronically hospitalized patients;[35] some clinicians refer their individual therapy patients to a T-group for "opening-up"; and finally, some T-group techniques have been adopted by clinicians, resulting in a gradual shift in the practice of group therapy. For example, the increased emphasis on the here-and-now, the concept of feedback, the greater leader transparency, the use of group "gimmicks," both verbal and nonverbal, and the time-extended meeting, have in part been the legacy of the T-group to group therapy.

Interface of the T-group and Therapy Group

Starting from their widely different points of origin, the recent course of the T-group and the therapy group have shown a convergence to the point where there is a considerable interface between the two fields. Indeed, so many similarities are present that many observers wonder whether there are any intrinsic differences between the two types of group work.

DEVELOPMENT OF THE INDIVIDUAL'S POSITIVE POTENTIAL

The traditions from which each have derived have undergone considerable evolution, which has resulted in a major shift in group goals, theory, and technology. Human relations education, as we have shown, has changed its emphasis from the acquisition of specific theory and interpersonal skills to the present goals of total enhancement of the individual. Human relations education now means that the individual becomes educated about his relationship to others as well as to his various internal selves. In the field of psychotherapy there has been a gradual evolution from a model of personality development based on the transmutations of the individual's libidinal and aggressive energies to the current emphasis on ego psychology. Many theorists have posited the existence of an additional positively valenced drive which must perforce be allowed to unfold rather than be inhibited or sublimated: thus Hendrick's "instinct to master," [36] Berlyne's "exploratory drive," [37] Horney's "self-realization," [38] White's "effectance motivation," [39] Hartmann's "neutralized energy," [40] Angyal's "self-determination," [41] and Goldstein's, Rogers' and Maslow's "self-actualization." [42] The development of the individual entails more than the inhibition or sublimation of potentially destructive instinctual forces. He must, in addition, fulfill his creative potential, and the efforts of the therapist should be directed toward this goal. Horney [38] states that the task of the therapist should be to help remove obstructions; given favorable circumstances the individual will realize his own potential, "just as an acorn will develop into an oak." Similarly Rogers refers to the therapist as a facilitator. A closely related trend in psychotherapy, beginning perhaps with Fromm-Reichmann, Erickson, Lindemann, and Hamburg, has been the strategy of building on the patient's strengths. Psychotherapists have come to appreciate, for example, that individuals may encounter great discomfort at certain junctures in the life cycle, not because of

357

poor ego strength but because there have been inadequate opportunities for the learning relevant to that life stage to occur; psychotherapy may be directed toward the facilitation of this learning. Hamburg, in particular, has explored adaptive methods of coping with severe life challenges and has suggested strategies of psychotherapy based on the facilitation of coping.[43]

This shift in therapy orientation has brought the group therapist and the T-group trainer closer together. The T-group has always espoused the goal of acquisition of competence. To the T-group leader the reinforcement of strengths is no less vital than the correction of deficiencies.

OUTCOME GOALS

Hoped-for changes occurring in the individual as a result of his T-group experience closely parallel (despite differences in language) the changes that group therapists wish to see in their patients. For example, one T-group outcome study [44] investigated these fifteen variables: sending communication, receiving communication, relational facility, risk taking, increased interdependence, functional flexibility, self-control, awareness of behavior, sensitivity to group process, sensitivity to others, acceptance of others, tolerance of new information, confidence, comfort, insight into self and role.

SUPRA-INDIVIDUAL FOCUS

One important difference between T-groups and therapy groups present in their early phases but now diminished was that the T-group often had supra-individual goals, whereas the therapy group concerned itself solely with the personal goals of each individual member. For example, the first T-group described earlier had the goal of facilitating the operation of the Connecticut Fair Employment Practices Act. Other T-groups frequently have the supra-individual goal of increasing the effectiveness of the contracting agency. Group therapy, on the other hand, had no goals other than the relief of suffering of each of its members.

Both disciplines have altered their original positions. T-groups often consist of strangers each of whom have highly personalized goals, while many of the supra-individual goals are split off from the T-group and assigned to other activities of the human relations laboratory. Psychotherapy, on the other hand, has gradually become more aware of the importance of supra-individual goals. Stanton and Schwartz [45] in 1954 first noted that in a large group, the psychiatric hospital, the improvement or deterioration of the individual patient was a function of the structural properties of the large group. For example, if the large group had evolved norms which prevented the resolution of intrastaff conflict, then patients were more likely to have psychotic exacerbations. Similar observations have been made in military, prison, and community settings. Gradually an important principle of psychotherapeutic intervention has evolved: a supra-individual focus—the cohesiveness and norms of the large group—can facilitate the attainment of each member's individual goals. In fact, often there is little choice; for example, the great majority of therapists would agree that the individual treatment of the underprivileged adolescent drug user without involvement of his social group is a futile endeavor. The small therapy group analogue of this principle was fully described in Chapter 3 in the discussion of cohesiveness as a curative factor in group psychotherapy.

GROUP COMPOSITION

T-group and therapy group composition have also grown more similar over the years. No longer do psychotherapists solely treat individuals with major mental health problems. An increasing number of fairly well-integrated individuals with minor problems in living are seeking psychotherapy. A number of factors are responsible: increased public acceptance and understanding of psychotherapy, curiosity-arousing mass media depictions of psychotherapy, and increased affluence and leisure time which have resulted in a shift upward on the hierarchy of needs. Conversely many patients have erroneously considered the short intensive T-group, especially the weekend marathon variety, as crash psychotherapy programs. Indeed, as Rogers observed,[46] a new clinical syndrome—the group addict —has recently arisen; these individuals spend every weekend in some T-group, searching them out up and down the West Coast. (I recently attended a marathon group in which three of the members had, the previous evening, just completed another marathon group!)

THE COMMON SOCIAL MALADY

Both T-groups and therapy groups highly value self-disclosure, and the content of what is disclosed is remarkably similar from group to group.

359

Loneliness, confusion, and alienation haunt T-groups and therapy groups alike. The great majority of individuals, both patients and nonpatients, share a common malady, which is deeply imbedded in the character of modern Western society. In much of America the past two decades have witnessed an inexorable decomposition of social institutions which ordinarily provide for human intimacy; the extended family living arrangement, the lifelong marriage (one out of two California marriages ends in divorce), the small, stable work group and home community are often part of the nostalgic past. Organized religion has become irrelevant to many of the young, often little more than a "Sunday morning tedium," [47] while the neighborhood merchant and the family doctor are rapidly disappearing.

Modern medical practice is a case in point. Spurred on by advances in medical technology, the doctor has become an efficient scientist. But at what a price! The president of the American Medical Association stated recently:

In the future, the family doctor will be almost as extinct as a dodo. When you're hurt or sick, you'll go to the nearest hospital for emergency treatment, administered by physicians especially trained in these procedures.

You may not even see the doctor on your initial visits. Your case history will be taken by assistants—even, eventually, by computers. Trained aides may do some of the preliminary examination.

The kindly old gentleman with the bedside manner was wonderful in his day, but society can no longer afford him. The modern doctor is more efficient, more scientific and less subject to error.

Unfortunately, he is often more impersonal. But people are already beginning to accept this, as they are beginning to accept changes in all areas of personal service.

It's part of a normal trend in society. In all forms of human service, there is less concern for the individual. We are no longer served as well as we used to be in stores and restaurants. The relationship between people and those who provide them with services is deteriorating, and there is no chance of its return. [48]

In short the institutions which provide intimacy in our culture have atrophied and their replacements—the supermarket, dial-a-prayer, and the television set—are the accoutrements of the lonely crowd. Yet the human need for closeness persists and intimacy-sponsoring endeavors like the T-group have multiplied at a near astronomical rate in the past few years. As the future comes upon us, a periodic social immersion—a rehumanization station (God forbid)—may become a necessity if we are to survive the relentless dehumanizing march of a socially blind scientific technology.

Modern man is personally as well as socially alienated; he is separated from his own self and gropes for some sense of personal identity. The modeling process by which children establish their personal and sexual identity has been disrupted. The broken homes, the confused role of the mother-homemaker-career woman, the father whose occupation is invisible or incomprehensible to the child, the television teaching machine, the absent extended kinship, all contribute to the identity confusion. The current generation is the first in the history of the world which has nothing to learn from grandparents; in fact, the pace of change is such that children can scarcely learn from peers five years older. One can, in passing, only muse about the effects on the unused identificatory figures. What does it mean to the father who is unable to extend himself into the future through his son? *

Increased literacy, education, mass media, leisure time have made modern man, patient and nonpatient alike, more aware of a discrepancy between his values and his behavior. Many enlightened individuals who consider their chief life values to be humanitarian, esthetic, egalitarian, or intellectual find that, under self-scrutiny, they pay only lip service to these and instead base their behavior on the values of aggrandizement: the "philistine triumvirate" [50] of material wealth, prestige, and power. The awareness of this discrepancy may result in a pervasive anxiety, self-abrogation, and sense of emptiness which often beget a harried attempt to avoid reflection by compulsive working and hobbying.

Another discrepancy is experienced between work and one's sense of creativity; the great majority of individuals rarely experience a sense of pride, completion, or effectiveness in their work. The gap between the worker and the finished product, originally a blight of the industrial revolution, continues to widen as the technological maelstrom whirls man into an anonymous automation. These developments result in a growing sense of personal inadequacy. Although the individual may obtain some sense of

---

*Has the rapidity of change precluded the type of relationship that the Odysseus of Kazantzakis experienced with Telemacus?

> He who has borne a son dies not; the father turned,
> and his sea-battered vagrant heart swelled up with pride.
> Good seemed to him his young son's neck, his chest and sides,
> the swift articulation of his joints, his royal veins
> that from tall temples down to lithesome ankles throbbed.
> Like a horse-buyer, with swift glances he enclosed
> with joy his son's well-planted and keen-bladed form.
> "It's I who stand before my own discarded husk,
> my lips unshaven, my heart still covered with soft down,
> all my calamities still buds, my wars, carnations,
> and my far journeys still faint flutterings on my brow." [49]

pride from the achievements of his megagroup, generally the individual's sense of personal worth is inversely proportional to the size and power of the megamachine, to use Mumford's term,[51] in which he is ensconced.

Although any of these concerns may be more important to one group member than another, each is likely to have some real meaning to all, be they labeled patient, student, delegate, trainer, or therapist. All these factors, then, indicate that there is an enormous overlap between T-groups and therapy groups. Both types of groups have similar goals, similar views of man, rely on similar change or curative factors, have similar ground rules (here-and-now, inter- and intrapersonal honesty, feedback, admitting weaknesses and uncertainty, establishing mutual trust, understanding and analyzing behavior) and similar shared concerns. Obviously groups with so many shared properties will and must go through comparable processes.

The groups are so similar that practically any T-group meeting may be mistaken for a therapy group meeting; and yet the total course of the two types of groups may be distinguished from one another. There are, I believe, some fundamental differences between the therapy and the T-group.

Therapy Groups and T-Groups—Differences

I must make a few explicatory points before discussing these differences. First we must note that many of these issues are generalizations and need to be qualified. The nature of the T-group or the therapy group depends upon the goals and techniques of the leader. Certain trainers and therapists, particularly those who straddle both fields, may lead their groups in such similar fashion that differences between the two are blurred, whereas others operate so differently that even the unpracticed observer can readily enumerate fundamental differences. In other words, the differences *within* both the T-group field and the therapy group field may be greater than the differences *between* the two fields. Secondly there are both extrinsic and intrinsic differences. Extrinsic or procedural differences are expendable and arise from the different customs, settings, and traditions of the two fields from which the two types of groups originated and are not valuable indicators in understanding underlying principles of the groups. Intrinsic differences, on the other hand, are core differences and arise from the vital differences in the goals and composition of the two types of groups. Even here, however, we must acknowledge the overlap; many trainers and group therapists will contest the distinctions which I shall make.

EXTRINSIC DIFFERENCES

Setting. The T-group differs from the therapy group in size, duration, and physical setting. Generally it consists of twelve to sixteen members who may be total strangers or who may be associates at work. Often the T-group meets as part of a larger residential human relations laboratory lasting one to two weeks. The T-group, in this setting, usually meets in two- to three-hour sessions once or twice a day. The members usually spend the entire day with one another and the T-group atmosphere spills over into other activities. Often T-groups meet like therapy groups, in shorter sessions spaced over a longer period of time. Almost always, however, the T-group's life spans a shorter period of time.

Unlike the therapy group, the T-group's ethos is one of informality and pleasure. The physical surroundings are often resort-like, and more consideration is given to the pursuit of fun. Laughter is heard more often in the T-group. The leader may often tell jokes to explicate certain issues in the group. Many leaders of the newer encounter groups emphasize that it is important to them that the group members have a good time. Not only does the group have more fun during the meetings, but it devotes more attention to the role fun occupies in the lives of each of the members. To the reasonably well-integrated T-group member, the ability to play and to enjoy the leisure his affluence has brought him is an issue of considerable import. To the more survival-oriented psychiatric patient, fun occupies a less pressing, more distant position on his hierarchy of needs.

Role of the Leader. Generally there is a far greater gap between the leader and the members in a therapy group than in a T-group. This is a result both of the leader's behavior and the characteristics of the members. Although T-group members may, as we have mentioned, overvalue the leader, generally they tend to see him more realistically than do psychiatric patients. T-group members, due in part to their greater self-esteem and also due to a greater opportunity to socialize between meetings with the leader, perceive the leader to be similar to themselves, except insofar as he has superior skill and knowledge in a specialized area. Whatever prestige he enjoys in the group the trainer earns as a result of his contributions. Eventually he begins to participate in a similar manner to the other members and in time assumes full membership in the group although his technical expertise continues to be appreciated and employed.

Part of the trainer's task is to transmit not only his knowledge but also his skills; he expects his group members to learn methods of diagnosing and resolving interpersonal problems. Often he explicitly behaves as a teacher; for example, he may, as an aside, explicate some point of theory and may introduce some group exercise, verbal or nonverbal, as an experiment for the group to study. It is not unusual for T-group members to seek further human relations education and subsequently to become trainers. (Occasionally this has had some unfortunate repercussions resulting in excesses since some members, without the necessary skills and background, have considered one or two experiences as a group member sufficient training to launch them on new careers as group leaders.)

Group therapists are viewed far more unrealistically by their group members. (See Chapter 5.) In part the therapist's deliberately enigmatic and mystifying behavior generates this distortion. He has entirely different roles of conduct from the other members in the group; he is rarely transparent or self-disclosing and too often reveals only his professional front. It is a rare therapist who socializes or even drinks coffee with his group members. In part, however, the distortion resides within the patients and springs from their hope for an omniscient figure who will intercede in their behalf. They do not view the therapist merely as an individual similar to themselves aside from his specialized professional skills; for better or for worse they attribute to him the archetypal abilities and powers of the healer. Often the group members and the therapist conspire together then to define his role: the leader often chooses, for technical reasons, to be perceived unrealistically, and the group members, for survival reasons, do not allow his real personage to emerge. Although, as the group proceeds, the therapist's role may change so that he behaves more like a member, he never becomes a full group member: he almost never presents his personal problems in living to the group; his statements and actions continue to be perceived as powerful and sagacious regardless of their content. Furthermore, the therapist is not concerned with teaching his skills to the group members; it is a rare instance for a therapy group member to use his group experience to launch himself on a career as a group therapist.

INTRINSIC DIFFERENCES

Beyond the Common Social Malady. Most of the fundamental differences between T-groups and therapy groups derive from the difference in composition. Although overlapping may occur, the T-group is generally composed of well-functioning individuals who seek greater competence and growth, whereas the therapy group has a population of individuals who often cannot cope with minor everyday stress without discomfort; the latter seek relief from anxiety, depression, or from a sterile and ungratifying intra- and interpersonal existence. We have described a common social malady that to a greater or lesser degree affects all individuals. However, and this is a point often overlooked by clinically untrained T-group leaders, psychiatric patients have, in addition, a set of far deeper concerns. The common social malady is woven into the fabric of their personality but is not synonymous with their psychopathology.

To illustrate, consider the concept of self-alienation—one of the common results of the "culture game" described above. Horney's formulations, to use one of several available personality constructs, also postulates an alienation from the self as a core problem of many individuals. (She defines neurosis as a "disturbance in one's relationship to self and to others.")[38] However, whereas the "culture game" concept describes self-alienation as a commonplace phenomenon emanating from the façade-wearing ritual of the adult world, Horney describes self-alienation as a defensive maneuver occurring early in the individual's life as a response to basic anxiety stemming from severe disharmonies in the parent-child relationship. The child is faced with the problem of dealing with parents too wrapped up in their own neurotic conflicts to conceive of him and treat him as a separate individual with his own needs and potential. As a survival mechanism the child diverts his energies, which would ordinarily be devoted to the task of actualization of his real self, to the construction and realization of an idealized self—a self the individual feels he should and ought to become for the sake of survival. Horney then proceeds to delineate a complex development of the individual in terms of the relationship between his ideal self, his potential self, and his actual self (the person he perceives himself to be), but this need not concern us now. *The important point is that this split occurs early in life and profoundly influences all aspects of subsequent development.* The individual attempts, all his life, to shape himself in the form of the idealized (and unattainable) self, develops a far-reaching pride system based on idealized characteristics, blots out opposing trends in himself, experiences self-hatred when the discrepancy between the idealized and actual selves seems particularly great, and evolves a pervasive network of claims on the environment and restrictive demands on himself. In light of the far-reaching consequences of these developments on the neurotic person, it would seem that little benefit could accrue from a brief human relations training group, such as a twelve-hour (six two-hour meetings) course recently advertised in the newspaper,[52] which was entitled "The Courage to be Real" and which planned to ". . . deal with such problems as telling the difference between phoniness and reality in one's self and in others . . ."

To return to the central issue, the fact that patients and nonpatients alike share many common concerns should not obscure the point that patients have, in addition, a far deeper basis for their alienation and dysphoria.

Orientation to Learning. The basic task of the T-group—the acquisition of interpersonal competence—requires a degree of interpersonal skill which most psychiatric patients do not possess. T-group trainers ordinarily make certain assumptions about their group members: they must be able to send and receive communications about their own and other members' behavior with a minimum of distortion; they must, if they are to convey accurate information and be receptive about themselves, have a relatively high degree of self-awareness and self-acceptance. Furthermore, participants must desire interpersonal change. They must be well intentioned and constructive in their relationship to the other members and must believe in a fundamental constructive attitude on the part of the others if a cohesive, mutually trusting group is to form. The members must be willing, after receiving feedback, to question previous cherished beliefs about themselves (unfreezing) and be willing to experiment with new attitudes and behavior, which may replace older, less successful modes of behavior.

The participants must then transfer these modes of behavior beyond the group situation to interpersonal situations in their "back-home" life. Generalized adjunctive learning is also necessary; for example, Argyris [53] notes:

. . . if the individual learns to express his feelings of anger or love more openly, he may also have to develop new competence in dealing with individuals who are threatened with such openness. It is important, therefore, for the individual to learn how to express these feelings in such a way that he minimizes the probability that his behavior will cause someone else to become defensive, thereby creating a potentially threatening environment.

These intra- and interpersonal prerequisites which trainers take for granted in their group members are the very attributes sorely deficient in the typical psychiatric patient, who generally has lower levels of self-esteem and self-awareness. The stated group goals of increased interpersonal competence are often perceived as incompatible with their personal goals of relief from suffering. Their initial response to others is often based on distrust rather than trust and, most important of all, their ability to question their belief system and to risk new forms of behavior is severely impaired. In fact, the inability to learn from new experience is central to the basic problem of the neurotic. To illustrate with a classic example, consider Anna Freud's study of Patrick, who during the London blitz in 1943, was separated from his parents and developed an obsessive-compulsive neurosis. In the evacuation center he stood alone in a corner and chanted continuously, "Mother will come and put on my overcoat and my leggings, she will zip my zipper, she will put on my pixie hat," etc.[54] Consequently Patrick, unlike the other children, could not avail himself of the learning opportunities in the center. He remained isolated from the other adults and children and formed no other relationships which could have relieved his fear and permitted him to continue his growth and the development of his social skills. The frozen compulsive behavior did provide some solace for Patrick by preventing panic but so tied up his energy that he could not appraise the situation and take new, adaptive action.

Not only does the neurotic defense preclude reality testing and resolution of the core conflict, but it characteristically generalizes to include an ever-widening sphere of the individual's life space. Generalization may occur directly or indirectly. It may operate directly, as in traumatic or war neuroses in which the feared situation takes an increasingly broader definition. For example, a phobia once confined to a specific form of moving vehicle may generalize so as to apply to all forms of transportation. Indirectly the individual suffers since, as with little Patrick, the inhibition prevents him from exploring his physical and interpersonal environment and developing his potential. A vicious circle arises since maladaptive interpersonal techniques beget further stress and may preclude the formation of gratifying relationships.

The important point is that the individual with neurotic defenses is frozen into a closed position; he is not open for learning, he is generally searching not for growth but for safety. Argyris[53] puts it nicely when he differentiates a "survival orientation" from a "competence orientation." The more an individual is competence-oriented the more receptive and flexible he is. He becomes an "open system" and in the interpersonal area is able to use his experience to develop greater interpersonal competence. On the other hand, an individual may be more concerned with protecting himself in order to survive. Through the use of defense mechanisms he withdraws, distorts, or attacks the environment.

This, in turn, begins to make the individual more closed and less subject to influence. The more closed the individual becomes, the more his adaptive reactions will be controlled by his internal system. But since his internal system is composed of many defense mechanisms, the behavior will not tend to be functional or economical. The behavior may eventually become compulsive, repetitive, inwardly stimulated, and observably dysfunctional. The individual becomes more of a "closed" system.[53]

The survival-oriented individual does not give or accept accurate feedback; if left to his own devices he will generate those kinds of experiences which will strengthen his defensive position. He may, for example, be particularly attentive to feedback that confirms the rationality of his having to be closed. Similarly the feedback he gives to others may be highly colored by his survival orientation: he may be far more concerned with engendering in others certain attitudes toward himself than with giving accurate feedback.

Individuals are neither all open or all closed, they may be closed in specific areas and open in others; nor, as we have stated, are all therapy group members more closed than all T-group members. There is little data bearing on this point and one must be cautious about overgeneralization. Consider for a moment the vast scope and diversity of the group therapies; it is possible, for example, that the affluent members of an analytic group in Manhattan may be as integrated and congruent as the members of an average T-group. The label of "patient" is often a purely arbitrary one which is a consequence of the request for help, not of the need for help. (It is possible that once the therapist has labeled an individual as a patient he initiates a self-fulfilling prophecy: by expecting, and unwittingly reinforcing, patient-like behavior he elicits closed rather than open behavior.) Generally, however, the therapy group is composed of individuals with a survival rather a competence orientation and who therefore cannot readily take advantage of the interpersonal learning opportunities of the group. Therapy group members cannot easily follow the simple T-group mandate to be open, honest, and trusting when they are experiencing profound feelings of suspicion, fear, distrust, anger, and self-hatred. A great deal of work must be done to overcome these maladaptive interpersonal stances so that patients can begin to participate constructively in the group. Jerome Frank came close to the heart of the matter when he said that "therapy groups are as much or more concerned with helping patients to unlearn old patterns as they are with helping them to learn new ones." [6] Accordingly in therapy groups the task of interpersonal competence acquisition goes hand in hand with (and sometimes straggles far behind) the task of removing maladaptive defenses.

Differences Early and Late. Thus there are two intrinsic differences between T-groups and therapy groups, both emanating from the composi-

368

tion and goals of the group. First, therapy group members are in a greatly different state of readiness to learn. Secondly, although they share many aspects of a common social malady with T-group members, they nevertheless have deep highly personalized splits within themselves explicable only on the basis of each one's developmental history. Each member must be helped to understand the form, the irrationality, and the maladaptive implications of his behavior. This type of exploration can only occur once a highly cohesive, mutually trusting group with highly therapeutic norms has been formed. In one sense this work begins at a point where many T-groups end. The improved interpersonal sensitivity and communication which may be the goal of the T-group is a means to an end for the intensive therapy group. Frank, while acknowledging he was overstating the point for purposes of explication, noted, "The therapy group reaches maximal usefulness at the point where the T-group ceases to be useful." [6]

The therapy group, then, differs from the T-group early and late. It differs early by beginning more painfully and laboriously. T-group members may begin a group with trepidation; they face an unknown situation in which they will be asked to expose themselves and to take risks. Nevertheless, they are generally backed up by a relatively high self-esteem level and a reservoir of professional and interpersonal success. Psychiatric patients, on the other hand, begin a therapy group with dread and suspicion. Self-disclosure is infinitely more threatening in the face of a belief in one's basic worthlessness and badness. The pace is slower; the group must deal with one vexing interpersonal problem after another. The T-group after all does not often have to face the problem of an angry paranoid patient, or a suicidal depressive one, or a denying patient who attributes all his difficulties in living to his spouse, or a fragile borderline schizophrenic individual, or the easily discouraged members who constantly threaten to leave the group. The therapist, unlike the trainer, must constantly modulate the amount of confrontation, self-disclosure, and tension the group can tolerate.

The therapy group differs later by having a different termination point for each member. Unlike the T-group which invariably ends as a unit and generally at a predetermined time, the therapy group continues for each member until his goals have been reached. In fact, as Frank points out, one reason that the therapy group is so threatening is that its task, "broad personal modification," has scarcely any limit and furthermore there is no restriction as to what can, and perhaps must, be discussed.[6] Often in a T-group it is enough for the group to recognize and to surmount a problem area; not so in the therapy group in which problem areas must be explored in depth for each of the members involved.

For example in a twelve-session T-group of mental health professionals which I recently led, the members (who were also my students) experienced great difficulty in their relationship to me. They felt frightened and inhibited by me, vied for my attention, addressed a preponderance of their comments to me, overvalued the wisdom of my remarks, and harbored unrealistic expectations of me. I responded to this issue by helping the group members recognize their behavior,* their distortions, and unrealistic expectations. I then helped them appreciate the effects of their unrealistic and dependent attitudes toward me on the course of the group and called their attention to the implications of this phenomenon on their future role as group therapists. Next we discussed some of the members' feelings toward the more dependent members of the group: for example, how it felt to have someone ostensibly talk to you but at the same time fix his gaze on the leader. Once these tasks were accomplished, I felt that it was important that the group move past this block and proceed to focus on other facets of the group experience, for it was abundantly clear that the group could spend all of its remaining sessions attempting to resolve fully its struggle with the issue of leadership and authority. One way in which the leader can facilitate this process is to be reality-oriented and transparent in his presentation of self. I shared with the group my feelings of uncertainty and anxiety and my response to being feared and overvaluated; I discussed the issue of my double role, that of teacher-evaluator and of T-group leader, and helped them distinguish the real from the irrational. For example, many members felt that they must conceal their feelings of inadequacy or confusion from me lest I "grade" them unfavorably and thus influence their future careers. I pointed out to them that not only was my administrative power overestimated but that, given my own still vivid and still present struggle with similar feelings, and my belief in the value of self-exploration and self-understanding, it was unthinkable for me to behave as a critical judge. I helped to focus the group's attention on other current but untouched group issues—for example, their feelings about three silent and seemingly uninvolved members, the hierarchy of dominance in the group, and the general issue of intermember competition and competence, always a specter looming large in T-groups of mental health workers.

In a therapy group the leader would approach the same issue in a different fashion with different objectives in mind. He would encourage

---

* During the height of this phase I scheduled a leaderless meeting in order to allow the group to sample the sense of liberation and disinhibition which occurred without me. This helped the group to be quite clear that it was my presence, rather than some other factor, which was oppressive.

the patients especially conflicted in this area to discuss in depth their feelings and fantasies toward him. Rather than consider ways in which to help the group move on, he would help plunge them into the issue so that each member might understand his overt behavior toward him, as well as his avoided behavior and the fantasied calamitous effects of such behavior. Although he would, by a degree of transparency, assist the members in their reality testing, he would attempt to modulate the timing of this behavior so as to allow the formation and full exploration of their feelings toward him. (See Chapter 5 for a detailed discussion of this issue.) The goal of clarifying other facets of group dynamics is, of course, irrelevant for the therapy group; the only reason for changing the focus of the group is that the current issue is no longer the most fertile one for the therapeutic work: either the group has pursued the areas as far as possible at that time or some other more immediate issue has arisen in the group.

To summarize, the basic intrinsic difference between T-groups and therapy groups arises from the differences in composition (and thereby the goals) of the groups. As a general rule psychiatric patients have different goals, more deeply disrupted intra- and interpersonal relations, and a different (closed, survival-based) orientation to learning. These factors result in a number of process and procedural differences both in the early stages and in the late working-through stages of the group.

REFERENCES

1. "Sensitivity Training," *Congressional Record—House,* June 10, 1969, pp. H4666–H4679.
2. C. Rogers, "Interpersonal Relationships: Year 2000," *J. Appl. Behav. Sci., 4:* 265–280, 1968.
3. *Int. J. Group Psychother., 17:* 419–505, 1967.
4. L. Horwitz, "Transference in Training Groups and Therapy Groups," *Int. J. Group Psychother., 14:* 202–213, 1964.
5. S. Kaplan, "Therapy Groups and Training Groups: Similarities and Differences," *Int. J. Group Psychother., 17:* 473–504, 1967.
6. J. Frank, "Training and Therapy," in L. P. Bradford, J. R. Gibb, and K. D. Benne, (eds.), *T-Group Theory and Laboratory Method; Innovation in Education* (New York: John Wiley and Sons, 1964).
7. E. H. Schein and W. G. Bennis, *Personal and Organizational Change Through Group Methods: The Laboratory Approach* (New York: John Wiley and Sons, 1965), pp. 329–334.
8. H. Coffey, personal communication, 1967.

371

9. A. Bavelas, personal communication, 1967.
10. A. Marrow, "Events Leading to the Establishment of the National Training Laboratories," *J. Appl. Behav. Sci., 3:* 144–150, 1967.
11. L. P. Bradford, "Biography of an Institution," *J. Appl. Behav. Sci., 3:* 127–144, 1967.
12. K. Benne, "History of the T-Group in the Laboratory Setting," in Bradford, Gibb, and Benne, *op. cit.,* pp. 80–135.
13. K. Lewin, R. Lippit, and R. K. White, "Patterns of Aggressive Behavior in Experimentally Created Social Climates," *J. Soc. Psychol., 10:* 271–299, 1939.
14. K. Lewin, "Forces Behind Food Habits and Methods of Change," *Bull. Nat. Res. Council., 108:* 35–65, 1943.
15. D. Stock, "A Survey of Research on T-Groups," in Bradford, Gibb, and Benne, *op. cit.,* pp. 395–441.
16. R. R. Blake and J. S. Mouton, "Reactions to Intergroup Competition Under Win-Lose Conditions," *Management Science, 7:* 420–435, 1961.
17. Schein and Bennis, *op. cit.,* p. 41.
18. *Ibid.,* p. 43.
19. A. Camus, cited in *ibid.,* p. 46.
20. J. Luft, *Group Processes: An Introduction to Group Dynamics* (Palo Alto, Calif.: National Press, 1966).
21. I. R. Wechsler, F. Messarik, and R. Tannenbaum, "The Self in Process: A Sensitivity Training Emphasis," in I. R. Wechsler and E. H. Schein (eds.), *Issues in Training* (Washington, D.C.: National Education Association, National Training Laboratories, 1962), pp. 33–46.
22. M. Rosenbaum and M. Berger (eds.), *Group Psychotherapy and Group Function* (New York: Basic Books, 1963).
23. A. L. Kadis, J. D. Krasner, and C. Winick, *A Practicum of Group Psychotherapy* (New York: Harper and Row, 1963).
24. H. Mullan and M. Rosenbaum, *Group Psychotherapy; Theory and Practice* (New York: Free Press of Glencoe, 1962).
25. Rosenbaum and Berger, *op. cit.,* p. 5.
26. E. W. Lazell, "The Group Treatment of Dementia Praecox," *Psychoanal. Rev., 8:* 168–179, 1921.
27. L. C. Marsh, "Group Therapy and the Psychiatric Clinic," *J. Nerv. Ment. Dis., 32:* 381–392, 1935.
28. L. Wender, "Current Trends in Group Psychotherapy," *Am. J. Psychother., 3:* 381–404, 1951.
29. T. Burrows, "The Group Method of Analysis," *Psychoanal. Rev., 19:* 268–280, 1927.
30. P. Schilder, "Results and Problems of Group Psychotherapy in Severe Neurosis," *Ment. Hyg., 23:* 87–98, 1939.
31. S. Slavson, "Group Therapy," *Ment. Hyg., 24:* 36–49, 1940.
32. J. L. Moreno, *Who Shall Survive?* (New York: Beacon House, 1953).
33. L. Bradford, in *Human Relations Training News, Vol. 1,* No. 1 (May 1967).
34. L. Horwitz, "Training Groups for Psychiatric Residents," *Int. J. Group Psychother., 17:* 421–435, 1967.
35. R. Morton, "The Patient Training Laboratory: An Adaptation of the Instrumented Training Laboratory," in Schein and Bennis, *op. cit.,* pp. 114–152.
36. I. Hendrick, "Instinct and the Ego During Infancy," *Psychoanal. Quart., 11:* 33–58, 1952.
37. D. E. Berlyne, "The Present Status of Research on Exploratory and Related Behavior," *J. Indiv. Psychol., 14:* 121–126, 1958.
38. K. Horney, *Neurosis and Human Growth: The Struggle Toward Self-Realization* (New York: W. W. Norton, 1950).

39. R. White, "Motivation Reconsidered," *Psychol. Rev., 66:* 297–333, 1959.
40. H. Hartmann, "Notes on the Psychoanalytic Theory of the Ego," *Psychoanal. Stud. Child, 5:* 74–95, 1950.
41. A. Angyal, *Foundations for a Science of Personality* (New York: Commonwealth Fund, 1941).
42. K. Goldstein, *Human Nature in Light of Psychopathology* (Cambridge, Mass.: Harvard University Press, 1940).
43. D. A. Hamburg and J. Adams, "A Perspective on Coping Behavior: Seeking and Utilizing Information in Major Transitions," *Arch. Gen. Psychiat., 17:* 277–284, 1967.
44. D. Bunker, "The Effect of Laboratory Education Upon Individual Behavior," in Schein and Bennis, *op. cit.,* pp. 257–267.
45. A. Stanton and M. S. Schwartz, *The Mental Hospital* (New York: Basic Books, 1954).
46. C. Rogers, personal communication, 1967.
47. J. D. Rockefeller, "In Praise of Young Revolutionaries," *Saturday Review of Literature, 51:* 18–20, 1968.
48. D. Wilber, *Palo Alto Times,* October 24, 1968.
49. N. Kazantzakis, *The Odyssey: A Modern Sequel* (New York: Simon and Schuster, 1958), Book One, l. 135–145, p. 6. © 1958 by Simon & Schuster, Inc.
50. I. Sarnoff, *Society with Tears* (New York: Citadel Press, 1966), p. 17.
51. L. Mumford, *The Myth of the Machine: Techniques and Human Development* (New York: Harcourt, Brace and World, 1967).
52. *Palo Alto Times,* October 12, 1968.
53. C. Argyris, "Conditions for Competence Acquisition and Therapy," *J. Appl. Behav. Sci., 4:* 147–179, 1968.
54. A. Freud and D. Burlingham, *War and Children* (New York: Medical War Books, 1943), pp. 99–104.

373

15

CONCLUDING REMARKS: TRAINING AND RESEARCH

❧

This book has had two purposes: the training of therapists and the exploration of the scientific basis of group therapy. Together, training and research will shape the future of the field. The development of effective training programs is an especially timely issue; group therapy is currently experiencing an unprecedented popularity which has produced a sharp increase in the number of prospective therapists. The approach to therapy outlined in this book is based upon the best current research evidence; but as continued investigation leads to new conceptualizations of the therapeutic process, the principles of therapy must be changed accordingly. In the educational process, as this chapter will show, research and training are closely interrelated; not only is good clinical training essential in the development of the researcher, but the acquisition of a research orientation is necessary in the development of the mature therapist.

Training

This text, like any text, is only a partial training guide; the student group therapist requires complementary experiences in order to develop into an effective therapist. My experience as a teacher has taught me that neophyte group therapists profit from a personal experience in a group, a personal psychotherapeutic or self-exploratory experience, the observation of an experienced group therapist at work, and close clinical supervision.

A personal group experience has become widely accepted as an integral part of a training program; for example, the accreditation committee of the American Group Psychotherapy Association has recommended a minimum requirement of sixty hours as a participant in a group. My own practice has been to offer students, early in their course of training, an opportunity to participate in a human relations "T-group."* Such an experience may offer many types of learning not elsewhere available. The student is able to learn at an emotional level what he may previously have known intellectually: he realizes the power of the group, how it can wound or heal, how important group acceptance is; he learns what self-disclosure really entails, how difficult it is to reveal one's secret world, one's fantasies, one's feelings of vulnerability, hostility, and especially tenderness; he appreciates his strengths as well as his weaknesses; he learns about his own preferred role in the group; and perhaps most striking of all, he learns about the role of the leader as he becomes aware of his own dependency and his own unrealistic appraisal of the leader's power and knowledge.

A caveat to the group leader: groups of mental health professionals, and especially psychiatric residents who will continue to work together throughout their training, are extremely difficult groups to lead. The pace is slow, intellectualization is common, and self-disclosure and risk taking minimal. The neophyte therapist realizes that his chief professional instrument is his own person and generally is doubly threatened by requests for self-disclosure: not only his personal competence but his professional competence is at stake. In training programs the group leader is often placed in a double role in the student groups: he is both teacher-evaluator and T-group leader. Generally this compounds the problem and forces undue attention to authority issues. Eventually the group's problem with the leader must be resolved around the issue of trust; resolution is facilitated if the leader can eventually disclose himself and take risks of the same magnitude demanded of the members.

In my experience, a training group is most effective if it is voluntary. The group may be presented to the students in such a way as to insure near unanimous participation. I generally frame the group experience within the students' education by attempting to project the field into the future. It is quite likely that mental health practitioners will spend an

---

* Many training programs advise students, following a sensitivity group experience, to participate for an extended period of time as a patient in a therapy group.

increasingly greater amount of their time in groups as leaders of therapy groups and as members and leaders of treatment teams; to be proficient the mental health practitioner of the future will simply have to know his way around groups. He will have to learn to work in groups and he will have to understand his group behavior and his presentation of self. The threat of the group is further reduced if the teacher reminds the students of the total here-and-now focus of the group and discourages the discussion of past or current private material outside the boundaries of the group. I have led psychiatric resident T-groups since 1961 and without exception found them to be a valuable teaching technique; indeed many residents when reviewing their residency curriculum have rated the T-group as the most valuable aspect of their first year of training.

It would be presumptuous to attempt to specify how much and what type of individual psychotherapy the student group therapist requires. Few would dispute, however, that some self-exploratory venture is necessary for the maturation of the group therapist. An inability to perceive countertransference responses, to recognize personal distortions and blind spots, to use his own feelings and fantasies in his work limits the effectiveness of any therapist. The therapist who lacks insight about his own motivations may, for example, avoid conflict in the group because of his own proclivity to mute his feelings; or he may unduly encourage confrontation because of his search for aliveness in himself. He may be overeager to prove himself, to make consistently brilliant interpretations and thereby emasculate the group; he may himself fear intimacy and prevent open expression of feelings by premature interpretations. He may do the opposite: overemphasize feelings, make too few connections, and so overstimulate his patients that they are left in agitated turmoil.[1] He may so need acceptance that he is unable to challenge the group and, like the members, may be swept along by the prevailing group current; he may be so devastated by an attack on himself and so unclear of his presentation of self that he is unable to distinguish the realistic from the transference aspects of the attack. A supervisor-observer, a co-therapist, or a video-recording playback may help to provide feedback for the student group therapist which may assist him in discovering many of these blind spots; however, some type of guided self-exploration is usually necessary for full understanding and correction.

A supervised clinical experience is a *sine qua non* in the education of the group therapist. This book posits a general approach to therapy, delineates broad principles of technique, and, primarily when discussing the opening and closing stages of therapy, suggests some specific tactics. The laborious working-through process which comprises the bulk of therapy cannot, however, be comprehensively described in a text; there are an infinite number of situations which arise, each of which may require a rich, imaginative approach. The neophyte therapist's first group is a highly threatening experience; without an experienced clinician as guide, he may develop a limited, stereotyped clinical approach. Recently my colleagues and I [2] studied twelve nonprofessionals who led groups in a psychiatric hospital. Half of the leaders received ongoing supervision as well as an intensive training course; the others received neither. Naïve observers rated the therapists at the beginning of their groups and six months later. The results indicated that not only did the trained therapists improve but the untrained therapists at the end of six months were less skilled than at the beginning. Sheer experience, apparently, is not enough; without ongoing supervision and evaluation, original errors may be reinforced by simple repetition.

Group therapy supervision is generally more taxing than individual therapy supervision. Mastering the cast of characters, a formidable task in itself, is facilitated if the supervisor observes the group periodically or at least once. The students' written or verbal summary of the session often fails to capture the emotional flavor of the group, and ongoing audio or preferably videotapes are invaluable supervision aids. It is particularly important for the supervisor to focus on the student therapist's behavior in the group. Are his verbal and nonverbal interventions congruent with his feelings and do they help to establish the types of group norms he considers useful to the group? At the same time the supervisor must avoid making the student so self-conscious that his spontaneity is stunted. Groups are not so fragile that a single statement markedly influences their direction; it is the therapist's overall gestalt which counts. Every supervisor will, at times, tell the supervisee what he would have said at some particular juncture of the group. This is a useful and perhaps essential part of the modeling process; however, the majority of student therapists are inclined to ape the supervisor's comments at some not entirely appropriate spot in the following group meeting. The next supervisory session generally begins with "I did what you said, but . . ." Therefore I have learned to preface my comments with a caveat: "Don't say this next meeting . . ."

One particularly common error of neophyte therapists is an impatience with the developmental progression of the group. The students fail to realize how threatened many patients are by self-disclosure, by confrontation, and by conflict. Some therapists grow particularly impatient at the lack of mutual caring and concern among the members. They overlook the fact that the expression of affection is often a late development in the group; for some period of time patients nourish the assumption that others are competitors with whom they will have to share the gifts bestowed by the therapist.

The overall training sequence which I have developed for psychiatric residents consists of: (1) a T-group experience at the onset of the residency; (2) four to six months of group observation—the students observe, through a two-way mirror, an experienced clinician leading a group and then join him in a post-meeting discussion; (3) a series of seminars in which the material covered in this book is presented; (4) a supervised group experience; midway through the first year of residency, the residents form an outpatient group with a co-therapist. This group continues for the remaining two and one half years of residency. Supervision is once weekly; supervisors are changed annually. (5) During their second and third years the residents lead, with supervision, a number of inpatient groups.

One additional training adjunct which I have employed is a multiple therapy format [3] in which four to five residents and two senior clinicians treat one patient. This teaching technique, in my opinion, is an efficacious method of increasing the resident's sensitivity to group process and countertransference phenomena.

Obviously group therapy training should be conducted by experienced and dedicated clinicians; a skeptical closed attitude toward group therapy, or any treatment modality, is readily apparent to the student. Furthermore, this training should be an integral part of the planned curriculum; to my mind a training program with absent or optional group therapy training is an anachronism and fails to prepare the student for the field of the future.

The emergence of the new groups discussed in the previous chapter, the blurring of the boundaries between training or education and therapy, between patient and nonpatient, between leader and member, has resulted in considerable confusion about the proper training of the group therapist. Two opposing trends have emerged. Some traditional therapists have experienced the new groups as a threat and have responded territorially. They have not integrated potentially valuable contributions from the human relations field and have tended to conceptualize the group therapist's task, role, and consequently his training as more complex than it need be.

The other position claims that no training at all is necessary; that, in fact, training may be antithetical to the development of the therapist. This point of view stems from several sources. The encounter group field, especially the recent noninstitutional segment, espouses an anti-establishment *Weltanschauung*. The emphasis is on youth, vigor, and innovation. Every leader must develop his own methods, do "his own thing."* Similar trends exist in a number of other fields: young composers scoff at the thought of mastering counterpoint or harmony; painters bypass training in traditional techniques and media in favor of "expressionistic" paint dripping and undisciplined collages. Those in psychotherapy opposing systematic training have cited the views of Rogers,[5] who states that a good therapist-patient relationship is a necessary and sufficient condition for change. Research [6] has shown that three important qualities of the therapeutic relationship—accurate empathy, positive unconditional regard, and genuineness—are significantly correlated with positive therapeutic change. These qualities, it is argued, reside within the therapist and are independent of training. Thus, an overly literal interpretation suggests, therapists should be selected, not trained. Furthermore, the proponents of no training cite research which documents the efficacy of nonprofessional therapists.

To my mind this position is a dangerous one, which requires careful evaluation. Parloff [7] points out that the evidence relating therapy outcome and therapist regard, genuineness, and empathy is far less substantial in group therapy than in individual therapy. In fact, three recent research studies demonstrate a *negative* correlation between each of these three dimensions and group therapy outcome; [8, 9, 10] these findings have resulted in the dubious assumption that only two of the three necessary and sufficient conditions need be present in group therapy. The group therapeutic process is rich and complex. It seems overly simplistic to assume that a circumscribed set of therapist behaviors—the emanation of warmth, empathy, and genuineness—will effect all levels and types of change.[7] Many of the curative factors depend upon patient-patient relationships and upon total group forces; in addition to his personal qualities, the therapist must be skilled in the complex tasks of group maintenance and culture building (see Chapter 5). In addition, diagnostic skills, gained through training, play an important part in the therapeutic process; therapists must learn which patients to include in group therapy and how to evaluate the different needs, defenses, and resources of each patient.

Furthermore, the therapist's sensitivity and his ability to convey empathy and positive regard for the patient are clearly influenced by training. Truax,[11] for example, has designed a systematic program for training therapists in these qualities. Consider also Fiedler's research [12] which demonstrated that senior clinicians of different schools of therapy resemble each other far more closely than they resemble less experienced

---

* One Free University instructor advertised his course by claiming that the best teacher creates little distance between himself and others. Since, he pointed out, he knew nothing at all, he therefore made the best possible teacher![4]

379

therapists in their own school. As one example of this point, I recall an initial interview of a psychiatric patient conducted by a sensitive, empathetic medical student. Because of his inexperience, the student did not perceive that the patient was panicked by a fear of insanity; the interview was a shambles, with both patient and doctor the worse for it. An analysis of the interview with his supervisor made it most unlikely that he would repeat that particular error.

The fact that nonprofessionals sometimes do effective therapy should not be interpreted as evidence against the need for training. Generally nonprofessional therapist programs entail considerable training. The best known work, Rioch's program for housewives,[13] consisted of an intensive two-year training course. The students, by the end of training, were competent enough to pass the clinical part of the American Psychiatric Association Board examinations! [14]

Research

That the question of the need for training even arises demonstrates the imperative need for substantial research in group therapy. Unless research firmly establishes the basic principles of the field, there will be continued flux, sectarianism, and compulsive innovation. Clearly the most pressing need is for imaginative and rigorous outcome research. The lack of outcome criteria and results has served to discourage research in such areas as the following: curative factors, group composition, selection of patients, and the relative efficacy of specialized techniques and formats. The theory presented in this book that the curative factors posited in the first four chapters constitute the vital agents of therapeutic change is by no means conclusive. Although there is considerable research support for this assumption, far too much of the evidence stems from research based on indirect sources: the intervening variables and nontherapy groups.

A new approach to the measurement of outcome is needed. I fully agree with Parloff [7] that traditional designs of outcome studies share a common error: they fail to individualize outcome. Clearly the conventional approach of applying one or several outcome measures to all patients and scoring each on the same "worse-improved" continuum has proven to be unsatisfactory. A recent study by Jewell [15] demonstrates that when judges were asked to examine patients and to evaluate, at the onset of therapy, which direction of change would be considered positive for each patient,

they determined that only 37 per cent of the patients should have decreased anxiety as a goal of therapy. In fact, the judges decided that 10
per cent of the patients required anxiety elevation. Obviously in this
sample the common research strategy of measuring anxiety pre- and post-
therapy and equating anxiety reduction with successful outcome is fore-
doomed to failure. Bergin [16] and Truax and Carkhuff [6] have marshaled
considerable evidence to demonstrate that treated patients as opposed to
nontreated controls show a greater variation about the mean on a number
of outcome measures. They have interpreted this finding to indicate that
some patients improve while others deteriorate in therapy; that some therapists help their patients while others harm them. An additional explanation may be that positive outcome is not unidirectional for all patients.

Improvement in therapy means something different to each patient. I
can conceive of instances in which being more unsettled, tense, depressed,
or inefficient may in some particular individual accompany improvement
or reflect a stage of improvement. Consider, for example, the common
outcome criterion of self-esteem which is generally evaluated pre- and
post-therapy by a self-administered questionnaire which measures absolute self-esteem or the discrepancy between the real self and the ideal self.
Silber and Tippet [17] compared traditional self-administered questionnaires
with thorough clinical evaluations and discovered that a high questionnaire self-esteem score (or a low self-ideal self discrepancy) could reflect
either a genuinely healthy regard of self *or* a defensive posture in which
the individual maintained a high self-image at the expens? of self-awareness; the individuals with defensive high self-esteem denied many difficulties and areas of limitations. On questionnaires these individuals, as a result of successful treatment, would most likely experience less (but more
accurate) self-esteem.

Chassan makes a similar observation about hostility: ". . . moderate
hostility is generally regarded, and in most cases probably rightly so, as
sicker than minimal or no hostility. Yet, a patient who is finally capable of
showing an observable degree of hostility following a lifelong history of
complete repression of hostility may quite likely be getting healthier." [18]

In summary, the standardized (nomothetic) approach to therapy outcome has severe limitations. I can think of no alternative except a laborious individualized (ideographic) approach to outcome. Shapiro,[19]
Phillips,[20] and Kellam and Chassan [21] have demonstrated the feasibility
of an individualized outcome scale for each patient. Malan [22] has proposed an outcome strategy in which each patient is interviewed pretherapy and a judgment made by experienced clinicians of what types of
changes would occur if that patient were to improve in therapy. At the

conclusion of therapy the patient is re-examined and each of the predictions is examined. Although unwieldy, this approach offers maximal individualization; and if video-recorded interviews were used for pre- and post-ratings, then proper editing would permit the use of naïve judges and controls—patients both in other treatment modalities and a no-treatment condition. It is highly desirable to construct a design which would permit comparison of group therapy and individual therapy outcome since another source of error in outcome research may be that group therapy outcome is traditionally measured with instruments originally designed for individual therapy outcome. I suspect that, although group and individual therapies may be equivalent in overall effectiveness, each modality may affect different variables and have a different type of outcome. For example, group therapy graduates may be more interpersonally skilled, more inclined to be affiliative in times of stress, more capable of sustaining a number of meaningful relationships, more empathetic, etc., while individual therapy patients may be more self-sufficient, introspective, and attuned to inner processes. These speculations, however, have not yet been tested by research.

Not only must the general strategy of assessing outcome be re-examined but the criteria for outcome must also be reformulated. The traditional dimensions of removal of discomfort, neutralization of target symptoms, improvement of social effectiveness and self-esteem elevation have proven to be of limited value and may be incomplete reflections of the effects of group therapy. For years group therapists have considered therapy as a multidimensional laboratory for living, and it is time to acknowledge this in outcome research. As a result of therapy some patients, for example, alter their hierarchy of life values to decathect values of material wealth and influence and to stress humanistic or aesthetic ones; others may make a major decision which will influence the course of their lives; others may be more interpersonally sensitive and empathetic and more able to communicate their feelings to others; still others may become less petty and more elevated in their life concerns; others may have a greater sense of commitment to other individuals or projects; others may experience a greater flow of ideas and a greater energy level; others may come to terms in a meaningful manner with their own mortality; while others may find themselves more adventuresome, more receptive to new concepts and experiences.

Parloff [7] suggests similarly that outcome measures be made more consonant with group therapists' goals, which no longer are simply concerned with amelioration of suffering and the restoration of functioning. He recommends that outcome measures be devised for such variables as: the ability to attain such subjective states as joy, ecstasy, peak experiences, love, or the ability to use capacities in a creative, energetic fashion. Relief of suffering and self-fulfillment ("headshrinking and mind-expansion," as Parloff irreverently puts it) may not be on the same continuum. An individual may improve in some spheres and not others; he may become more alive and creative but continue to experience considerable discomfort.

Lieberman [23] in a study assessing outcome of the encounter group experience, suggests several criteria (which to my mind are equally applicable to therapy groups): (1) unsettling (the creation of a psychological set of more questioning, doubting, less certainty, and perhaps more anxiety); (2) a peak experience (a deep conviction that the experience was a landmark which may serve in the future as an anchor point, a goad to further experience, or as a catalyst for life planning; (3) humanization (a reorientation of feelings toward people; the individual may become less critical, more tolerant, and view others in a more complex framework); (4) self-experience (increased self-consistency, congruence, self-esteem); (5) life decisions (important decisions may be made about life directions, activities, important relationships); (6) changes in coping styles (a shift in the approach to stress; the individual develops new styles of dealing with problems and his own growth); (7) changes in specific behavior (a change in his manner of relating to others, expressing feelings, self-assertion, etc.).

Research plays as crucial a role in the development of each individual group therapist as it does in the development of the field at large. The primary purpose of research training in the educational process is not, however, to train researchers. The great majority of group therapists will never do substantial research: few therapists will have the available time, funding, or the large numbers of groups necessary for adequate research.

Rather, the purpose of a research orientation in the curriculum is to instill an inquiring or research attitude in the student. The student must be encouraged to question the basic assumptions of the field and to evaluate objectively the sources and validity of the underlying data. He must be taught to regard each patient, each group, indeed his whole career, as a learning experience. Furthermore, the student must acquire the skills to evaluate the research of others and to assess the generalizability and clinical applicability of basic research. Research can enhance the acquisition of therapy skills; an extremely valuable experience for beginning therapists is to participate in outcome research in which they interview patients who have concluded group therapy in order to evaluate the degree and types of improvement as well as the mechanism whereby the group experience effected the improvement.

For an individual to grow and develop he must be able to tolerate a position of uncertainty. However, this demands a great deal from the developing therapist; to live with uncertainty and ambiguity is difficult and anxiety-provoking. Moreover, patients beset with suffering often demand a pose of infallibility from the healer; to resist the temptation of accepting this role requires a high degree of commitment and integrity. History teaches us that healers who lack a definitive treatment do not long tolerate self-doubts. Lévi-Strauss [24] graphically describes the self-deceptive techniques used by the shamans to keep their self-concept in good repair; comfort is gained at the expense of growth. The modern equivalent is for the therapist to embrace a school of conviction which offers not only a comprehensive system of explanation but also methods of screening out discrepant facts and discounting new evidence. This commitment usually entails a lengthy apprenticeship and initiation. Once within the system the student finds it difficult to disengage himself: first, he has usually undergone such a lengthy apprenticeship that denouncement of the school is equivalent to denouncing a part of himself; secondly, it is extremely difficult to abandon a position of certainty for one of uncertainty. Clearly, however, such a position of certainty is antithetical to growth and particularly stunting to the development of the student therapist.

There are certain potential dangers in the abrogation of certainty. For example, there is some evidence that a therapist with a firm sense of conviction in his beliefs is more effective.[25] There is also a danger of therapeutic nihilism in the student who consequently may refuse to master any organized technique of therapy. The teacher, by his personal example, must offer an alternative model: that the best evidence available leads him to believe that a particular system is effective and that as new information becomes available he would expect to improve his approach. Furthermore, he takes pride in being part of a field which attempts to progress and is honest enough to know its own limitations.

Without a research base the developing practitioner is in a difficult position. How is he, for example, to react to the myriad of recent innovative approaches? Unfortunately the current state of affairs is that the adoption of a new method is a function of the vigor, persuasiveness, or charisma of its proponent. Some new methods have been extraordinarily successful in obtaining both visibility and adherents. Approaches such as marathon groups, nude therapy groups, and body awareness groups have received considerable favorable (as well as unfavorable) mass media attention shortly following their inception. Many therapists without a commitment to research have found themselves unreasonably unreceptive to all new approaches or, on the contrary, swept along with a current fad and then, dissatisfied with its limitations, they have gone on to yet another.

The critical problem facing the field, then, is one of balance. A traditional, conservative sector is less receptive to change than is optimal; an innovative, challenging sector is less receptive to stability than is optimal. The field is swayed by fashion, whereas it should be influenced by evidence. Psychotherapy is a science as well as an art and there is no place in science for uncritical orthodoxy or for innovation solely for its own sake. Orthodoxy offers safety for adherents but leads to stagnation; the field becomes insensitive to the *Zeitgeist* and is left behind as the public goes elsewhere. Innovation provides zest and a readily apparent creative outlet for proponents but, if unevaluated, results in a kaleidoscopic field without substance, a field "which rides off madly in all directions." [26]

Group therapy has had a succession of attractive wrappings: it was, during World War II, the economical answer to the shortage of trained therapists; later it became the logical treatment arena of the interpersonal theory of psychiatry; and currently it is a medium for alleviating individual and social alienation. At present, groups, self-disclosure, interpersonal closeness, touching are "in." Yet the medium is *not* the message. Group therapy is not primarily a vehicle for closeness and human contact. It is a method for effecting therapeutic change in individuals. All other goals are metaphenomena and secondary to the primary function of the group.

REFERENCES

1. B. B. Wassel, *Group Analysis* (New York: Citadel Press, 1966).
2. G. O. Ebersole, P. H. Leiderman, and I. D. Yalom, "Training the Nonprofessional Group Therapist," *J. Nerv. Ment. Dis., 149:* 294–302, 1969.
3. I. D. Yalom and J. H. Handlon, "The Use of Multiple Therapists in the Teaching of Psychiatric Residents," *J. Nerv. Ment. Dis., 141:* 684–692, 1966.
4. Catalogue, Mid-Peninsula Free University, Menlo Park, Calif., Winter 1968.
5. C. Rogers, "A Theory of Therapy, Personality and Interpersonal Relationships," in S. Koch (ed.), *Psychology: A Study of Science, Vol. 3* (New York: McGraw-Hill, 1959), pp. 184–256.
6. C. Truax and R. Carkhuff, *Toward Effective Counseling and Psychotherapy* (Chicago: Aldine Press, 1967).
7. M. Parloff, "Assessing the Effects of Headshrinking and Mind-Expanding," paper presented at the American Group Psychotherapy Association Convention, New York, February 1969.

8. C. Truax, R. Carkhuff, and F. Kodman, Jr., "Relationships Between Therapist-Offered Conditions and Patient Change in Group Psychotherapy," *J. Clin. Psychol.*, 21: 327–329, 1965.

9. C. Truax, J. D. Frank, S. D. Imber *et al.*, "Therapist Empathy, Genuineness, and Warmth and Patient Therapeutic Outcome," *J. Consult. Psychol.*, 30: 395–402, 1966.

10. C. Truax, D. G. Wargo, and R. Carkhuff, "Antecedents to Outcome in Group Psychotherapy with Outpatients: Effects of Therapeutic Conditions, Alternate Sessions, Vicarious Therapy Pretraining, and Patient Self-Exploration," unpublished manuscript, University of Arkansas, 1966.

11. Truax and Carkhuff, *Toward Effective Counseling and Psychotherapy*, pp. 243–336.

12. F. Fiedler, "A Comparison of Therapeutic Relationships in Psychoanalytic, Non-Directive and Adlerian Therapy," *J. Consult. Psychol.*, 14: 436–445, 1950.

13. M. J. Rioch *et al.*, "National Institute of Mental Health Pilot Study in Training Mental Health Counselors," *Am. J. Orthopsychiat.*, 33: 678–689, 1963.

14. M. Parloff, personal communication, 1968.

15. W. O. Jewell, cited by T. Volsky, T. M. Magoon, W. T. Norman, and D. P. Hoyt (eds.), *The Outcomes of Counseling and Psychotherapy: Theory and Research* (Minneapolis: University of Minnesota Press, 1965), p. 154.

16. A. E. Bergin, "The Effects of Psychotherapy: Negative Results Revisited," *J. Counsel. Psychol.*, 10: 244–250, 1963.

17. E. Silber and J. S. Tippet, "Self Esteem: Clinical Assessment and Validation," *Psychol. Rep.*, 16: 1017–1071, 1965.

18. J. B. Chassan, *Research Design in Clinical Psychology and Psychiatry* (New York: Appleton-Century Crofts, 1967), p. 254.

19. M. B. Shapiro, "The Measurement of Clinically Relevant Variables," *J. Psychosom. Res.*, 8: 245–254, 1964.

20. J. P. N. Phillips, "Techniques for Scaling the Symptoms of an Individual Psychiatric Patient," *J. Psychosom. Res.*, 8: 255–271, 1964.

21. S. Kellam and J. B. Chassan "Social Context and Symptom Fluctuation," *Psychiatry*, 25: 370–381, 1962.

22. D. H. Malan, H. A. Bacal, E. S. Heath, and F. H. G. Balfour, "A Study of Psychodynamic Changes in Untreated Neurotic Patients. I. Improvements that are Questionable on Dynamic Criteria," *Brit. J. Psychiat.*, 114: 525–551, 1968.

23. M. Lieberman, personal communication, March 1969.

24. C. Lévi-Strauss, *Structural Anthropology* (New York: Basic Books, 1963), pp. 167–185.

25. J. Frank, *Persuasion and Healing, A Comparative Study of Psychotherapy* (New York: Schocken Books, 1963).

26. S. Leacock, "Gertrude the Governess or Simple 17," in *A Treasury of the Best Works of Stephen Leacock* (New York: Dodd Mead, 1954).

INDEX